INJECTION MOULDING OF PLASTICS

INJECTION MOULDING OF PLASTICS

Written By :

EIRI Consultants and Engineers

ENGINEERS INDIA RESEARCH INSTITUTE

4449, Nai Sarak, Main Road, Delhi-110 006 (India)

Ph. : 91-11-23918117, 23916431, 23840361

Fax : 91-11-23916431, 23918117

* **E-Mail :** eirisidi@bol.net.in

* **Website :** www.eiriindia.org

Sole Distributors :

INDIAN INSTITUTE OF CONSULTANTS

4/54, Roop Nagar, Delhi-110007

Printed and Published by :

ENGINEERS INDIA RESEARCH INSTITUTE

4449, Nai Sarak, Main Road, Delhi-110 006 (India)

Ph. : 91-11-23918117, 23916431, 23840361

Fax : 91-11-23916431, 23918117

✶ **E-Mail :** eirisidi@bol.net.in

✶ **Website :** www.eiriindia.org

Distributed by :

SMALL INDUSTRY RESEARCH INSTITUTE
INDIAN INSTITUTE OF CONSULTANTS

ISBN : 978-81-89765-20-0

Printed in New Delhi (India)

Rs. 750

Printed and Published by Sudhir Gupta for
"Engineers India Research Institute", 4449, Nai Sarak, Main Road,
New Delhi-110 006 and Printed at Swastik Offset, Delhi

Preface

The book **'Injection Moulding of Plastics'** covers various methods including Injection Moulding, Setting-up Mould and Machine,Effect of Processing on Mechanical Properties, Mouldflow, Computer Controlled Automatic Injection Moulding Machine, Maintenance of Injection Moulding Machine, CAE and CAD Technology in Moulds Making, Injection Moulding Process, Specialised Injection Moulding Process, Troubleshooting in Injection Moulding, Injection Moulding of Thermosets, Injection Moulding Machine Design for Injection Moulds, Designing Moulds for Thermoset Processing, Injection Moulded Plastic Components, Plastic Moulded Toys, Plastic Injection Moulding Products, Plastic Injection Moulding Items (like Bucket, Plastic Chairs, Bathing Tub).

The book has been written for the benefit and to prove an asset and a handy reference guide in the hands of new entrepreneurs and well established industrialists.

Director

ENGINEERS INDIA RESEARCH INSTITUTE

Nai Sarak, Main Road,
Delhi-110 006 (India)
E-mail : eirisidi@bol.net.in

CONTENTS AND SUBJECT INDEX

1

Injection Moulding

Injection Moulding is the process where plastics granules or powder, with the addition of heat and pressure, are physically changed to form usable finished parts.

This is done by heating the plastics ganules or powder to a melt condition in an injection cylinder and forcing the melt out of the cylinder under high and forcing the melt out of the cylinder under high pressure to insure that it will not open during the injection process. When the melt has reached a solid state, the mould is opened and the solid parts is removed.

An injection moulding machine basically consists of two main sections the injection System and the clamping System. Because both of these systems operate under high pressure Extreme caution should be observed. Each machine comes with Safety instructions stickers, devices and guards. Under no circumstances should these be removed or modified in order to facilitate ease of operation or for any other reason.

The injection System consists of —

- The material hopper
- The barrel/cylinder heating system
- The barrel/cylindr and screw
- The screw drive system

The Material Hopper

This unit contains the unprocessed plastics granules and should always be cleaned before use and when changing colours or other types of materials. At the bottom of this unit, is a material shut off slide which prevents the materials from failing into the screw/barrel. Do not open this slide until the cooling valve has been opened underneath the hoper (this will prevent the material from caking or forming lumps of the screw inlet), and you have checked the rear temperature zone on the barrel/cylinder to make sure it has reached the desired temperature. The addition to material to a cole barrel/ cylinder can cause damage.

The Barrel/Cylinder heating system

In injection moulding, the barrel/cylinder must be heated, in order to help the melting process. The barrel/cylinder is divided into four heating zones. Each zone is controlled by a pyrometer which is mounted on the moulding machine or the main control panel. Because of the different melting temperatures of plastics moulding materials, temperatures setting will vary from material to material. Every material manufacturer has recommended settings that should be used for his particular material. Trial and error for each job will allow the operator to arrive at the best settings. These settings shoule be recorded on a Job operation sheet to be used for future runs. Variations from these settings in future runs can indicate that a problem exists. The four zones are the Rear, Centre, Front and Nozzle. Always set these zones at temperatures lower than required (especially the rear zone) a they can easily be raised as required. it is easier to raise the temperature of the barrel/cylinder than to lower it.

In order to heat the barrel/cylinder, Band Heaters are used. They come to all sizes and types, some of the more common ones are : Mica band heater, mineral insulated band heater and ceramic band heaters. The use of proper size and the installation of band heaters are very important as imprope heaters can waste energy, cause material melt problem and barrel/screw problems because of uneven heat distribution. Operators should make sure that, once the barrel/cylinder is up to heat, all heater hands are securely fastened. Pyrometers should be checked periodically to make sure that they are not overriding. Nozzle heaters, because of their closeness to the mould have a tendency for short life due to material leakage, wire damage and burning plastic.

The Barrel/Cylinder and Screw

The injection unit which consists of the barrel/cylinder and screw has two functions: to melt the plastic granules or powder and to force that melt into the mould, thereby forming a finished part. The most common system in use today is the reciprocating screw system. Here, as the screw rotates, the plastic material is forced down the length of the screw and, due to the heat conduction from the barrel/cylinder wall and the shearing action, is melted. As the material travels the length of the screw, it passes through three zones; the feed zone, the compression zone and the metering zone, and builds up in the front of the barrel/cylinder. As this buildup occurs, it forces the screw to reciprocate rearward until the required load and shot size is located in the front of barrel/cylinder. The size of the load of the material is conditioned by the feed or shot setting which is located on the machine. Once this required amount of material is reached, the screw will stop rotating and will back up as far as the back off the limit switch. This is done in order to relieve the pressure that has built up in the front of the screw. A distance of once quarter to one half of an inch will usually be sufficient to relieve the pressure. Upon injection, the screw move forward and forces the material through the nozzle and into the mould, forming a part. In order to hold the required injection pressure and, to keep the plastics materials from working its way back through the barrel/cylinder, a check valve or ring is fitted to the front of the screw and prevents material flow back during the forward movement of the screw.

Never attempts to start the inejction unit until it reaches the required temperature. If the material has been let in the barrel/cylinder unit, wait for an additional ten minutes before attempting to rotate the screw. When the unit has reached the required temperature, start the screw rotating (Do not move the screw forwards and backwards). If the screw is rotating at a reasonable speed and the material is not coming from the nozzle, slowly raise the nozzle temperature until it does, being to add material. The screw will not move backwards until the feed limit switch is reached. Inject the old material through the unit. Repeat this process several times. Safety glasses should always be worn in case the heat or pressure settings were miscalculated.

Purging of colours or changing materials is the barrel/cylinder unit can be done by rotation of the screw itself. The screw should be in the maximumm forward position during this procedure. When the majority of the material is removed, the screw can be allowed to return backwards and forwards but not while it is rotating. When the previous material used happens to have been a heat sensitive material and new material requires high temperatures, use a third material such as plypropylene, acrylic or styrene to purge with, before using the new material. When going from a high heat material to a low heat material purge at the lowest temperature at which the high heat material will move. When shutting the machine down. It is recommended to purge it. Certain materials, upon reheating, can become dangerous, causing harmful gases and dangerous pressure levels in the barrel/cylinder unit.

Most injection moulding machines with general purpose screws which can be mould most materials, but, in order to get the maximum out of the material that is being used, specially designed screws are sometimes needed. Every material manufacturer will tell you what type of screw is best for his material.

Screw geometry consists of three factors :

- L/D Ratio. The length over diameter ratio is used to determine the length of a screw. It is determined by dividing the flighted length of screw by the outside diameter of the screw.
- Compression Ratio is that which gives the approximate amount the screw compresses the plastic. It is developed by dividing the depth of the feed section by the depth of the metering section.
- Zone length. Changing the length of the feed, compression or the metering zones, elimination of the metering zone or the addition of the mixing devices can provide the best processing of a given material.

The screw steel must be tough, wear resistant and able to be easily polished. It is recommended that the tops of the screw flights be hard faced with such materials as Satellite. Colmonoy and Xaloy 830, in order to prevent wear.

Besides the proper screw design, to bring the material to its optimum, that is, completely melted, mixed and at the proper temperature, the screw torque and speed play a very important part. Torque and speed range are determined by the type of the material that is going to be used. For materials of a low viscosity, such as polystyrene, polypropylene and polyethylene, low torque and high speed should be used. For materials of high viscosity, such as acetals, ABS, nylon, polycarbonate and PVC, high torque and low speed should be used. As a rule of thumb, try and use as low a screw speed as possible.

The barrel/cylinder, in which the plastic material is mixed, melted and moved, must be able to withstand high injection pressure and resist wear. Barrel/ cylinders are usually either nitrated or constructed with a bimetallic abrasive and/or a corrosion resistant liner. Due to their superior length of life and excellent resistance to wear, bimetallic barrel/cylinders are highly recommended.

Every injection moulding machine, old or new, is subject to Barrel/Cylinder and Screw Wear. With every gramme of material that leaves the barrel cylinder, the efficiency of that machine is reduced, the cost of the operation is increased, and the quality of the end product is diminished. These effects may not be noticeable for weeks, months and, in some cases, years, but they occur nevertheless. The increased use of fillers, reinforcements and additives in the moulding materials lead to a greater Wear in the barrel/cylinder and screw injection unit.

Wear is a generic term covering the broadest range of actions within the barrel/cylinder and the screw unit. Mechanism at work include abrasion, adhesion, corrosion and delamination, and anyone or several of these mechanisms may be operating at one time with the various formulations and machine components. In fact, the interaction of these mechanisms can sometimes prove to be the most challenging problem in combating wear.

Adhesion

Any metal-to-metal contact, rubbing between the barrel/cylinder and screw can cause adhesive wear.

Abrasion

This form of wear takes place between two bodies in the process, one of which is harder than the other. In plastics processing, hard particles in the formulation gradually erode the metal surface of the barrel/cylinder and the screw. Small particles of metal produced by adhesive wear can also act abrasively once they are free in the melt.

Corrosion

A more insidious form of wear that is sometimes forgotten because it functions on a molecular level. It can, however, do severe damage to barrel/cylinders and screws. Certain resins and additives can react with oxygen, water and sometimes with each other to produce acids (PTFE, hydrofloric, PVDC and PVC hydrochloric are a few examples) that will attack the surface of the metal barrel/cylinder and screw components. Even moisture can cause pitting.

Delamination

In it, shearing action is thought to cause fracture of hard particles below the metal surface. Cracks progressively grow towards the surface to produce spalling or chipping of the wear resistant surface. Proper processing, careful monitoring of conditions, materials and the correct selection of a bimetallic barrel/cylinder will allow the processor to minimize the costs associated with 'Wear' and get the most use and profit from his barrel/cylinder and screw unit.

The Screw Drive System

In order for the screw to rotate while plasticizing and move forwards during injection, hydraulic motors and pumps are used because of the large force that is required to reach and maintain the injection speed or fill and pressure.

Injection speed or fill: Each inaction moulding machine is equipped with controls that allow the operator to control the speed with which the screw move forwards while forcing the material into the mould. Some machines allow *far* more than one speed during this operation.

Injection pressure is that pressure in the moulding barrel/cylinder that forces the material into the mould and remains until:

- The 'cushion' micro switch is activated.
- The injection timer control times out.
- The use of pressure of *force* transducer in the mould shows that a proper cavity pressure has been attained. This pressure reading will be *from* 500 to 2000 PSI. (Remember these readings must be multiplied by ten to get the actual pressure). Always set injection pressure below what is needed and work upto the required amount. At this point, the holding pressure will take over.

  Holding pressure is normally 1/4 to 1/3 of injection pressure and is the pressure that remains in the barrel/cylinder during the 'injection and holding' portion of the overall moulding time period or cycle. When the injection hold timer times out, the cooling or solidifying of the moulded part portion of the moulding cycle begins. It is at this time that the screw begins to rotate, forcing a new load of melted material to the *front* of the barrel/cylinder to be ready *for* the next injection into the mould. As with injection pressure, there may be more than one holding pressure used.

  Back pressure is that pressure, during the part cooling cycle, that remains in the barrel/cylinder when the screw is rotating the new material to the *front* and forcing the injection piston back. Back pressure, depending on the material being used, varies *from* 50 to 500 PSI. Always use as low a back pressure as possible.

All material manufacturers supply the processor with their recommended screw torque, speed, and moulding pressure. The finished moulded part will indicate to the processor what variations will be necessary in order *for* him to produce the best possible part. All final times and settings should be noted on the job information sheet. Deviations *from* these during future runs is an indication of a problem.

- The clamping system consists of
- The stationary platen.
- The mould.
- The moving platen and tie rods. The clamping unit.

The Stationary Platen

The stationary platen is that portion of the injection moulding machine where the mould and the nozzle of the barrel/cylinder unit meet. The platen has a hole in the centre of it, where the mould, which has a locating ring mounted on its *front* half, is fitted. After making sure that the mould is level, it is fastened to the stationary platen using least four clamp bolts, with these bolts in holes as close as possible to the mould so that maximum clamp is exerted on the mould without excessively straining the bolts or the clamps.

The Mould

The mould is a steel tool designed to *form* plastics material into the desired shape or size. In choosing the correct mould steel, the processor must take into account the plastics material being used, the hardness of the steel, the wear resistance, machinability, ease of polishing, shock resistance, etc. No one steel is perfect *for* all moulds. Careful consideration is needed in choosing the steel that will give the processor the longest lasting tool. With a good mould, you can make a good part on a bad machine, but a bad mould in a good machine will give you nothing but *a* bad part.

The basic injection mould is made in two halves: The back half, and the *front* half.

- *The locating ring:* This fits in the hole of the stationary platen and lines up the nozzle of the barrel/cylinder unit with the mould.
- *The front bushing:* This provides a conical channel through which the melted material passes *from* the nozzle into the mould.
- *The front clamp plate:* This is used to secure the mould by the use of clamps and bolts to the stationary platen.

- *The cavity:* This is the depression in the mould that *forms* the outer surface of the moulded part. Moulds can contain single or multiple cavities.
- *The cavity retainer plate·* This plate holds the cavity which can either be inserted into the plate or cut into the plate. This plate also contains interconnecting drilled holes through which circulating warm, hot or chilled water is passed. In order to cool the mould. This cooling time is the longest portion of the overall moulding cycle.
- *Leader pins:* These four pins are used to provide a proper alignment for the mould when it is closed (these should be checked for wear).
- *Runner System:* This system receives the material that has passed through the sprue bushing and leads to the cavity. Runner shapes will differ in size and geometry depending on the type of the plastics material used. Runner systems should be balanced so that all cavities fill at the same time.
- *Gate:* This is the section at the end of the runner at which point the plastics material passes into the cavity. The correct type of gate that is to be used depends. on the geometry, material flow and product end use. As a rule of thumb, gates should be as short as possible because large gates can cause longer cycles, marred part surfaces, sinks and stresses in the part. Yet, if the gates are too small, splay marks, premature freeze off of the material or just plain difficulty in filling the part can result.
- *Core:* The element which fits into the cavity and forı ns the inner portion of the moulded part.
- *Sprue puller pin:* When the mould opens, this pin, by means of an undercut, pulls the hardened plastics material (which is called the sprue) out of the sprue bushing. The sprue remains attached to the runner system and, in most cases, the runner system to the moulded parts.
- *Ejector pin:* A rod, pin or sleeve that, once the mould is opened, pushes the moulded part off the force. It also pushes the sprue off the sprue puller pin and the runner out of the runner system.
- *Ejector pin retainer plate:* The plate upon which the ejector rods, pins of sleeves are assembled and held in place.
- *Ejector plate:* The plate that is fastened to the ejector pin retainer plate and is used to push the eject or pins through the support plate and core

retainer plate, knocking the finished part off the core. This can be done either manually or hydraulically.

- *Ejector plate return pins:* As the mould closes, these pins come in contact with the front half of the mould and push the ejector plate back to its original position.
- *Core retainer plate:* This is the plate which holds the core element which fits into the cavity. It also contains the leader pin bushings and interconnecting drilled holes through which circulating warm, hot or chilled water is passed in order to cool the mould.
- *Support plate:* This plate is used to add strength and rigidity to the mould.
- *Support pillars:* These round pillars are used to give added support to the support plate.
- *Ejector housing:* This housing contains the support pillars, the ejector pin retaining the plate and the ejector plate.

Injection moulds can be divided into three basic classes:

- The conventional two plate or two half moulds which we have just seen. This type of mould ejects the sprue, the runner system and the finished parts all connected together. Parts must be clipped or broken away from the runner which is then reground or discarded.
- The three plate mould where the core is on the back half of the mould and the cavity is on one side of a moving plate. As the mould opens, the runner system automatically breaks away from the moulded parts, with the moulded part able to drop free.
- The insulated or hot runner mould where the runner system is inside the cavity retainer plate and remains fluid. The material is forced through small gates into the cavity. When the mould opens, the parts are ejected.

The Moving Platen and Tie Rods

The back half of the mould is mounted to the moving platen by the use of clamps and bolts. This platen is supported on the tie rods and moves forwards to close the mould and backwards to open the mould.

The Clamping Unit

This unit has three basic functions:

To close and open the mould

The mould closes under high speed and pressure until the two halves almost meet (the speed at which the platen and the distance between the two halves is adjustable). At this point, the moving platen switches to low speed and pressure as the two mould halves close. The clamp or lock up is now completed and held clamped under high pressure in order to keep the mould closed with, sufficient force to resist the pressure in the mould that is trying to open the mould as it is filled.

The mould is first opened under slow and high pressure and then continues to open under high speed switching back to slow speed and pressure right before the ejector unit comes into play.

To *eject the parts*

Due to the material packing of the part during injection and the shrinkage of the moulded part, an ejector system must activate the ejector plate in order for the ejector pins to remove the parts from the core. This can be achieved by mechanical means using knockout bars that push the ejector plate forward or by hydraulic knockouts that push the ejector plate forward and automatically return it to its original position.

To *keep the mould closed during the injection cycle*

There are three basic types of clamps:

- *Mechanical* : Most mechanical clamps are toggle clamps. The links of the toggle are activated by the use of a small hydraulic cylinder. Since the extended toggle is always the same, the nuts on the tie rods are used to adjust the clamp for different mould heights. Adjustments normally have to be made after the moulding cycle has begun because of the heat transferred to the mould.
- *Hydraulic:* Straight hydraulic clamping is relatively easy and trouble free. Most machines using hydraulic clamping are larger than those using toggles because of the larger cylinder and ram. The clamp force is easily adjustable.
- *Hydromechanical:* These types of clamps combine the best attributes of the previous two. After the toggle links have been fully extended, hydraulic force is exerted to build up the clamp tonnage. As with the straight hydraulic, the clamp force is easily adjustable.

Determining the proper size of the moulding machine that is needed to produce a part depends on the design the material used and the projected area of the part. As a rule of thumb, 3 and ½ tons/sq. in will determine the tonnage required. Never useful clamp tonnage if the mould is less than half of the platen area to be used.

Check these item for trouble-free moulds

- For safety and speed in running, subsequent setup and maintenance, be sure that
- Hot runner connectors and thermocouple jacks are located on the back of the mould away from the operator.
- Pull back arms are located away from the operator.
- Mould does not extend beyond the press platen.
- Mould will not hit the press gate.
- Mould fits the maximum and the minimum shut height of the press.
- Locating ring dimension matches that of the moulding machine.
- Clamp slots are of proper width to suit mounting.
- Mould has a knockout pattern that machines the press.
- Back plate is thick enough (31 mm minimum) to hold the clamps.
- Mould assembly has a safety strap to keep it together during installation.
- Inlet and outlet water lines connect on the same side of the mould.
- Mould has 'quick coupling' water and hydraulic connections.
- Water lines are cross drilled to eliminate external plumbing.
- Hydraulic cylinders are connected in parallel for fast hook-up.
- Hydraulic cylinders have guards to protect them from damage.
- Interchangeable cavity inserts can be changed without dismantling the mould.
- Backside of guide pins has 9 or 12 mm dia threaded holes 25 mm deep to permit guide pin removal without removing the die from the press.
- Slide faces are large enough to permit correction of errors in locating holes being cored by slides.
- Leader pins are longer than any standing cores.
- Wire ways in mould are large enough for all hot runner wires and thermocouple leads.

- Ejector plate is properly guided to prevent excessive wear on ejector pins and holes.
- Sprue bushing can be removed without taking the die out of the press.
- Electrical connector for the hot runner is recessed into the mould.
- Eyebolts are on mould centerline to facilitate installation.
- To insure the strength of the mould, check that:
- Mould has a minimum of 101 mm between the cavity and the edge of mould.
- Mould has an adequate number of support pillars.
- Ejector plate is thick enough to prevent deflection during ejection stroke.
- Large slides are backed up by heel blocks large enough to withstand the pressure of injection.
- Mould has properly designed die locks. Lock at ejector system to see that:
- Ejector pin layout is adequate to eject part, even in a short shot.
- Ejector stroke is long enough to move part completely off core.
- Contoured ejector pins are locked to prevent rotation.
- Part is designed to remain on the ejection side of the mould.
- If possible, large, deep ribs have ejector pins.
- Lifters extend beyond part, and can be pushed back into place by the opposite half of the mould.
- For sprues, runners, gate: The 'Of' dimension of the sprue matches material and part.
- Sprue bushing is locked in place.
- Sprue bushing pocket has a minimum dia of 3¼ in.
- Sprue and runners have cold slug areas.
- Direct sprues have bubblers or other cooling arrangements.
- If possible, the sprue has cooling ribs.
- Hot runners have a minimum dia of 18 mm.
- All submarine gates are on the ejector half of the mould, if possible.

- Scan the part configuration to see that:
- Ribs and thick sections are less than 70% of nominal wall thickness to prevent sink marks.
- Mould and cavities have identification numbers
- If possible, ribs and walls are generously drafted to aid ejection.
- No inserts are more than twice as tall as they are wide.
- Any grain or pattern stops short of part edges.

General check list for new moulds

- Is part drawing approved?
- Have you read all correspondence about job?
- Is type of plastics, additives, & colour specified? Is function of part understood?
- Can changes be made to make simple, better, easier to mould part ?
- Are number of cavities correct for the volume requires?
- Are tolerances indicated on critical dimensions?
- Can these tolerances be maintained?
- Is cycle time realistic?
- Are dimensions given including or excluding shrinkage?
- What shrinkage factor was used? Has adequate draft been specified?
- Where does draft start and stop?
- Have tapers been specified?
- Has gate location been approved?
- Is stripper mechanism sufficient?
- Has mould finish been specified?
- Has engraving master or art work been approved by customer?
- Is engraving specified for size, type, and depth?

Machine

- Is clamp tonnage sufficient for parts.
- Is swing radius sufficient

- Will moulds (Blow & Inj.) physically fit in machine specified and clear safety gate.
- Is injection capacity of plasticizer sufficient.
- Are spacers needed for stack height.
- Do wate lines interferes with the bars.
- Is system for stripper-tipper and ejector pins needed.
- Does machine need mixing nozzle.
- Is special screw needed.
- Is process control recommended.
- Do parts hit safety gate when stripped.

Mould Design

Injection

- Is cavity steel specified right for part.
- Is type of plating specified.
- Is nozzle size correct.
- Is nozzle seat inserted or air gaped.
- Are water ports located in right place.
- Are there a sufficient number of water ports.
- Are water ports drilled as we want.
- Are moulds vented proper amount for type of plastics to be moulded.
- Is number of cavities correct.
- Is cavity width correct.
- Are cavities marked with numbers, top or bottom, and job number.
- Has heat treat been specified.
- Has heat expansion been calculated.
- Are alignment pins in correct half of mould.

Blow

- Is cavity material specified suitable for parts.
- Is cavity finish specified (e.g. polish, sand blast etc.)

- Are water ports drilled as we want.
- Are moulds vented properly and sufficiently
- Are alignment pins needed.
- Are alignment pins securely installed and spaced corrected.
- Are cavities marked with numbers, top or bottom, and job number.
- Is number of cavities correct.
- Is width of cavities correct.
- Is draft indicated and is it sufficient.
- Is draft beginning and end specified.
- Has customer approved art work or masters for engraving.
- Is all engraving specified exactly for depth, size, type, and location.
- Is bottom plug material specified.
- Are bottom plugs correct - Push-up, shape, and / or special.
- Is cooling of bottom plug necessary.

General

- Have spare parts been specified. Are quantities for all parts specified.
- Chart for bolts, 'Of' rings, nozzles, heaters, and special mechanisms.
- Are all parts numbered & identified.
- Scheduled completion dates for mould fixed.
- Are metric sizes specified for parts.

Mould - Analysis Software

Generally flow analysis and cooling analysis is done separated and the results displayed for the entire part at one point in time, for example, the point of mould fill. In newer versions, it is possible to pick a series of points during the process display the results.

The features include:

- True thickness display of cooling lines and runners, which is highlighted in colour.
- Choice of American or Metric units.

- Ability to handle frozen fronts thereby providing information about short shots.
- Plots vectors on the screen showing flow direction in addition to fill pattern.
- Multiple Gate capability to enable to specify that the consistent pressure at all gate has to be maintained.

Analysis to move complex geometrix is also possible by using more number of finite elements.

The system can predict through warp and shrink analysis the quantitative deformations from moulded-in-stresses and the degree of sink as a percentage of total thickness.

Provision of packing simulation gives more accurate prediction of the total clamp pressure requirements and the quantity of material required to fill the cavity. It also helps in shrinkage analysis. The cooling software helps to evaluate the thermal effects of inserts and slides.

Co-ordinate Measuring Machines

CMM's are being used more and more all over the world as quality tools in plastics processing. CMM's can make multiple measurements on parts with contours and irregular surfaces in a fraction of the time required for conventional manual gauges. The use of this facility totally eliminates rejections at the QC and inspection stages thereby reducing rejection in the production of precision components.

Typical CMM consists primarily of a 3 D measuring are with a touch sensitive probe arm attached vertically to an overhead gantry or horizontally to a vertical guide bar. The probe arm can move in two directions, while the gantry or the guide bar moves in only one, resulting in three axes of motion for the probe.

When a tool or a part is placed within the measuring area, usually on a table, the probe is moved along the objects surface by servo motors, either manually or under automatic control.

For automatic control, the user first directs the probe manually and stores the measuring sequence in computer memory for later recall. In a manual operation, the user has to direct the probe by a joystick for each workpiece. Whenever the probe actually touches the workpiece, the point of contact is defined in terms of x-y-z axis of a coordinate system. This is repeated for several points and with the aid of a computer, successive data are interpolated to determine the distances between points. The distance are then automatically translated into part dimensions for comparison with specifications.

Benefit to Processors

CMM allows processors to greatly increase the number and accuracy of measurements being performed on parts and tooling. The CMM can be used during the initial production set-ups, capability studies and annual measurements lay-outs required particularly by the automobile manufacturers. Although shrinkage is forecast during die designing, it is quite common to have several shots to optimize the mould. The CMM provides a shot-to-shot history of dimensions during set-up enabling the tool maker to adjust the mould and bring the dimensions within tollerance. Most CMM's depend on the probe physically touching the workpiece for the measurements, since contact measurement is still the best choice for many applications although for parts that are flexible, fragile or highly contoured, a non-contact method of measurements using lasers or video cameras is preferred.

The CMM's have a great promise for the future and the investment in them is certainly going to be beneficial as well as economical in the long run.

Granulator - Check List

- Will it produce the desired product at the required capacity?
- Will it accept the largest feed stock currently available?
- What is the horsepower demand per Kg. per hour of use?
- Is it economical to operate with minimal maintenance?
- What is the availability of spare parts?
- It is safe to operate ?
- Is it versatile ?
- Are the rotor and the knives of hardened (Rockwell-C 53 to 61 steel?
- How Noisy?
- Am I buying the latest technology?

The films and the flexible materials cannot be directly granulated on such machines. They are first passed through an aglometer to form lumps, which could then be fed to the conventional granulator.

Metal Separators

Magnetic metal separators are used on the machine hoppers to remove metal contaminants from the plastics raw materials, particularly the reprocessed ones, and to.

- Protect processing equipment from serious and expensive damage to the machine parts.
- Reduce expensive down-time resulting from break-downs and equipment repairs.
- Eliminate worry by removing metal contaminants from the plastics processing product,

In a recent development, Electronics of India Inc. U.S.A. for example, are offering Electronics All metal separator which is able to detect and remove any metal-iron, steel, brass, aluminium, copper etc. from the processing product, even if the contaminate is embadded in the product. It is electronic circuit is adjustable for various materials to yield optimum sensitivity with a minimum of waste.

Geneal Performance Data

- The horse-power provides basic information about the capacity of a machine with respect to speed of its movements. It indicates power input to the pumps.
- More meaningful information is provided by plotting power in-put versus shot capacity, because the power in-put is generally adjusted to the total power in-put changes with the capacity of the injection unit if more than one unit can be combined with one clamping unit in a modular system.
- Moulding machines designed exclusively for processing Thermosets and Elastomers have about 50% less power input tan comparable machines for Thermoplastics.
- One also has to consider that the heating capacity is included in the total power input, which, therefore, can be increased by 40 to 90% over the pump input data.
- An electro-mechanical screw drive has to separately provided the power rating.
- The installed capacity of heating for Thermoplastics should be 0.4 to 0.5 KW for each grammed per second of plasticizing capacity to be

able to provided a great portion of heat to material by conduction if need.

- The dry Cycle time is a measurement of the basic velocity of the machine and comprises all stages of a cycle except plastication, mould filling and cooling of the part.
- Floor space requirement is the area calculated by multiplying length and width of the machine.
- Machine weight factor also needs to be correctly understood. Heaviest machine is not necessarily the most valuable machine nor of Superior Technology. As a general rule, weight should not be saved with respect to-
  - Thickness of machine platens'
  - Dimensions of toggles and links to ensure rigidity and long service life
  - Design of bars and sliders to prevent any deformation
  - Support of movable platens
- Weight can, howeve, be reduced with respect to
  - All components the deformation of which does not affect processing
  - All movable components of the hydraulic system which are accelerated or braked down
  - All components of the injection unit which move during injection
- The logical consequence of such a value-oriented concept is neither a very light or an extremely heavy machine.

2

Setting-up Mould and Machine

Each mould and each machine call for individual commiserations and should be accordingly handled. Following are the general guidelines:

- Strictly follow the precautions outlined in the manufacturers manual to prevent malfunction and hazards.
- Preferably disconnect the main supply whenever operator's hands are within the working area of the machine to eliminate any accidental operation of a contact switch.
- Mould placement
    - Adjust the positive stripping bars to zero ejecting action.
    - Maintain the barrel in retracted position.
    - Set clamp opening to the required daylight.
    - Set the selector Switches-mould setting, hand and auto-in set up position
    - Lower the mould from the Top or slide from the side depending on the size and facility available, after ensuring that main supply is off.
    - Reconnect power supply, retract moving platen, place ejection rods in position, move platen against mould, disconnect power and clamp mould to the platen.
    - Set the pyrometers and swtich on the heat.

- Set timers
- Adjust stripping bar for ejection
- Reconnect power and open and close the press by manually operating to ensure that everything is in order.
- Set limit switches for controlling speed of clamp closing and opening.
- Check cylinder temperatures as well as Nozzle temperature.
- Clean the cylinder of the inside material by purging till clean material comes out.
- Ensure correct fitting of Nozzle with the sprue bush.
- Start water cooling for mould and the Hydraulic Unit.
- Machine is now ready for operation.

\- Removal of mould from the Machine

- Record all the set conditions for future.
- Record whatever corrections that may be required on the mould.
- Keep all the jigs accessories, etc. in one box to save time during the next run.
- Before sending the mould for storage, clean the surfaces, dry and apply good quality grease to protect from corrosion. The great should be applied after the mould has come to room temperature.

\- Starting the machine.

- Ensure that the hopper is clean.
- Ensure that the material is completely dry, adequately preheated, if necessary.
- Check all the temperatures.
- Check all the water connections.
- Clean the cylinder by purging-may be by using the same material to be run.
- Adjust the feed, till a complete shot is obtained.
- Re-set all the culces to ensure optimum quality and shortest possible cycle time.

- Follow the instructions of the machine supplier for operting various controls.
- Store sprues, runners, short-shots and rejected mouldings separately in a clean polyethylene bag for re-use after grinding.
- Ensure that the adequate quantity of the required raw material is kept ready for uninterrupted production run as per the schedule.
- Record all the processing conditions for future references.
- At the end of the shift, record the product report on the prescribed forms.

Moulding Set-Up Time

Material	Cylinder °C	Mould °C	Heat Distortion °C	Factor
ABS	230	50	80	190
PE	230	30	90	200
PP	250	60	120	338
PS	200	30	90	340
ACETAL	225	100	140	305

Moulding Set-up time (seconds) = factor x Max. thickness (cm^2)

Maximum Ejection Temp. = indicated in column Heat Distortion °C.

For example, the factor for PS is 340 and assuming component thickness of 2mm the set up time can be estimated as :

340 x 0.2 x 0.2 = 13.6 seconds.

To obtain the overall cycle time, the injection time, the mould opening time, mould closing time and the pause must be added.

CHECK-LIST FOR START-UP

Assuming that the machines are fully ready for startup

- Chain - Pulley Block for lifting the Mould
- Silicone Aerosol Mould Release
- Brass Rods (25 mm Dia) for removal of parts sticking in moulds. The ends to be ground for flat end.
- Silicone High Temperature Grease
- Teflon Tapes

- Emery Paper for polishing of moulds
- Diamond Paste for the above
- Plastics mugs with handle and Buckets for material handling
- Knife for opening the bags of raw materials
- Hack Saw Blades sharpened for removing sprue from moulded parts
- Hand Gate cutters
- Asbestos Gloves
- Nylon Headed Hammer
- Insulation Tape
- Araldite Adhesive

INJECTION MOULDING CYCLE

A BREAK-UP OF MOST COMMON MOULDING CYCLE

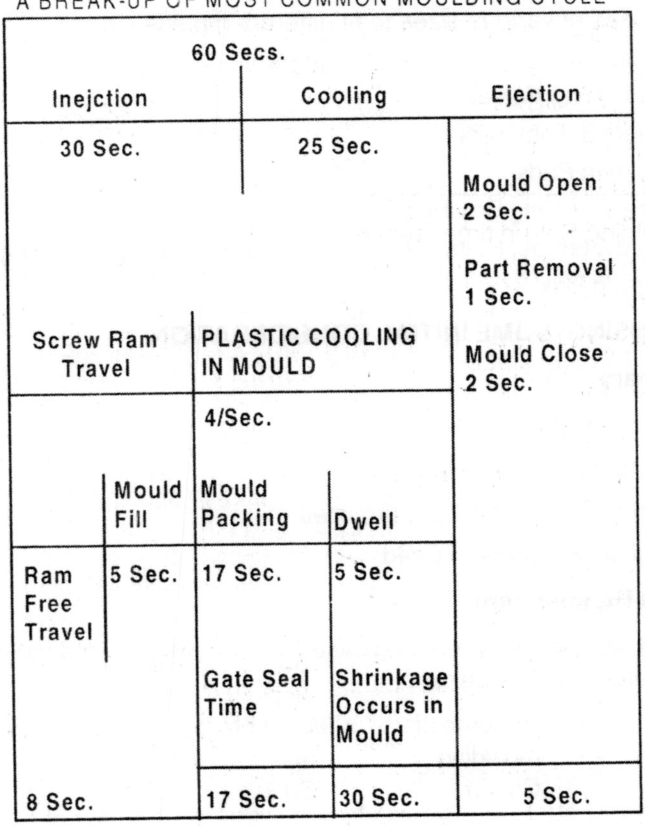

- Blow Lamp for removal of parts sticking in the moulds
- Chemical Fire Extinguishers for any emergency
- Plastics/Rubber Tubes, Hoses, Nipples etc. spares for oil/water connections in case of replacement.
- Insurance for equipments possibly to cover the Trial Runs
- One strong wooden table for mould keeping for working
- Inspection Lamps, portable
- Tool Box with complete set of spanners, screw Drivers, etc.
- Electrical Testing Machines
- Machine and Engineering Spares
- Plastics open crates for collecting sprues and Runners as well as moulded components.
- Plastics Bags (Poly) for packaging of production
- Nozzles of various sizes to fit different moulds
- Heater Bands and Cartridge Heaters
- Check Ring Valves
- Cutters & Trimmers
- Moulding Pads
- Barrel Cleaning Brushes
- Mould Clamps, Bolts, Washers Nozzle & Bushing Refacing Tools
- First-aid Box

PROCESSING: SOME INITIAL CONSIDERATION

Preliminary

- Shot weight
- Clamping Tonnage Required
- Number of cavities to be provided
- Position and Type of Feed

Machine Requirement

- First, shot capacity required based on total weight of the moulding which is determined as below :

Shot-Capacity = (Volume of moulding Cu.in.) x (Wt of plastics mateirals in Cu.in.) x (no. of impressions)

As a Guide, weights or moulded plastics per Cu. In for major materials are :

Materials	g/Cu.in
Polystyrene	17
High Impact PS	17
LDPE	15.1
HDPE	15.8
PP	14.8
ABS	18
SAN	23
Polycarbonate	20

Number of Shots / Cycle Time

This is very difficult to predict being dependent on various factors such as:

- Polymer's Thermal Characteristics
- Part Weight
- Part Design, Wall Thickness
- Efficiency of Cooling
- Mould Design, Ejector System
- Inserts, etc.

This, also can be estimated more out of experience and very close to the actual calculation

Theoretical Max. no. of cycles per minute

$$= \frac{\text{(Effective Plasticizing Rate in Kg/hour}}{\text{Weight of total shot in Kgs x 60)}}$$

Plasticizing Capacity/Rate

This is given by the machine supplier in terms of Kgs/hour based on Polystyrene. If for any material other than Polystyrene (A), Say (B) :

$$\text{Plasticizing} = \text{(M/c Plasticizing Rate)} \times \frac{\text{(Sp. Heat of 'A'}}{\text{Sp. Heat of 'B')}} \times \frac{\text{(Moulding Temp of A}}{\text{Moulding Temp of B)}}$$

The above formula can be used for calculating Plasticizing Rate for any Polymer. For maximum efficiency, it is recommended to operate machine upto 80% of its rated capacity to ensure uniform plastification.

Clamp Tonnage

The clamp tonnage for any given moulding is determined as below:

(Clamping Force Required (Tons)]	=	(Projected Area Moulding (Sq. inches)]	x	(Clamping Force Required to resist cavity pressure (ton/sq. inches)]

A rule of thumb is 2 to 3 Tons per Sq. inches of projected area is the Clamping Tonnage required for General Moulding.

For Structural Foam and Gas Moulding, this requirement is as small as 0.7 to 1.0 Sq. inches of projected area.

MOULDABILITY FEATURES

This relates to the mould designing and can be expressed as A Group of Features that are incorporated in a mould for the purpose of ensuring repeatability of operation, properties and other performance and design requirements of a product.

Such features are briefly covered only as a reference:

Part Removal

Even a slight tendency to stick in any portion of the cavity causes, warpate, stresses, dimensional distortion of parts and increases the Cycle Time. This can be overcome by additional taper, polishing the lines in the direction of withdrawal and may be, manipulation of mould temperature.

The Sprue

The Sprue has to be of such dimensions that the pressure drop is minimal and that its ability to deliver material to even the extremes is not impaired.

Runner System

The surface finish to the runner system should be as good as that of cavity. The preferred cross section of a runner is circular. The sharp edges should be avoided. The pressure drop should be kept to a minimum.

Cold-Slug Well

A Well is provided an extension of a sprur to receive the cool material lying in the nozzle zone due to inadequate heating and prevent it from entering the runner system. The well is equal in diameter to the sprue at the parting line and is about 1 to 1.5 times diameter in depth.

Gate Location

The gate can have a number adverse effect on part quality, if improperly place. It can cause weak weld lines, gas trapping and jetting. If the highest weldstrength is required, gate should be placed closest to the area of weld.

Gate Size

The gate size and its location has a very direct influence on the quality and the appearance of a moulded part. The recommended gate size is specified as a percentage of part-thickness with a width of twice the depth of a gate. Round gates about 10% larger in diameter than the Specified generally give a satisfactory result.

Cores

Are generally provided in a mould to form holes in a product or to support insets.

Vents

Lack of proper venting may cause excessive pressure for injection of the material, short shots, burn marks, poor weld-lines, splay marks and a high degree of internal stresses.

Undercuts

The guidance for successful undercuts is that the mould halves be apart so that movement can take place to free the part from the groove. The undercut should be less than one third of the material thickness; the moulded component should be ejected when the material is hot enough to permit it to stretch or collapse during ejection and the steel edge that forms the groove should have a radius against the moving of the part to prevent shearing.

Melt Rheology

Rheology is connected with flow of the material through the ducts. If the passages are not correctly proportioned for the Polymeric materials which are viscoelastic in flow, they may cause short, shots, poor surface finish, distortion, voids and bubbles, brittleness, poor welds, poor dimensions and varying shrinkages.

PURGING

Purging of injection machine cylinder is necessary if there is a change in material, colour or if the mouldings have a problem of brown or back steaks because of thermal degradation of the material in the cylinder or contamination.

This can be done in the following steps :

- Shut the slide of the hopper to stop feeding the material into the cylinder.
- Empty the hopper.
- Fill into the hopper, the purging material.
- Continue production till the moulded part shows presence of purging material.
- After the purging material starts coming through the nozzle, reduce the cylinder temperature to the permissible lowest. This gives a better scouring action being a harder material.
- More the nozzle away from the mould.
- Injection pressure may be reduced by 25 to 30%.
- Cylinder should be purged rapidly.
- About 1.5 times the capacity of the cylinder, the purging material is required to fully flush the cylinder.
- New material may now be filled in the hopper.
- Atleast two airshots with the new material should be taken and this material can be ground and reused.

This systematic approach will certainly give effective saving of expensive raw materials.

TABLE 2.1
THE INJECTION MOULDING MACHINE OPERATION

Item : Material :	Part No. : Pc. Wt. :	Mould No. : Shot Wt.:
Mould type : Overall Cycle Pcs/Hr.:	Pcs. /Mould: Clamp & Shot size :	Mould Drwg. No.: Make & No. of Press. :

Set Clamp Cycle
Clamp Fwd. slow
Pressure Buildup
Clamp Fast Reverse
Clamp Slow down

Clamp Reverse stop
Clamp Overstroke
Hyd. Eject

Clamp Data
Press Daylight
Clamp High-Clamp Low
Clamp Open-Slow/Fast

Pressures, Feed, Speeds
Injection High
Injection High-Squeeze
Injection Hole
Setting
Back Pressure
Injection Feed
Cushion
Injection Speed Setting
Screw RPM

Timers in Sec.
Injection High or Total Injection
Injection Low
Cooling-Cure
Melt Decompress
Clamp-Open
Air Ejection on/off
Temp. Cylinder, Nozzle & Nozzle Valve
Front, Zone # 1
Middle, Zone # 2
Rear, Zone # 3
Rear, Zone # 4
Time to reach settings
Melt Temp.
Nozzle Temp.
Nozzle Valve Temp.
Nozzle Vactuated
Throat Temp.

First Shot
First shot feed 'or runnerless mould

Mould Warm-up time
Hot runner warm-up time

Mould Mounting Data
Eye Bolts Size & No.
Mould Shot Height-In
Horizontal-in (eye Bolt Side)
Vertical-in
Spacer Size
Pull backs or
K.O. Rods size & No.
Mould Weight
Time to place Mould

Mould Placement
Sling Type Size & No.
Lift Size
Type of Hold down clamps
Heels
No. of Hold down clamps
Hold Down Clamp Spacing Cavity
Hold Down Clamp Spacing-Core
"Screw Jacks" Bottom Supports
Torque on clamp bolts

Removal
Core & Cavity Temp.
Cover with Mouldsaver
Time to Remove Mould
Water Hose & Size No.

Water Data
Water Temp. Cavity
Water Temp. Core

Temp. Cavity Position
1.
2.
3.
4.

Temp. Core Position

1.
2.
3.
4.

Misc. columns as needed

Table 2.2
Principal Conditions in Moulding

Stage of cyle	Typical results of Variations of Moulding Conditions	Action of Moulding Materials
Injection plunger or screw moves forward forcing plasticized material through nozzle.	Too start a cycle does not plasticize material sufficiently. Too low a cylinder temperature increases pressure losses, material may exceed or degrade if in cylinder too long at too high a temperature.	Injection Approximately 20 per cent pressure loss compressing cold material. External lubricant on power facilitates compression. Pressure squeezes air out from between granules which is vented back along cylinder. Heating increases volume of plastics but pressure increases volume.
Material enters sprue bush passing through runners to gate.		Cold material a front of plastics flow from nozzle is trapped in cold well. Out skin of flowing material chilled on runner walls. Cold material at front of plastics flow in runners trapped in runner cold wells (if provided). Pressure loss due to viscous friction of approx. 10% of original plunger pressure

Table 2.2 (Cont.)
Principal Conditions in Moulding

Stage of cyle	Typical results of Variations of Moulding Conditions	Action of Moulding Materials
Material passes through gate and enters cavity.	Low material temperatures increases orientation in moulding.	If cold front of material not trapped, may freeze on mould face opposite gate, causing surface scab. Pressure loss through gate of 10-20% of original plunger pressure depending on design. Steady steamline flow with possible fidgeting from restricted gates increases material velocity and thus reduces viscosity through gate. On other side, this velocity falls rapidly, increasing viscosity which together with cooling, seals gate when mould full. Small gates increase temperature of material but give higher orientation to the incoming material.
Material commences to fill cavity.	To low an injection pressure or temperature will not fill mould. Too high an injection ram speed may Material hamper venting of mould, and	Internal lubricate in material facilitates flow and ultimate mould release, Material at mould surfaces cools, increasing viscosity and

Table 2.2 (Cont.)
Principal Conditions in Moulding

Stage of cyle	Typical results of Variations of Moulding Conditions	Action of Moulding Materials
	cause excessive orient action on moulding. Too low a pressure or temperature can lead to low lines or bad knitlines. High moulding temperatures decrease material viscosity, give faster filling less shear strain Frozen strains are increased by the added cooling due to slow filling. At low material velocity rate, the shear rate of the material is also low and hence melt viscosity is high. At the same temperature but high material flow rate viscosity falls. Thus modifying size of runners will not improve flow if material velocity is too low. Poor weld lines caused by too low injection pressure, injection speed, cylinder temperature or mould temperature.	decreasing flow velocity. Hotter internal material continues to flow at faster rate thus settingup shear stress and orientation through material from coolest outer skin to hottest at center. These stresses are increased in this section due to the faster cooling rate arising from greater surface-to-volume ration. Flow of material fastest along easiest path (e.g. thickest section). Flow path divides at pins or raised characters. Cold front of flowing material joins up with other flow paths leading to knit lines at junction. Air is displaced ahead of incoming plastics material-if this cannot escape may lead to burning or weak welds. Hottest material from cylinder is last to enter cavity. Heat leaves plastics as it enters cavity increasing

Table 2.2 (Cont.)
Principal Conditions in Moulding

Stage of cyle	Typical results of Variations of Moulding Conditions	Action of Moulding Materials
		temperature of mould until removed by cooling water. As the plastics cools it viscosity increases and hence its flow viscosity decreases. Greatest heat around spur and near gate due to constant inflow of fresh hot material. Uneven cooling of the mould causes uneven shear rates to be set up in the flowing material thus causing differing frozen strains in the flowing material thus causing differing frozen strains in the moulding, leading to warpage and brittleness. Thus most cooling required near gate (hottest material) and least at extermities of mould (coolest material) to even a shear strains.
Cavity full. Packing pressure.	Poor surface on moulding from cold material or mould. Too high a temperature or pressure causes mould to flesh.	Cavity under full pressure. As material in cavity commences to cool it shrinks and further materials forced in. This packing causes

Table 2.2 (Cont.)
Principal Conditions in Moulding

Stage of cyle	Typical results of Variations of Moulding Conditions	Action of Moulding Materials
		displacement of cooling, viscous material in gate area, causing molecular orientation and shear strain between cold outer skin and hot internal care. As material cools still further, continued packing causes thermo elastic deformation instead of plastic flow. This deformation causes further frozen strain in the component and reduces heat distortion of moulding.
Gate freezes. Injection ram withdrawn	If ram withdrawn before gate freezes some back flow of material out of cavity will occurs. Surface shrinkage or voids caused by too high a material temperature, too short a ram forward time, or gate freezing too soon. Too long a packing time and or too high an injection pressure can lead to residual mould pressure and high moulding weight. Alternatively, it may require longer cooling quire	Material continues to cool and shrink cold outer layer retain frozen strain-hot inner core relaxes (thus thicker mouldings more strain free shrinkage is offset by residual elastic pressure within material. Excess shrinkage frees moulding from contact with female tool and grips male (setting up stress in mouldings). Excess residual

Table 2.2 (Cont.)
Principal Conditions in Moulding

Stage of cyle	Typical results of Variations of Moulding Conditions	Action of Moulding Materials
	longer cooling period to facilitte ejection by allowing shrinkage to offset higher cavity pressure, this lengthening cycle. Too low an injection temperature leds to weak mouldings. Minimum shrinkage in moulding from low cylinder and mould temperature, maximum pressure, long packing time, low injection speed (cools as it fills). With male tools, long cooling time causes cold drawing of material thus reducing shrinkage but increasing internal stress. Warpage may be high cylinder and mould temperature (low melt viscosity leading to lower shear strain and orientation and allowing more relaxation), low injection pressure and short packing time (also allowing less shear strain and more relaxation)	pressure seixes moulding between male and female tools causing difficult ejection. Cooling of heat sections can lead to internal voids or surface sinking.
Mould opens.	Too short a cooling time can lead to distortion by ejectors. Mould too hot lengthens cycle time.	Ejectors move forward and under pressure eject mouldings and tool leading to distortion and

Table 2.2 (Cont.)
Principal Conditions in Moulding

Stage of cyle	Typical results of Variations of Moulding Conditions	Action of Moulding Materials
	Sticking of moulding on male tool controlled by cooling rate, modulus of elasticity and tensile strength of material-if exceeded may cause cracking.	resistence to ejection). Sprue with drawn from sprue bush.
	Mould too hot lengthens cycle time. Stiking of moulding on male tool controlled by cooling rate, modulus of elasticity and tensile strength of material-if exceeded may cause cracking.	Hot mouldings continues to shrink in size on removal from press internal-stresses may lead to some distortion. With some materials mouldings may continue to shrink at room temperature for some time. Shrinkage on to insert set up local stresses in bosses etc.

The Injection moulding cycle

The sequence of event of during the ejection moulding of plastic part, is called the ejection moulding cycle. The cycle begins when the mould closes, followed by the injection of the polymer into the mould cavity. Once the cavity is filled, a holding presure is maintained to compensate for material shrinkage. In the next step, the screw turns, feeding the next shot to the front of screw. This causes the screw to retract as the next shot is prepared. Once the part is sufficient cool, the mould opens and the part ejected. Figure presents the sequence of events during the Injection moulding cycle. The figure shows that the cycle time is dominated by the cooling of the part inside the mould cavity. The total cycle time can be calculated using.

$$T_{cycle} = t_{closing} + t_{cooling} + t_{ejection}$$

where the closing and ejection times $t_{closing}$ and $t_{ejection}$, can last from a fraction of second to a few seconds, depending on the size of the mould and machine.

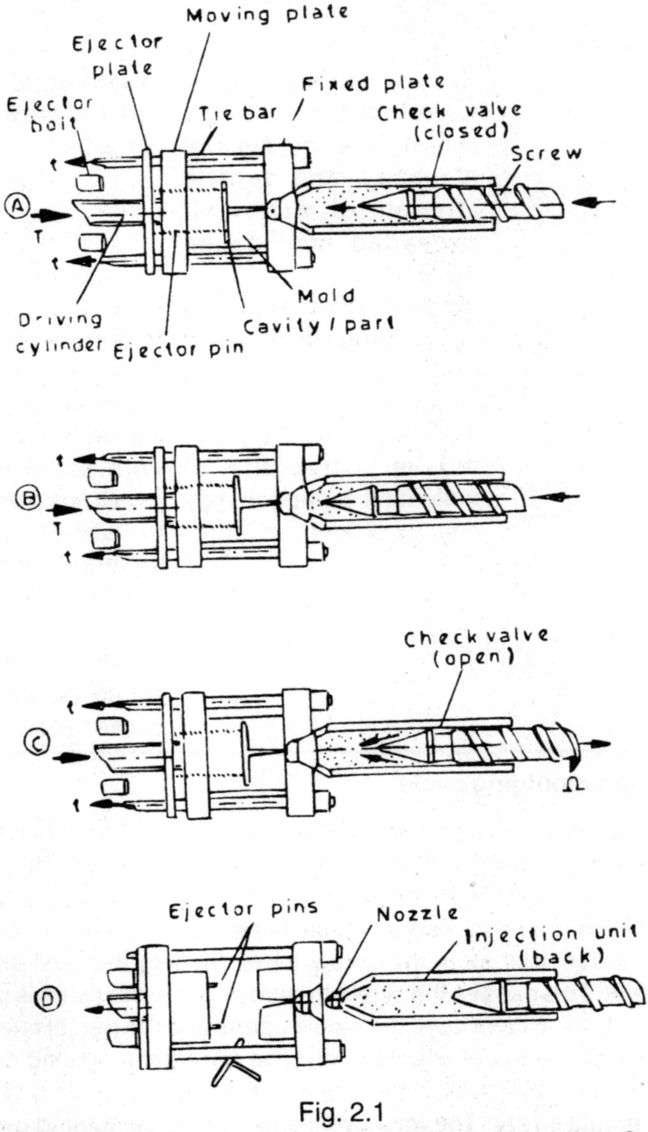

Fig. 2.1

Sequence of events during An Injection Moulding Cycle

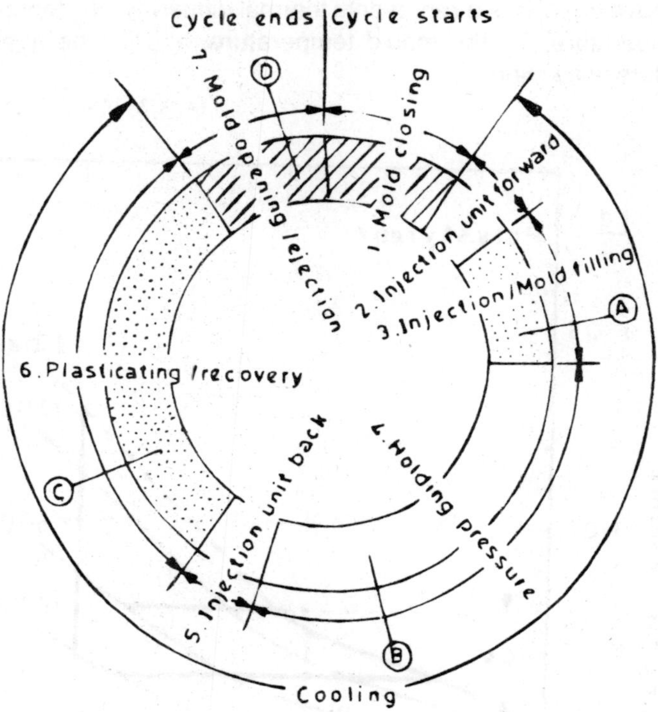

Fig. 2.2
INJECTION MOULDING CYCLE

Estimating cooling time during injection moulding

The cooling time for a plate like part of thickness h can be estimated using

$$t_{cooling} = \frac{h^2}{\pi\alpha} \ln \left[\frac{8\,T_M - T_W}{\pi^2\,T_D - T_W} \right]$$

and for cylindrical geometry of diameter D using

$$t_{cooling} = \frac{D^2}{23.14a} \ln 0.692 \quad \frac{T_M - T_W}{T_D - T_W}$$

In above equations a represents thermal diffusivity, T_M represents that melt temperature, T_W the mould temperature, and T_V the average part temperature at ejection.

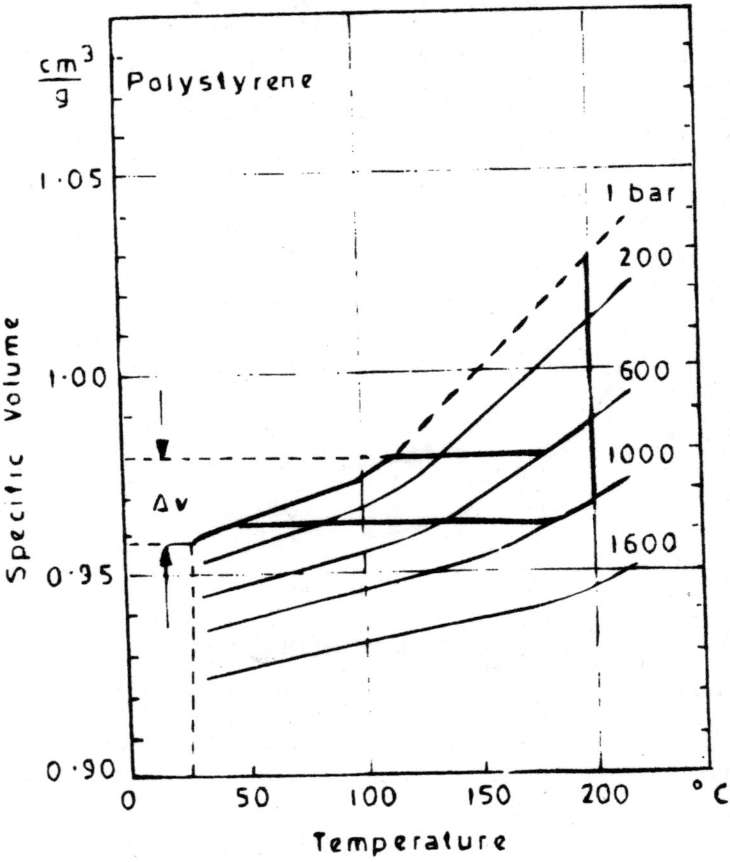

Fig. 2.3

TRACE OF TWO DIFFERENT INJECTION MOULDING CYCLES IN A PVT DIAGRAM

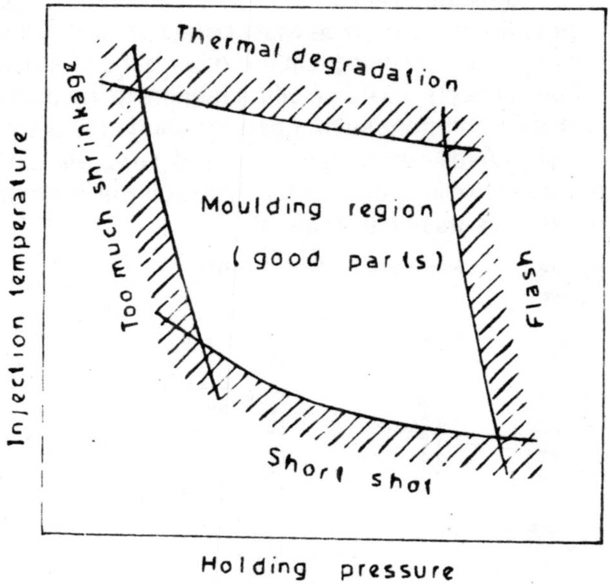

Fig. 2.4
HOLDING PRESSURE

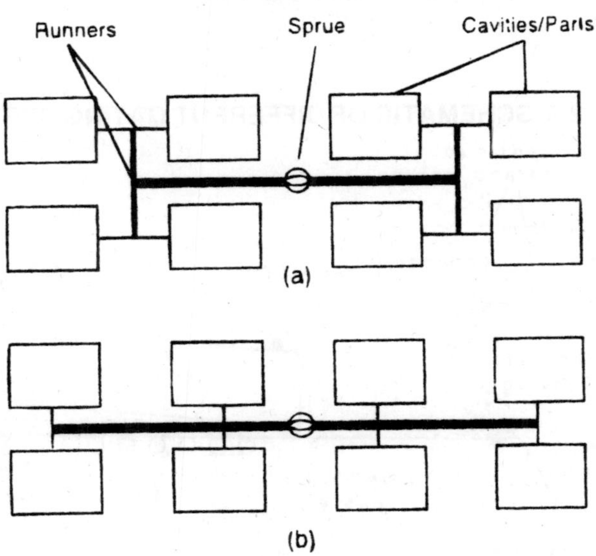

Fig. 2.5
SCHEMATIC OF DIFFERENT RUNNER SYSTEM ARRANGEMENTS

When large items are injection moulded, the sprue sometimes serves as the gate as in figure. The sprue must be subsequently trimmed, often requiring further surface finishing. On the other hand, a pin type gate is a small orifice that connects the sprue or the runners to the mould cavity. The part is easily broken off from such a gate, leaving only a small mark that usually does not require finishing. Other types of gates, also shown in figure, are film gates, used to eliminate orientation and disk or diaphragm gates for symmetric parts such as compact discs.

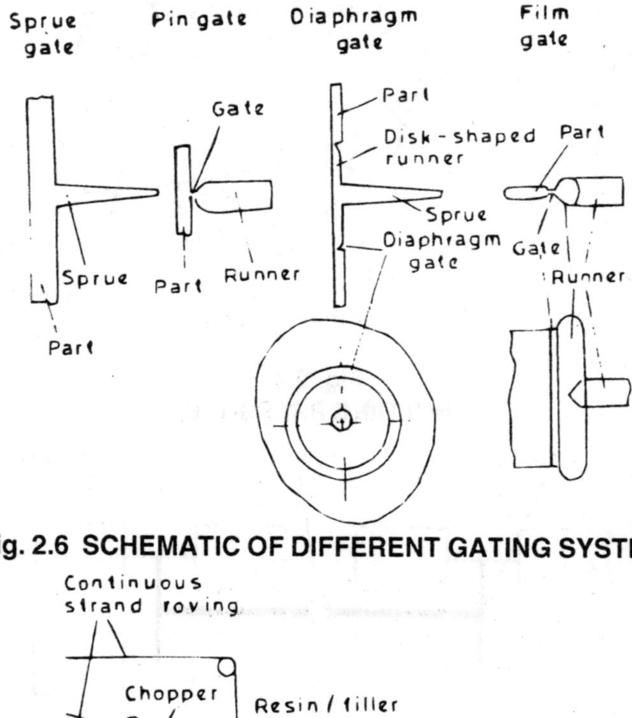

Fig. 2.6 SCHEMATIC OF DIFFERENT GATING SYSTEM

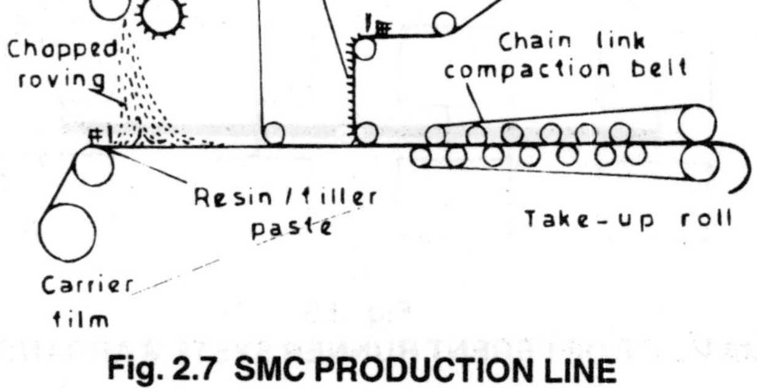

Fig. 2.7 SMC PRODUCTION LINE

One of the main advantages of the compression moulding process is the low fiber attrition during processing. Here, relatively long fibers can flow in the melt without the fiber damage common during plastication and cavity filling in injection moulding.

An alternate process is injection-compression moulding. Here, a charge is injected through a large gate followed by a compression cycle. The material used in the injection compression moulding process is called bulk moulding compound (BMC), which is reinforced with shorter fibers, generally 1 cm long, with an unsaturated polyester matrix. The main benefit of injection compression moulding over compression moulding is automation. The combination of injection and compression moulding leads to lower degrees of fiber attrition compared to injection moulding.

As in any polymer process, in compression moulding there is a direct relationship between deformation and final orientation in the part. Figure depicts the fiber orientation distribution within a plate were the initial charge coverage was 33% (11). Such distribution functions are very common in compression or transfer moulding and lead to high degrees of anisotropy throughout a product. To illustrate the effect of fiber orientation on material properties of the final part, figure shows how the deformation and resulting orientation from 33, 50, 66 and 100% mould coverage affects the stiffness of the plate.

Similar to injection moulding, today, there are commercially available codes that can be used to predict mould filling, fiber orientation and warpage of compression moulded parts. To predict fiber orientation in realistic parts, the Folgar - Tucker model has been implemented into commercially available compression mould filling simulation programs. The predicted fiber orientation distribution field for a compression moulded automotive fender is shown in figure.

SETTING UP A MOULDING SHOP

Accessories for the Injection Unit

Standard equipment with standard functions (without controls) includes:

- stainless steel feed hopper with shutoff against barrel, sight glass, cover, vent provision for draining.
- rotatory screw drive
- hydraulically (pneumatically for mini equipment) actuated injection

cylinder.

- controllable carriage movement (nozzle retraction eventually time delayed).
- complete plasticating unit (barrel head, band heaters, open nozzle, screw, nonreturn valve), exchangeable
- screw cooling installation with lateral (version A) or end inlet and exit (version B) of coolant.
- safeguard of screw against rupture
- non-reversing lock on screw
- screw return device before and/or after feeding cooling jacket in feeding section with sight control
- mechanism for alignment of nozzle.
- optical control of screw position
- back pressure relief
- instruction hookup (optional),
- safe guards in accordance with regulations

Special equipment (without controls) includes:

- plasticating unit for PVC, thermosets and elastomers
- selection of rotatory screw drive (electromechanical or hydraulic),
- option of accumulator connection for injection
- shut-off nozzles
- variable pull-in force for careful treatment of nozzle and sprue bushing
- variable speed control

Other Auxiliary Equipment

- drying tray oven for pre-drying materials
- hopper loader
- mould temperature control unit
- scrap grinder
- compressor
- water cooling / chilling plant
- double cone SS blender
- platform balance
- materials handling particularly for the moulds

Hygroscopic Plastics

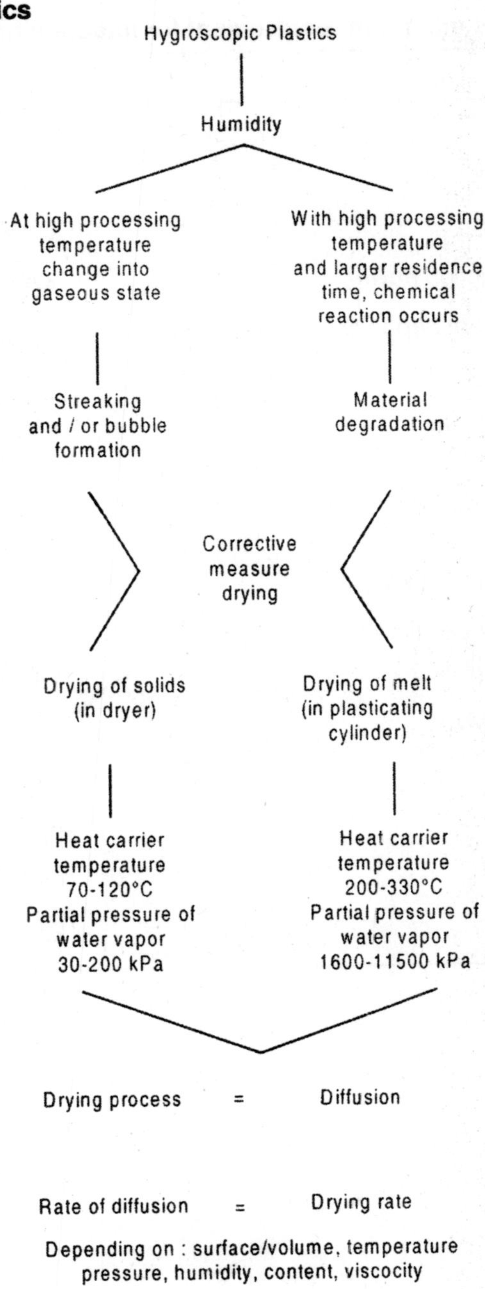

Table 2.3
Measurable minimum requirement for injection moulding machines

Features	Unit
Dry cycle	s
Recovery rate	g/s
Injection rate	cm^3/S
Available injection power	kW
Injection or shot capacity	cm^3 or g
Torque of screw	Nm
Injection pressure	MPa
Clamping force	kN
Opening Force	kN
Platen/size (height x width)	mm x mm
Distance between tie bars (horizontal x vertical)	mm x mm
max./min. daylight	mm
Max. stroke	mm
Drop chute	m^2
Floor space	m^2
Weight	kg

TABLE 2.4
FREQUENTLY EMPLOYED CLAMPING SYSTEMS FOR INJECTION MOULDING MACHINES

Clamping unit		Closing and opening	Clamping force	Maximum force buildup	Mould height adjustment
Mode of clamping	Design				
Mechanical	Vise	Mechanical with spindle*	Mechanical	Mechanical	Mechanical
	Single-toggle	Mechanical or hydro-mechanical	Mechanical or hydro-mechanical	Mechanical	Mechanical
	Double-toggle	Hydro-mechanical	Hydro-mechanical	Mechanical	Mechanical
Hydraulic	Direct hydraulic	Hydraulic	Hydraulic	Hydraulic	Hydraulic and automatic
	Hydraulic with rigid mechanical look	Hydro-mechanical	Hydraulic	Hydraulic	Hydraulic
		Hydro-Mechanical	Hydraulic	Hydraulic	Mechanical
Swivel arm	Hydraulic cylinder on	Hydro-mechanical	Hydraulic	Hydraulic	Hydraulic
	Toggle with hydraulic cylinder	Hydro-mechanical	Hydraulic	Hydraulic	Hydraulic

*Mini Machines only

TABLE 2.5
INJECTION PRESSURE REQUIRED FOR VARIOUS PLASTICS

Material	Necessary injection pressure (MPa)[a]		
	Easy Flow material[b] heavy sections	Medim flow material[b] standard sections	High viscosity material thin sections, small gets
ABS	80-110	100-130	130-150
POM	75-100	100-120	120-150
PE	70-100	100-120	120-150
PA	90-110	110-140	>140
PC	100-120	120-150	>150
PMMA	100-120	120-150	>150
PS	80-100	100-120	120-150
Rigid PVC	100-120	120-150	>150
Thermosets	100-140	140-175	175-230
Elastomers	80-100	100-120	120-150

[a]-Not Identical withlisted maximum injection pressure

[b]-Definition depends on flow properties of the material, temperature, and resistance to flow.

TABLE 2.6 COMMON GATING SYSTEMS AND THEIR APPLICATIONS

Gate type	Principal	Gate Removal	Application
Sprue type	Direct central feed	Part must be degrated manually	Single-cavity moulds, parts with heavy sections, demand for good appearance, requires post operation.
Pinpoint gate	Direct central or edge feed	Part is torn off	Most common gate for single and multicavity moulds, generally no post operation With runner systems : Separation during mould opening and removal of runner in the plane of an additional parting line. Three plate mould
Fan gate	Direct feed through fanned out thin channel	Manual separation	Need for symmetrical or linear filling, especially to prevent warpage.
Tunnel gate (submarine gate)	Runner with pinpoint gates machined into cavity steel, without additional parting line.	Gate is shorn off during mould opening	Multicavity mould with automatic gate removal
Hot tip, hot manifold	Hot runner or probe filled with melt, temperature- cntrolled feed through sprue, or pinpoint gate	Separation at the melt-solid interface sprue remains with parts	Multiple gating of parts with long flow distances and multicavity mods (stack moulds)
Insulated runner	Runner with large cross section, melt in its centre, feed generally with pinpoint gate	Separation during mould opening	Multiple gating of large parts and multicavity mouls.

TABLE 2.7
RECOMMENDATION FOR TEMPERATURE SETTINGS ALONG A VENTED BARREL FOR VARIOUS THERMOPLASTICS

T Melt°C	Control Setting°C				T Melt°C	Control Setting°C		Material
230-245	230	230	230	230	225	225	240	ABS
260-270	265	265	260	250	255	235	250	ABS/PC
210-220	210	210	210	210	210	215	225	Cellulosics
220-245	220	230	230	210	230	220	230	PA 6
260-280	260	250	250	230	250	240	250	PA 66
250-260	245	245	240	240	250	235	250	PBTP
300-315	300	300	290	280	280	280	310	PC
240-255	240	240	240	240	230	220	240	PMMA
280-310	280	290	290	290	275	290	290	PPO
250-265	250	260	260	255	235	240	260	SAN

TABLE 2.8
SPHERICAL RADII AND OF-DIMENSIONS OF NOZZLES ACCORDING TO EUROPEAN STANDARDS

Clamping force (kN)	Spherical radium (mm)			Of-Dimension (mm)		
	Thermoplastic Processing	Thermoset Processing	Elastomer Processing	Thermoplastic Processing	Thermoset Processing	Elastomer Processing
<500	10 (35)	10 (35)	10 (35)	3-5	5-8	4-6
500-1000	10 (35)	15 (35)	15 (35)	4-6	6-8	5-7
1000-5000	15 (35)	20 (35)	20 (35)	5-8	8-10	6-8
5000-10000	35	35	35	6-10	8-10	8-10
More than 10000	35	35	35	10-12	-	-

Table 2.9
INJECTION MOULDING -PARAMETERS FOR COMMON PLASTICS

Material	Density (g/cc)	Avg. Sp. heat [KJ/ (Kg x K)]	Avg. Processing Temp. (°C)	Avg. Mould Temp. (°C)	Shrink age (%)
Polystyrene	1.05	1.3	180-280	10-40	0.3-0.6
ABS	1.06	1.4	210-275	80-90	0.4-0.7
SAN	1.08	1.3	180-270	50-80	0.5-0.7
LDPE	0.92	2.0-2.1	160-260	50-70	1.65-5.0
HDPE	0.95	2.3-2.5	260-300	30-70	1.5-3.0
PP	0.91	1.84-2.5	250-270	50-75	1.0-2.5
PVC Soft	1.38	0.85	170-200	15-20	<0.5
PVC-Rigid	1.38	0.83-0.92	180-210	30-50	Around 0.5
Acrylics	1.18	1.46	210-240	50-70	0.1-0.8
PPO	1.06	1.45	250-300	80-100	0.5-07
Poly-carbonate	1.2	1.3	280-320	80-100	0.8
PET	1.37	-	260-290	140	1.2-2.0
NYLON-6	1.14	1.8	240-260	70-120	0.5-2.2
Thermo-plastic PU	1.2	1.85	195-230	20-40	0.9
Phenol Formaldehyde	1.4	1.3	60-80	170-190	1.2
Melamine	1.5	1.3	70-80	150-165	1.2-2.0

Operations and Controls in Injection Moulding

The total moulding cycle is as below

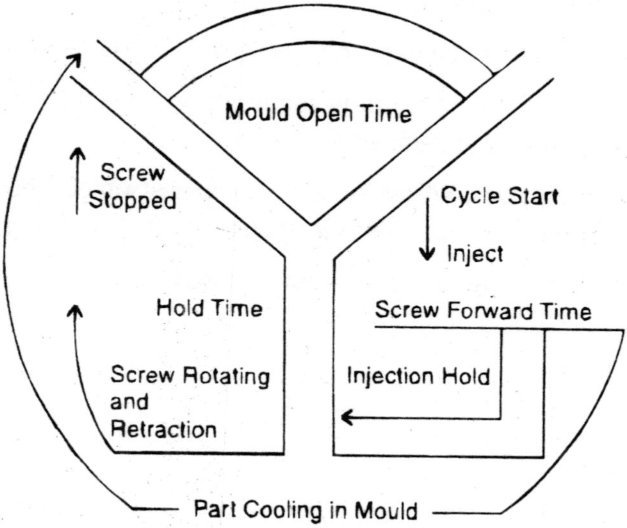

The key paratmeters to control the process are Temperature of the melt, Mould Temperature, Injection Pressure and Various Time cycles such as Injection time, Dwell time and dead time.

- The heating temperature is generally below the melting point of the resin to prevent thermal degradation due to over heating in case of any extended cycle and should match the requirements of the resin, The Machine and the Shot size being moulded.
- The nozzle should act merely as a melt conveying pipe and should not affect the melt temperature. Ideally, melt temperature entering and leaving the nozzle should be more or less the same.
    - The Nozzle temperature setting depends on nozzle design, type of resin and the sot size.
- Cooler moulds give faster moulding cycles. A compromise, therefore, has to be struck between Resin Flow and the Mould Temperature. The factors that affect the System Temperatures are :

- Shot Size-larger shot require more heat
- Injection Rate-faster filling creates higher melt temperatures because of shearing
- Size of Runner System-long runners require higher temperatures
- Part thickness-thick parts require more cooling time and are moulded at lower temperatures

- Injection and Holding Pressures should be lowest without getting a short shot. The pressure should be high enough to prevent shrinkage.
- The resin should be injected as fast as possible.

3

Effect of Processing on Mechanical Properties

The mechanical properties of a plastics product depend greatly on the manufacturing process. The variation in properties,of a product occur as a result in changes in temperature, pressure and raw materials. Certain properties that are influenced, particularly in the injection moulding are :

Molecular Orientation

This occurs in every process and there is no easy, rapid and economical way of finding out the extent nor there is any method to accurately predict the orientation that may occur.

Residual Stresses

These are developed within the moulded parts, as the polymer melt at high temperature flows into a mould at a much lower temperature. The plastics cool rapidly and residual stresses are generated by the following sequence

- The material in contact with the mould walls cools rapidly and shrinks either as a result of solidification shrinkage or solely due to thermal contraction.
- This surface contraction causes the interior to be compressed. Since the interior is still hot, it has little mechanical strength and the applied stress produces permanent deformation of the interior material.
- The centre then cools and contracts, tending to generate compressive stresses on the exterior. However, the exterior is frozen and the resultant stresses are resisted by elastic contraction of the exterior.

Residual stresses affect the fatigue life and impact strength of the moulded products, the major effect being due to residual stresses at the surface, where fatigue cracks initiate and propagation of these cracks begin.

Melt Elasticity

During processing, hydrostatic stresses develop within the melt. When these are removed as the extruded material leaves the die, the liquid swells considerably. This is called DIE SWELL. It is described by the swell ratio function

$$B = \frac{\text{Diameter of extradate}}{\text{diameter of the die}}$$

The parameters that increase 'B' are :

- Increased extrusion rate
- Increased die length/diameter ratio
- Decreased ratio of the die diameter to liquid pool diameter

Melt Fracture

If the flow rate through the die is increased excessively, surface imperfections known as Melt Fracture occurs.

Weld Lines

Weld Lines are generally generated in injection moulding due to inadequate gates or whenever the plasticized polymer is forced to diverge and reunite in flow around an insert. The weld lines often result in stress concentration at a location of inherant weakness as well as unpleasant appearance.

Provision of sufficient gates to ensure that the plastic will join while it is not enough for proper welding to occur. Another way to avoid weld-lines is to mould holes only partway through the product, so that the plastic flow will be unimpeded by a core running entirely across the plastic flow pattern. The holes are then drilled out after moulding.

Accurate Dimensions

The shrinkage due to thermal contraction and crystallization results into change in dimensions depending on temperature at which the gates freeze shut, the rate of cooling of the product and the moulding pressure. The shrinkage will vary with direction in the finished part, since the extent of molecular orientation depends on flow direction within the mould.

Shrinkage can be reduced by adding materials with low shrinkage. Typical fillers used for this purpose are calcium carbonate, talc, mica, etc.

The post moulding shrinkage may be reduced by annealing at slightly elevated temperatures to speed up the process. Annealing temperatures should be kept low, since annealing may affect other mechanical properties unfavourably.

Cooling Rate

The cooling rate of the part must be uniform to avoid distortion and uneven shrinkage. The cooling rates is a function of the coolant supply to the mould but is also dependent on heat transfer through the molten polymer. Due to the increased crystallization, the density often increases towards the centre. Similarly increasing the mould temperature also increases the crystallinity.

The residual stresses generated by the unequal cooling rate also affect the density. The variation in density in an moulded product is attributed to the variation in the cooling rate within the product.

Weigh Feeding And Blending

Gravimetric feeders and blenders are used in compounding and primary processing operations. Their function is to accurately and continually proportion resin and additives by weight, according to recipe. Compared to the traditional blend-by volume approach, gravimetric operation offers several important improvements. Quicker start-ups, improved blend/product quality, gravimetric extruder control, material cost savings, reduced scrap/regrind, and the availability of weight-based material use data for accurate inventory control are some advantages of the continuous gravimetric approach.

Feeders

Gravimetric feeders chiefly used by the compounder include the weigh-belt (usually for pelletized base resins) and the loss-in-weight feeder (typically for additives and low feed rates).

Weigh-belt feeders control flow rate by continuously weighing the resin pellet or other material as it is transported along the feeder's short conveyor. By combining the measured weighed with sensed conveyor belt speed, actual gravimetric flow rate is computed. Differences between actual and desired flow rate are then eliminated through an automatic, proportional adjustment of conveyor speed.

Loss-in-weight feeders are composed of a hopper, feeder (e.g. single or twin augers, vibratory tray, liquid pump), weighing system, and controller. In operation, the hopper, material, and feeder are collectively and continuously weighed. For liquids, a holding tank and pump replace the hopper and feeder. As material is discharged, the actual rate of weight loss is measured and compared to the desired rate of weight loss (setpoint). Deviations from setpoint are automatically corrected through adjustment of feeder speed. Periodic manual or automatic hopper refill is needed.

Weigh Blenders

Weigh blenders are designed for primary processors. Today, weigh blenders are found in continuous processing applications such as extruded profiles, sheet, cast film, blown film, wire and cable coating and filament pigmentation.

Two basic approaches are taken in weigh blender design: semi-continuous. In semi-continuous weigh blenders, volumetric (speed-controlled) feeders sequentially batch out their materials in recipe proportion. Discharge is to a common weigh hopper. When all material have been layered, the batch is discharged to a central mixer triggers the next batching cycle. In this way, the extruder is constantly supplied with the blend (although the ingredient feeders operate as batchers), but some possibility of segregation exists.

Fully continuous gravimetric blending involves individuals loss-in-weight control of each ingredient's flow. All ingredients are fed simultaneously in desired proportion to a continuous mixin.g hopper open to the extruder throat. Minimizing segregation. Level probes in the mixer sense extruder demand. These level data are then used to automatically change the weigh blender's total throughput as needed, to precisely follow extruder demand. Alternatively, in gravimetric extrusion control applications, the same level information can control extruder speed to maintain a specified weight based throughput.

Controls

Today's microprocessor-based control systems afford the user of feeders and weigh blenders a strong measure of operating convenience, performance flexibility, and data communications capability.

(By Bruce Lowden, General Marketing Manager, K. Tron Vertech. Inc. a K- Tron International Company, Route 55 & 553, Pitman, Ns 08071. Book - Modern Plastics Encyclopedia Handbook)

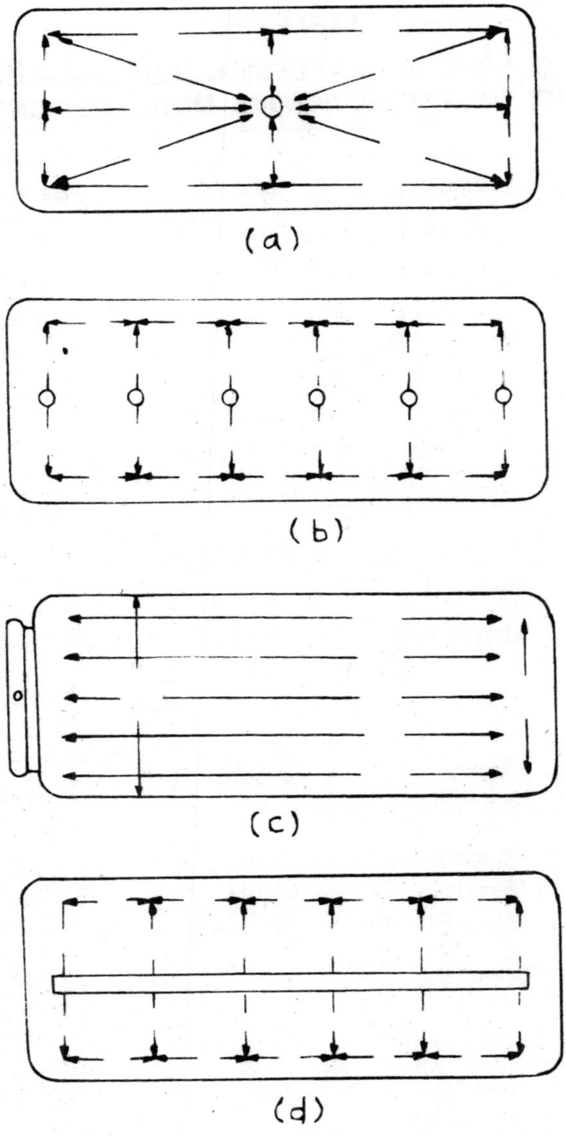

a. Central sprue or pin-point gate b. Ring rate c. Row of pin -point gates d. Diapharagm gate

Fig. 3.8

SHRINKAGE IN DIRECTION OF FLOW (A) AND TRANSVERSELY TO IT (B) WITH VARIOUS TYPES OF GATE

TABLE 3.10

INTERRELATIONSHIP OF PART DESIGN, MOULDING CONDITIONS, POLYMER SELECTION AND MOULD DESIGN

Part Design	Moulding Conditions	Polymer Selection	Mould Design
Properties:-	Process Control :-	Properties :-	Gate Size/ Location
Mechanical	Melt/Mould Temp	Mechanical	Runner/ Cavity Layout
Thermol	Cycle	Thermol	
Chemical	Pressure	Chemical	
Electrical	Ram Speed	Electrical	Draft angles
Dimensional	Materials handling	Diimensional	
Stability	Use of Regrind	Stability	Undercuts
Outdoor exposure			Tolerances
Bearing Area	Effects of Moulding :	Processng :	
Ribs	Toughness Mould Mould Shrinkages	Flow Mould Shrinkages	Mould Shrinkage
Bosses	Weld Lines		Location of Parting line
	Post Mould	Ejection	
Sharp & Radii	Shrinkage Part Surface	Cycle	Vent Size & location
Undercuts			Side Actions
Sections Thickness	Post Moulding		

TABLE 3.10 (CONT.)

INTERRELATIONSHIP OF PART DESIGN, MOULDING CONDITIONS, POLYMER SELECTION AND MOULD DESIGN

Part Design	Moulding Conditions	Polymer Selection	Mould Design
	Operations		Surface Finish
Surface Finish	QualityControl Preheating		Coring for Finish
Surface Finish	Quality Control Preheating		Coaring for Water Cooling
Tolerances	Annealing Finishing		
Gate Size/ Location	Assembly Decorations		

TABLE 3.11

SPECIFIC GRAVITY AND BULK FACTOR FOR PLASTIC MATERIALS

Material	Specific gravity g/cc	Specific weight lb/cu.in	Specific volume cu.in/lb	Bulk factor
ABS	1.02-1.25	0.037-0.045	27.2-22.2	1.1-1.2
Acetal	1.41-1.42	0.050-0.051	19.6-19.5	-
Cellulose acetate	1.20-1.34	0.044-0.048	21.9-20.7	1.8-2.6
Cellulose acetate butyrate	1.15-1.22	0.041-0.044	24.1-22.7	1.8-2.4
Cellulose nitrate	1.35-1.40	0.049-0.050	20.5-19.8	-
Cellulose proponate	1.17-1.24	0.042-0.045	23.7-22.44	-
Fluorocarbon:PTEF	2.10-2.22	0.75-0.080	13.2-12.5	-
FEP	2.12-2.17	0.076-0.078	13.0-12.8	2.0
Polyamide	1.09-1.15	0.043	23.2	1.7-5.5

TABLE 3.11 (CONT.)

SPECIFIC GRAVITY AND BULK FACTOR FOR PLASTIC MATERIALS

Material	Specific gravity g/cc	Specific weight lb/cu.in	Specific volume cu.in/lb	Bulk factor
Polyethylene :				
Low density	0.910-0.925	0.032-0.033	30.4.30.0	2.0-2.5
Medium density	0.926-0.940	0.033-0.034	29.9-29.5	-
High density	0.941-0.965	0.034-0.035	29.4-28.7	-
Polymethyl methacrylate	1.17-1.20	0.042-0.043	23.7-23.2	1.6-2.0
Polyphenylene oxide	1.06	0.038	26.1	2.0-3.5
Polypropylene	0.086-0.906	0.032-0.033	31.5-30.6	2.0-2.4
Polystyrene	1.04-1.100	0.037-0.040	26.6-25.2	1.6-2.4
Poiysulfone	1.24	0.045	22.4	1.8-2.2
Polyvinyl acetate	1.10-1.14	0.040-0.041	25.2-24.3	-
Polyvinyl Chloride :				
Rigid	1.35-1.45	0.049-0.052	20.5-19.1	2.0-2.3
Flexible	1.16-1.35	0.042-0.049	23.9-20.5	2.0-2.3
Polyvinylidene chloride	1.65-1.72	0.059-0.062	16.8-16.1	2.0
Polyurethane	1.11-1.25	0.040-1.045	25.0-22.28	2.4-2.8

TABLE 3.12

WATER ABSORPTION OF COMMON PLASTICS (PER CENT)

Plastics	Per Cent
Allyl resins :	
Cast moulded	0.03-0.44
Glass filled	0.12-0.35
Mineral filled	0.20-0.50
Synthetic fibre filled	0.20-0.22

TABLE 3.12 (CONT.)
WATER ABSORPTION OF COMMON PLASTICS (PER CENT)

Plastics	Per Cent
Cellulose plastics :	
Cellulose nitrate	1.00-2.00
Cellulose acetate	2.00-7.00
Cellulose acetate butyrate	0.90-2.20
Cellulose propionate	1.20-2.80
Ethyl cellulose	0.80-1.80
Eposy resins :	
Cast :	
No filler	0.08-0.15
Aluminium filled	0.10-4.00
Laminated :	
Glass fibre	0.04-0.30
Paper base	0.15-0.50
Ionomer Melamine :	
Alpha cellulose filled	0.10-0.60
Cotton flock filled	0.16-0.30
Asbestos filled	0.08-0.14
Macerated fabric filled	0.30-0.60
Glass fibre filled	0.09-0.21
Phenol formaldehyde	
No filler	0.10-0.20
Wood flour filled	0.30-1.20
Asbestos filled	0.10-0.50
Mica Filled	0.01-0.05
Macerated or cored filled	0.40-1.75
Glass filled	0.13
Laminated :	
Fabric base	0.20-2.50
Mat base	0.10-0.80
Cotton fabric base	1.30-3.50
Paper base	0.10-5.00
Polyphenylene oxide	0.06-0.07
Urea formaldehyde	0.040-0.80

THERMAL CONDUCTIVITY OF MATERIALS
(BTU/°F/ft²/hr)

Copper (pure)	222
Copper alloy*	187
Aluminium 2017	95
Brass	69
Beryllium Copper	64
Steel (1% C)	26
Tool Steel P 20	21
Tool Steel H13	12
Stainless 316	10
Water	0.39
Polystyrene	0.07
Polyethylene	0.18
Nylon	0.14
Polypropylene	0.07
Air	0.14

* This alloy consists of 99.14% copper, 0.85% Chromium and 0.01% silicon. It has a 70,000 psi tensile strength and is produced by Resistance Welding Assoc.

TABLE 3.13
MINIMUM ACTUAL COOLING TIME IN SECONDS

Wall Thickness Maximum Mil.	Inch	Abs.	Nylon	Low Density Poly-ethy-lene	High Density Poly-ethy-lene	Poly-Propy-lene	Poly-styrene	Poly-vinyl Chloride
20	1/32				1.8	1.8	1.0	
30	1/32	1.8	2.5	2.3	3.0	3.0	1.8	2.1
40		2.9	3.8	3.5	4.5	4.5	2.9	3.3
50	3/64	4.1	5.3	4.9	6.2	6.2	4.1	4.6
60		5.7	7.0	6.6	8.0	8.0	5.7	6.3
70		7.4	8.9	8.4	10.0	10.0	7.4	8.1

TABLE 3.13 (CONT.)

MINIMUM ACTUAL COOLING TIME IN SECONDS

Wall Thickness Maximum Mil.	Inch	Abs.	Nylon	Low Density Poly-ethy-lene	High Density Poly-ethy-lene	Poly-Propy-lene	Poly-styrene	Poly-vinyl Chloride
80	5/64	9.3	11.2	10.6	12.5	12.5	9.3	10.1
90		11.5	13.4	12.8	14.7	14.7	11.5	12.3
100		13.7	15.9	15.2	17.5	17.5	13.7	14.7
125	1/8	20.5	23.4	22.5	25.5	25.5	20.5	21.7
150		28.5	32.0	30.9	34.5	34.5	28.5	30.0
175	13/64	38.0	42.0	40.8	45.0	45.0	38.0	39.8
200		49.0	53.9	52.4	57.5	57.5	49.0	51.1
225		61.0	66.8	65.0	71.0	71.0	61.0	63.5
250	1/4	75.0	80.8	79.0	85.0	85.0	75.0	77.5

TABLE 3.14

PROCESSING TEMPERATURES, MOULD TEMPERATURES, AND SHRINKAGE OF MOST COMMON PLASTICS USED IN INJECTION MOULDING

Material	Symbol	Density [g/cm3]	Glass foner content [%]	Average Specific heat [kJ/(kg x k)]	Proce-ssing temper-ature [°C	Mould temper-ature [°C]	Shrin kage* [%]
Polystyrene	PS	1.05		1.3	180-280	10-40	0.3-0.6
Styrene-butadiene	SB	1.05		1.21	170-260	5-75	0.5-0.6
Styrene-acrylonitrile	SAN	1.08		1.3	180-270	50-80	0.5-0.7
Acrylonitrile-butadiene-styrene	ABS	1.06		1.4	210-275	50-90	0.4-0.7
Acrylonitrile-styrene-acrylate	ASA	1.07		1.3	230-260	40-90	0.4-0.6
Low-density polyethylene	LDPE	0.954		2.0-2.1	160-260	50-70	1.5-5.0
High-density polyethylene	HDPE	0.92		2.3-2.5	260-300	30-70	15.3.0

TABLE 3.14 (CONT.)
PROCESSING TEMPERATURES, MOULD TEMPERATURES, AND SHRINKAGE OF MOST COMMON PLASTICS USED IN INJECTION MOULDING

Material	Symbol	Density [g/cm3]	Glass foner content [%]	Average Specific heat [kJ/(kg x k)]	Processing temperature [°C	Mould temperature [°C]	Shrinkage* [%]
Plypropylene	PP	0.917		0.84-25.	250-270	50-705	1.0-2.5
Polypropylene-GR	PP-GR	1.15	30	1.1-1.35	260-280	50-80	1.5-1.2
Polyisobutylene	PIB	0.93		-	150-200	50-80	-
Poly (4 methylpentene-1)	PMP	0.83		-	280-310	70	0.5-3.0
Poly (vinyl chloride)	PVC soft	1.38		0.85	170-200	15-20	< 0.5
Poly (vinyl chloride)	PVC rigid	1.38		0.83-0.92	180-210	30-50	-0.5
Poly (vinylidene floouride)	PVDF	1.2			250-270	90-100	3-6
Polytetrafloroethylene	PTFE	2.12-2.17		0.12	320-360	200-230	3.5-6.0
Poly (methyl methacrylate)	PMMA	1.18		1.46	210-240	50-70	0.1-0.8
Polyxymethylene, polyacetal	POM	1.42		1.47-1.5	200-210	> 90	1.9-2.3
Poly (phenylene oxide)	PPO	1.06		1.45	250-300	80-100	0.5-0.7
Poly (phenylene oxide)-GR	PPO-GR	1.27	30	1.3	280-300	80-100	> 0.7
Cellulose acetate	CA	1.27-1.3		1.3-1.7	180-230	50-80	0.5
Cellulose acetate butyrate	CAB	1.17-1.22		1.3-1.7	180-230	50-80	0.5
Cellulose propionate	CP	1.19-1.23		1.7	180-230	50-80	0.5
Polycarbonate	PC	1.2		1.3	280-320	80-100	0.8
Polycarbonate-GR	PC-GR	1.42	10-30	1.1	300-330	100-120	15-.55
Poly ethylene terephthalate	PET	1.37			260-290	140	1.2-2.0
Poly ethylene terephthalate-GR	PET-GR	1.5-1.53	20-30		260-290	140	1.2-2.0

TABLE 3.14 (CONT.) PROCESSING TEMPERATURES, MOULD TEMPERATURES, AND SHRINKAGE OF MOST COMMON PLASTICS USED IN INJECTION MOULDING

Material	Symbol	Density [g/cm3]	Glass foner content [%]	Average Specific heat [kJ/(kg x k)]	Proce-ssing temper-ature [°C°	Mould temper-ature [°C]	Shrin kage* [%]
Poly butylene terephthalate	PBT	1.3			240-260	60-80	1.5-2.5
Poly butyelene terephthalate-GR	PBT-GR	1.52-1.57	30-50		250-270	60-80	0.3-1.2
Polyethyeretherketone	PEEK	1.32			350-390	120-150	1.1
Polyethere-therketone-GR	PEEK-GR	1.49	30		350-400	120-150	0.2-1
Polyamide 6 (nylon-6)	PA 6	1.14		1.8	240-260	70-120	0.5-2.2
Polyamide 66-GR	PA 6-GR	1.36-165	30-35	1.25-1.7	270-290	70-120	0.3-1
Polyamide 66 (nylon-66)	PA-66	1.15		1.7	260-290	7.-120	0.5-2.5
Polyamide 66-GR	PA 66-GR	1.20-1.65	30-35	1.4	280-310	70-120	0.5-1.5
Polyamide 11	PA 11	1.03-1.05		2.4	210-250	40-80	0.5-1.5
Polyamide 12	PA 12	1.01-1.04		1.2	210-250	40-80	0.5-1.5
Polyamide-imide	PAI	1.4		-	330-380	230	-
Poly (phenylene sulfide)	PPS	1.64	40	-	370	>150	0.2
Poly (thermimide)	PEI	1.27		-	340-425	65-175	0.4-0.7
Poly (ether sulfone)	PES	1.6	30	-	360-390	140-190	0.2-0.5
Polyethere ketone	PEK	1.3		-	330-380	110-180	0.7
Polyurethane (thermopl.)	PUR	1.2		1.85	195-230	20-40	0.9
Phenol-formaldehyde resin	PF	1.4		1.3	60-80	170-190	1.2
Melamine-formaldehyde resin	MF	1.5		1.3	70-80	150-165	1.2-2
Melamine-phenol-formaldehyde resin	M PF1.6		1.1	60-80	160-180	0.8-1.8	
Unsaturated polyester	UP	2.0-2.1		0.9	40-60	150-170	0.5-0.8
Exoxy, epoxide	EP	1.9	30-80	1.7-1.9	ca.70	160-170	0.2

*Note difference in shrinkage in flow direction and transverse, processing influence.

TABLE 3.15

GENERAL

Polymer	Density at Room temp. g/cm³	Density at Processing Temp. g/cm³	Shrinkage Z	Cavity Pressure Range Bar	Max.Flow Ratio for 1 nm
ABS	1.06	0.95	0.4-0.7	500-1500	140
CA	1.2-1.3	1.10	0.4-0.7	-	100
POM	1.42	1.16	2	400-1200	100
PMMA	1.18	1.09	0.4-0.8	350-1400	100
PRO	1.05-1.1	-	0.5-0.7	-	140
PA 6/6	1.14	0.95	1 to 3	350-1400	100
PC	1.22	1.08	0.7-0.8	700-1400	60
PES	1.37	-	0.6	-	60
PBT	1.30	1.15	1.3-1.5	350-1400	125
PPS	1.5-2.1	-	0.2	-	150
PETP	1.38	1.20	1.3-1.5	350-1400	125
PS	1.05	0.95	0.45	350-1400	130-150
HDPE	0.96	0.74	1.5-2	850-1050	170
LDPE	0.92	0.74	1-2	350-1000	200
PP	0.91	0.73	1.5-2.2	700-1400	170
RPVC	1.3-1.6	-	1.2	700-2800	60
SPVC	1.1-1.14	-	0.5	650-1750	180
SAN	1.08	0.99	0.50	500-1500	140
TPU	1.20	-	1.15	-	-

TABLE 3.16

MEASURABLE MINIMUM REQUIREMENTS FOR INJECTION MOULDING MACHINES

Features	Unit
Dry cycle	s
Recovery rate	g/s
Injection rate	cm^3/s
Available Injection Power	kW
Injection or shot capacity	cm^3 or g
Torque of screw	Nm
Injection pressure	MPa
Clamping force	kN
Opening force	kN
Platen/size (height x width)	mm x mm
Distance between tie bars (horizontal x vertical)	mm x mm
Max./min. daylight	mm
Max. stroke	mm
Drop chute	m^2
Floor space	m^2
Weight	kg

TABLE 3.17
DRY CYCLE TIMES OF INJECTION MOULDING MACHINES- A THUMB RULE

Clamping force (kN)	Dry cycle force times for processing of	
	Thermoplastics (s)	Thermosets and elastomers (s)
25	0.8-1.8	-
50	0.9-1.5	up to 3
100	1.1-2	up to 6
200	1.7-4	up to 12
500	2-7	up to 25
1000	5.5-10	-
3000 & above	15-25	-

TABLE 3.18
INJECTION PRESSURE REQUIRED FOR VARIOUS PLASTICS IN GENERAL

Material	Necessary injection pressure (MP_a)[a]		
	Easy flow material, [b] heavy sections	Medium flow material, [b] standard sections	High viscosity material, [b] this sections small gates
ABS	80-110	100-130	130-150
POM	85-100	100-120	120-150
PE	70-100	100-120	120-150
PA	90-110	110-140	> 140
PC	100-120	120-150	> 150
PMMA	100-120	120-150	> 150
PS	80-100	100-120	120-150
Rigid PVC	100-120	120-150	> 150
Thermosets	100-140	140-175	175-230
Elastomers	80-100	100-120	120-150

[a] Not identical with listed maximum injection pressure.

[b] Definition depends on flow properties of the material, temperature, and resistance to flow.

TABLE 3.19

INJECTION PRESSURE RANGES FOR MODULAR SYSTEM OF INJECTION UNITS

Employed for processing of	Injection pressure (MPa)	Hydraulic Unit	Pressure ratio
Special cases	Highest pressure		10-12
Thermosets, PC, PMMA and rigid PVC under difficult conditions	200-250	same as above	9-11
Standard processing of thermoplastics and elastomers	170-180[a]	same as above	7-9
Easy flow materials and cases with low resistance to flow	120-140[a]	same as above	6-8
Special cases	100-120[a]	same as above	6-7

a Increase necessary if pressure loss in hydraulic servo and control system is larger than 20% of maximum pressure.

TABLE 3.20

EFFECTS OF PROCESSING PARAMETERS ON PART DIMENSIONS

Processing parameter	Effect	Part dimension an invariable mould dimension	resulting from a mould dimension by breathing of the mould
Increasing melt temperature	(a) increasing in volume (b) Better pressure transmission	(a) (b)-	(a)-(b)

TABLE 3.20 (CONT.)

EFFECTS OF PROCESSING PARAMETERS ON PART DIMENSIONS

Processing parameter	Effect	Part dimension an invariable mould dimension	resulting from a mould dimension by breathing of the mould
Increasing mould temperature	Higher releases temperature		
Increasing Injection speed	Better pressure transmission during holding pressure stage		
Increasing holding pressure	Better compensation of volumentric shrinkage during cooling stage; better compression of the melt		
Increasing holding pressure time	Same as above, before gate is frozen		
	After gate is frozen		
Increasing mould deformation from cavity pressure	Packing of areas of large deformation affecting dimensions by breathing		
Gate geometry; increasing cross section of gate	Indirect effects, (refer to injection speed, holding pressure, melt temperature)		

TABLE 3.21
PROCESSING LIMITATIONS FOR VARIOUS POLYMERS - GUIDELINES

Polymer	Predrying Temp. °C	Process Time Hrs.	Mould Temp. °C	Injection Temp. Hrs.	Peripherel Volume Z	Back Pr. Screw Speed	In Speed Range Bar	Inj. Press	Material bar	Custom nm
ABS	8-100	2-4	180-260	10-90	30-80	0.5	<200	High	,1500	2-6
CA	-	-	200-220	40-80	15-85	0.5	<100	High	800-1200	3-8
POM	90-110	2	170-210	60-120	15-75	0.6	<200	High	<1500	2-6
PMMA	70	4	170-240	40-80	20-75	0.5	<400	Low	High	2-6
PPO	100	2	240-270	80-105	15-85	-	<50	High	<1200	3-5
PA6/6	80	16	250-290	60-90	15-80	0.8	<80	High	<1500	2-6
PC	120	3	260-320	80-120	20-80	0.5	<150	High	<2000	2-6
PES	150	3	330-790	130-200	-	-	<400	High	<2000	4
PBT	120	3	240-270	90-140	15-80	0.6	<50	Low	<1500	3-5
PPS	150	6	300-360	130-160	15-70	-	-	High	<1500	4-6
PETP	120	3	240-270	90-140	15-80	0.6	<50	Low	<1500	3-5
PS	70	1-3	180-270	10-50	5-95	1	<150	High	<1500	2-6
HDPE	NR		150-280	10-50	5-95	1	<200	High	<1000	2-6
LDPE	NR		150-220	20-50	5-95	1	<200	High	<1000	2-6
PP	NR		160-250	20-60	10-90	1	<200	High	<1800	2-6
RPVC	NR		170-190	20-60		0.2	<50	Low	<1700	4
SPVC	NR		180-200	20-80		-	<250	Low	<1200	4
SAN	70	1-3	220-280	30-80	50-80	0.4	<150	High	<1000	2-6
TPU	80-110	3	180-220	30-80	40-80	-	<150	Low	<1000	3

TABLE 3.22

RECOMMENDED NOZZLES FOR PLASTICS MOULDING MACHINES

Plastic Material	Types of Nozzle: Open nozzle	Sliding shut-off nozzle[1]	Spring-loaded needle shut-off nozzle[2]	Hydraulic needle shut-off nozzle	Hydraulic bolt-type shut-off nozzle[3]
ABS	●	○	○	○	○
CA	●	○	○	○	○
CAB	●	○	○	○	○
PA	○	○	○	●	●
PAI	○	○	○	○	●
PBT	○	○	○	●	●
PET	○	○	○	●	●
PC	●	○	○	○	○
PE	●	○	○	○	○
PEEK	○	●	○	○	●
PMMA	●	○	○	○	○
POM	●	○	○	○	○
PP	●	○	○	○	○
PPO	●	●	○	○	○
PPS	○	○	○	○	●
PVC	●	-	-	-	-
SAN	●	○	○	○	○
TSG	-	-		●	●
Thermoset	●	-	-	-	-
Elastomer	●	-	-	-	-

- recommended 1 resistant to flow, poor temperature control

○ feasible throttle, high shear stresses

- nicht geeignet channel cross section = nozzle-opening cross section

TABLE 3.23

PERCENTAGE BY WEIGHT OF PERMISSIBLE MOISTURE AND THE RECOMMENDED DRYING TEMPERATURES OF VARIOUS PLASTICS MATERIALS

Material	% by weight of permissible moisture		Drying temperature	
	Injection	Extrusion	°F	°C
Acrylic	0.02-0.10	0.02-0.06	160-180	71-82
Nylon	0.04-0.08	0.02-0.04	160	71
Polyallomer	0.10	0.10	160-200	71-93
Polyethylene	0.05-0.10	-	160-175	71-80
Polypropylene	0.10	-	160-200	71-93
ABS resin	-	-	170-190	77-78
Cellulosics	Max. 0.40	Max. 0.30	150-190	66-88
Ethyl cellulose	0.10	0.05	170-190	77-88
Polystyrenes	0.10	0.05	160	71
Polycarbonate	Max. 0.02	0.02	250 at hopper	121
Vinyl	0.08	0.08	140-200	60-93

TABLE 3.24

INJECTION MOULDING-PROCESSING TEMPERATURE RANGE

Material	Processing temperature range	
	(°C)	(°F)
ABS	180-240	356-464
Acetal	185-225	365-437
Acrylic	180-250	356-482
Nylon	260-290	500-554
Polycarbonate	280-310	536-590
Polyethylene		
Low density	160-240	320-464
High density	200-280	392-536
Polypropylene	200-300	392-572
Polyester	160-180	356-500
Polyvinyl chloride, rigid	160-180	320-356

TABLE 3.25

INTERRELATIONSHIP OF PART WITH DESIGN, MOULDING CONDITIONS, POLYMER SELECTION AND MOULD DESIGN

Part Design Conditions	Moulding Selection	Polymer Design	Mould
Properties :	Process Control :	Properties :	Gate Size/ Location
Mechanical	Melt/Mould Temp.	Mechanical	Runner/ Cavity Layout
Thermol	Cycle	Thermol	
Chemical	Pressure	Chemical	
Electrical	Ram Speed	Electrical	Draft angles
Dimensional	Materials Handling	Dimensional	
Stability	Use of	Stability	Undercuts
Outdoor exposure	Regrind	Tolerances	
Bearing Areas	Effects of Moulding	Processing	
Ribs	Toughness Mould Shrinkage	Flow Mould Shrinkage	Mould Shrinkage
Bosses	Weld Lines Post Mould	Ejection	Location of Parting line
Sharp Corners & Radii	Shrinkage Past Surface	Cycle	Vent Size and location
Undercuts			Side Actions
Section	Post Moulding		
Thickness	Operations :		Surface Finish

TABLE 3.25 (CONT.)

INTERRELATIONSHIP OF PART WITH DESIGN, MOULDING CONDITIONS, POLYMER SELECTION AND MOULD DESIGN

Part Design Conditions	Moulding Selection	Polymer Design	Mould
Surface Finish	Quality Control		
		Preheating	Coring for Water
Tolerances	Annealing		Cooling
		Finishing	
Gate Size/ Location	Assembly Decoration		

TABLE 3.26

SUGGESTED WALL THICKNESS FOR COMMON THERMOPLASTICS MOULDING MATERIALS

	Minimum	Average	Maximum
Acetal	0.35	1.50	3.10
ABS	0.75	2.25	3.10
Acrylic	0.60	2.30	6.25
Nylon	0.40	1.55	3.10
Polycarbonate	1.00	2.30	9.40
LDPE	0.50	1.50	6.25
HDPE	0.90	1.50	6.25
PP	0.60	2.00	7.50
Polystyrene	0.75	1.50	6.25
PVC Rigid	1.00	2.30	9.50

(All in mm)

TABLE 3.27
COMPOSITION OF MATERIAL (%)
AFTER BEING PROCESSED SEVERAL TIMES
(NUMBER OF THROUGHPUTS AND WITH
DIFFERENT RATIOS OF VIRGIN -REGRIND)

	Composition of Material (Amount processed 0-4 Times)									
90 Parts New 10 Parts Recycled Number of throughplus						60 Parts New 40 Parts Recycled				
	0	1	2	3	4	0	1	2	3	4
1.	100	-	-	-	-	100	-	-	-	-
2.	90	10	-	-	-	60	-	-	-	-
3	90	9	1	-	-	60	24	16	-	-
4.	90	9	0.9	0.1	-	60	24	9.6	6.4	-
5.	90	9	0.9	0.09	0.01	60	24	9.6	3.84	2.56

Note : the above data will be a useful guideline for processors to know the effect of mixing recycled material with fresh material in repeated usage.

Processes Control Method in Injection Moulding

- manual control
- control by electromechanical components after manual setting
- Controi by electronic circuits and manual setting
- control by definite programmes
- open-loop control of some important parameters (speed and pressures) with manually programmed sequence control
- programmed open-loop control
- closed-loop control

Factors that Affect Reproductive Behaviour of Injection Moulding Machine

- Reproductibility of valve positions or control of their characteristics by integrated readjustment
- Consistancy of clamping force

- Wear resistance of plasticating unit
- Functioning of non-return valve
- Consistency of melt temperature
- Consistancy of initial material temperature
- Uniformity of material-bulk density, melt-index, etc.
- Reproducibility of mould sealing along parting lines, mould temperature, affecting clamping force and hot runner system.
- Consistancy of ambient conditions, especially temperature and humidity.

In-Line Injection-Compression Equipment

This development is by Remplan, Germany particularly for moulding the pallets in the sizes upto 1500 m x 1100 mm. The mould is a combination mould, which can produce four types of pallets from one basic mould and thereby giving on saving of atleast 50% on the Tooling cost alone. The inserts are provided for producing different types.

This Remplan system has also introduced an innovative features by using glass fiber compound for the pallets. By using glass-fiber and recycled HDPE or PP, a cheaper product using up in-house scrap or bought out scrap can be produced gaining a cmpetitive advantage. Remplan's is a combo injection. Compression moulding system for making pallets and large plastics parts like garbage bins, often from recycled material. The standard presses are three-platen units increasing the stroke and allowing large moulds to be used. This uses slide-mould technology where slides are mounted on the moving on the moving platen enabling manufacture of more intricate design.

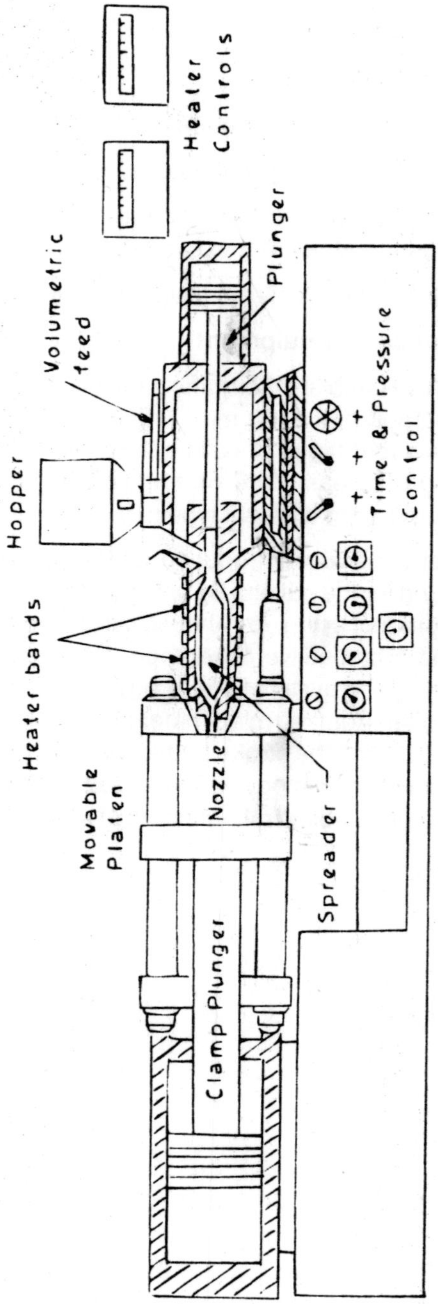

FIG. 3.7
CONVENTIONAL INJECTION MOULDING MACHINE

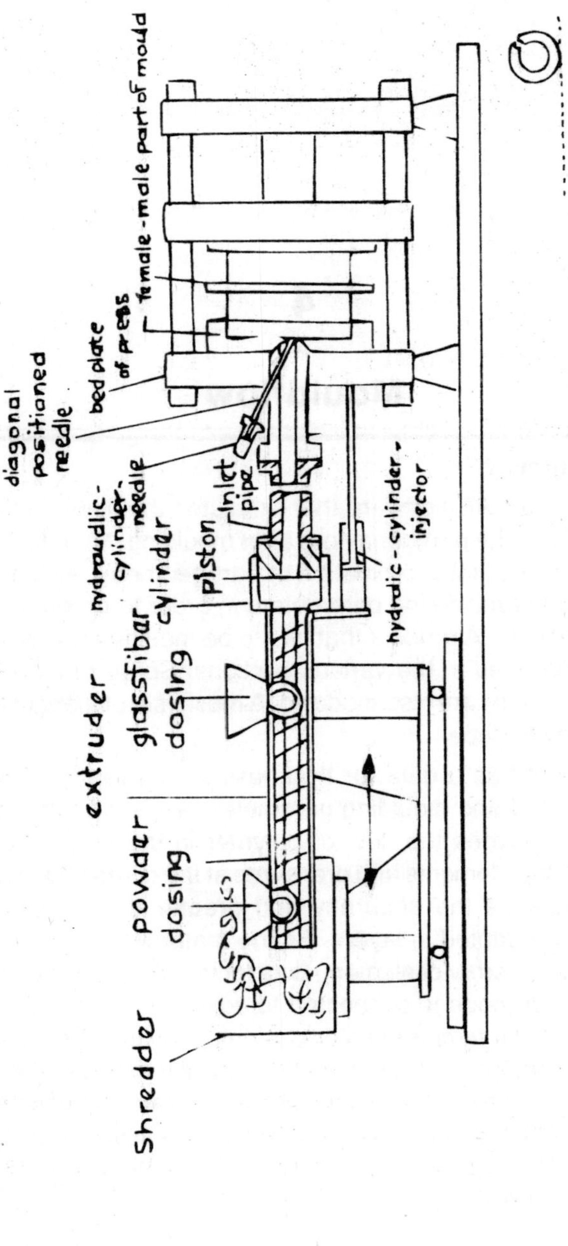

FIG. 3.8
REMPLAN'S IN-LINE INJECTION COMPRESSION SYSTEM

4

Mouldflow

What is Mouldflow ?

Mouldflow is a CAE software that simulates the flow of plastics in the mould and predicts the part behaviour after moulding. Mouldflow alloys one to determine the optimal combination of part geometry, selected material, mould design and processing parameters in order to produce high quality finished components. A product that has to be moulded is modelled in 2-D. Thickness is assigned to the various sections. Sprue runner & gates are modeled. Cooling lines are also modeled. A mesh (set of triangular elements) is created on the surface.

Each element has a data for thickness in that region. The moulding material is selected and moulding parameters are set on the system. The software now simulates the flow of polymer in the mould by simulating temperatures in the elements and pressures at the corner of elements. Finer the mesh, greater is the accuracy and greater the computation time. Thickness is represented in layers. As the material flows into an element through the nodes (corner of element) data for temperature, pressure velocity is calculated. Each node is connected to adjacent node and the software calculates the data for temperature drop & pressure drop. The surface mould temperature is computed considering the type of temperature & flow rate of coolant. The temperature at each element is calculated across the thickness using finite different method and corresponding pressure drop, shear stress are computed. The results of non-uniform shrinkage & the thermal stress are used to predict warpage.

How Mouldflow can help Part Designers, Mould Maker & Processor

- By optimizing part geometry
- By optimizing part weight
- Location of Ribs, and optimising its dimensions
- Material selection
- Choosing the best plastic material
- Alternate plastic material selection

How Mouldflow can help Mould Designer

- Helps to determine type of gate, gate positions, no. of gates
- Design optimized feeding system
- Design effective cooling system
- Design mould with optimum possible cycle time
- Improvement in overall quality of the product

How Mouldflow can help a Processor

- Can set optimized processing parameters
- Can determine minimum possible cycle time
- Determine clamping tonnage
- Improved quality of finished part by minimizing shrinkage, warpage & weld-lines
- Eliminate the moulding defects

How To Improve Quality & Productivity using Mouldflow

A mould designer may visualize various options to design a mould but he can practically select only one design. The selected design may or may not be the best. The gate location is also critical. The area near the gate will be highly pressurized and the shrinkage near the gate will be minimum for the material to be moulded. If the gate location is not correct, the component cannot be uniformly packed and will cause differential shrinkage and result in part warpage.

It is also a common fact to first design ejector pins and then provide cooling lines in the available space. This may either lead to insufficient cooling and result in higher cycle time or lead to warpage due to differential cooling which induces thermal stresses.

Another important fact is that when a new mould is to be tried on a machine, the criteria is to 'fill the mould' and get moulded component. Most of the time no consideration is given to built in stress or the high injection pressure requirement or the higher tonnage of the machine. A good mould design can result in lower injection pressure, lower tonnage and lower energy costs.

The injection pressure increase with increase in flow length. Long flow paths can be avoided by strategic location of gates or designing multiple gates. Size of gate is also critical. The function of the gate is to shear heat the material which cools down as it flows from the nozzle in to the gate area. The gate has to be small enough to shear heat the material without exceeding the shear rate limit and should be sufficiently large to fill the component and provide sufficient hold time to pack the material. Once a mould is made, it goes to processing shop, where all efforts are made to get a full shot and a warp free product. In most cases we do not know what should be an ideal cycle time and whatever settings are set on the control panel are assumed to be the best settings.

To overcome the problem of warpage, generally cooling time is increased so that the component cools down completely in the mould. The cause of warpage is not known and efforts to overcome the problem lacks direction.

Mouldflow can help identify problems, analyse and suggest remedies. There are innumerable examples where Mouldflow has helped to overcome problem, reduce cycle time and reduce costs.

Mouldflow also offers a 'Process Wide Simulation' i.e. it bridge a gap between the product designer, a mould designer and the processors.

The advent of CAE technology for injection moulding of plastics components is having a rapid growing impact on the plastics on the plastics industry. Using the technology effectively has helped the industry to produce quality components and improve productivity. Mouldflow has been successfully used to improve the quality and productivity of injection moulded components. With the growing competition and shorter time to market, use of a scientific tool like Mouldflow has become a necessity.

TABLE 4.1

COMPARISON OF COLOURING METHODS

Factor	Colour Con-centrate	Liquid Colour-ants	Dry Pigment	Precoloured Polymer
Cost	1	2	3	1
Dispersion	1 - 2	1 - 2	3	1
Ease of handling	2	1	3	1

TABLE 4.1 (CONT.)
COMPARISON OF COLOURING METHODS

Factor	Colour Concentrate	Liquid Colourants	Dry Pigment	Precoloured Polymer
Inventory Required	1	2	3	1
Colour Matching Difficulty	2	3	1	3
Ease of Colour change	2	1	3	1-2

(Key: 1 - Higher; 2 - Medium; 3 - Lowest)

TABLE 4.2
WALL THICKNESS OF MOULDED PARTS

Polymer	Minimum (mm)	Maximum (mm)	Average (mm)
LDPE	0.5	6.4	1.6
HDPE	0.9	6.4	1.6
Rigid PVC	1.0	9.5	2.4
Polystyrene	0.76	6.4	1.6
Polypropylene	0.64	7.6	2.0
Acrylics	0.64	6.4	2.3
ABS	0.76	3.2	2.3
Nylons	0.76	3.2	1.6
Polycarbonate	1.00	9.5	2.4
Polysulfone	1.00	9.5	2.5
Polyurethane	0.64	38.1	12.7

(Ref.: Plastics Products Design)

TABLE 4.3

QUALITY OF MOULDED PARTS - FACTORY THAT AFFECT

Quality Feature	Effective Parameters
Mechanical Properties	Injection Speed Melt Temperature Mould Temperature Cavity Pressure Holding Pressure
Dimensional accuracy	Melt Temperature
Absence of distortion	Mould Temperature Cavity Pressure Holding Pressure
Surface quality	Injection Speed Melt Temperature Mould Temperature
Other	Pressure Temperature

HYDRAULIC SYSTEM-NOISE SUPPRESSION

The main causes of noise are-

- Fan of the electric motor
- The hydraulic motor
- The hydraulic pump
- Switching valves
- The oil flow in narrow pipelines and elbows
- Sound of impact from opening and closing of mould

Some suggestions for Noise Reduction

- Reduce speed of electric motors
- Mount drive unit on vibration damping pads
- Use flexible supply and return lines for hydraulic drive units
- Employ valves without bouncing features by ramp like action
- Use pumps and motors of low noise
- Employ submergible pumps in the tank
- Encase drive units in the sound-absorbing enclosure.

INJECTION MOULDING SECTION

Estimating Cooling Time

The cooling time for a flat -sheet-like part of thickness 'h' can be estimated using the following formula

$$\underset{\text{(cooling time)}}{t} = \frac{4^2}{\pi\alpha} \quad \frac{8\ Tm - Tw}{P^2\ TD - Tw}$$

and for cylinderical parts, Diameter 'D'

$$t = \frac{D^2}{23.14\alpha}\ 0.692\ \frac{Tm - Tw}{TD - Tw}$$

a	=	Thermal diffusivity of polymer
TM	=	Melt temperature
Tw	=	Mould temperature
Td	=	Average temperature of the part at ejection

IMPORTANCE OF COOLING IN INJECTION MOULDING

Good Cooling vs. Bad Cooling

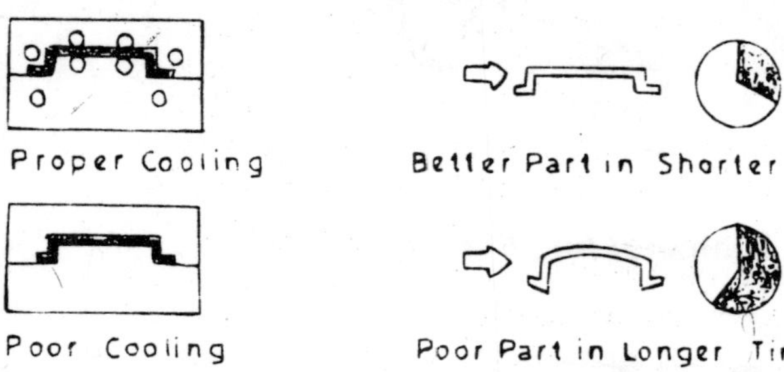

Why is Turbulent Flow Important

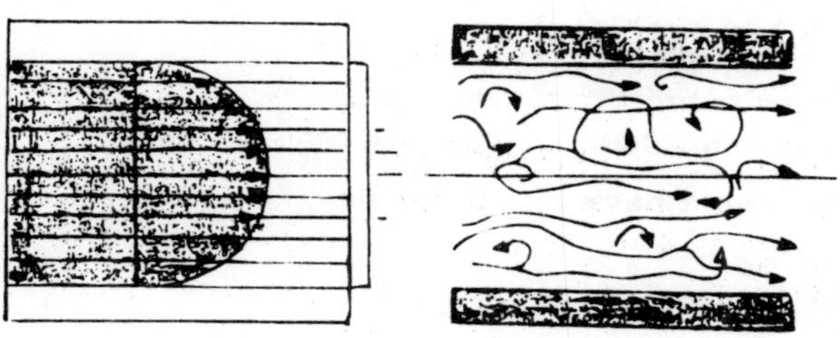

Laminar Flow Turbulent Flow

How Cooling Affects the Cycle Time

Reduce Cycle Time

Imcrease Profit Margins

Reduce Cooling Time

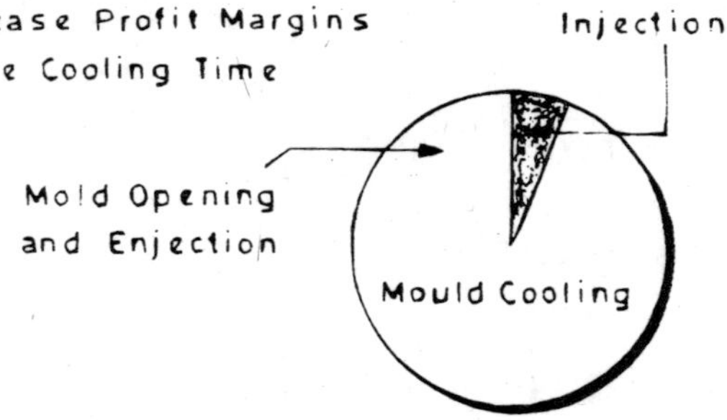

How Wall thickness Impacts Cooling Time

$$\text{Cooling Time} \sim \frac{(\text{Heaviest Wall Thickness})^2}{\text{Thermal Diffusivity of the Melt}}$$

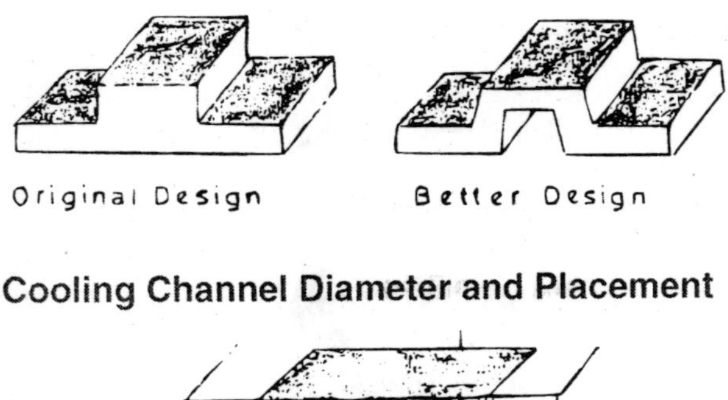

Original Design   Better Design

Cooling Channel Diameter and Placement

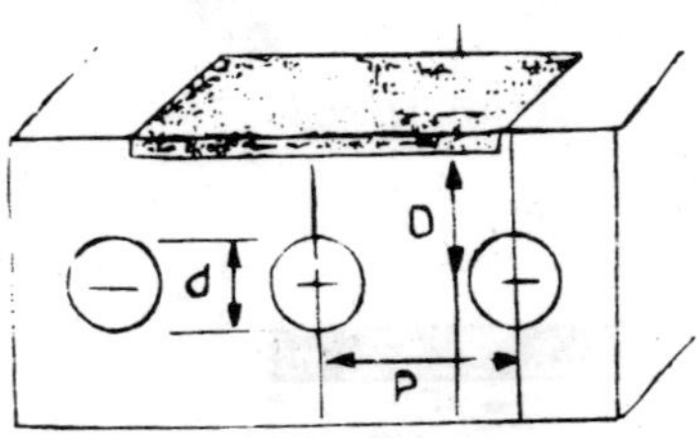

d = Diameter of Cooling Channel = 10-14mm

D = Depth of Cooling Channel = d to 2d

P = Pitch = 3d to 5d

How Turbulent is Enough ?

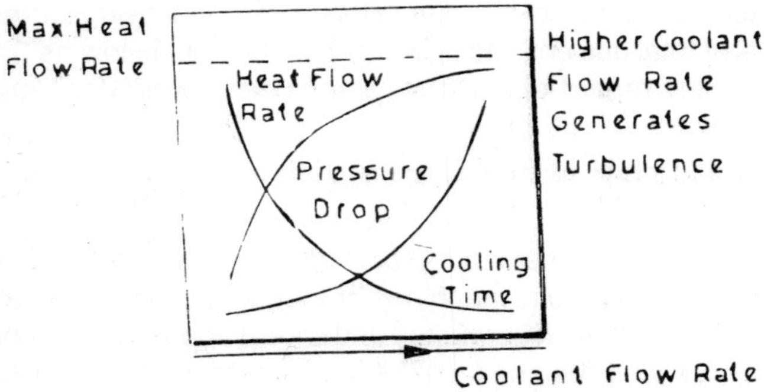

[Credit : IPI Journal - Jan/Feb'98]

Energy Consumption in Injection Moulding

Power is rate of doing work. Time integral of rate of work done or power is energy. It is this energy that we pay for. Hence correct terminology should be energy consumption and not power consumption.

Some of the measure already taken for energy saving are -

- Matching of installed capacity and contracted demand
- Maintenance of power factor above 0.9

Overall power factor can be raised by providing capacitor banks to the factory. Further improvement in power factor is possible by installing shunt capacitors on individual machines.

Electric motors on injection moulding machines form inductive load whereas heaters constitute resistive load. Since heaters constitute only 10% of the energy consumed it is apparent that major load is inductive in nature.

Inductive load requires reactive energy or magnetising current in addition to active energy to do useful work. Motor cannot be run without magnetisi'ng current and this power is waste. Idea is to keep this as low as possible. Installation of shunt capacitors across inductive load causes load to receive reactive power of opposite nature from capacitors and thus captive power neutralises the inductive power requirement. Thus supply system is relieved of inductive power to some extent and motor is able 'to deliver greater active power. Reducing magnetising current means reducing installation cost of cables and transformers. The installation of shunt capacitors on individual machines is complimentary to capacitor bank of the whole factory. The actual energy consumed has nothing to do with installed power or connected load. However a over designed motor should be discouraged as when motor runs at full load power factor is near unity but at very low load magnetising current may represent 90% of total current and power factor may be as low as 0.1. Latest development in this regard is use of high torque motor which facilitates use of lower HP motor.

A general view is that toggle machines do consume less power compared to hydraulic machines.

However work done on polymers for mouldings remains same whether moulding is carried out on hydraulic machines or toggle machines and any additional energy requirement must be wasted and should appear as frictional heating of hydraulic oil. A well designed machine which is noiseless and has low piping losses should consume more or less same energy whether it is hydraulic type or toggle type. Noise indicate waste of energy and noiseless machines are power saving. The machines using variable delivery pump requires less volume of oil compared to fixed displacement pump where system unloads at pressure whenever oil requirement is less and hence machines with variable delivery pump require less energy. A well designed machine should have least piping losses and this can be achieved by reducing by pipe lengths and oil lines fitted with internal diameter slightly more than normal, reduce fluid velocities, reduce pressure losses and consequent frictional heat built-up. They make machines quieter running and consequently

TABLE 4.4

TYPICAL BREAK UP OF ENERGY IN INJECTION MOULDING CYCLE

Mould	:	5.67%
Clamp tonnage	:	2.82%
Injection	:	8.05%
Hold on	:	9.20%
Plasticizing	:	52.88%
Cooling and idling and Inj-unit retraction	:	10.00%
Mould open	:	4.37%
Ejector forward	:	2.15%
Ejector retraction	:	0.92%

TABLE 4.5

INJECTION MOULDING : PRODUCT TO PRODUCTION

S. No.	Component		Plastic Granules			Components Required Per Month	* Allowance	Number of Cavities in Mould	Nos. of Shots Per Minute	M/c Hrs Reqd. to produce Monthly Quantity	Projected Area of One Shot Sq. CM →
	Name	Code	Type	Grade	Colour	Nos.	Kg.				

→ Weight of One shot Gms	Looking Force Tons	Theoretical Machine		Practical Machine Selection			Compoent To be produeced Name/Code	Remarks
		Shot Weight Capacity in PS Gms	Plasticising Capacity Kg/Hr.	Locking Tonnage	Shot Weight Capacity in PS Gms	Nos of Machines		

Quantity (Kg.) of plastic Granules Required to produce 1000 Components (Practical)

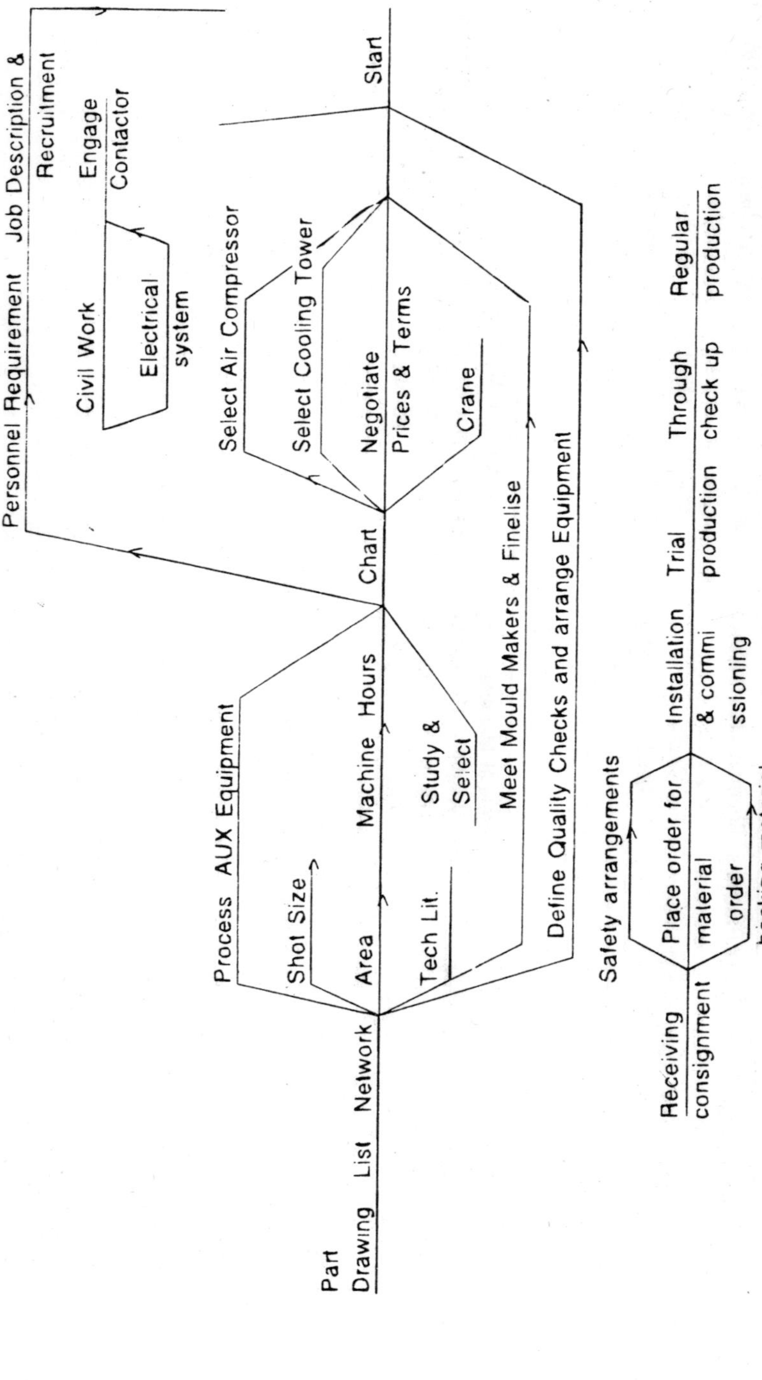

[Courtsey : Mr. M. Luqman]

FIG. 4.1

STARTING A NEW UNIT/NEW JOB

less energy consuming.

In general hydraulic power is directly proportional to product of pressure and flow. Large flow usually results during injection using all pumps and hence eleqtric motor capacity gets determined based on injection speed. Many times emphasis or undue

importance is given to connected load or pump motor capacity. However for comparing machine specification one must remember that injection moulding machines with higher electric motor capacity also offer higher injection speed. Besides electrical load and energy consumption are quite separate.

It can be seen that plasticizing takes maximum energy in injection moulding cycle. Here energy saving screw designs become important. As far as injection moulding machine design is concerned, a machine which creates less noise, less oil heating and low drain of oil in the entire cycle can be said to be energy efficient.

Irrespective of the type of hydraulic system used and the type of the pump (fixed or variable) used, AC variable drive reduces energy consumption by way of optimising the flow of oil through control of motor or pump rpm.

In general on processing side following things should be taken care of to reduce power consumption

- Avoid over setting of clamp tonnage.
- Optimise screw rpm Vs. energy consumption.
- Optimise injection rate against energy consumption and cycle time.

It should be remembered that injection pressure set on the machine is only a limit. Machine tries to achieve injection speed or rate and restrictions in the mould flow path causes injection pressure to develop. Thus it is injection rate that should be optimised and not injection pressure.

INJECTION MOULDING - CONTROL SYSTEM

The control system covers all equipment that control oil and barrel temperatures, clamping force, oil pressure and flow rates in such a way that they are available in the required magnitude and direction at the right time during the logical sequence of one cycle or several consequetive cycles. Mould temperature is also a very important parameter.

Quality of an moulded part is determined by :

Mechanical Properties

Injection Speed

Melt Temperature

Mould Temperature

Cavity Pressure

Holding Pressure

Dimensional Accuracy

Melt Temperature

Mould Temperature

Cavity Pressure

Holding Pressure

Surface Quality

Injection Speed

Melt Temperature

Mould Temperature

Basic Methods for control are:

- Manual Control
- Control by electromechanical components
- Control by electronic circuits and manual setting
- One loop control of some important parameters with manually programmed sequence control.
- Programmed open loop control. Close-loop control

Temperature Controls

The following temperatures influence the product

- barrel temperature
- melt temperature
- temperature of the hydraulic fluid
- temperature of the tie-bars
- mould temperature
- temperature of the hot-runner system
- even the ambient temperature, sometimes

Pressure Measurement

- Pressure in front of the screw tip provides information about the material flow between nozzle and mould during the holding pressure stage.

- Hydraulic Pressure provides a picture of the flow resistance in the nozzle-gate system during injection. The pressure rises with the increasing flow resistance during the cavity filling.
- Cavity pressure predominantly affects quality features such as voids, sink marks, weight shrinkage, etc.

Disturbing Factor that affect smooth operation are:

- disturbing the set controls for no reason
- unplanned corrective measures without waiting for outcome
- No clear/accurate displays
- Local temperature variations and humidity
- Mould problem
- Lot to lot variation of material

A microprocessor or multiprocessor system has to monitor the following functions

Standard	:	Sequence Control
	:	Timer Function
	:	Displacement actuator function
	:	Alphanumeric data display
	:	Limit value monitoring
	:	Malfunction indication
Monitoring	:	Self-diagnosis of malfunctions
	:	Screen display
	:	Control of setup procedure
	:	Calculation of operating data
	:	Input of data
	:	Correction via central monitoring
Control	:	Control of temperatures
	:	Control of speed and holding pressure
	:	Control of switchover point from injection to holding pressure
	:	Optimizing the process by selfadaptation

Computer controlled automatic injection moulding installation automatically execute and monitor the following steps:

Clamping

- preheating of moulds
- automatic mounting of mould
- automatic connection of oil lines (hydraulic circuit)
- automatic day-light adjustment
- automatic adjustment of clamping force
- automatic adjustment of opening stroke

Injection

- pre-heating of plasticizing unit
- automatic mounting of plasticizing unit
- automatic coupling of screw
- automatic adjustment of barrel retraction
- automatic device for supply with different material

TABLE 4.6

INJECTION MOULDING- PRESSURE CONVERSION TABLE

Nominal Value (psi)	Equiv Value (BAR)	Equiv Value (MPa)
10,000	689.5	68.9
15,000	1034.2	103.4
20,000	1379.0	137.9
30,000	2068.4	206.8
Nominal Value (MPa)	**Equiv Value (psi)**	**Equiv Value (BAR)**
100	14503.8	1000
150	21755.7	1500
200	39007.6	2000
Nominal Value (BAR)	**Equiv Value (psi)**	**Equiv Value (MPa)**
600	8702.3	60
1000	14503.8	100
1500	21755.7	150
2000	29007.6	200

MICRO PROCESS CONTROLS IN MOULDING

In a microprocessor control system, the software is designed to contain the instructions for the processor how he has to process the signals from the operator panel and link them with other process parameters stored in electronic memory modules. The heart of the microprocessor is the Central Processing Unit (CPU) which contains the control unit, which performs the basic operations. The ROM, Read Only Memory, contains fundamental data and instructions, while the RAM, Random Access Memory, stores all the additional data generated in the data-processing operation and the necessary instructions. From there they can retrieve any time.

A microprocessor or multi-processor system has to carry out the following control and monitoring functions -

Standard Functions

- Sequence control
- Timer functions
- Displacement actuator function'
- Alpha-numeric data display
- Malfunction indication

TABLE 4.7

INJECTION MOULDING -CLAMP FORCE CONVERSIONTABLE

Nominal Value (Tonnes)	Equivalent Valve (KN)
25	245.2
50	490.3
100	980.7
200	1961.3
300	2942.0
400	3922.7
500	4903.3
1000	9806.7
1500	14710.0
2000	19613.3
3000	29420.0

(Note : In some countries, 25 Tonnes are taken as equivalent to 27.6 Tons equivalent to 245.2 KN)

TABLE 4.8

INJECTION MOULDING-SHOT WEIGHT CONVERSION FACTORS

Polymer	Multiply Volume cm^3 by this factor to obtain shot weight (gms)
LDPE	0.79
HDPE	0.81
PP	0.85
PS	0.88
ABS	0.89
PPO	0.92
SAN	0.92
NYLON 66	0.95
PMMA	0.01
Polycarbonate	0.01
PBT	1.12
PET	1.15
PVC-U	1.15
Acetal	1.22

TABLE 4.9

INJECTION MOULDING-SHOT VOLUME CONVERSION TABLE

Nominal Shot Volume (cm^3)	Equivalent Shot Weight (gms)
25	22
50	44
75	66
100	88
125	110
150	132
175	154
200	176
300	264

TABLE 4.9 (Cont.)

INJECTION MOULDING-SHOT VOLUME CONVERSION TABLE

Nominal Shot Volume (cm^3)	Equivalent Shot Weight (gms)
175	154
200	176
300	264
400	352
500	440
1000	880
2000	1760
3000	2640
4000	3520
5000	4400

Monitoring Functions

- Self-diagnosis of malfunctions
- Screen display
- Dialog programme
- Control of setup procedure by means of operator guidance
- Calculation of operating data
- Input of data from a data carrier
- Connection to a central monitoring system and evaluation of data via central interface
- Corrections via a central monitoring station

Control Functions

- Control of temperature of barrel, mould and hydraulic system
- Process control of speed and holding pressure
- Filling index control
- Control of switch-over point from injection to holding pressure
- Optimizing the process by self-adaptation

Note

It must be remembered that the microprocessor controlled systems with either open or closed loops do not readily ensure the reproduction of good processing conditions. A number of factors, which may not be handled by a operator, affect the reproductive behaviour of an moulding machine.

5

Computer Controlled Automatic Injection Moulding Machine

On a conventional moulding m/c, the time generally spent for various operations is around 2 to 5 hours causing a loss of production and affecting the cost. This time can be considerably reduced to only minutes by various measures such as -

- prepare for the next job even before the machine is stopped for the changeover.
- mould change and even change of plasticating unit can be automated.
- Automation of machine setup and control circuits.
- Master Computer station for automatic operation of the machine.

All these features are now available for a Injection Moulding Machine, which can automatically execute and monitor the following steps -

Clamping Side

- Preheating of moulds.
- Automatic transport of the mould by conveyor.
- Automatic mounting of mould.
- Automatic connection with oil lines, etc.
- Automatic day-light adjustment.
- Automatic adjustment of clamping force
- Automatic adjustment of opening stroke

Injection Side

- Preheating of plasticizing unit
- Automatic connection to energy supply for plasticizing unit
- Automatic adjustment of barrel retraction
- automatic device for supply of different materials

Machine Maintenance

To keep you injection moulding machine in tip-top condition, there are some basic but often overlooked steps that you can take to reduce maintenance cost and downtime. Nine sure-fire ways to beat moulding machine blues are briefed below -

Simple machine maintenance over sights often cause injection moulders as many problems as mould and material-related issues. Here are nine recommendations that should help reduce machinerelated headaches, costs, and downtime:

Make Sure The Oil Is clean

Oil contamination is the common denominator for a myriad of machine performance problems and component failures. Pre-filter oil to 10 microns before adding it to your system and have a qualified lab analyse your hydraulic fluid every three months. Test for particulate contamination and chemical content to head off serious problems.

Change oil only when analysis indicates it necessary, not necessarily on the basis of an arbitrary date or number of hours. Every time you change fluid, you increase costs and risk introducing contaminants into the hydraulic system.

Likewise, watch out for oil supplied from tanker trucks. Their high-pressure pumps can trigger bypass valves in filters, pushing tanker contaminants into your machine reservoir.

In addition to maintaining the machine's built-in filtration system, consider using an electrostatic oil filter. They are so effective in removing insoluble contaminants that machine performance loss can be reversed. The importance of oil maintenance should never be overlooked.

Examine Control Cabinet Filters

Excessive control cabinet temperature will lead to premature electrical component failure. Check air filters weekly and clean or replace them when dirty. Clean the intake filters a minimum of once every four or six weeks and exhaust filter every 12 weeks. Good airflow is one of the best ways to combat cabinet temperature problems.

Check Water Quality

Regularly analyse your water, just like your oil. Mineral-laden or non-pH-neutral well water can clog heat exchangers, leading to damaged hydraulic oil and valves, but a closed water system is not always the answer.

Metals and foreign particles from pumps, manifolds, seals and hoses can build up in a closed system. Mould and hose changes can introduce cleaning compounds or surface rust particles. Here's the bottom line: no matter what type of system you have, you must regularly analyse your water to avoid equipment failure and downtime.

Pay Attention To Toggle Link Lubrication

Automatic lube systems certainly are convenient but not always faultless. Visually inspect your machine, 'listen' to it, and follow maintenance schedules. An automatic system is no substitute for good old observation and alertness to changes.

Monitor Machine Levelling

Periodically inspect machine level. Everything from rapid clamp cycling to minor earthquakes can change machine level. Out-of-level conditions cause hydraulic seals to leak, and moving components to bind and gall. This is an area where a little maintenance will save costly repairs.

Beware of How You Square

Changing ram spacers, dieheight chains, dieheight motors and eject cylinders can alter alignment. Square your machine the right way - use micrometers and a squaring block. Don't expect a mould to act as a squaring block.

Inspect Heater Bands

Expansion and contraction from heating and cooling tends to loosen heater bands. This can mean shorted out bands, blown cards and ruined controls. The solution? Check heater band every month to guarantee they are tight on the barrel. If you remove the bands, make sure you reinstall them to original specifications. Check and clean them after purging.

Watch safeties

Don't forget to check safety switches and guards if you remove or readjust them during repairs. The easiest way to avoid trouble is to inspect safety hardware during every shift.

Stop, Look, Listen

A routine checklist is no substitute for common sense. An experienced operator can usually tell when a machine is 'out of its groove'. Use that sixth sense, too.

Mould Placement

The following steps, not necessarily in the sequence as outlined, can be carried out for placIng the mould.

- The positive stripping bars should be adjusted to zero ejecting action.
- Plasticizing chamber should be in the retracted position.
- Set clamp opening to the required daylight. For hydraulic clamps, this is accomplished by a limit switch controlling the backward movement of the platen and on toggle pressure, by the threaded adjustment of the platen.
- Selector switches on the machine should be placed in setup position. There are thee basic selector-switch positions: "mould setting", "hand" and "auto" operation. Some machines have additional selector switches for a variety of purposes. In this chapter, we will be concerned with the three basic ones mentioned.
- Sprue Bushing. The nozzle seat and possibly irregularity of the entrance hole should be checked out. Also the smoothness of the holes and its correct tapes require attention. Two other. items to be checked are deformation of the hole at the junction of sprue and runner, and the proper functioning of the sprue puller.
- Cam Action. Each cam-action mould has its own peculiarities. The one feature to look for is that the competent of the cam embedded in plastic during operation should have nearly the same temperature as the remainder of the mould.
- Heaters. Whenever heaters are present, they should be in good working order. Their writing should be fully protected against short circuits and completely covered against accidental damage.
- Lubrication. Any lubrication on a mould should be so arranged as to keep the lubricant from the plastics and confine it to the area that needs it.

- Storage. Most moulds run 10,000 pieces, sometimes several times of that amount. A mould should be treated according to its value when stored. All accessory jigs, fixtures, and tools should be placed in a container and properly labeled so that repeat orders can be filled without loss of time. The last short should also be attached to the mould so that any question arising in connection with the last run' can be readily settled.
- Finally, before the mould is closed for storage, the moulding surfaces should be clean and dry and protected against corrosion. The corrosion-proofing materials, in most cases, are best applied to surface at room temperature which is readily attainable by circulating tap water through a mould.

Purging

The first step is to shut the slide on the hopper. The moulders deal with expensive materials so, to keep waste down to a minimum, they should attempt to use every bit of the material in the cylinder for productive purposes. This can be accomplished by a procedure in which the material in use of producing parts (after the hopper is empty) is followed through the cylinder by a distinguishable purging agent. The parts are run until the purging agent becomes noticeable. The two shots preceding the one in which the purging material is observed should be discarded.

Mould Removal from Press Moulding Machine

Every press usually has a job in it that requires removal of the mould and, quite frequently, purging of the cylinder. Before removal of a job, any additional information in addition to that shown on the setup sheet should be recorded so that any difficulties experienced will not be repeated. Furthermore, any details in the mould requiring repair or replacement should be noted and called to the attention of supervision for corrective measures.

Again, it should be emphasized that we are dealing with. a very expensive tool, and parts approaching the end of their useful life should be repaired or if necessary replaced in order to keep the mould in active and useful performance.

- Cavity of Core. Any leakage of coolant should be checked. A gate should be checked for wear or detraction, moulding surfaces should be checked for loss of polish or design details important for fitting configurations. Nicks or scratches that would spoil the Appearance of the product or interfere with withdrawal of the parts should also be removed. Any lands that provide for cores or other purposes, if damaged should be corrected to prevent flashing in the area.

- Ejection system. If springs are used, look for broken coils or lack of compression. Check the overall length against original specifications. When support pillars are checked, they should have a .001 to .002 lin. greater length than the space provided for them.
- Vents. The venting at parting lines and around the pins can be plugged by deposits from moulding operation. The depth of the vents around the parting line should be checked to see whether they conform to original specifications; if not they should be restored to same. Any deposits around the pin holes should be reamed out to standard clearances. If should be remembered that vents play a most important part in a quality product, and their maintenance during operation is a required feature on every mould. Some circumference vents may call for widening or even slight deepening so as to insure against plugging.
- Cooling channels. All cooling channels should be checked to make sure that the full flow of coolant is pumped through them.
- The mould should be lowered from the top or slid from the side so that the locating ring around sprue bushing finds its way into the corresponding opening in the stationary platen. The clamp is now moved slowly forward to hold the mould firmly in position while being clamped to the stationary platen. In the interest of safety, the power-supply switch should be disconnected during clamping of the stationary half. The preferred arrangement of clamp slots is horizontal in order to avoid accidental slippage of the moving mould half. If vertical slot mounting becomes necessary, an additional bottom support should be provided on the moving platen.
- Reconnect power, retract moving platen, place ejection rods in position, move platen against mould, disconnect power, and clamp back of mould to platen.
- Set chamber heat switches to "on" position, and make temperature settings on pyrometers.
- Set timers for cycle.
- Water connections for machine and mould should be made.
- Make setting of stripper bars for proper stripping action. Reconnect power, and with selector switch in "hand control", open and close press to see that everything is functioning properly.

- Set limit switches for controlling speed of clamp closing and opening. Closing of mould must be such that no banging or hammering will take place; the parting-line edges of mould halves must be protected against peening if flash-free parts are to be moulded.
- Change selector switches: (a) "mould set" switch of "off" and (b) "autohand" switch to "hand".
- The "extruder reverses top, should be set to a position that can be calculated as shown in "setup".
- The extruder "speed", "torque", and "back pressure" are indicated on the material processing sheet and should be set accordingly.
- Check cylinder temperatures to determine, whether setting have been reached. Also check nozzle temperature. "With the extruder unit in retracted position and extruder selector switch in "run-off-on" to "on" position, depress extruder "runbutton" until "extruder reverse stop" limit switch is actuated, indicating that the shot zone is filled with material.
- Depress "Injection forward" button to purge material into a suitable container, making sure it does not splatter. Repeat this operation until all new clean material is coming through.
- The needle value that controls the movement of the heating cylinder by means of the "pull-in" cylinder is opened, and the "seal valve" is moved so that it will cause the "pull in" cylinder to seat the nozzle against the sprue bushing. Depressing the "clamp forward" button will apply the full pump pressure to the "pull" cylinder and thus bring about a good seat between nozzle and bushing.
- Set "injection high pressure", "speed of injection", "low pressure injection", as indicated on set up specification.
- Set "full-semi-auto" switch to "semi". Set extruder switch to "on" and change "hand" to "auto". The press is now ready for normal operation.
- After a Final check to pyrometers to see that they are up to the setting, the press may be operated by opening and closing the gate.

MOULD STEELS

The use of plastics for the production of everybody commodities and technical components has become a matter of course today. This trend has required continuous developments in plastics processing tools which has in turn brought ever increasing demands on plastic mould steels with good dimensional stability, corrosion and high wear resistance,as well as resistance to scratching, good thermal conductivity, toughness, high comprehensive strength and good polishability and photo-etching properties.

Some of the new development are optimum solutions to the specific problems in the plastics processing industry.

One is a plastic mould steel produced by the powder metallurgy process with hitherto unequalled properties; Maximum corrosion resistance; maximum wear resistance; and excellent polisability. it is the optimum solution for high performance plastic moulds, particularly for the processing of highly abrasive and corrosive plastic materials with abrasive fillers.

Also available is a corrosion resistant mould carrier frame steel combining maximum machinability with good corrosion resistance. It is optimum solution for mould carrier frames in the processing of highly corrosive plastic materials.

The combination of mould insert material and as carrier frame material is the optimum solution to the problems in the processing of highly corrosive plastic materials.

The combination of mould insert material and as carrier frame material is the optimum solution to the problems in the processing of highly corrosive and abrasive plastic materials.

A pre-heat treated low-sulphur mould steel has good machining properties: no additional heat treatment required; very good machining properties; excellent photo-etching properties; and excellent polishability. They are the optimum solution for applications requiring excellent machining, polishing and photoetching properties.

A precipitation hardening plastic mould steel of high hardness (up to 44 HRC maximum). Properties include; condition as supplied; precipitation hardened (no additional); heat treatment required or solution annealed (uncomplicated heat treatment, high dimensional stability); very good nitriding properties; very good machinability; and good polishing, photoetching and spart erosion properties. It is the optimum solution for plastic moulds where the strength of the pre-heat treating steels, are not sufficiently high.

PLASTIC MOULD STEELS REQUIREMENTS

From the point of view of the tool manufacturers

When purchasing plastics mould steels, one looks for :

Good matching properties

- Good polishability.
- Good photo-etching properties
- Safe, uncomplicated heat treatment.
- Minimum inclusion level.
- Consistently high quality.
- Technical assistance and advice in tool manufacture and application

From the point of view of the plastic processing industry :

Plastic moulds steels should be featuring :

- Good dimensional stability.
- Good corrosion resistance.
- High wear resistance.
- Good resistance to scratching.
- Good thermal conductivity.
- Good polishability
- Good photo-etching properties.
- Good toughness.
- High comprehensive strength

New Mould Materials (Alloys and Powder Metals)

New high performance alloys and powder metals are debuting in the market, to meet the growing demand to quality mould material in the mould making industry. These new materials after higher mechanical strength, machinability, heat treatment and polishability. Some of those new materials are shown in the table.

Powder Metallurgy is a process in which raw steel is melted, degassed, treated and poured. Then, Nitrogen gas is sprayed into the molten stem to disperse the melt into million of tiny droplets. The droplets are then rapidly solidified and collected and packed into steel containers, which are then compressed by hot isomatic presses. These powder steels are normally used for granulator knives, pelletizer blades etc. but becuase of their extreme high wearability, hardness and toughness, they are now used for making mould inserts for corrosive and hightech moulding application.

Two-component Injection Moulding (Sandwich Moulding)

This technique has been known since the middle of the seventies and has proved itself in many areas. The origins of the process go back to the developments and patents of ICI in the United Kingdom.

TABLE 5.1
COPPER, ALUMINIUM ALLOYS

Alloys of Copper and Aluminium are increasingly being used in Injection Moulding due to its superior heat transfer abilities, thus help to reduce cycle-times and Warpage.

Grade	Manufacturer	Important Properties	Remarks
Moldax XL	Copper and Brass Co.	Good Thermal Conductivity, Good Corrosion and wear resistance, Excellent polishability and weldability	It is a copper nickel tin alloy. Can be suplied in 30 and 40 HRc.
Protherm	Copper and Brass Co.	Excellent high thermal conductivity. Good yield strength	It is Beryllium Copper alloy suited for applications requiring rapid heat removal. Can be used for gates and nozzle tips.
Berylco Tool 1 and Berylco Tool 2	NGK Metals	Good tensile strength comparable too tool steels	Suitable for moulding PVC. Can be supplied 26-32 HRc (Berylco Tool 1) and 36-42 HRc (Berylco Tool 2.) It is Beryllium Copper Alloy.
Pas 940	Performance alloys	Good texturability, weldability. Requires no heat treatment	Beryllium free copper alloy. Can be preferred for Injection mould cores, cavities, hot runner systems and pins.

TABLE 5.1
COPPER, ALUMINIUM ALLOYS (CONT.)

Grade	Manufacturer	Important Properties	Remarks
QC-7	Copper and Brass Co.	Good thermal conductivity, higher machinability, lower material cost.	It is an Aluminium alloy, Can be supplied upto 17 HRc. Can be used in high volume injection moulding application.
Alumec, 89	British Aluminium Plate	High strength-70% stronger comparable to other Aluminium materials. Good machinability.	It is an Aluminium alloy. Less machining time, hence quick delivery and cost savings.

TABLE 5.2
POWDER METALS

Grade	Manufacturer	Important Properties	Remarks
Porcerax II	International Mould steel	Good permeability enhance gas release in the mould, reduce burning, weld lines and other gas-related flaws. Higher homogeneity.	It is a 30% sintered powder steel. Supplied in 35HRc. 15 to 20% reduction of cycle times and lower part reject rates, reduced energy and material consumption and higher moulding precision
Elmax PM	Uddeholm	High corrosion and wear resistance	It contains 18% Chromium and 3% vanadium. Suitable for moulding engineering plastics with high filler contents in electronic/electrical applications
M390 Isomatrix	Bohier	Improved polishability and enhanced notched impact strength. Optimum corrosion and wear resistance	It contains 12 to 20% Chromium. 4% Vanadium. Can be preferred for wear tool components and inserts in high precision for compact discs and electroni
CPM V	Crucible materials	Good toughness and excellent wear resistance	It is Chromium-Vanadium Mould steel, available in different combinations. can be hardened upto HRc.Preferred for high wear, high intricate applications

TABLE 5.3
SOME VARIANT INJECTION MOULDING PROCESSES

Type	Two-material Injection moulding	Composite injection moulding	Multi-component injection moulding
number of moulds	2 for rotary table 1,5 for shuttle table	1 with moving inserts	1
number of injection units	2	2	2
clamp unit	- rotary table - shuttle table - conventional with rotating mould	conventional	conventional
cross section	2 layers	2 layers	3 layers
cycle time	short, finished parts from one mould	longer,only one mould needed	short
design options	wide	limited	wide

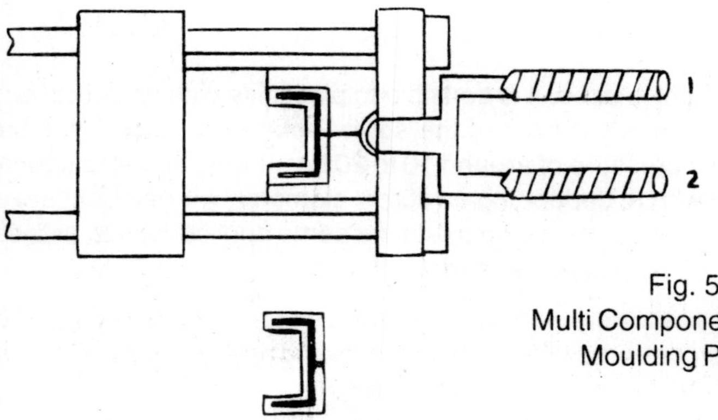

Fig. 5.1
Multi Component Injection Moulding Principle

Example for typical temperature are given below -

Polystyrene

				220	220	220	180	160	°C	B (core component)
			190							
nozzle	240	240							throat	
			210							
				250	250	250	240	240	°C	A (skin component)

ABS

				210	210	210	180	160	°C	B (core component)
			190							
nozzle	230	230							throat	
			210							
				240	240	240	230	210	°C	A (skin component)

Polypropylen

				220	220	220	180	160	°C	B (core component)
			200							
nozzle	240	240							throat	
			210							
				250	250	250	240	220	°C	A (skin component)

Modified PPO

				280	280	280	250	230	°C	B (core component)
			270							
nozzle	280	280							throat	
			270							
				290	290	290	280	260	°C	A (skin component)

Back Pressure

If a blowing agent is used, it is sensible to plasticise with back pressure so that expansion of melt in front of the screw before it is required is prevented. A hydraulic pressure of around 10 to 20 bar should be set to counter the melt pressure which, depending on screw diameter, will be about seven to fifteen times this value. It may be useful for some applications to process with as much as 40 bar back pressure.

Although not absolutely necessary to set a value for back pressure on the injection unit processing material without blowing agent, it has been found that a low back pressure of say, 5 bar is helpful.

Injection Techniques

It is possible to set any desired injection speed profile on each barrel. Thermoplastic should in principle be injected as fast as possible.

6

Maintenance of Injection Moulding Machine

From a view point of time maintenance may be classified into :

- **Daily maintenance** performed each work day by the operator before and after machine operation.
- **Periodic maintenance** conduced by PM (Preventive Maintenance) personnel at intervals of one month, three monghs, six months, and one year referring to the inspection data sheets prepared specifically this purpose; and
- **Overhaul,** which implies maintenance conducted after the machine has endured 25,000 hours (about three years) of service. The machine is disassembled and inspected to replace only worn out parts or replace parts with regard to abrasion.

The above mentioned maintenance is systematic work which requires a high level of technique.

It desirable to call in specialists to perform the task according to a definite programme.

DAILY MAINTENANCE

This maintenance must be conducted daily by the operator before and after machine operation.

- *Noise* : Is noise being produced by the motor pump piping, valve, gear housing etc.?

- *Vibration*; are vibrations being created by the machine body itself, the piping, gear housing etc.
- *Oil leakage*; Does oil leak from the mounting surfaces of the hydraulic components screwed portions, joints, packings etc."
- *Lubrication*; are the slide ways, gear housing etc. properly lubricated; Does the lubricating pump rotate normally?
- *Oil level*; are the hydraulic oil gear housing, electromagnetic clutch thrust bearings, etc. being fed with a sufficient amount of oil?
- *Vacuum gauge*; confirm by the pump vacuum gauge that a vacuum valve of 10 cm-Hg is being maintained.
- *Clamp pressure rise* : by causing the clamp pressure to rise at a point short of the mould clamp limit, check for the time consumed in pressure rise.
- *Oil temperature*:ascertain that the oil temperature is within 68-140°F (20-60°C)
- *Cleaning*: after machine operation, be sure to clean the slide ways, hydraulic components, machine surrounding etc. If this procedure is neglected, the slide ways may be damaged, accuracy of the machine deteriorated and as, a result, an early detection of oil leakage, etc. will be possible.
- *Pressure gauge*: if equipped with cock, close it when not in use.
- *Lock* : When setting the relief valves etc is completed, tighten their lock nuts, Bolts, nuts, etc. check for possible loosened condition.
- *Temperature indicating controller*: Check for ON/OFF action using the setting needle.
- *Heater band failure*: by switching on the heater and referring to the ammeter, does the current rise to the specified value?
- *Water leaks*; are there any leaks in the cooling water line (for the mould and heating cyliner?)
- *Control box*; is there any abnormal heating in the electromagnetic box? Is anywear visible on the electromagnetic switch contacts?

Since there are no set standards for vibrations, noise etc. their identification must depend on the checker's skill, experience and intution.

DAILY MAINTENANCE

Monthly maintenance

- *Checking lubricating oil :* Check on the lubricating oil for the gear housing thrust bearings, electromagnetic clutch etc. replenishing or replacing when necessary. Particularly, lubricating oil for the electromatnetic clutch and thrust bearings is for heavy-duty service and must be rigidity checked. Never fail to clean the section strainer of the gear housing.
- *Cleaning in-line filter :* When the indicator has turned yellow, the inliner filter must be replaced. Replace the cartridge.
- *Disassembling and cleaning cylinder head and screw tip.* :This procedure helps check on the interior wear and worn plating of such components. At the same time, it helps prevent rust from accumulating on the cylinder head mounting bolts and their screwportions and on the screw is finished spread heat resistant lubricant (lubricants containing molybdenum sulfide such as Mollicoat, Molliub, etc.) over their threaded parts and tighten them.

Additional tightening: Bolts and nuts on the hydraulic piping union joints, - cylinders, etc. which are affected by force must be additionally tightened.

- *Cleaning the machine:* Clean the entire machine once a month. If any dents are visible on the slide way, tie rod surface, etc., smooth them down with a smooth-cut file or a whetstone until surfaces are even.

  Those parts of the machine covered solid by a thin layer of congealed grease or hydraulic oil are liable to collect particles of dirt, metal, etc. This will affect accuracy of the machine and accelerate its wear.

  Resin in pellets scattered around the hopper are liable to find their way into the hydraulic oil while repairing the machine, damaging the pumps and valves.

  Appropriately clean the power board once a month with compressed air, removing dust particles accumulated on the relay contacts. Tighten all loose screws (if any) on each power board terminal.

Inspection at three-month intervals

Check the hydraulic oil for quality

Inspection at six-month intervals

- Since the duration of guarantee on the pressure gauge, vacuum gauge, oil temperature gauge. V packings, etc. and some electrical parts (timer and heater) is specified as six months, their service life is considered expired when this inspection is made, requiring their replacement.

- Check the heater wiring thermocouple for cover loss, and replace if necessary.
- Lubricate the coupling, motor shaft, pump shaft, etc.

Annual inspection

- Service life of the thrust bearings, bearings in the gear housing, magnetic clutch, V-packings, and O-rings, terminates after a lapse of a year. Consider replacing them.
- The cooling jacket of the oil cooler or heating cylinder may sometimes be clogged by "fur".
- Remove it by running compressed air or a diluted solution of sulphuric acid through the jacket.
- To reconfirm overall accuracy of the machine, at 'least measure the parallel condition of the mould, correcting any existing out-of-parallel condition.

Daily Maintenance Attention Piping installation

- Use pipes for high-pressure service. Purchase those that have been subjected to a pickling process Never use those that have a rust accumulation on their inner walls.

  Pipe for high-pressure service implies OST2 (precision steel pipe) and STP-38 (carbon steel pipe for general high-pressure service). They must be pressure rated at 3000 p.s.i. (210kg/cm^2).
- When bending a pipe, it should be cold processed. If hot-processing is unavoidable, pickle it after bending.
- When welding a pipe, use electrodes for mild steel, and do not create too much metal filling at a time.
- When closing a crack that has developed in the welded part, scrape off part of the former filling metal with a sander before applying new filling.
- When installing a pipe line, be sure to clean its interior walls and completely protect the inside against dust etc.
- When replacing an O-ring etc., and mounting or demounting a pipe, thoroughly clean the ring or mounting surface with the bare hands. Do not wear gloves, leave dirt on the mounting surface, or wash the ring or surface dirty oil.
- Hydraulic equipment is vulnerable to dirt. Make a habit of preventing dirt from infiltrating the hydraulic oils.

Controls of Hydraulic and Lubricating Oils

For long service life of a machine, the inspections described above are absolute necessities. In addition, the control of hydraulic and lubricating oils is equally important. Inspite of its apparent simplicity this control poses a most difficult problem, the lack of it having caused many accidents. It is worthy of special mention since it can prevent more than 70% of the accidents inherent in hydraulic machines.

TROUBLE SHOOTING OF HYDRAULIC CIRCUIT

Problems and Possible causes

Noisy Pumps

Cavitation (Pump starving)

- Clean inlet strainer filter
- Check inlet piping for checking
- Fluid viscosity too high
- Operating temperature too low

Pump picking up air

- Low oil level
- Loose or damaged intake pipe
- Worn or damaged shaft seal
- Aeration of fluid in reservoir

Other possibilities

- Worn or sticking valves
- Worn ring
- Worn or damaged gears and housing
- Shaft misalignment
- Worn or faulty bearings

Low or erratic pressure

Fluid contamination

Worn sticking relief valve

Dirt or plastic holding valve partially open

Pressure control setting too low

No Pressure

Low oil level

Pump drive reversed or not running

Pump shaft broken

Relief valve stuck open

Full pump volume by passing through faulty valve or actuator.

Actuator fails to move

Faulty pump operation

Directional control not operating

- Failure of solenoid, limit switch
- Inadequate Pilot pressure
- Interlock device not actuated

Operating pressure too low

Worn or damaged cylinder or hydraulic motor

Slow or erratic operating

Air in fluid

Low fluid level

Viscosity of fluid very high

Internal Leakage

Worn Pump

Pump drive speed too low

Erratic Feed Rates

Stickling warped or binding ways

Air in fluid

Faulty or dirty flow control valve

Overheating of System

Water circulation clogged

Continuous operation at relief setting

- Stalling under load
- Fluid viscosity very high

Excessive slippage or internal leakage

Check stall leakage past motors and cylinders

Fluid viscosity rather high.

MACHINE MAINTENANCE IN GENERAL

Pressure gauges and pyrometers

The pressure gauges and pyrometers are the means by which machine parameters are set for the moulding operation. These instruments should be checked once at the beginning of each week or at least once at the start of each month with a master pressure gauge and a master pyrometer to insure that accuracy is maintained.

Hydraulic Oil

The hydraulic system performs all the important functions of the machine. The hydraulic oil must be in top notch condition not only to transmit power but also to lubricate and prolong the life of pumps and valves. Cleanliness and oil fortified with necessary additives and of proper viscosity are prerequisites to proper functioning of the press. A good-quality hydraulic oil should have a broad useful viscosity range, befortified with antioxidants, be free from tar like material, be noncorrosive, and have good lubricating characteristics.

Filters

When recognize that sliding spools have to seal against pressure of 2000 or 3000 psi and that rotating vanes also have a seal under these conditions, we can readily see that the hydraulic fluid has to provide good lubricating properties. Consequently, it must be free from any foreign particle size that would interfere with the free movement of spools, vanes, etc. or cause abrasive effects. The fluid must not only be contained in clean and dust-free receptacles, but it also must be continuously filtered. The filtering agents must have openings not larger than 200 mesh screen.

Coolers (heat exchangers)

Since the control of oil temperature is so vital to the proper functioning of a hydraulic system, it is necessary to examine the heat exchange between the oil and the cooling medium. A typical heat. Its function is too cool the incoming oil by means of circulating water through the multitude of tubes. The oil flows aver the water-cooled tubes, thus losing some of the heat to the moving water. When in good functioning condition, these exchangers do an outstanding job in maintaining oil temperatures at prescribed levels. In addition, the oil tank plays a major part in heat dissipation. It is imperative that tank walls as the inside of the heat exchanger be free from sludge or other substances that may from on the conducting surface. Any substance on a heatconducting area will act as heat insulation and thus minimize the effectiveness as a cooler. Therefore, periodic thorough cleaning of heat exchangers and tank surface should follow oil inspection.

Oil leaks

Wherever an oil leak develops, it should be stopped immediately. Leaks cause pumps to work harder and thereby generate additional heat in the system. In addition, they are a potential hazard to machine attendants, and they contribute to poor appearance of the shop.

Leaks may be result of worn "O" rings, loose connections, or improperly adjusted packings. A. U or V-shaped packing should be free enough in its space so that the arms of the U or V will flex under pressure, thus bringing about good sealing action. It is best to obtain information on a specific type of packing from the manufacturer and to follow recommendations for adjustments to seal.

Troubleshooting of a hydraulic circuit

While analyzing a malfunction of a hydraulically actuated machine, we should keep in mind some general principles, namely, that a pump makes oil flow but that there must be resistance to flow to generate pressure. Determine where fluid is going. If actuators fail to move or move slowly, the fluid must be by passing them or going somewhere also. Trace it by disconnecting lines if necessary. No flow (or less than normal flow) in a system will indicate that pump or pump drive is a fault.

BRIEF MOULD DESIGN CHECK LIST

Press

- Is the weight of the moulding, runners and sprue within the shot capacity of the press?
- Is the expected output well within the plasticising capacity of the press.
- Is the clamping pressure of the press sufficient for the projected area of the moulding and runners?
- Will the mould pass between the press tie bars?
- Do the clamping arrangements for the tool suit the platen bolt holes?
- Is the closed thickness of the tool above the minimum and below the maximum required for the press?

- Is the press opening stroke sufficient for the ejection and extraction of the moulding?

Moulding

- Is the flash line at the tool parting line position visually acceptable on the moulding?
- Are the positions of any print line arising from tool blocks, cores, ejectors, etc., visually acceptable on the moulding?
- Is the gate position visually acceptable on the moulding?
- Will the position of any flow or knit lines that may occur be acceptable in appearance?
- Will any knit lones cause weakness in a critical area?
- Will any heavy section in the moulding cause unacceptable sink marks?
- Is the design free of any undercut areas that. will prevent ejection?

Tool

- Is the tool parting line chosen the most efficient for mould operation and tool construction?
- Have the punch and cavity been designed in the easiest manner of machining on the available equipment?
- Will any slender blades or pins deform under cavity pressure or flow?
- Is the cavity of adequate strength to resist internal cavity pressure?
- Are all tool components exposed to side thrust from cavity pressure, located by solid steel and not only by screws or dowels?
- Is the tool construction free from any chance of horizontal flash?
- Does the ejector packing provide sufficient support to the die plate to prevent distortion under cavity pressure?
- Can all parts of the tool be dismantled and separated in the event of tool breakdown or modification?
- Are all necessary parts hardened?
- Have all allowance for moulding shrinkages been provided?
- Has sufficient moulding taper been allowed on all parts forming moulding surfaces?
- Will the tools dimensions produce mouldings within component tolerances?
- Will the mouldings remain on the ejection side when the mould opens?

- Is the ejection stroke sufficient to clear the moulding?
- Have sufficient ejectors been provided to prevent sticking, cracking or distortion of the moulding?
- Are the ejector and ejector bars sufficiently strong?
- Is the ejector mechanism suitable for the particular press ejector system?
- Has the ejector return mechanism been provided?
- Have adequate guide pins been provided between the tool halves?
- On split tools are moving cores is the opening movement provided by cams, cylinders, etc., sufficient to clear the undercuts on the component?
- Are all inserts positively located for position and prevented for displacing themselves during tool closing or under plastic flow in the cavity?
- On split tools are moving cores is the mechanism sufficiently fool proof to prevent damage by faulty operation?
- On all split and moving cores, is the cavity pressure resisted by solid steel locking faces and bolt by the split or core operating cam or ram?
- Have adequate cooling channels been provided?
- Is the cooling too close or too distant form the mould surfaces?
- Are the runners of sufficient size?
- Has a sprue puller hook and sprue cold well been provided ?
- Are runner hooks and runner colds wells necessary ?
- On three-plate tools has sufficient opening been provided between the plates to allow extraction of mouldings and runner system?
- Is the mould sufficiently vented?
- On offset designs is the out-of balance force too great?
- Has an injection side platen location spigot been provided?
- Do the spherical nose and orifice of the cylinder nozzle match with the spherical seating and bore of the sprue bush?
- On split tools can all ejectors be in the forward position without interfering with the closing of the splits?
- Is sufficient clearance provided between ejector chains or links to withdraw the component through them without difficulty?
- Have tool lifting eye bolts been provided?

A CHECKLIST-MOULD VISA-VIS MACHINE

- Is the mould strong enough to withstand the closing force.

- Is the mould having enough bearing area on the platen to avoid indentation on the mould platen? Bearing load should not exceed value of 10 to 15 kg/mm2.
- Is the size of the mould very much smaller than the moulding platen size? Small moulds when loaded full given rise to undue deflection of mould platen, resulting in flashing.
- Will the mould physically fit into the machines being used? Check that mould overall dimensions permit fitment of the same, through the gap between tie bars.
- Is the mould thicker than the minimum mould height? If the mould is too thin, bolster plates can be added.
- Is the opening stroke of the machine long enough to allow for part removal.

  This should be critically reviewed. When there is minimum amount of room the overall cycle may be longer and this should be considered while quoting the piece part.
- Is the ejection stroke of the machine long enough to allow for part removal?

  If the stroke is insufficient it may be overcome by extending the knockout plates and attaching pneumatic or hydraulic cylinders to it on both sides.
- Can the mould be clamped on the mould platen?

  Sometimes additional holes might have to be drilled in the platen. If cylinders or other equipment are to be attached to the mould they will not interfere with the clamping of the mould.
- Is the clamping force of the machine enough for the parts?

  The actual pressure exerted within the mould cavity is considerably less than the theoretical value of the injection pressure. Hence for the purpose of working out mould separating force, projected area of mould along with runners and effective injection pressure transmitted to the cavity (may be taken between 35% to 50% of the theoretical) are used. It is generally desirable that clamping force exceeds the separating force by 10% to 15%.
- Is the injection capacity of the machine enough for the parts?

  The shot capacity for a given pressure head is normally given for polystyrene. For different materials, this figure is to be calculated based on density of the material at operating temperature. It is recommended not to exceed 85 to 90% of calculated value.
- Do the major ejector holes correspond to the ejector mechanism of the machines to be used?

Since all the machines do not have standard ejector hole pattern, list should be prepared of the likely machines and possibility of making a suitable mould should be reviewed.

- Are knockout mechanism needed on the injection side?

  As the ejector cylinders are not offered on injection plates as standard supply, if such a system is required, make sure to include the same in the purchase of new machines. Mould design may open be simplified for some articles.

- Are water hoses located so that they will not be in the way of the operator, or the removal of the part and movement of the safety gate?

  Care has to be taken to avoid the same. Also for heated moulds, keep the hoses out of the operators reach to avoid burning. When refrigerated water is used the mould should be designed so that the condensation does not fall where it can cause damage.

- Do water lines interfere with the bars or other mechanism?
- In the events of requirements of heating the mould, are the heating elements and control units placed safely to be out of the operators way.

CHECK THESE ITEMS FOR TROUBLE-FREE MOULDS

For safety and speed in running in the subsequent setup and maintenance, be sure that:

- Hot runner connectors and thermocouple jacks are located on back of mould away from operator.
- Pull back arms are located away from the operator.
- Mould does not extend beyond the press platen.
- Mould fits maximum and minimum shut-height of press.
- Locating ring dimension matches that of the moulding machine
- Clamp slots are proper width to suit mounting.
- Mould has a knockout pattern that matches the press.
- Back plate is thick enough (31 mm minimum) to hold clamps.
- Mould assembly has a safety strap to keep it together during installation.
- Inlet and outlet water lines connect on same side of the mould.
- Mould has quick coupling water and hydraulic connections.
- Water lines are cross drilled to eliminate external plumbing.
- Hydraulic cylinders are connected in parallel for fast hook up
- Hydraulic cylinders have guards to protect them from damage

- Interchangeable cavity inserts can be changed without dismantling the mould
- Backside of guide pins have 9 for 12mm dia threaded holes 25mm deep to permit guide pin removal without removing die from press.
- Slide faces are large enough to permit correction of errors in locating holes being cored by slides.
- Leads pins are longer than any standing cores.
- Wire way in mould are large enough for all hot runner wires and thermocouple leads.
- Ejector plate is properly guided to prevent excessive wear on ejector pins and holes
- Sprue bushing can be removed without taking the die out of the press
- Electrical connector for hoot runner is recessed into the mould
- Eyebolts are on mould centreline to facilitate installation
- To insure the strength of the mould check that:
  - Mould has a minimum of 101 mm between cavity and edge of mould
  - Mould has an adequate number of support pillars
  - Ejector plate is thick enough to prevent deflection during ejection stroke
  - Large slides are backed up by heel blocks large enough to withstand the pressure of injection
  - Mould has properly designed die locks
- Look at ejector system to see that:
  - Ejector pin layout is adequate to eject part, even in a short shot
  - Ejector stroke is long enough to move part completely off core
  - Contoured ejector pins are locked to prevent rotation.
  - Part is designed to remain on the ejection side of mould
  - If possible, large, deep ribs have ejector pins
  - Lifters extend beyond part, and can be pushed back into place by the opposite half of the mould.
- For Sprues, runners, gates: The "O" dimension of the sprue matches material and part
  - Sprue bushing is locked in place
  - Sprue bushing pocket has minimum dia of 3 1/4 in

- Sprue and runners have cold slug areas
- Direct sprues have bubblers or other cooling arrangements
- If possible, the sprue has cooling ribs
- Hot runners have a minimum dia of 18 mm

- All submarine gates are on ejector half of mould, if possible, Scan the part configuration to see that :

- Ribs and thick sections are less than 70% of nominal wall thickness to prevent sink marks.
- Mould and cavities have identification numbers.
- If possible ribs and walls are generously drafted to aid ejection
- No inserts are more than twice as tall as they are wide
- Any grain or pattern stops short to part edges.

Mould making Using Computer Integrated Manufacturing (CIM)

The new facilities and infrastructure available with some mould makers and in- house tool rooms makes it possible to use information technology and make fast precision moulds.

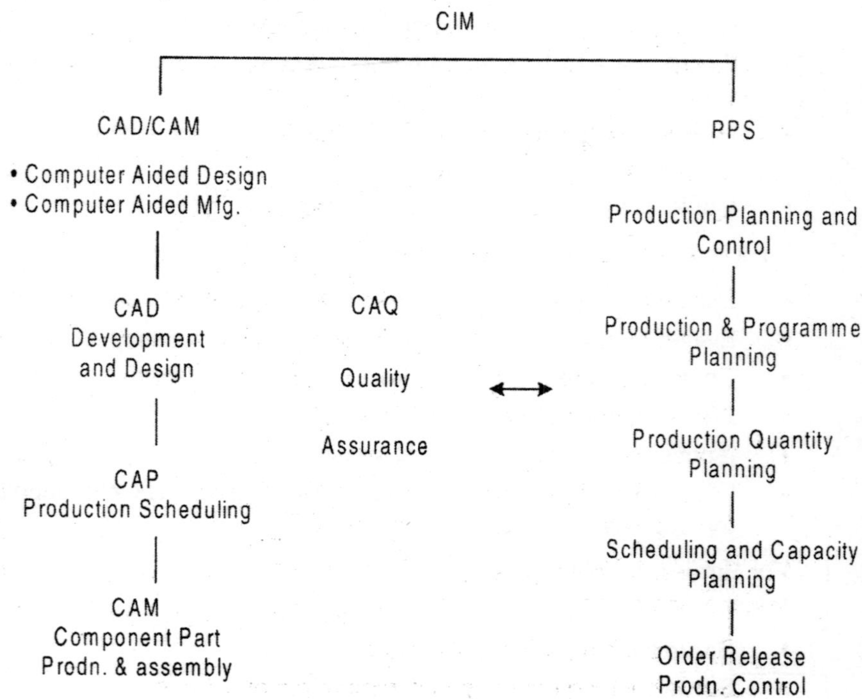

CAD for Part Designing

CAD means computer aided design on a monitor. The part designer draws a product with aid of the computer software. The work on the monitor is converted into a 3-D master pattern through creation of a machine programmed from the surface data of the part. The approved master pattern is completely digitized. The software now describe the product in the computer language Mould production sequence is described below -

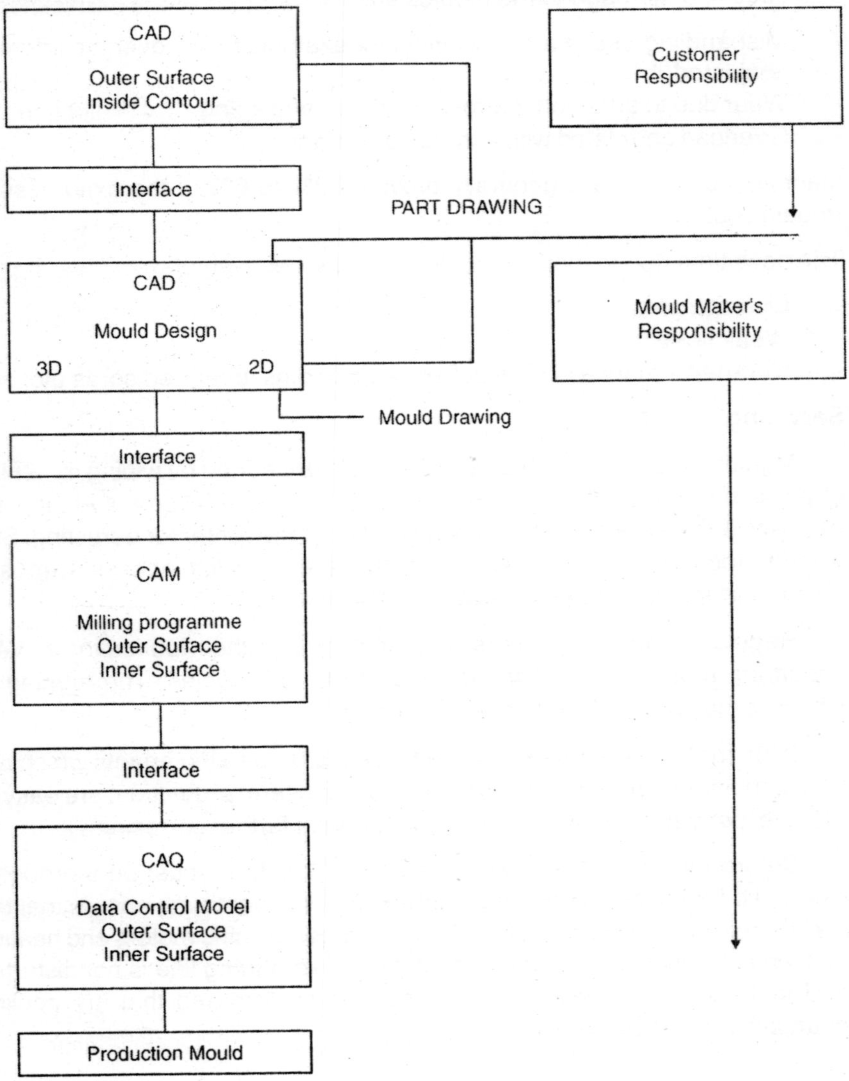

Maintenance and Care of Moulds

Maintenance plan include

- Servicing
- Inspection
- Repairs

The causes of damage to the moulds are -

- Mishandling-use of a screw-driver for example to remover the part that is ejected.
- Wear due to abrasion, corrosion, fatigue and aging.
- Overload correlated with enhanced damage

Maintenance costs are generally provided 3% to 6% of the fixed assets, (mould costs)

The downtime due to moulds problem may be becuase of-

- Operator error
- Weak links
- Non-performance of core pullers, ejector pins, threaded cores etc.

Servicing

Moulds must be kept clean and the cavities cleaned by wiping, brushing or polishing. Some cleaning agents that are used are Isopropyl Alcohol for Deposits & Degreasing; Emery Paper and Rust Preventer for derusting. Soft wooden rods are useful to clean areas that are difficult to access. Deposits on the surface can be removed by a soft brush.

Regular cleaning of sliders and ejectors and their lubrication is very important, may be at the interval of 30 to 40,000 cycles. The topping of lubricant may be required during this period.

If the moulds are to be preserved, use the preserving agents which are free of moisture, are easy to apply, provide long term protection, are easy to remove, convert corrosion products are prevent further corrosion.

Before the moulds are taken for production, they must be thoroughly examined for residue in cleaned cavities, crack in contours, ensure that the connections for the hot runner, hydraulic cylinder, electric motors and heating - cooling channels are all sound, that the mould parting line is not distorted and that there is no leakage in the cooling system and that are cooling channels are not blocked.

Repairs -Most Common

- Damage to sealing surfaces causing flash can be corrected by-
  - Reforging
  - Welding
  - Grinding
  - Resinking the sealing surface
- Chipping or Grainy Surfaces can be corrected by welding and if welding is not possible, new sections will have to be inserted.
- Repairs to ejector system (chipping, seizing, and readjustment or new insert).
- When cooling system requires rapairs the channels must be rebored separating, plated must be re-inserted into the vertical channels and new seals must be installed.

7

CAE and CAD Technology in Moulds Making

Difficulties and benefits of CAE and CAD technology.

In fact, total quality and productivity of injection moulding depend more on perfection of part design and mould design.

- Superficial knowledge of injection moulding process is not enough to appreciate this technology. This technology demands good understanding of fundamentals of physics. Injection moulding process and computer skill in handling CAE and CAD. It may be difficult to combine these skills in one man to begin with. It is knowledge-centered technology. Therefore, it also demands teamwork and new work culture.
- It requires higher investment and higher salaried knowledgeable personnel.
- Design time is reduced to a great extent. Perfection is achieved in the first trial itself. Therefore higher investment is compensated by perfection in first trial and further trials are not necessary.
- Standard pre-machined to size plates and guide pins are used to reduce the mould fabrication time.

What is CAE?

This is software for analysis program that enables the designer to test the design before it is produced. This software bridges the gap between the part designer and mould designer. As explained earlier, the plastic part requires the following basic analysis.

Flow Analysis

Filling analysis to determine the extent of imbalance in melt flow, so that part geometry can be modified till the melt flow is at least 90% (if not 100%) balanced. It also present variation of temperature, shear and stress over part surface and across thickness.

Cooling Analysis

It enables to design the cooling circuits, which will give, uniform temperature all around the mould surface.

Structural Analysis

It gives information on structural deficiencies like moulded-in stresses. There can be analysis for shrinkage, warpage, etc.

Powerful Tool For Moulder and Learning Environment

CAE software is a powerful tool for achieving perfection in part design, mould design and even for determining the optimum cycle time of the newly designed mould as well as existing mould. Therefore, it is a must for all the mould makers, if they want to survive in their business in future. It reduces drastically the design time and enables you to get perfect moulding during first trial itself.

It is also very useful to the moulder for getting the data of optimised processing for a given mould. It also enables you to know the shortcomings in the existing mould. That prompts you to take possible corrective improvements in the mould for improving the quality as well as productivity. If the shortcomings are impossible to correct on a given mould, then you do not waste time and money on correcting the mould by trial and error. In short, you will be able to assess the capability and performance of your existing mould. This powerful tool would save you from wasting time and money on irrational developmental as well as corrective activities.

In addition to all these, it provides a learning environment for the users of software to master the moulding process in very precise engineering terms.

It enables you to learn more details of the process in an iterative manner. It provides a learning environment for you and you will be thrilled to discover the causes of many mysteries of moulding. You will be delighted to know more and more complexities of the process and you will be wondering how you thought in the past that moulding is the simplest of all process.

Usage of CAE

You will have to provide (input) the following information

About Material -

- Melt density
- Heat capacity
- Thermal conductivity
- Viscosity of melts as a function of shear rate, temperature and pressure as determined by capillary rheometer.

(These details are available in the data bank of standard materials of various manufacturers).

User Specified Values

- Temperature of mould:
- Cooling channels details of mould.
- Sprue bush details, hot runner details of mould.
- Part runner, gate details of mould.
- Time to fill, pack, cycle time.
- Maximum pressure at screw tip of machine.

You get the following output from the analysis

- Pressure, temperature distribution in cavities and runners.
- Flow front advance, weld line location, air trap.
- Flow rate at any point and at any time.
- Freezing rate.
- Velocity profile.
- Velocity directions.
- Minimum and maximum clamp force during fill.
- Shear stress.
- Shear rate.

These results are shown as colour shaded pictures, colour plots, tables of data or wire form diagrams. There are set norms for acceptability of the result of these analysis. If the result of the analysis is within the set norms, then the part design becomes acceptable. Otherwise the designer has to modify the part design to overcome the constraints visible in the analysis. This way the analysis is literative in nature.

Is It Not An Expensive Showpiece?

The design of mechanical part involves quite accurate calculations of stress, strain, bending moment, heat transfer, whereas the formulas for plastic parts are quite complex; therefore the thumb rule prevails while designing plastics parts. Dimensional stability of plastic parts and creep behaviour under load condition is quite complicated. They can not be easily estimated manually. Therefore, it calls of the use of Computer Aided Engineering - based on sound engineering principles. Now PC and CAE software prices are affordable to even rationally thinking small entrepreneurs involved in development of trouble free moulds.

Plastic moulders are called upon to develop automobile parts on the basis of sketches at a very short notice. CAE be a very useful tool, as it can predict the quality problems during shaping up of the part itself. CAE also ensure precision of the part. It reduces the development time for moulds.

CAE technology is also referred as prediction technology. While developing the plastic parts, many unforeseen problems can occur that will have a major influence on delivery. These problems can be foreseen and eliminated by having an accurate predictive ability during the product development. The rectification of the problem can be swift and low cost. By integrating prediction into the design process in the early stages, most potential problems can be eliminated in a virtual environment -created in the computer - without any need to waste resources in a factory environment. The predictive ability of CAE enables elimination of the problem of subsequent stages. In other words, CAE predicts the manufacturability of the part design and helps in eliminating the constraints of moulding the parts.

The form, fit, function and cost of plastic components can now be optimised, in terms of part weight, part strength and manufacturing cost.

This CAE software must be expensive. We may not be able to afford its high cost

If it allows you to perfect your mould and production, improves quality with zero defect, then your initial expenses would be recovered quite soon. The cost of CAE is the one time investment for quality and productivity. With this, you will be spreading scientific work culture in your organisation, which is desirable.

You will be able to run production automatically without an operator and may be with a robot. Since quality is inbuilt in part design and mould design, there may not be any need for separate quality supervisors. There is no need for post moulding corrections on mouldings. The production supervisor need not have a technical background, but he should be more a statistician and a good organiser of the shifts.

You will realise that with the employment of few people of good technical caliber and less number of unskilled personnel you will be able to improve the efficiency of your operations. The cost of CAE will definitely be justified, when overall productivity, quality of production and efficiency of operation is drastically improved.

Mouldflow & C-Mould are CAE software. They are available in modules. You need not buy all the modules at one time. You may buy every year some modules and build up your R&D capabilities. In two or three years you might have mastered the technology.

CAE helps you to master the moulding process in greater depth. It deals with the quantified process parameters - direct as well as indirect. Only CAE software can make you expert in plastic moulding technology. With the help CAE software, it is possible to incorporate quality at the part design stage itself. It identifies problems with part geometry and enables to find a solution to the problem. It enables to perfect the part geometry and makes it 90% - 100% mouldable.

It provides the following useful parameters for mould design - which is carried out with CAE software.

- Optimised dimensions for runner and gate and also placement of gates.
- Optimised cooling channel dimensions, flow rate of coolant, positioning of channels.
- Shrink corrected dimensions for core and cavity.
- Identified warpage and its causes, which enables the designer to remove or minimise cause for warpage.
- Optimised process parameters and reduced cycle time.
- Quick set up/start-up without wastage.
- Zero defect parts possible with the first trial of new mould - reduced mould development time.

Now it is possible to evaluate the performance (process parameter for a combination of mould, machine and material) of an existing mould and find out whether it is possible to improve. We can even know what can be the best possible cycle time for a given set up. With this knowledge, we need not waste time for doing impossible things on the given set of mould, machine and material.

COMPUTER AIDED DESIGN AND COMPUTER AIDED MANUFACTURING

CAD systems have been available for about 20 years. There are three types of CAD system

2D System

It replaces the drawing board with a computer system. It can create engineering drawings. When drawing needs modification it can be carried cut without redrawing the entire drawing.

3D Interactive graphics system

This enables the designer to produce 3D assemblies. It has capability to zoom in on any details. It can also rotate the models to enable view the assemblies from different directions. Isometric views can be produced easily. Parts can be scaled and also duplicated easily. Colour graphics improves the clarity of assemblies. Different components, notes, dimensions can be put on different layers. These layers can be selectively presented without losing information.

Solid Modellers

It uses basic 3D shapes like blocks, cylinders, cones, toroids, spheres and prisms, and 3D edges based on construction made by rotating line and arcs. These are added or subtracted until the model is over. It can calculate area, volume, and weight.

Well-known CAD systems are Pro-Engineers, Unigraphics, Ideas, Cimatron, Solid Works, Solid Edge, Deloams Power Shape, Mechanical Desktop.

CAM - Computer Aided Manufacturing

Computer aided manufacturing is the automatic machining of parts by numerically controlled machine tools. CAM system can be integrated with CAD systems so that it can generate the tool paths automatically.

CAM software creates roughing and finishing toolpaths to optimise the productivity of CNC machine tools, while at the same time ensuring the highest quality matching of models and tooling.

CAM software offers high speed calculation, powerful integrated visualisation and verification facilities, which allow the user to compare alternative strategies with any combination of cutting tools and check all toolpaths before they are sent to the machine. As a result, machine idle time and wasted materials and resources are eliminated.

Well-known CAM software are Unigrapnics, Cimatron, Delcams PowerMill, Command, Mastercam...... Actually, is it possible to imagine a good tool room without such a marvellous technological tool?

Solid modeling has replaced the drawing board and usage of 2D software.

When the part is designed in solid, the same model can be used for CAE analysis, mould design and for CAM. This integrated approach - of automated design to manufacturing - saves lot of time. All the leading software offers integrated modules for solid modeling, mould design and CAM.

CAE analysis software (Mouldflow and C-mould) provides useful design parameters of part as well as mould in order to ensure perfect mouldability (manufacturability) of plastic parts. This analysis is carried out after solid modeling and before mould design.

Speed of designing and time saving is because of parametric and associative nature of the solid modelers. They are some kind of in-built intelligence. Therefore, changes made to one element of the mould design update the dimensions and locations of all the related elements. For examples, resizing of a mould plate will also update the size and location of all the holes, bushings, and other features associated with that plate. Changes also carry through to the bill of materials and production drawings, providing greater time saving.

The mould design software is not a stand-alone package but is run within the specific CAD system.

Mould design (CAMD) modules available are -

A mould design system has a great time saving feature in automatic extraction core and cavity from a part model. It produces parting lines and parting surfaces. A single value shrinkage obtained from CAE analysis is applied to core and cavity dimensions to get the perfection of the moulding stage. It easily generates details assembly drawings, sectional drawings and automatically produces the bill of materials which is linked to the database of few leading manufacturers of mould bases and mould components like leader pins, screws, guide pins, electors, support pillars, sprue bushes, etc., (DME Hasco, etc.). Non standard components can also be added by the users in the data bank.

How Does the Mould Design Software Expedite the Work?

All the software products require the same steps to produce a solid of a mould assembly.

- After creating or importing a 3D part model, you create core and cavities around that model, using automated routines. Shrinkage values obtained from CAE analysis is applied to compensate for the shrinkage in the ultimate mlouldings.
- Thereafter you pick a mould base size in which core and cavity insert fit. In fact, in Cimatron it recommends the suitable size of plate automatically.
- Through a dialog/menu interface, you add all the tool's functional components - from gates, runners, ejection cooling, (all from CAE systemand slides right down to individual screws, pins, and bushes. As these components are added, the mould base software also creates the associated holes and features for those components, keeping track, all the while, of relations between features.
- The mould base package creates four-view production drawings and on automatic bill of materials. These programs also set the stage for CNC code generation.

Experienced users of this software claim that there is in all 25 to 75% time saving.

How does CAM Software Work?

CAM-(Cimatron) is used for programming the solid model created earlier. After the completion of programming, it is sent to the CNC machine's computer located on the shop floor adjacent to CNC machine. CNC is computer Numerical Control. CNC machine Center picks up the programmed cutter tool and removes the metal from the job

It is programmed to cut one region on the job at a time. It roughs out the edges, preparing them for semi-finishing stage. CNC machine continues to cut each region one after another till the whole job is finished.

During the next stage, the job is smoothened, but not entirely. At the last stage the job is completed with all the finest details and is made ready for assembly. Ball nose cutter with carbide tool insert, give good finish.

The machine picks up the job and places it on the CNC machine. Then x, y, x, z axis are picked out to match the design of the programmed shape. The machine picks up the required tool and performs the machining operation as programmed.

CAM (Cimatron's NC Machining) is designed to maximise productivity. It works on solid model data and generates automatically precise tool paths for any complex shape for 2.5 to 5 axis milling, drilling, turning and wire EDM. It provides control over creation, modification and display of all NC operations. It also facilitates the machinist to operate and generate tool path on the shop floor. Verifier performs QA checks on entire machining process.

Assembly and Testing of Mould

Assembly of mould becomes quite easy as parts produced are very precise and standard mould bases and other components fit precisely without any rework for fitment. Since mouldability is taken care of during part design, you will find that the mould produces good parts in the first trial itself.

It can be observed that by using new technologies, you can achieve-

- Faster design and drafting through CAD and CAMD software.
- Good selection of most suitable material and grade of material for the defined service condition of plastic part, by using SENSAN software.
- Mouldability and precision through CAE software
- Precision and perfection in manufacturing through CAM software.
- Ease of assembly of mould because of accuracy and precision of manufactured parts of mould.

There is some hesitation in absorbing the new technologies in our working system. This is because the new technology is based on knowledge of physics and engineering and not based on hunch or intuition.

These new technologies provide a learning environment and hence it is possible to absorb them by the people, who have good understanding of basics of physics and engineering.

In the design office, the draft-men's job has become easy, precise and much faster. Therefore, this job has been integrated with the job of junior design engineer. At the shop floor, the manual skill of the machinist is replaced by the programming skill of the CAM programmer. CNC machines provide very good repeatability. whereas it is not easy to get good repeatability by manual skill. However, the experienced machine operator can give very valuable inputs to the machining strategy for CAM programming

8

Injection Moulding Process

Fundamentally the injection moulding of thermoplastics, compared to the compression, moulding of thermosets, is a simple process. Thermoplastic pellets are heated until fluid, then forced into a mould where the plastic re-solidifies to reproduce the shape of the mould. In practice, however, injection moulding is not a simple and easy process, and many details must be successfully worked out to circumvent difficulties. Time, pressure, and temperature are the basic variables that must be controlled, given the poor thermal conductivity of the thermoplastics. Heating a thermoplastic until fluid is not necessarily easy; it is possible to degrade ,the surface by heat before the interior of the plastic mass is warm. That the plastic mass will necessarily fill the mould is also an innocent assumption; it may have voids, blisters, sinks, and shorts, and some cavities in a multicavity mould may not receive any plastic at all. Finally, of course, the part must be ejected, and thermoplastics, like thermosets, are adhesive and, given any scope for doing so, will stick.

The plunger type of injection moulding machine is shown in Fig. 8.1. The cycle begins with a feed mechanism. This meters out a constant amount of material for each moulding cycle.

The hydraulic plunger pushes the plastic through the plasticating chamber, which is a heating cylinder, and then through the nozzle into the mould. The torpedo or spreader (Fig. 8.2), provides an increased surface-to-mass ratio by reducing the cross section of the passages, thus improving the rate of heat transfer into the plastic.

The fluid plastic is forced into the mould though a nozzle connecting the cylinder and the mould. The area of contact between mould and cylinder is small to minimise the flow of heat from the cylinder to the mould.

Besides a cavity or cavities, the mould must contain passages to connect the cavities to the nozzle. These connecting passages which supply the cavities are the sprue, runners, and gates. The sprue is the passage between the nozzle and the runners. It is usually tapered. Each cavity is connected to the sprue by a runner. The gates are very short, restricted passages at the entrance to the cavity.

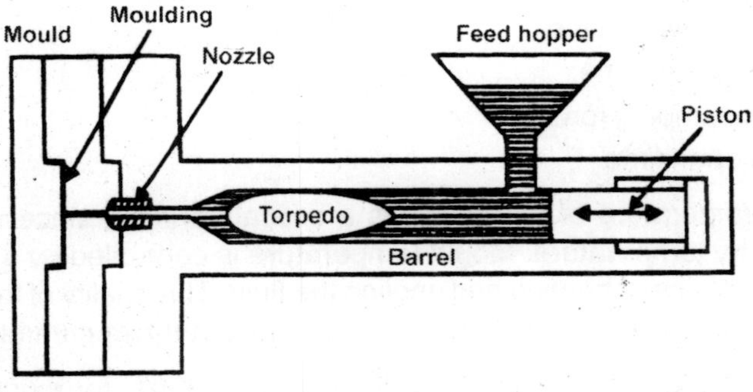

Fig. 8.1 Injection moulding machine, plunger type.

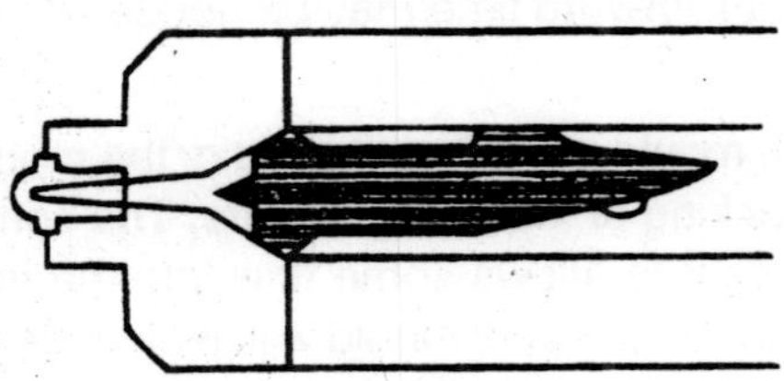

Fig. 8.2 The spreader (torpedo).

The plastic that freezes in the sprue and runners is removed from the part and reground to be fed again into the moulding machine. Time, temperature, and pressure controls indicate whether performance requirements of a moulded part are met. Time factors include rate of injection, duration or ram pressure, time of cooling, time of plastication, and screw RPM. Pressure factors are injection high and low pressure, back pressure on the extruder screw, and pressure loss before the plastic enters the cavity, which can be caused by a variety of restrictions in the mould (Fig. 8.3). Temperature factors are mould (cavity and core),.barrel, and nozzle temperatures, as well as the melt temperature due to back pressure, screw speed, frictional heat, and so on (Fig. 8.4).

The principal variables that must be controlled are nine in number. There may be additional controls also, depending on the uses to which the machine is put:

1. The amount of plastic introduced into the cylinder.
2. The pressure applied to the plunger.
3. Plunger speed.
4. Temperature of the heating cylinder. (Nozzle temperature also may be controlled).
5. Temperature of the mould.
6. Plunger-forward time.
7. Mould closed time.
8. Mould clamping force.
9. Mould open time.

The temperature of the plastic is a critical variable, since viscosity is controlled by temperature. Mould temperature is controlled by a circulating fluid and a means of heating and cooling the fluid. The quality of the moulded product is highly dependent on the ability to adjust these control settings.

Many of the above variables influence the others; for example, if the temperature of the heating cylinder is increased, then the gate freeze more slowly and a longer plunger-forward time may be needed if sinks and voids are to be prevented.

Immediately after the mould is filled with plastic, the mould pressure is greatly increased, and packing of the mould occurs. The compressibility of the plastic under high pressure allows some flow into the mould after the filling stage. Also, the plastic in the cold mould will at once begin to cool and therefore to occupy less volume and allow more plastic to enter from the gate. The usual practice is to time the ram to return after the gate to the cavity is sealed, in order to prevent any discharge from the mould.

The plastic granules are metered into the process either by volume or by weight. The usual arrangement is a volumetric feed, in which the plastic falls from the hopper into a box, which may be adjusted to the desired volume. The measured volume of material then drops into the heating cylinder in front of the ram.

Volumetric feeding is sufficiently precise for most injection-moulding operations. More complex parts, or high-speed operation may require more precise method of feeding by weight, Slight difference in granule geometry, granule friction, or even static electricity may cause variations in volume.

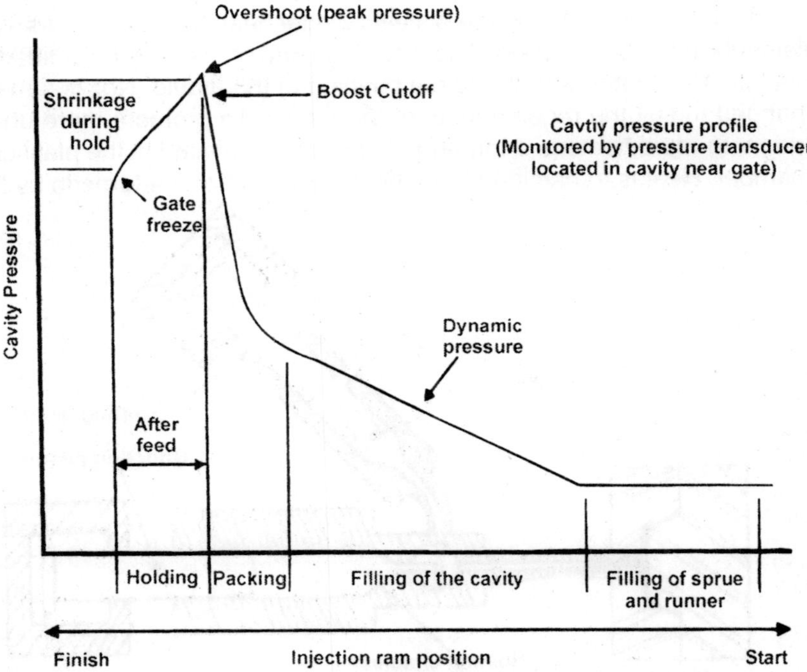

Fig. 8.3 Cavity Pressure profile

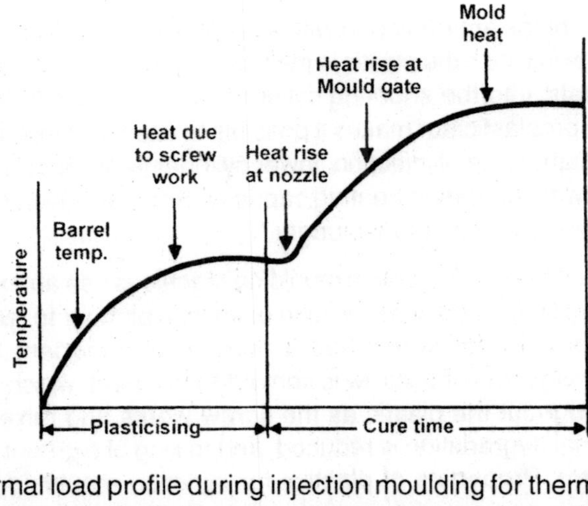

Fig. 8.4 Thermal load profile during injection moulding for thermosets (TSs). (For TPs the curve is similar from the start to the heat rise at the gate; there after it descends during its cooling time period.

The plasticating chamber is a steel cylinder heated by electric resistance elements in the outer jacket. The discharge end of the cylinder is fitted with a nozzle that mates with the sprue bushing of the mould. Nozzles may be changed to suit the requirements of the mould. To promote more uniform and more rapid heating, a torpedo or spreader is placed in the plasticating chamber. Heat is transmitted from the cylinder wall to the torpedo by fins.

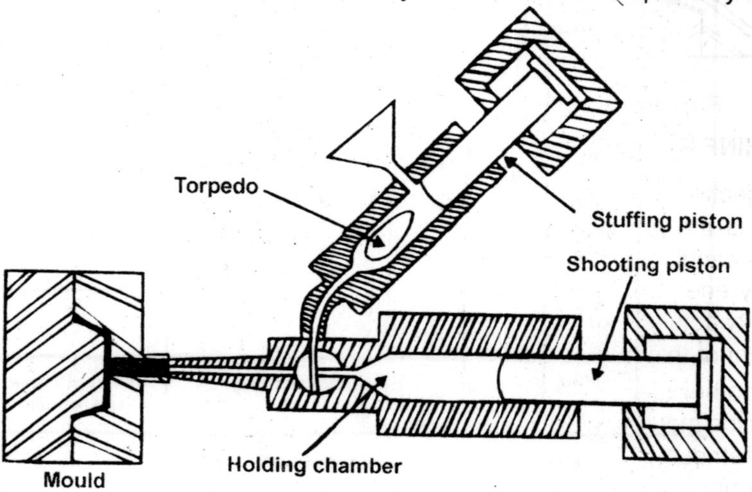

Fig. 8.5 Piston type preplasticating machine

Some machines are equipped with a preplasticator, which is an auxiliary heating cylinder in which the plastic is melted. The plunger of the preplasticator forces the plastic into the shooting cylinder, which shoots it into the mould (Fig. 8.5). The preplasticator makes it possible to use lower injection moulding pressures, a higher rate of injection, lower cylinder temperature, and a larger shot capacity with increased heating capacity. Some preplasticators use an extruder screw instead of a ram plunger.

The newer designs of injection moulding machines use an extruder screw for melting the plastic. The screw is also used as a plunger to feed the mould (Fig. 8.6). The extruder screw has a number of important advantages. Mechanical energy from the screw is converted into heat, which is distributed uniformly throughout the plastic as the screw works and mixes it. Heating time and thermal degradation is reduced, and mixing of pigment in the plastic is more uniform. Properties of plastics for injection moulding are given in Table 8.1.

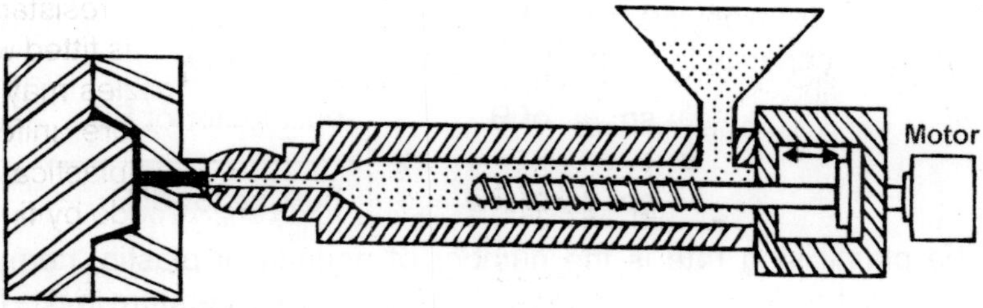

Fig. 8.6 Reciprocating screw injection moulding machine.

MACHINE RATINGS

Injection moulding machines are rated in several ways. The conventional rating is the shot capacity, which is the heating capacity of the heating cylinder and the amount displaced by the plunger in one stroke, in ounces of polystyrene per cycle. This may range from 1 ounce to 1000 ounces. The capacity actually used in any moulding operation would not exceed 75 to 80 per cent of this rating.

Another rating is the clamping force, the rated maximum tonnage that closes the mould during the injection stroke. Limitations on clamping pressure may restrict the projected area of the moulding. For example, suppose that the clamping force of the machine is 350,000 lb and that polycarbonate is to be moulded at 20,000 psi. Then the permissible mould area is limited to a theoretical maximum of 350,0001 /20,000 or 17 1/2 sq. in. However, only a fraction of the pressure produced by the injection cylinder is actually transmitted to the mould cavity, since various pressure losses occur in the heating cylinder, the nozzle, the runners, and the gate. These losses are about one half of the cylinder pressure.

Thin sections require high injection pressure if they are to be filled. Less viscous plastics such as polyethylene of high melt index flow readily and require less clamping force.

The shot capacity in ounces of polystyrene (or any other plastic) is calculated as follows:

Shot capacity in PS =

(volume of moulding in cu in.) x (weight of material per cu in.) x (number of impressions).

Allowance must also be made for runners and sprue. The weight of the material in grams cu in. = 16.4 x specific gravity. The weight of the material in oz cu in. = 0.578 x specific gravity.

To convert from any plastic to the shot capacity in PS, use the following formula. Shot capacity in plastic B = Shot capacity in PS

$$\times \frac{\text{sp. gr. of B}}{\text{sp. gr. of PS}} \times \frac{\text{bulk factor of PS}}{\text{bulk factor of B}}$$

The plasticising rate is the number of pounds of plastic, nominally Polystyrene, that the machine can heat to moulding temperature in one hour. For any plastic, the plasticising rate will depend on moulding temperature and specific heat. Using PS as the standard and again designating the other plastic as B, we find that:

Plasticising rate using B

$$= \text{Plasticising rate with PS} \times \frac{\text{sp. heat PS}}{\text{sp. heat B}} \times \frac{\text{moulding temp PS}}{\text{moulding temp. B}}$$

Table 8.1. Properties of plastics for injection moulding.

Type of plastics	*Bulk / factor*	*Speçific gravity*	*Specific heat*
Acetal	1.8-2.0	1.4	0.35
ABS	1.8-2.0	1. 0-1.1	0.35-0.4
Cellulose Acetate	2.4	1.24-1.34	0.3-0.4
PMMA	1.8-2.0	1.17-1.20	0.35
Nylon	2.0-2.1	I. 09-1.14	0.4
PC	1.75	1.2	0.30
PE, low density	1.84-2.3	0.91-0.94	0.55
PE, high density	1.72-1.9	0.94-0.965	0.55
PP	1.92-1.96	0.90-0.91	0.46
PS	I. 90-2.15	1.04-1.06	0.32
UPVC	2.3	1.35-1.45	0.2-0.28
PVC, flexible	2.3	1.16-1.35	0.3-0.5

Clearly no machine should be pushed to the limit of its plasticising rate but should have some reserve capacity preferably 20 per cent.

Plasticising rate, lb/hr = weight of moulding, lb x number of moulding per hour

The number of mouldings that the machine will produce in an hour is somewhat difficult to predict. The moulding cycle is chiefly depended on the cooling period necessary before the mould can be opened. This cooling period is governed by such factors as the weight of the moulding, specific heat, temperature of the plastic, thickness of the moulding, and its surface area.

INFLUENCE OF MATERIAL PROPERTIES ON THE MOULDING

All thermoplastics have a low thermal conductivity. This makes them susceptible to overheating, particularly at a surface in contact with a heat source. If the polymer is exposed to an excessive temperature for a sufficient period of time, the material will degrade. The degradation usually appears as reduced molecular weight and therefore lower viscosity. It is not unknown for a moulder who is excessively profit minded (or simply in order to make any profit) to use a plasticising temperature that is excessively high, thus improving productivity. The result to such practice is poor mechanical properties and surface defects. If the surface defects are not too serious, the customer may accept the parts,' though the poor mechanical properties may not be disclosed until much later. Fortunately, the screw extruder type of machine greatly reduces the hazard of overheating.

As the plastic cools in the mould, it contracts, so the moulding is smaller than the mould in which it was formed. When the mould is being designed from a dimensioned drawing of the part, a shrinkage allowance must be added to the dimensions of the mould. Shrinkage allowances are obtained from the plastics resin producer, usually given as a range of shrinkage values, the exact value depending on the shape of the moulding and the injection moulding conditions. Rigid PVC has only a slight shrinkage 0.001 to 0.002 in. per inch, while polyethylene of low or high density has a shrinkage range of 0.015 to 0.030 in per inch. Polyethylene, PP and acetal all have very high shrinkage allowances. These materials are crystalline plastics, and in thick sections will cool sufficiently slowly to develop considerable crystallinity.

On the other hand, thin sections of such plastics cool quickly, thus developing little crystallinity and therefore less shrinkage. Tensile strength, density and modulus of elasticity increase with the amount of crystallinity, while elongation and impact strength are reduced. Thus in these crystalline plastics the shape of the moulding has a strong influence on properties.

Shrinkage transverse to the flow direction of the polymer in the mould will be somewhat less than in the flow direction because the long polymer chains become oriented and packed closer together in the flow direction.

Shrinkage is minimised by increased temperature and pressure, by a longer cycle, and by keeping the mould cool.

NOZZLE

Nozzles usually have a spherical nose. This nose must be accurately machined to obtain a satisfactory seal with the mould. The mating spherical recess on the sprue bushing in the mould is usually made 1/32 in, larger than the radius of the nozzle in order to reduce leakage by ensuring positive seating of the two spherical surfaces at the region of the orifice, and to reduce heat loss from the nozzle to the mould.

The orifice diameter of the nozzle varies with the size of the mould and with the plastic to be moulded, but is commonly 1/8 to 9/16 in. Normally this diameter is slightly smaller than that of the sprue orifice.

A number of special types of nozzles are in use, including a nozzle with a ball check valve. Reversetapered nozzles are used for moulding crystalline polymers. These plastics have a sharp melting point, and if too hot they may drool from the nozzle between shots, or if cold will freeze in the nozzle. The reverse-tapered nozzle makes easier the extraction of chilled plastic from the nozzle tip and avoids the necessity of raising nozzle temperature to the point where drooling may occur.

The mixing nozzle as shown in Fig 8.7, is used in dry-blend colour operations. The breaker-plate inserts in the nozzle disrupt the streamline flow pattern to give improved mixing of the pigment.

RUNNERS AND GATES

From the nozzle, the plastic flows through the sprue bushing in the fixed half of the mould. The sprue is cone-shaped for case of extraction of the solidified plastic. The flow of plastic is distributed to the mould cavities through runners. The runners end just short of the cavities and are connected into the cavities by very short channels of small cross section called gates. Each gate preferably feeds into the thickest section of the cavity. Vents are required to exhaust air from the cavity.

The injection mould has a more complex construction than the compression mould, chiefly because of the necessity for sprue and runners. Unlike compression, moulding, no flash should form during the injection moulding process.

The gate is given a smaller cross section than the runner so that the moulding can be easily degated (separated from the runners). The positioning

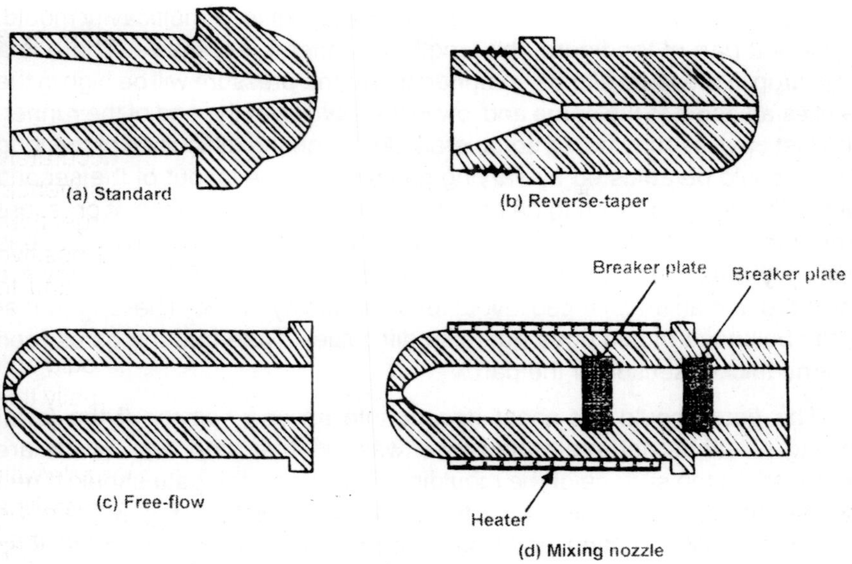

Fig. 8.7. Types of nozzles for injection moulding.

and dimensioning of the gates is critical, and sometimes the gates must be modified after initial trials with the mould. Feeding into the centre of one side of a long narrow moulding almost always result in distortion, the moulding being distorted concave to the feed. In a multi cavity mould, some items the cavities closest to the sprue fill first and the farther cavities later in the cycle. This condition can result in sink marks or shorts in the outer cavities. The condition is corrected by increasing the size of some gates so that simultaneous filling of all cavities will result.

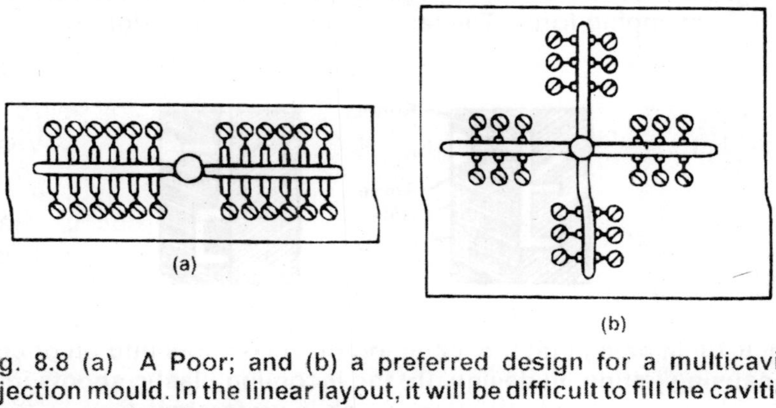

Fig. 8.8 (a) A Poor; and (b) a preferred design for a multicavity injection mould. In the linear layout, it will be difficult to fill the cavities at the ends of the lung runners.

Fig.8.8, shows a poor and an acceptable layout for a multicavity mould. In the first part of the figure, the length of runner is excessive. There is a large drop in pressure along the runner; therefore, pressure will be high in the cavities adjacent to the sprue and low in the cavities at the end of the runner. The last cavities may not fill completely. Although the difficulties of the long runner could be adjusted by varying gates sizes, the layout of the second part of the figure is much to be preferred. Besides this problem of pressure drop, the mould layout must be symmetrical so that the clamping force is uniformly balanced over the whole area of the mould. Fig. 8.9 shows a balanced and an unbalanced layout for a two-cavity mould. The long runner of the balanced mould does not raise difficulties. Note that the gates feed into the thicker section of the part.

The gate should not shoot directly into an ope~ cavity. If the jet of flowing plastic is not interrupted by a wall or other stoppage, swirls are produced on the surface of the moulding. Therefore, the gate should direct the material against some obstruction to break up the flow. Fig. 8.10 shows a layout that allows jetting, and also an improved gating system to break up the flow.

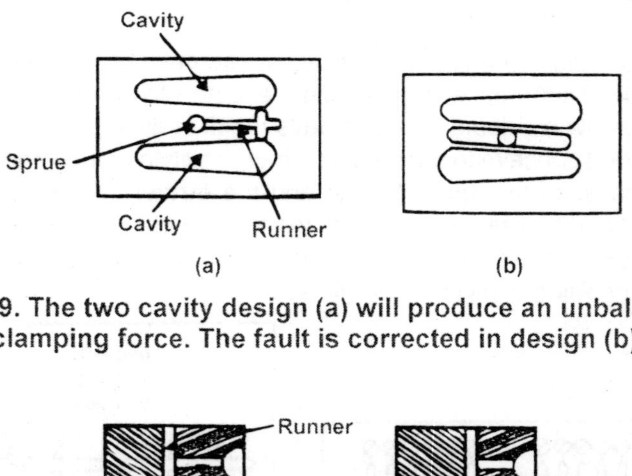

Fig. 8.9. The two cavity design (a) will produce an unbalanced clamping force. The fault is corrected in design (b)

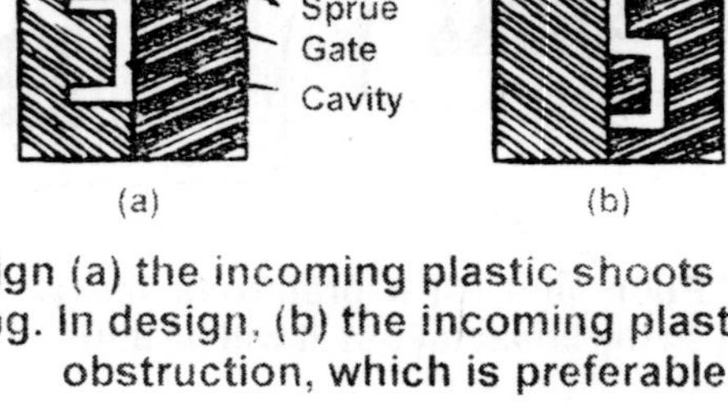

Fig. 8.10. In design (a) the incoming plastic shoots into on open cavity, causing jetting. In design, (b) the incoming plastic shoots into an obstruction, which is preferable.

MOULD

The simplest mould is the two-plate mould with a fixed and a moving platen (Fig. 8.11). The three-plate mould has a third plate, which is called the floating or centre plate. This centre plate carries the gate and some of the runner system.

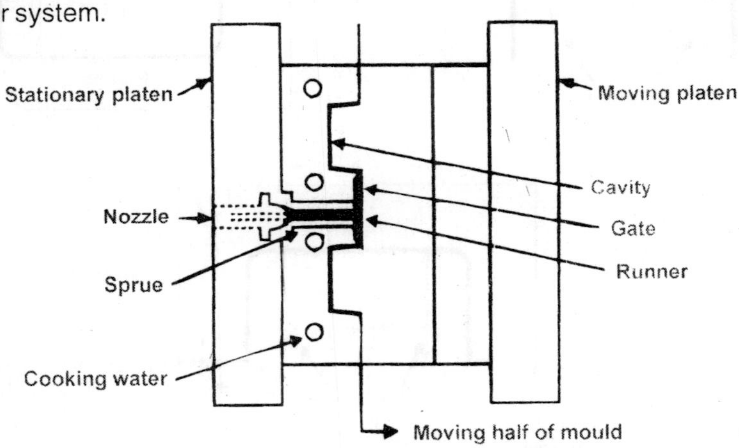

Fig. 8.11 Standard two-plate mould.

When the mould is opened, the centre plate is separated from the other two plates in order to allow the mouldings to be ejected on one side and the sprue and runners on the other. A three-plate mould is shown in Fig. 8.12. Three-plate moulds are frequently used in the production of small articles, but in the case of large moulding the centre plate becomes too massive. The three-plate mould requires a large opening stroke; the availability of the necessary stroke must be checked.

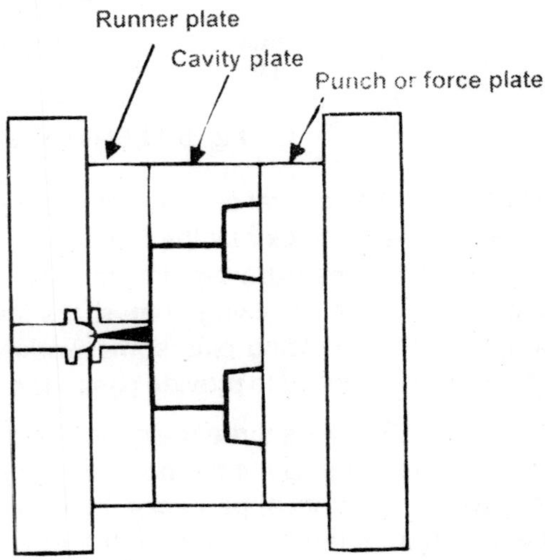

Fig. 8.12 Standard three-plate mould.

The overall dimensions of the mould construction must suit the injection press

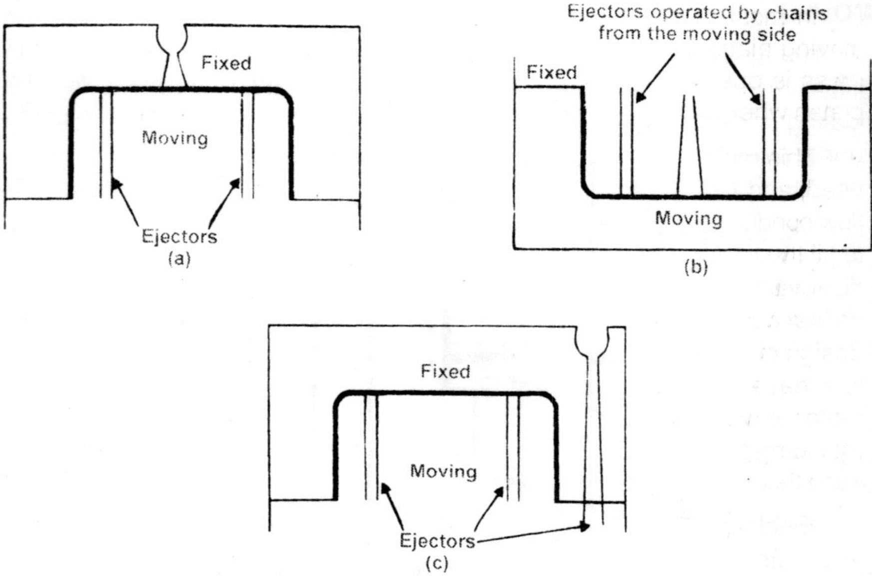

Fig. 8.13 Various methods of feeding a mould.

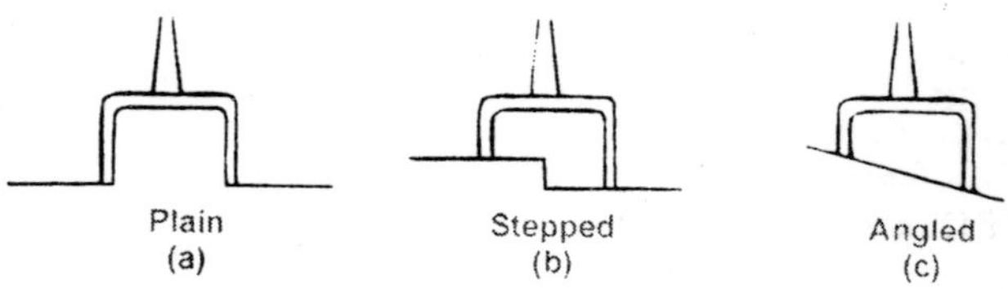

Fig. 8.14 Flash line layouts.

to be used. The critical dimensions are the closed height of the mould, the opening needed to extract the moulding, the width, and the depth. To allow the moulding to be extracted, the opening stroke must not be less than twice the height of the moulding, that is, the length of the male punch plus the length of the moulding plus some working clearance. Both plates of the mould may be drilled to provide passages for water-cooling.

Fig. 8.13, shows three methods of feeding a mould. The first method is the preferred one. But if the positioning of the sprue on the exterior of the part will detract from appearance, then the second or the third method must be adopted. In the first method, the moulding shrinks on the male punch mounted on the moving platen.

In most mould designs the male part of the mould is located on the moving platen, with the moulding remaining on the male mould when the press is opened. In the second method the part will be held on the fixed platen when the mould is opened.

This method requires a longer sprue. In the third method a side gate is used, and the moulding shrinks on to the moving plate of the mould. The flow conditions are less advantageous, and a higher pressure will be required to fill the mould. This may result in increased distortion of the part. Another disadvantage is that the cavity is not symmetrical with the axis of the platens, so that clamping pressure is eccentric. One of the first considerations in the design of the mould is the location of the parting line or flash line. This split line leaves a small witness line on the moulding, since a small amount of material will be able to crepe between the two faces of the mould under moulding pressure. Consequently, the flash line must be so located that any such flash will be visually acceptable. Some layouts are shown in Fig. 8. 14.

Ejector pins for ejecting the moulding from the mould are usually attached to a master bar or ejector plate. The pins are normally on the moveable section of the mould. A central pin is required to eject the sprue.

Various types of inserts may be needed in an injection moulding. These may be classified as : (i) blind or through female threads; (ii) blind or through holes; (Hi) using an insert with a male thread; (iv) special inserts, such as pins, metal stampings, etc. (v) male threads.

PRODUCT DESIGN FOR INJECTION MOULDING

Unless both the product and the mould are capably designed, mouldings will be rejected on grounds either of appearance or properties. Even with good designs, production without rejects .or faults is not easily achieved; sometimes the mould must be modified, or the product design modified, or even both. The moulding must eject readily from the mould; therefore, undercuts should be avoided and a draft of at least 1 degree should be employed on the walls of the moulding.

There should be no region in the mould where material will solidify before injection of material has been completed. The necessary injection pressure will depend on section thickness, length, and cross section of runners and gates, and also on the flow characteristics of the thermoplastic.

Large thicknesses are difficult to produce by the injection-moulding process because of difficulties in filling and cooling the mould, blisters, and sink marks. Products should be hollowed and stiffened with ribs rather than

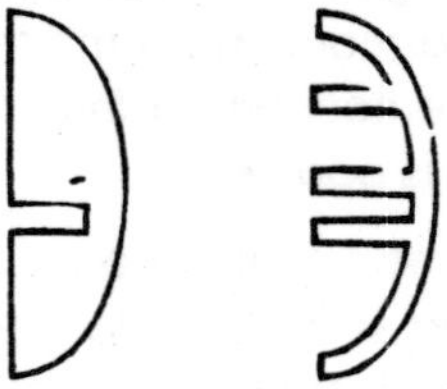

Fig. 8.15. Redesign of a component for injection moulding by adopting ribs and uniform thickness.

formed in heavy sections. A thick component and its redesign for moulding are shown in Fig. 8.15. A uniform thickness results in a more satisfactory part.

For a successful mould to be obtained from the mould maker, he must have more information than a sketch of the part. He needs to know the critical dimensions, tolerances, the special service requirements of the component, how it will be ejected, limitations on gating, and the machine for which the mould is designed.

If the moulded surface of the part must be free of blemishes, then internal gating must be used. The mould maker may adopt either subgating or edge gating. For subgating, the gate goes to the component from the parting line, and when the part is ejected, the gate automatically separates. For edge gating, the part, gate, and runner separate as a unit, and the gate and runner must be separated in a second operation.

COLOURED MOULDING

Often a product must be produced in several colours. Such changes in colour are expensive because it is impossible to clean the previous colour from the heating chamber. When a second colour is used, some of the former colour is absorbed, and mouldings of mixed colour must be produced until the former colour disappears. This interim production of mixed colouring may continue through as many as 50 shots.

Lost production due to colour mixing may be reduced by using a clear and colourless grade of the same thermoplastic. The procedure is the following. Suppose that white resin has been used, and a change is to be made to green. All white material is cleaned out of the hopper, which is then loaded with a quantity of clear resin with green resin on top of the clear material. When the clear material reaches the nozzles, it has picked up white pigments and therefore will be pigmented white. After a time the white colour is suppressed and a mix of clear and green material appears. The number of shots of mettled colour is greatly reduced by this procedure.

The clear material thus serves as a cleaner between one colour and the following colour. Pigments and dyes are added as powder to plastic granules and mixed by tumbling in a drum. Each drum must be restricted to its own colour. Alternatively, special moulding pellets with a high percentage of blended colour may be tumbled into the plastic granules. Such coloured pellets do not cake like powders and provide a better dispersion of colour.

MOULDING PROBLEMS

It is not difficult to blend foreign objects or material into plastic granules. The contamination of one polymer by another is a chronic problem because there are so many possibilities for it. Broken bags, spillage, open containers, unclean containers, reuse of containers, and poor housekeeping practices are only a few of the circumstances that lead to mixing of thermoplastic materials. Sprues and runners are reground and used again for moulding, and it is easy to mix such regrind material with the wrong resin.

Surface blisters are produced by hot gas in the plastic. Such gas may be produced by solvents, plasticizing agents, moisture, release agents, or even thermal degradation of the thermoplastic. Moisture can be absorbed by pellets in the machine hopper, especially when humidity is high. The cellulosics, acrylics, polycarbonate, nylons and ABS readily absorb moisture.

Internal voids or bubbles are more common in thicker sections than thin sections. Opaque plastics are preferred because they hide this defect. These voids are caused by trapped gases in the material.

Flash may have a number of possible causes, such as improper closing of the dies, material too hot, excessive pressure, or too heavy a feed. Products with thin walls must be moulded at a higher temperature to resist premature chilling in the mould; hence the viscosity is lower and the material' can penetrate the parting line.

Sticking of the part to the mould is often corrected by cooling the part of the mould where sticking occurs. Dirt, slight undercuts, or a rough mould surface also result in sticking.

Burn marks, which are charred areas, are caused by hot volatile material such as entrapped air.

Sink marks are of concave depressions, usually at thick sections or on the opposite side to a rib. To prevent sink marks, the gate should be located at the heaviest section of the part. Sometimes the gate must be enlarged to reduce sinks, or pressure may be increased. Often small sink marks cannot be avoided, or may even be acceptable.

Lightweights or shorts are incompletely filled cavities. They may result from inadequate pressure or temperature or too narrow a gate. Other causes may be a clogged nozzle or entrapped air.

A weld line occurs when material flows together from two directions, as around as insert. Weak weld lines result in a defective product, and may be corrected by faster mould filling.

Warping usually results from changes of section. Thinner sections cool fast, and then the thicker sections shrink and pull against the hardened thin sections.

FINISHING AND REGRINDING

Flash and fins must be removed from mouldings. Defining and deflashing are done in tumbling barrels, the operation also giving a polish to the mouldings. Steel stars or balls are used for defining, and sawdust for removing the dust of the defining operation. Pumice, shoe pegs, wax, and other media are used for polishing.

Another difference between compression and injection moulding is that in injection moulding the waste material, sprues, runners, and rejects, can be regranulated and used a second time. Grinders, also called granulators, are rated by the number of pounds per hour that can be reground.

PURGING

Purging has always been a necessary evil, consuming substantial amounts of materials, labour, and machine time, all nonproductive. In 1M (extrusion, blow moulding, etc.), sometimes it is necessary to run hundreds of pounds of resin to clean out the last traces of a dark colour before changing to a lighter one. Sometimes there is no choice but to pull the screw for a thorough cleaning. Although there are few generally accepted rules on how to purge, the following tips should be considered: (i) try to follow less viscous with more viscous resin; (ii) try to follow a lighter colour with a darker colour resin; (iii) maintain the equipment; (iv) keep the material handling equipment clean; and (v) use an intermediate resin to bridge the temperature gap (such as that encountered in going from acetal to nylon), and use a PS as a purge.

Ground/cracked cast acrylic and PE-based materials are the main purging agents, but others also are commercially available for certain machines and materials. Cast acrylic, which does not melt completely, is suitable for virtually any resin. About one pound for each ounce of injection capacity will be needed (5-10 lb/in. of screw diameter in an extruder). With extruders, special conditions and preparations are required, which suppliers of the purging compound can recommend (remove dies, screen packs, etc.)

PE-based compounds usually contain abrasive and release agents. They are used to purge the "softer" TPs (polyolefins, styrene, some PYCs, etc.). With extruders, many of the requirements/restrictions do not apply.

These purging agents function by mechanically pushing and scouring residue out of the machines. Others also apply chemical means. Table 8.2 and 8.3 provide information on purging.

Table 8.2. Guidelines for purging agents.

Material to be purged	*Recommended purging agent*
Polyolefins	• HDPF
Polystyrene	• Cast acrylic
PVC	• Polystyrene, general-purpose, ABS, cast acrylic
ABS	• Cast acrylic, polystyrene
Nylon	• Polystyrene, low-melt-index HDPE, cast acrylic
PBT polyester	• Next material to be run
PET polyester	• Polystryrene, low-melt-index HDPE, cast acrylic
Polycarbonate	• Cast acrylic or polycarbonate regrind; follow with polycarbonate regrind; to not purge with ABS or nylon.
Acetal	• Polystyrene; avoid any contact with PVC
Engineering resins	• Polystyrene, low-melt-index, HDPE, cast acrylic
Fluoropolymers	• Cast acrylic, followed by polyethylene
Polyphenylene sulphide	• Cast acrylic, followed by polyethylene
Polysulphone	• Reground polycarbonate, extrusion-grade PP
Polysuphone/ABS	• Reground polycarbonate, extrusion-grade PP
PPO	• General-purpose polystyrene, cast acrylic
Thermoset polyester	• Material of similar composition without catalyst
Filled and reinforced materials	• Cast acrylic

Flameretardant compounds • Immediate purging with natural, non-flame-retardant resin, mixed with 1% sodium stearate

PROCESS CONTROL

Process controls can range from unsophisticated to very sophisticated devices. Their cost includes the equipment and using them correctly (they take time, patience, and a willingness to learn new ways of moulding.

Table 8.3. Guidelines for resin changes.

Material in machine	*Material changing to*	*Mix with rapid purge and soak*	*Temperature bridging material*	*Follow with*
ABS	PP	ABS	-	PP
ABS	SAN	SAN	-	SAN
ABS	Polysulphone	ABS	PE	Polysulphone
ABS	PC	ABS	PE	PC
ABS	PBT	ABS	PE	PBT
Acetal	PC	Acetal	PE	PC
Acetal	Any material	PE	-	New material
Acrylic	PP	Acrylic	-	PP
Acrylic	Nylon	Acrylic	-	Nylon
TPE	Any material	PE	-	New material
Nylon	PC	PC	-	PC
Nylon	PVC	Nylon	PE	PVC
PBT	ABS	PBT	PE	ABS
PC	Acrylic	PC	-	Acrylic
PC	ABS	PC	PE	ABS
PC	PVC	PC	PE	pvc
PE	Ryton	PE	PE	Ryton
PE	PP	PP	-	PP
PE	PE	PE	-	PE
PE	PS	PS	-	PS
PETG	Polysulphone	PETG	-	Polysulphone
Polysulphone	ABS	Polysulphone	PE	ABS
Polysulphone	ABS	Cracked acrylic	-	ABS
PP	ABS	ABS	-	ABS
PP	Acrylic	Acrylic	-	Acrylic
PP	PE	PE	-	PE

PP	PP	PP	-	PP
PS	PP	PP	-	PP
pvc	Any material	LLDPE OR HDPE	-	New material
pvc	pvc	LLDPE OR HDPE	-	pvc
PPS	PE	PPS	PE	PE
SAN	Acrylic	Acrylic	-	Acrylic
SAN	PP	SAN	-	SAN

The development of powerful computer controls and programmes has greatly accelerated integrating process variables with a goal of zero defects at the lowest cost. The computer simplifies the fine-tuning of machine settings with moulding variables. Examples include establishing melt conditions for moulding filling and packing, which involves the simultaneous measurement and control of two or more critical variable parameters. It is during this phase of operation that most variations make themselves evident and can be easily detected. A change in melt viscosity is reflected as a change .in ram speed and can be detected by measuring the ram position with respect to time. A change in resin viscosity is reflected as a change in melt pressure and can be detected by measuring mould or cavity pressure with respect to time. Other variations that similarly display themselves and can be detected include melt temperature, hydraulic pressure, oil temperature and so on.

COMPUTER INTEGRATED INJECTION MOULDING

The ultimate result of Computer Integrated Injection Moulding (CIIM) in software packages is to translate the results of computer simulation of the moulding of a specific part into machine setting for specific microprocessor-controlled machines (Fig. 8.16). CIIM automates the entry of a large number of set points in microprocessor-controlled machines and maximises their efficiency, on the basis of extensive development.

Microprocessor Control Systems

Microprocessor control systems (MCS) make it possible to completely automate an 1M plant. They control machines, automatically, enabling them to achieve high quality and zero defects. These systems readily adapt to enhancing the ability of processing machines. There are many mouldings that would be difficult, if not impossible, to produce at the desired quality level without this feature.

Once processing variables are optimised through computer simulation, these values are entered in computer programmes in the form of a large number of machine settings. Establishing the initial settings during start-up is inherently complex and time-consuming. The many benefits of these systems are well

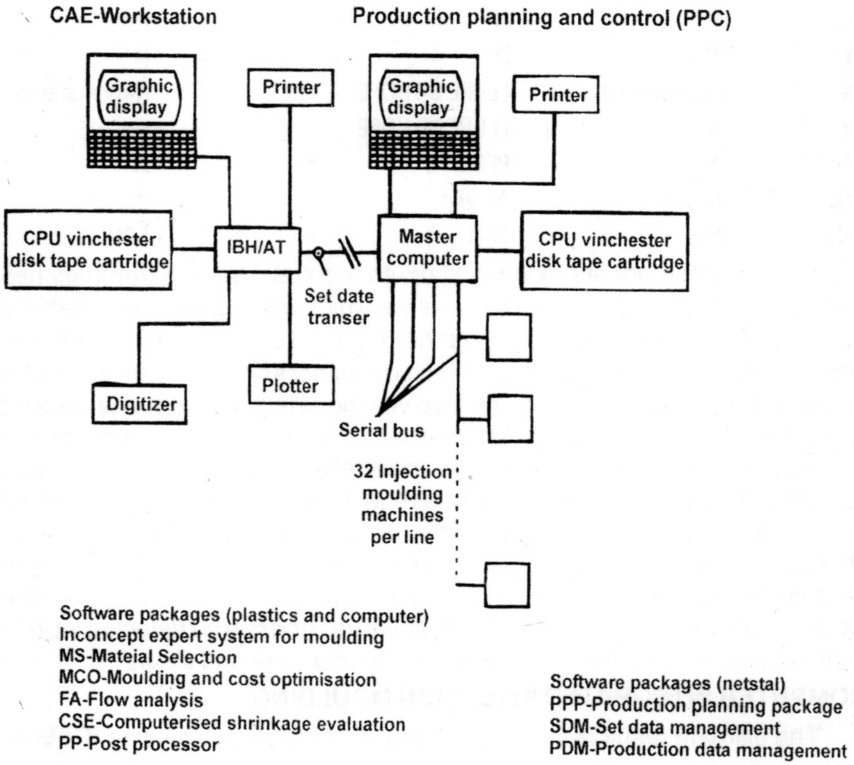

Fig. 8.16 Overview of Computer Integrated Injection Moulding (CIIM)

recognised and accepted, but it is evident that self-regulation of 1M can be effective only when the design of the part and the mould is optimised, and when the correct processing conditions for the operation have been predetermined. Otherwise, a self-regulating machine is confused and can provide conflicting instructions. The results could be disastrous, damaging the machine or the mould. Therefore, the efficient utilisation of microprocessor-control systems depends on the success of utilising correct and optimum programmes.

Computerised Process Simulation of 1M

The simulation approach replaces the traditional trial-and-error method. Programmes, such as the Barnnardt TM Concept, are packaged for the complete moulding process, including material selection, moulding and cost optimisation, flow analysis, computerised shrinkage evaluation, and mould thermal analysis. The programmes include mould filling, packing, and so forth, which accurately model the performance of microprocessor programmed injection. Major 3D CAD systems for part and mould design, as well as for structural and flow analysis, are integrated with these systems.

9

Specialised Injection Moulding Process

CO-INJECTION MOULDING

Co-injection basically means that two or more different plastics are "laminated" together. These plastics could be the same except for colour. When different plastics are used, they must be compatible in that they provide proper adhesion (if required), melt at approximately the same temperature, etc. Two or more injection units are required, with each material having its own injection unit. The materials can be injected into specially designed moulds-rotary, shuttle, etc.

The term co-injection can denote different products, such as sandwich construction, double-shot injection, multiple-shot injection, structural foam construction, two-colour moulding, in moulding, etc. Whatever its designation, a sandwich configuration has been made in which two or more plastics are "laminated" together to take advantage of the different properties each plastic contributes to the structure.

This form of injection has been in use since long and has become more commercial. Many different advantages exist. For example: (i) it combines performance of materials; (ii) it permits use of a low-cost plastic such as a regrind; (iii) it provides a decorative "thin" surface of an expensive plastic; and (iv) it includes reinforcements, etc. Co-injection moulding is being redefined today in light of the approaches now available for moulding multicomponent parts (automotive tail-lights, containers, business machine housings, etc.).

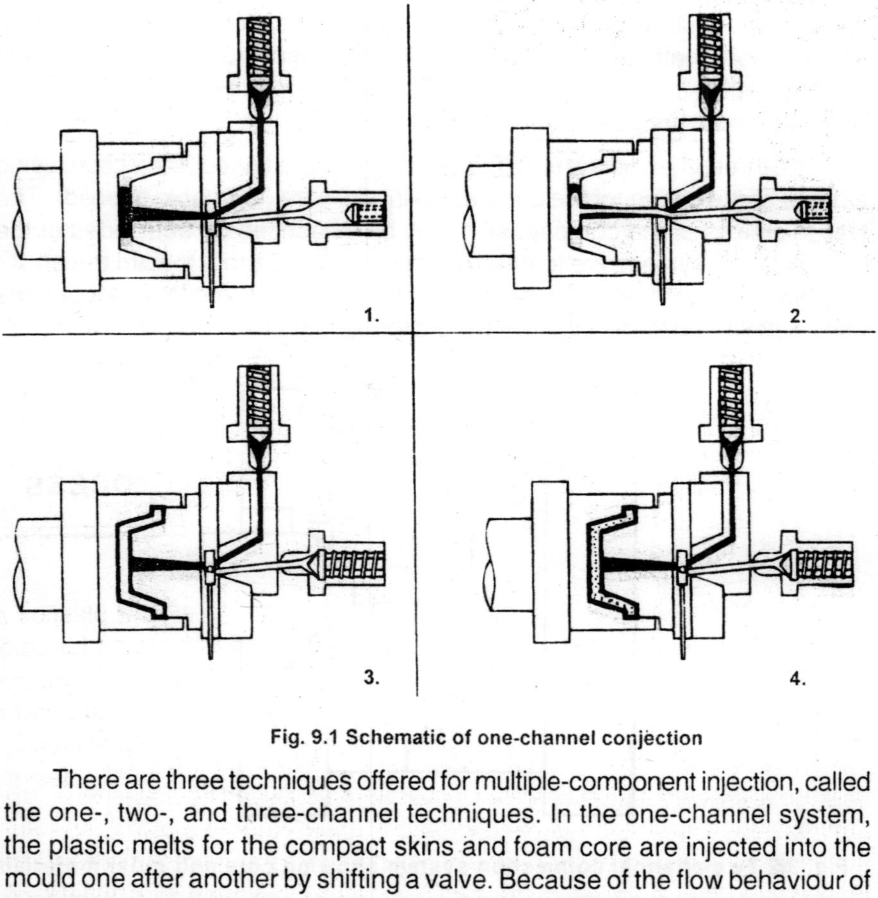

Fig. 9.1 Schematic of one-channel conjection

There are three techniques offered for multiple-component injection, called the one-, two-, and three-channel techniques. In the one-channel system, the plastic melts for the compact skins and foam core are injected into the mould one after another by shifting a valve. Because of the flow behaviour of the plastic melt in the tool and since the. first injected plastic for the compact skin cools off under the cooler mould surface, a closed compact skin and core are formed under proper parameter settings. The thickness of the compact skin may be changed by varying the process parameters, This single-channel technique can incorporate either a solid or foamed core. As shown in Fig. 9.1. in the one-channel coinjection system, the sequence of mould filling starts with the skin being injected, then the core. In the third stage, the skin polymer is injected again to clear the sprue and seal the skin on the injection side of the part. In this application, a foam core is used. Up to stage 3 all melts have been injected at the conventional high pressure of injection moulding. After the skin solidifies, the mould opens to a preset amount and permits the core to foam as shown in stage 4.

The two-channel system (Fig. 9.2) allows the formation of the compact skin and core material simultaneously. With this technique, the thickness of the compact skin in the gate area can be easily controlled (representing a difference from the one-channel system).

The three-channel system (Fig. 9.3) allows simultaneous injection, using a direct sprue gating, of the compact skin and core (foamable or solid). The wall thickness of the compact skin may be influenced on both sides of the part. With this system, the foamed core progresses farther toward the end of the flow path, compared to the one- or two-channel technique. Also, parts can be designed to be lighter in weight for the structural foam product.

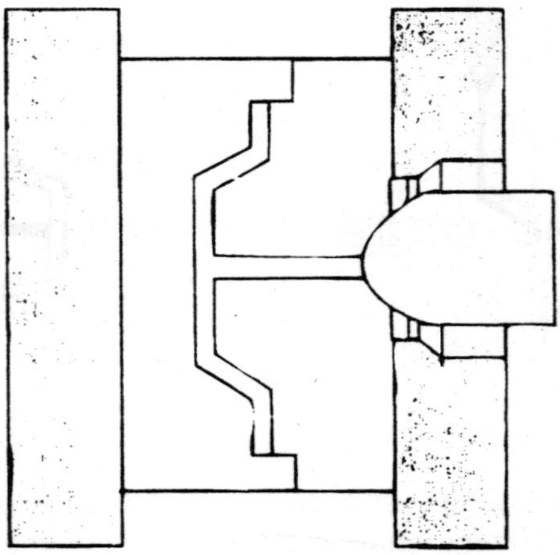

Fig. 9.2 Two-channel coinjection system showing core and outer materials.

TWO-COLOUR MOULDING

This is sometimes called double-shot moulding. It uses an injection moulding machine for making two colour moulded parts by means of successive moulding operations. This is accomplished by first moulding the basic case or shell and then, using this as an insert, with the next shot around or in the original moulded part. These steps can be accomplished using two separate machines or have two injection units (with the different plastics) delivering melts in sequence into a shuttle or rotary mould held between platens.

GAS INJECTION MOULDING (GIM)

Parts can be moulded by gas injection moulding (GIM), also called injection gas pressure (IGP), using injection moulding machines. This process is most effective and economical when used for large parts. It offers a way to mould parts with only 10 to 15% of the clamp tonnage that would be necessary in conventional injection moulding.

The technique-practiced in several variations, such as the usual internal system but also an external system (gas between filled cavity melt and cavity wall just prior to melt solidifying), with some patented involves the injection of an inert gas, usually nitrogen, into the melt as it enters the mould. This is not structural foam, as no foam core is produced; instead, the gas forms a series of interconnecting hollow channels in the thicker sections of the part. The gas pressure is maintained through the cooling cycle. In effect, the gas packs the plastic into the mould without a second-stage high-pressure packing in the cycle as used in injection moulding, which requires high tonnage to mould large parts.

Moulded-in stresses are minimal. The thick but hollow sections provide rigidity and do not create sink or warpage problems. The cycle time is reduced because the thick sections are hollow. As the gas is not mixed with the melt, there is no surface splay, which is typical of low-pressure structural foam moulding. The finished part exhibits an excellent surface finish with minimum distortion. The nitrogen tank gas pressure is usually about 4,300 psi (30 MPa). Gas injection is being used with commodity and engineering plastics.

Advantages and Disadvantages

Gas injection moulding (GIM) is a solution to many problems associated with conventional high-pressure injection moulding and structural foam moulding. It significantly reduces volume shrinkage which causes the sink marks in injection moulding.

Advantages

1. No moulded-in stresses (and no sink marks) due to low cavity pressure exerted by gas.
2. Lower mould cost because undercuts can be avoided "and there are savings on slide actions when required.
3. Simplification in certain mould designs.
4. Part design flexibility such as mixed thick and thin walls, box sections possible without movable cores, allowing part consolidation and larger complex parts to be moulded.

5. Lowers clamp force and thus costs for operating injection moulding machine (lower energy).
6. A shorter cycle time above all for mouldings with large wall-thickness variations.
9. Material savings up to 40%, depending on the part configuration.
8. Significant reduction of sink marks over ribs and bosses.
9. Improved surface finish.
10. Part weight reduction, higher strength-to-weight ratio.

Parts produced by the GIM method are stiffer in bending and torsion than equivalent conventional injection moulding parts of the same weight.

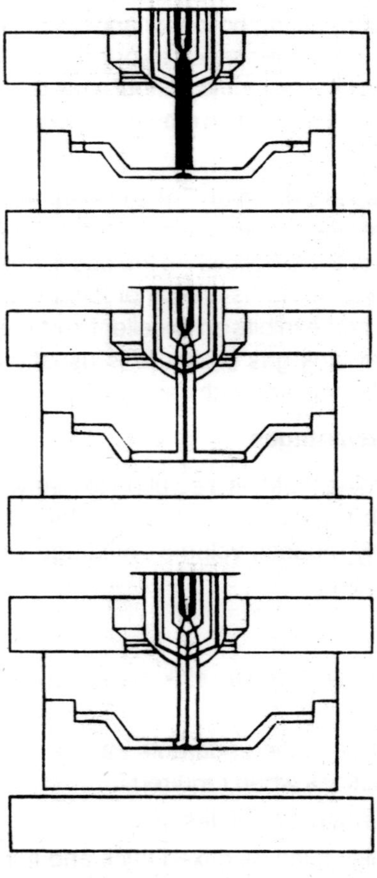

Fig. 9.3 Three-channel coinjection system simultaneously inject two different plastic melt.

Longer production-development lead time is required, it is difficult to control multi-cavity moulds (usually greater than four cavities), precision and programmable mould-temperature control is required for consistent wall thickness, and the part has to be designed to place a vent hole on a non-visible portion of the part.

Basic Processes and Procedures

It is well known that in the conventional injection moulding process, the pressure required to advance the plastic melt increases with the amount of plastic injected (or equivalently, the flow distance). It should be noted that the gap-wise averaged melt viscosity is proportional to the magnitude of the pressure gradient and melt fluidity. Therefore, as the flow length of the melt increases, the inlet pressure has to increase to maintain a certain pressure gradient if the flow is to be kept constant.

Disadvantages

With GIM, the pressure requirement is the same as that for the conventional process during the plastic injection stage. Upon the introduction of gas into the cavity, the gas starts to displace the viscous melt, pushing it to fill the extremities of the cavity. Because the gas has essentially zero viscosity, it can effectively transmit the gas pressure without a significant pressure drop to the advancing gas/melt interface. Therefore, as the gas advances toward the melt front, the pressure required to keep the melt ahead of the gas moving at the same velocity decreases, since the effective flow length decreases.

Consequently, the gas pressure required to fill the mould cavity can be lower than the entrance melt pressure needed for the conventional injection moulding process. Further, the resulting pressure distribution is more uniform in a gas-injected part. This action induces less residual stresses as the plastic cools down during the postfilling stage. Accordingly, the GIM part can be produced with a lower gas-pressure requirement that leads to lower clamping tonnage.

Owing to the unique mould design with a built-in gas channel network and dynamic interaction between gas and plastic melt, gas penetration can become very complicated. For example, during the melt injection stage, it is typical that the melt will flow preferably along the gas channel, which serves as a flow leader that leads to the so-called "racetrack" effect. The significance of the racetrack effect depends on the material properties and processing conditions, as well as cavity geometry. Improper combinations of these parameters will give rise to an air trap and gas permeation into the thin section near the air trap. The gas will take the path along which the plastic melt has the least resistance and largest pressure gradient. Since the pressure drop from the gas tip to the presumably vented melt front is approximately a constant, the flow path that has the least flow length (between the gas tip and melt front) wilt result in a high-pressure gradient and thus can be permeated by the gas. This is the reason why the gas starts permeating into the thin section moving toward the air trap.

Another common complication associated with uneven gas permeation is the melt-front position immediately before the gas injection. After the gas is introduced into the cavity, typically it starts penetrating the thick-sectioned gas channels. However, once the lower portion of the cavity becomes filled, the pressure over that region 'starts to build up because the melt can no longer fill in that region, giving its place to the incoming gas. The result is that the gas can hardly penetrate into the lower portion further until the whole cavity gets filled and the plastic starts to shrink. In the meanwhile, the gas penetration continues in the upper part of the cavity until it is filled.

In addition to problems like air trap, gas permeation into the thin section, and uneven gas penetration, other flow-related problems include gas blow-through. This is an insufficient amount of plastic melt ahead of the gas, switch-over or hesitation marks occurring along the suddenly decelerated melt front at the switch-over time due to delay of gas injection. It is also due to the material degradation associated with the acceleration of the melt driven by the advancement of gas, as well as short shot resulting from low gas pressure or inadequate tool design.

Processes

There are basically two types of processes: gas through the nozzle and gas through the runner or cavity (sequential type). In both cases, the mould is partially filled with plastic melt as a short shot. The gas can be introduced simultaneously and/or subsequently with the plastics after some delay time or the plastic flow is completely stopped by a specially designed shut~off gas nozzle, and a controled volume of inert gas (usually nitrogen) is injected into the centre of the melt flow. The combination of high melt surface tension and lower viscosity of the hotter molten plastic in the centre of the thicker sections, such as ribs, confines the gas to form hollow areas in the thicker sections of the part. The melt that is displaced by the gas is pushed into the extremities of the tool (mould), packing out the moulded part.

The outer surface of thicker sections do not sink because gas has cored them out from the inside and gas pressure holds the plastic against the mould surface during rehardening. The sink in thes sections takes place internally rather than on the exterior surfaces of the part, eliminating sink marks. Since the pressure used for final filling of the part is confined to an area defined by the system of gas channels, the resultant force against the sections of the mould is relatively modest so that lower clamping forces on the mould are adequate.

When comparing a gas through nozzle vs. gas through cavity process, each has its own pros and cons. Gas through nozzle is good for symmetrical multi cavity moulds and basically is not used with a hot-runner system. Also, the gas cannot be injected simultaneously; plastic flow is stopped, then the gas is injected. The existing moulds can usually be employed without much change for this mode, depending on part design.

Gas through a cavity or runner mode has more flexibility. The hot-runner systems can be easily used. Simultaneous plastic/gas injection is possible. This tends to be a more versatile technique.

In regard to part/tool design guidelines, it is well understood that simultaneous part design, mould design, and process design are important features for the success of any part gas-moulded. For GIM as for conventional injection moulding, some guidelines have been established for different plastics, but may not hold true for all geometries and wall thicknesses. The usual gas channel geometry is either symmetrical or unidirectional relative to the injection gate.

The balance for the plastic and gas flow from the gate is critical. Computer-aided mould fill analysis (short shot) can be a very helpful approach for gate design and location. As a rule of thumb, the width of a rib should be equal to or less than three times the nominal wall thickness and the depth (height) of a rib should be equal to or greater than three times the nominal wall thickness.

A gas flow channel must be continuous and should not loop back upon itself. The plastic melt displaced from the gas flow channel must have some place to go, and the material displaced must be sufficient to pack out the mould. One should provide spill-over space in the mould for fine-tuning the flow distance to achieve desired hollow channels.

Procedures

There are two basically different GIM-controlled moulding procedures: (i) with volume-controlled gas metering, a predetermined quantity of gas is injected, after which the gas pressure decreases slowly and (ii) with pressure-controlled gas metering, the gas pressure is either constant from the beginning or with a defined profile, (e.g., low at the start, high during the holding phase).

Some general comments can be made regarding these processes. The most important precondition from the reproducible operation of the process is homogeneous melt. High gas pressure during the cooling period gives smooth gas channel surfaces, whereas a pressure drop before the melt has fully solidified gives rise to a rough or foamed inner wall structure.

Gas blowing takes the path of least resistance. Thus, parts with wall thickness differences and large areas of uniformly thin walls have to be prefilled with a large proportion of the total quantity of melt. With higher gas pressure, the lighter the moulding. Also, the achievable wall thicknesses and surface effects can be more strongly influenced by material modifications than by changes in processing parameters.

The processes can be adopted for use on the usual type of injection moulding machines without major expenditures. The gas is introduced through a needle seal nozzle specifically modified for the process. The processes are based on the control of pressure. The pressure and length of the gas injection are regulated during gas introduction. The control of the duration of gas introduction and pressure can be accomplished by not only the signals of the injection moulding machine, but also the use of external programmers and signal transmitters.

It appears reasonable to obtain the signal for the injection and then control the time delay and length of the gas introduction through external regulators. The nitrogen has a maximum pressure of 300 bar (4,350 psi). Gas pressure in the usual application is 200 bar (2,900 psi). The pressure can be produced continuously, for example, by compressors. As an alternative, the gas can be injected intermittently using a hydraulically operated piston.

Measurements with transducers placed in the mould as well as theoretical considerations have shown that a simultaneous gas injection is not possible. During the injection of the melt, the pressure at the flow front is about I bar (14.5 psi). However, the gas pressure remains mostly constant throughout the entire expansion of the cavity. The flow front has to absorb the full difference between the pressure of the gas and that of the atmosphere. The moulded part is thus blownup. To prevent the blowout of the part, there must be significant mass accumulation between the gas bubble and flow front. This means that at the boundary a sufficient amount of melt must be supplied during the blowing stage.

However, this is not possible when the gas and melt are injected simultaneously, because in locations where the melt touches the mould, the pressure gradient is the same. Reinforcement with ribs in the part can be incorporated. Ribs must be designed in such a way that the gas has a free passage in the centre from the sprue to the outside. The ribs should not be brought together because this could cause material entrapment.

The gas-filling profile has to be finely tunable with the simultaneous as well as sequential method. Gas introduction is a function of the screw position, with the gas flowing to the internal gas pressure nozzle via a valve. Through the proportional valve, a gas profile can be set on the machine's control system. The screw-position-dependent start of gas injection ensures that from this moment, the mould has always been filled with an identical amount of melt.

Moulding Aspects

The position of gas bubbles determines the dimensional stability and thus the precision of reproduction of the moulded part. Control of the gas bubble is complicated. With simple designed parts it can be adequate, but with other parts it is a critical matter. The weight scatter with GIM when no holding pressure is used is currently±0.3 to ±1.0%. With conventional injection moulding, it is ±0.1 %. This large weight variation has no negative implications for part quality. In contrast to the example with conventional injection moulding, even light parts are properly filled and heavy ones not over filled.

The repeatability of geometry in the hollow space is essentially dependent on the material and geometry of the mould cavity. Process parameters and process stability have only a small effect. However, surface quality does depend very largely on them.

In general, GIM parts require moulds designed specially for the specific process. Faults are more difficult to correct than with conventional injection moulding. Also, the optimisation phase on commissioning a new mould usually takes longer with GIM moulding. The surface quality of thick-wall GIM parts depends above all on the injection technique, and jetting should be avoided during filling.

Marking, even when switching to gas metering, can result if cross sections are too small. With reinforced plastics, the external surfaces are rougher than with conventional injection moulding; the reason is that the gas holding pressure is lower.

From an environmental viewpoint, no special difficulty arises with GIM. Actually, the level of residual monomers in the nitrogen is extremely negligible. Gas-recovery systems are available and, in terms of the environment and nitrogen consumption, ought to be used.

The holding pressure drops as is usual in the conventional injection moulding process. It is replaced by the internal pressure of the gas. The gas presses the solidified melt against the wall of the mould. In conventional injection moulding, the holding pressure acts only up to the point of sealing the sprue. Beyond that action, it is no longer effective. This is especially critical for parts with thick walls that have only relatively small gates. During the GIM process, however, the sprue remains open due to a gas channel (or with the gas into the runner or cavity); this means that the pressure can be considered constant within the entire cavity. Thus, the space far from the sprue has the same internal pressure as that which is close to the sprue. This way shrink spots are eliminated even in these areas.

Generally, the usual parameters for the material, moulds, and machine can be adjusted. The effect of several processing parameters on gas expansion exists. As an example, the increasing temperature of the plastic material can have the following effects. The wall thickness of the moulded part diminishes, reproducibility becomes a problem, and increased risk of blow-out occurs. A higher mould temperature results in the reduced occurrence of sink marks, reduced amount of shrinkage, and improved efficiency of gas injection.

A reduction of the injection rate causes the increased risk of blow-out and a reduced material cushion in front of the gas bubble. When the metering passage is extended, the results will be as follows: increased plastic cushion in front of the gas bubble, reduced gas volume, and diminished risk of blow out.

The choice of gas pressure must be suited to the particular moulded-part. The minimum and maximum pressures can be determined by measuring pressures in a screw tab using a solid part. The minimum pressure should be chosen so that the gas pressure is higher than the melt pressure during two thirds of the total gas injection period. The maximum pressure has to be adjusted in such a way that there is no gas disturbance in the melt.

Shrinkage

Compared to conventional injection moulding, plastic shrinkage depends greatly on viscosity. The reason for this action is that with high mould wall or melt temperature, the resultant wall thickness is minimal and the inside of the wall of only a slightly higher temperature during demoulding than the mould surface. The shrinkage that then takes place is proportional to the difference between the mould and ambient temperature. If one compares a conventional injection moulding part of amorphous plastic with one produced by the GIM process, the shrinkage of the GIM part is reduced by one-third.

With crystalline plastics, the pressure during the cooling phase has a strong effect on the spherulite formation and thus shrinkage. Investigation has shown a gas-pressure-dependent shrinkage increase at low gas pressure, compared to conventional injection moulding. Thin walls result from the formation of hollow space. -They possess amorphous outer layers on the mould side, which are missing from the hollow side. The spherulite structure therefore transfers straight into the hollow space without any visible amorphous outer layer.

Thus, in, principle, all injection-mouldable plastics are suitable for the GIM process, whether they are transparent, coloured, filled, reinforced, etc. Their freeze characteristics are decisive for hollow space creation. Difficulties can arise with quickly solidifying plastics and large, thick-walled cavities. In these examples, good, crease-free surfaces can only be achieved with difficulty. Gas and plastic melt intermix in the border area and are due to gas pressure. These gas/melt mixes are the result of turbulences occurring when a certain gas pressure is exceeded. As a guideline for the maximum value that the gas pressure may serve, the melt pressure should be at least twice as high.

With a reduced gas pressure period, the whole of the hollow space is filled with foam. As previously reviewed, this foaming occurs because the only incomplete cooled melt (mixed with gas) expands along the wall of the hollow space at the start of gas feedback. This effect occurs with polyotefins in particular. In order to prevent this foaming effect, a low gas pressure should be applied during the gas-filling phase. A stepwise increase of the gas pressure should be programmed for the gas holding pressure phase.

Each GIM process (gas through nozzle and gas through cavity) has its own benefits and limitations based on the part design, complexity, number of cavities, type of mould, tolerance requirements, cost, equipment life, and necessary modifications needed on the injection moulding machine.

The part must be designed for the process, but at this stage, engineering know-how and experience for part design, tool design, and process optimisation are continually being advanced in development and experience. To reduce the cost of the trial-and-error approach, it is strongly recommended that conventional computer-aided plastic flow analysis with available gas flow analysis be performed.

For each process, many improvements are under way for the improved control of gas pressure, volume, injection speed, and time. The new gas equipment now available is more sturdy, thus minimising day-to-day production problems and having longer production life. The growth of this GIM technology will depend heavily on the cooperation between equipment suppliers, product and mould designers, and plastic moulders. This technology has brought about breakthrough innovations in injection-moulding related applications.

MULTI-LIVE MOULDING

The patented "Scorim" process is a moulding method to improve the strength and stiffness of parts by eliminating weld lines and controlling the orientation of fibres. A conventional injection moulding machine uses a special head that splits the melt flow into the mould into two streams (Fig. 9.4). During the holding stage, two hydraulic cylinders alternately actuate pistons above and below the head, compressing the material in the mould in one direction and then the other. This action aligns the fibres, removes weld lines, and induces orientation in liquid crystal polymers (LCPs). Used with thermoplastic and thermoset plastics, this process is similar to the push-pull method.

COUNTERFLOW MOULDING

With conventional thermoplastics injection moulding, the melt is injected from the injection unit into the cavity of the closed injection mould via a sprue bushing and the attached runner system. After the cavity has been filled, shrinkage is eliminated by means of holding pressure and the introduction of additional melt, after which the moulded part solidifies during the cooling time until ejection takes place.

The same approach in the filling and holding pressure phases is employed in multishot and multicolour injection moulding with two or more injection units, in which case a special rotary mechanism in the mould transfers the initially moulded parts into the cavities for the final moulded parts.

Since plasticated material is injected into what is essentially a closed cavity in classical injection moulding, considerable injection pressures and correspondingly high mould clamping pressures are sometimes required, depending on the moulded part design, in order to achieve dimensionally accurate moulded parts with good properties.

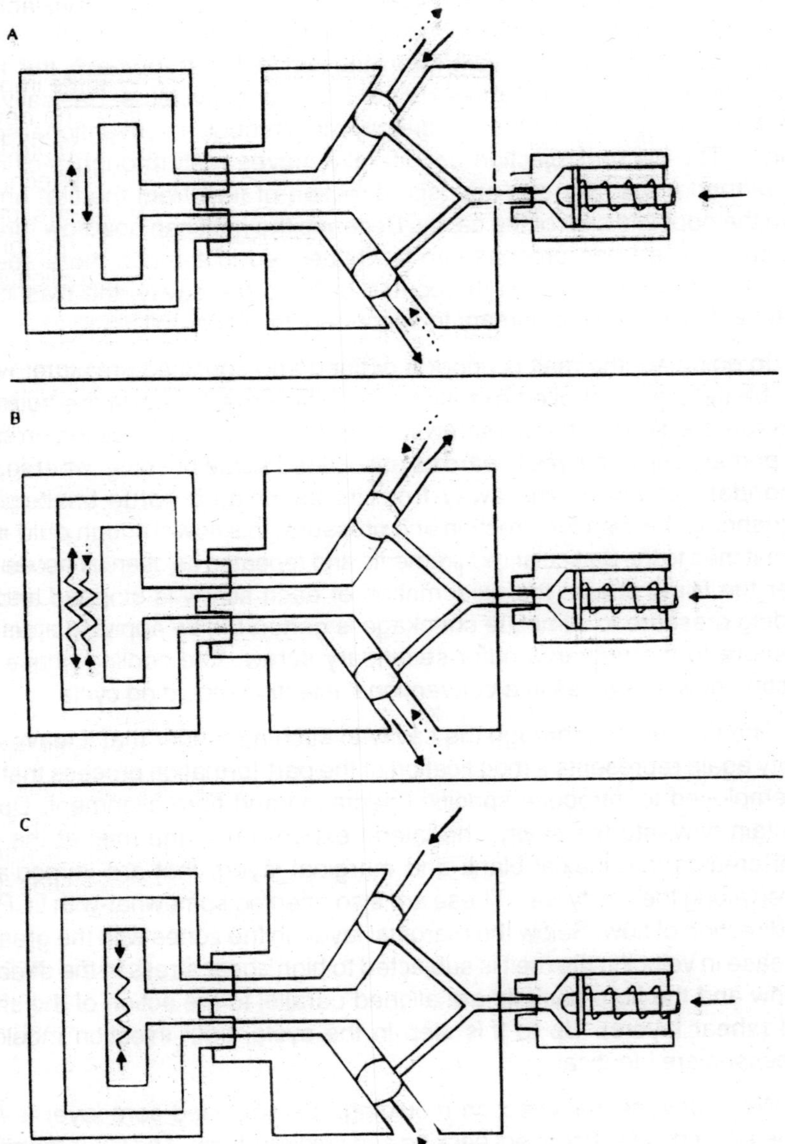

Fig. 9.4 In the multilive feed moulding process: (a) two packing pistons oscillate 180 deg out of phase; (b) two packing pistons oscillate in phase; and (c) two packing pistons compress melt with equal constant pressure.

The principle of counterflow injection moulding employs the machine technology of multi shot injection moulding with appropriately modified control electronics. In a complete reversal from the conventional approach, the mould is so designed with two or more runner and gating systems. Basically, two injection units are used. One can directly melt through a conventional sprue/ runner. The second injection unit literally moves melt through a different sprue/runner that is in the opposite direction of flow from the first unit, or from the opposite side of the cavity. Because the melt can now flow through the cavity, the filling process can be influenced in a much more specific manner than previously. In the course of filling the cavity, the plasticated material flows from the primary to secondary injection unit.

In doing so, the melt is under a defined and specified pressure; which can be set and controlled exactly by the difference between the hydraulic pressures acting on the two screws. During the injection moulding process, the primary screw moves toward its associated sprue bushing, whereas the secondary screw moves away from its associated sprue bushing. By exchanging the data for direction and pressure, this flow-through phase can be matched to the particular requirements and repeated as often as necessary. After the filling phase, the axial motion of each screw is stopped and the holding pressure to eliminate shrinkage is generated by applying a defined pressure to the primary and/or secondary screw. The cooling phase and ejection now follows as in a conventional injection moulding cycle.

The flow of melt through the cavity in such a manner that it leaves the cavity again represents a modification of the part-formation process that can be employed to introduce specific orientation and fibre alignment. During fountain flow into the cavity, the lateral expansion of the melt at the flow front creates thin biaxial blank and marginal layers that are immediately frozen along the cavity wall. These are also oriented somewhat-with LCPs-in the direction of flow. Below the marginal layer, in the zones with the greatest increase in velocity, the melt is subjected to high shear stress in the direction of flow and the fibre packets are aligned parallel to the action of the shear field (shear layers). Up to this step in the cycle, both injection moulding processes are identical.

With conventional injection moulding, the so-called core layer is now formed during the subsequent packing and holding phase. The layer-formation phase is characterised by orientation processes resulting from the decrease in shear to zero toward the centre of the moulded part. Shear displacement inward is, in part, responsible for the formation of additional layers oriented in the direction of flow contiguous to the original shear layers. Because of the cooling processes in the interior of the moulded part and with slower movement of the molt, coarser-fibre structures can sometimes be formed with LCPs. The actual melt core in the centre of the moulded part, which becomes oriented with the introduction of additional plasticated material into the cavity under holding pressure, shows in its frozen structure—especially for LCPs with their slight tendency for relaxation—a strong dependence of the flow geometry as well as gate position and design.

OSCILLATORY MOULDING FOR OPTICAL DISKS

An oscillatory moulding technique is a method used with optical compact disks. Optical disks use laser light to read digital information stored on the surface of a substrate. Light passes through the substrate twice as it reflects off the information that is typically on the order of a submicron spot. Optical path difference, or birefringence, needs to.be minimised in order to assure that light will focus on a small spot and remain focused as it returns to the sensor.

Compact disks (CDs) use normal incident light that is reflected from pits (0.1 μm deep) moulded into the plastic substrate during the injection moulding process. The pit side of the substrate is subsequently metalised with aluminium or gold that, in turn, is spin-coated with a polymer to protect against physical damage. Billions of pits are moulded into the substrate in a spiral pattern. The ultimate quality of this disk format is dependent on the precision of the pits and level of optical distortion introduced by the polymer substrate. The sputtering of a 400-A reflective film on the pit side of the substrate is generally not a major problem.

Rewritable disks are not commercially available with polycarbonate substrates. Several different technologies for data storage have been under development, with magneto-optical (MO) the front runner. This technology coats a transparent substrate that is nearly birefringence-free with a 20-μm-thick alloy (amorphous magnetic layer). Both materials and processing steps contribute to the total birefringence. Even though material systems can be developed with very low levels of birefringence, orientational birefringence and surface stress, along with thermal stress birefringence, develop when these materials are injection-moulded.

A novel disk mould with a movable cavity wall was used to reduce birefringence. The cavity measures 52 mm in diameter and is 1.85 mm deep with a centrally located sprue gate on the stationary side of the cavity. The moving cavity wall opposite the sprue can be rotated at a constant speed or oscillated at a fixed frequency and amplitude. Two different linear bis-phenol A polycarbonate resins were moulded, with low and high molecular weights.

All frequencies were relatively low, but the best results were obtained at the high end of the range, 0.73 cycle/see with an amplitude of 65 deg. The optical retardation in the moulded disks (substrates) was measured at three different radial locations (7, 14, and 21 mm). Both normal incident light and 30 deg off-normal incident light were used to characterise the optical properties. The birefringence was computed by dividing the retardation value by the disk thickness (1.85 mm).

The surface strain was measured by mounting bidirectional strain gages on the surface of the disks at two radial positions and then annealing the disks above 130°C for various lengths of time (hours).

Conventional injection moulding is characterised by strong shear and extensional flows with non isothermal boundary conditions. Velocity gradients in these flow fields orient the polymer chains. The orientation produces anisotropic properties in the moulded part.

Optical retardation describes a medium that exhibits a directional dependence or path difference for the transmission of light. Chain orientation in polymers creates such a path difference. The non-isothennal boundary conditions at the cavity walls of an injection moulding generate thermal stresses as the polymer cools, which in turn produces birefringence.

Once approach to reducing birefringence in plastic disk substrates has been to physically mix or blend two polymers with opposite orientational birefringence behaviour such "as PS and PC. However, this approach does not reduce thermal contribution. In order to mini mise birefringence in a moulded disk substrate, the polymers and process physics need to be considered together. Since orientational stress contributes heavily to the overall level of birefringence, processing techniques for altering chain orientation and reducing entanglements have the potential for producing significant improvements in optical properties.

This has been demonstrated by moulding substrates in a disk cavity with a moving wall during the filling step. Even at relatively low oscillations, 0.73 cycle/sec, retardation is reduced for normal incident light and 30 deg off-normal incident light. This relatively small disruption of diverging radial flow field has a dramatic effect on the resultant orientation and entanglements. In general, orientational stresses affect normal incident light retardation more, whereas thermal stresses have a greater effect on the 30 deg off-normal retardation. Since both retardation mechanisms are affected by a moving wall, it can be inferred from the results that the entanglement density of the network has been reduced.

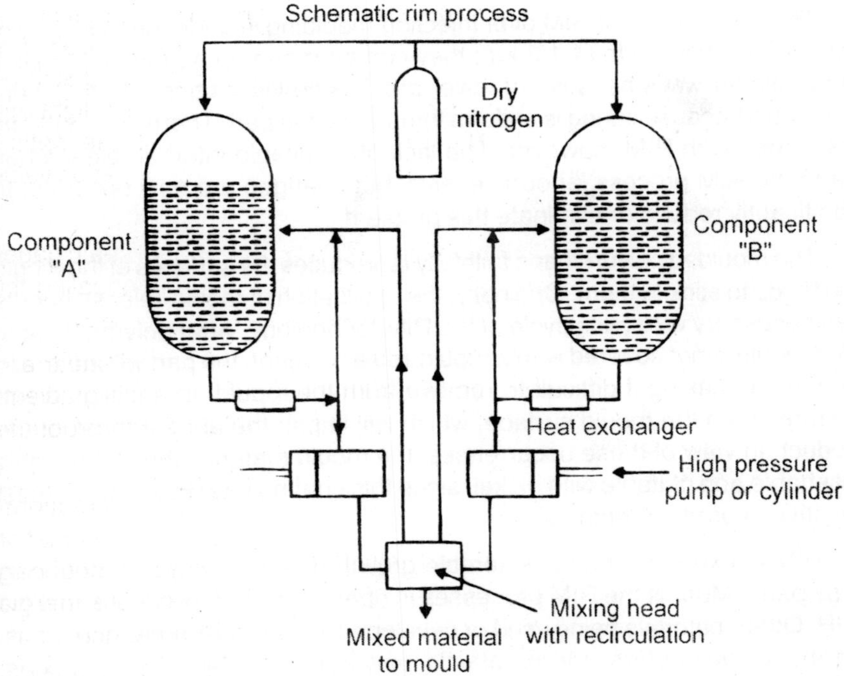

Fig. 9.5 Schematic of a polyurethane RIM Process

REACTION INJECTION MOULDING

Reaction injection moulding (RIM) is a process that involves the high-pressure impingement mixing of two or more reactive liquid components and injecting into a closed mould at low pressure. With RIM technology, cycle times of 2 min and less have been achieved in production for moulding large and thick [(4 in. (10.2 cm)] parts. The principal plastic used is thermoset polyurethane (PUR). Other materials used are thermoplastic nylon, thermoset polyester and epoxy etc. This RIM review only includes PUR.

As shown in Fig. 9.5, a typical polyurethane RIM process involves the precise metering of two liquid components under high pressure from holding vessels into the static impingement mix-head. The coreactants are homogenised in the mixing chamber and injected into a closed mould, to which the mixhead is attached. The heat of reaction of the liquid components vapourises the blowing agent, beginning the foaming action that completes the filling of the mould cavity.

The advantages of RIM over injection moulding include the moulding of parts larger than 10 lb (4 1/2 kg); they can be made on a production basis using thinner walls because of lower processing viscosities, or using very thick walls because curing is uniform throughout the part. There are problems associated with RIM, however. The lack of a suitable internal release has made the RIM process labourintensive, but changes are now occurring to significantly reduce or eliminate this problem.

The moulded polyurethane faithfully reproduces the surfaces of the mould and tends to stick to them. Originally, the application of mould-release agents was necessary with each cycle of the RIM technology. After polymerisation, if the mould is not covered with a mould-release agent, the part will adhere to the mould, making it difficult to remove from the mould. In addition, a film will remain on the mould surface, which will impair the appearances of the product. In view of these occurrences, the mould material should be highly polishable and platable with nickel, since this coating has proved to be most effective in product removal.

RIM is experiencing considerable growth due to savings in producing large parts. Most of the RIM processes in operation use flexible or semirigid PUR. Other materials being used or developed include thermoplastic nylons, thermoset polyesters, thermoplastic polystyrenes, thermoset epoxies, thermoplastic acrylics, etc.

In the processes of injection moulding of thermoplastic, injection moulding thermosets, structural foam moulding, and expandable polystyrene moulding, we are dealing with materials that are chemically complete compounds, ready for conversion into a finished product. The materials are received from suppliers with certain properties based on test bar information and recorded in material processing data sheets. The processors are expected to convert these materials into products with similar mechanical, electrical, and environmental characteristics, as indicated on the data sheets.

The processors are also furnished with a range of moulding parameters that should be optimised to attain the desired product properties. In brief, they are given a material along with guidelines for its conversion, but they can do little to change the processing behaviour of the material, since they are dealing with a finished raw material that is fully prepared for conversion into a finished product by the application of time, temperature, and pressure.

In RIM, the starting point for the conversion process are liquid chemical components (monomers, not polymers). These components are metered out in the proper ratio, mixed, and injected into a mould where the finished product is formed. In reality, it is a chemical and moulding operation combined into one system of moulding in which the raw material is not a prepared compound, but chemical ingredients that will form a compound when moulded into a finished part. The chemicals are highly catalysed to induce extremely fast reaction rates. The materials that lend themselves to the process are urethane, epoxy, polyester, and others that can be formulated to meet the process requirement. The system is composed of the following elements:

1. Chemical components that can be combined to produce a material of the desired physical and environmental properties. Normally, this formulation consists of two liquid chemical components that have suitable additives and are supplied to the processor by chemical companies (three or more are also used).
2. A chemical processing setup, which stores, metres, and mixes the components ready for introduction into the mould.
3. To facilitate smooth continuous operation, a moulding arrangement consisting of a mould, mould release application system, and stripping accessories.

The success of the overall operation will depend on the processor's knowledge of: (i) the chemistry of the two components and how to keep them in good working order; (ii) how to keep the chemical adjunct in proper functioning condition so that the mixture entering the mould will produce the expected result; and (iii) mould design, as well as the application of auxiliary facilities that will bring about ease of product removal and mould functioning within a reasonable cycle (e.g., 2 min).

RIM moulding is energy-conserving as compared to conventional injection moulding. The two liquid urethane components are injected generally at room temperature, and a typical mould temperature is 150°F (66°C). Also, since the material is expanded after injection, very low clamp pressures psi (690 kPa)] are required.

Since internal mould pressures would not normally exceed 100 psi, the clamping requirements for RIM are substantially lower than those for thermoplastic processing. Calculations have been done on a part and show that a clamp requirement of 2,500 to 5,000 tonnes necessary to produce a part from conventional injection-moulded thermoplastic polyurethane can be reduced to less than 100 tonnes for RIM. The production of polyurethane elastomers involves the controlled polymerisation of an isocyanate, a long-chain-backbone polyol and a shorter-chain extender or cross-linker. The reaction rates can be controlled through the use of specific catalyst compounds, well-known in the industry, to provide sufficient time to pour or otherwise transfer the mix, and to cure the polymer sufficiently to allow handling of the freshly demoulded part. The use of blowing agents allows the formation of a definite cellular core (thus, the term "microcellular elastomer"), as well as a non-porous skin, producing an integral sandwich-type cross section

In RIM, all necessary reactive ingredients are contained in two {or more) liquid components: an isocyanate component, A, and a resin component B.

The choice of isocyanate, as well as variations within isocyanate families, exerts a profound effect on the processing and final properties of the elastomer. The chemical structures of two of the major diisocyanate types, 4,4' diphenyl methane diisocyanate (MDI) and toluene diisocyanate (TDI), are commonly supplied in an 80/20 mixture of the 2, 4 and 2,6 isomers. Early in the development of RIM systems, the MDI family was chosen over TDI, based on the following considerations:

1. *Reactivity:* Given the same set of coreactants, MDI and MDI types are more reactive than TDI. This can be used to advantage when short cycles are required.
2. *Available co-reactants:* The high reactivity ofthe MDI types also makes available a large number of coreactants. For example, when hindered aromatic amines yield a given level of reactivity, a variety of glycols can give equivalent reactivity, thus allowing more formulation versatility.
3. *Handling:* The MDI materials ofter excellent handling characteristics due to comparatively low vapour pressure.
4. *Green strength:* The ortho-isocyanate groups of TDI are less reactive than the para-groups. Thus, at the end of the reaction to form a polymer, the rate of reaction slows, resulting in green strength problems upon demoulding. MDI does not suffer this deficiency.

Reaction injection moulding involves very accurate mixing and the metering of two highly catalysed liquid urethane components, polyol and isocyanate. The polyol component contains the polyether backbone, a chain extender or cross-linking agent, and a catalyst. A blowing agent is generally included in either the polyol or isocyanate component.

In order to achieve the optimum in physical properties and part appearance, instantaneous and homogeneous mixing is necessary. Insufficient mixing and/or lead/lag results either in surface defects on the part or, at the time of postcure, delamination or blistering.

The urethane liquid components are stored at a constant temperature in a dry air or nitrogen environment. These components are delivered to high-pressure metering pumps or cylinders that dispense the respective materials at high pressure and accurate ratios to a mixing head. The materials are mixed by stream impingement. Additional mixing is generally encouraged via a static mixture (tortuous material path) incorporated into the runner system of the mould. Following the injection of the chemicals, the blowing agent expands the material to fill the mould.

The preferred route for high-volume RIM manufacturing is multiple clamps fed from a single metering pumping unit, the logic being that this is the most efficient way to utilise the capacity of the mould-filling equipment.

Mould

Since one of the ultimate objectives of the RIM process, for its major market of automotive exterior part production, was a cycle time of 2 min or less, a great deal of effort was applied to mould construction and design. The continuous automatic operation of a moulding station without interruption required improvements in mould-release and mould surface technology. Originally, mould preparation following a shot was required due to the build-up of external release agents, which were necessary to enable easy removal of the part from the mould. This problem was approached from the material side, through a search for suitable internal releases, and through the development of improved external mould-release compounds. From the equipment side, the development of automatic moulds was required if the RIM process was to compete with classical injection moulding with respect to mould cycle times and efficient production.

In the construction of moulds for RIM processing, it must be kept in mind that part quality and finish are roughly equivalent to the quality and finish of the mould surface itself. A common misconception is that because the clamp tonnage for a RIM setup is relatively low, low-quality tools can be used. This, however, is true only in-so-far as the pressure requirements for the mould are concerned. Experience has shown that the finish on the part surface is a direct function of the mould finish, and it is a direct function of the quality of the mould material. Excellent results have been obtained using high-quality, nickel-plated, tool steel moulds and electroformed nickel shells.

For production parts a P-20, P-21, or H-13 steel would be most appropriate, not only because of these steels' homogeneous nature, but also because of their excellent polishability and adaptability for a good plating job. The prehardened grades of 30 to 44 RC are preferable because of the degree of permanency that they impart to a tool. After machining, a stress-relieving operation is very important in order to avoid possible distortions or even cracking.

Nickel shells that are electro- or vapour-formed when suitably backed up and mounted in a frame are also excellent materials for large-volume runs. For activities of less than 50,000 parts per year, aluminium forgings of Alcoa grade No. 7075- T73 machines to the needed configuration will perform satisfactorily. They have the advantage of good heat conductivity, an important feature in RIM.

Cast materials are used for RIM moulds with reasonable success. One such material is Kirksite, a zinc alloy casting material. Kirksite moulds are easy castable, are free from porosity, will polish and plate well, and have been used with favourable results.

For consistent quality and moulding cycles with PUR, the mould temperature should be maintained within ± 4°F (± 2°C). The mould temperatures will range from 101 to 150°F (66°C), depending on the composition being used.

The cooling lines should be so placed with respect to the cavity that there is a 3/4-in. (1.91-cm) wall from the edge of the hole to the cavity face. The spacing between passages should be 2.5 to 3 diameters of the cooling-passage opening. These dimensions apply to steel; for materials with better heat conductivity, the spacing can be increased by one hole size.

As with the chemical components, it is necessary to maintain constant surface temperatures in the mould for a reproducible surface finish and constant chemical reactivity. This temperature varies according to the chemical system being used and has been determined empirically.

The mould orientation should be such as to allow filling from the bottom of the mould cavity, permitting the escape of air through a top flange at a hidden surface. This allows controlled venting and positioning of vent pockets that can be trimmed from the part at a later time.

Process Controls

The chemical systems for RIM all have one characteristic in common: They require a RIM machine to convert liquid raw materials into quality plastic products. If we assume a properiy formulated chemical system, the quality of the end product results from the ability to measure, control, and adjust temperature, ratio, pressure, and other essential process parameters of the RIM dispensing machine. Such exacting control leads to a reduction in start-up time, minimal rejects and touch-up work, reproducible product quality, and the ability to pinpoint changes in product properties.

In the high-temperature RIM processing of nylon, temperatures are monitored and controlled within ±2°F using both electrical heat tracing and hot oil jacketing. The controllers contain high-low set points; all temperature zones must be at the required settings to permit machine operation. A graphic diagnostic panel, with light-emitting diodes (LED), associated with all key switches, valves, and pressures, aids in troubleshooting; if a malfunction occurs, the cause is pinpointed by a blinking light. Low- and high pressure circulation is monitored by transducers and displayed digitally; high/low pressure limits, if exceeded, will abort the RIM cycle for safety reasons.

LIQUID INJECTION MOULDING

(LIM) has been used much longer than RIM, but the processes are practically similar. The advantages it offers in the automated low-pressure processing of (usually) thermoset resins-fast cycles, low labour costs, low capital investment, energy saving, and space saving-may make LIM competitive to potting, encapsulating, compression transfer, and injection moulding, particularly when insert moulding is required.

Different resins can be used, such as polyester, silicones, polyurethanes, nylon, and acrylic. A major application for LIM with silicones is the encapsulation of electrical and electronic devices.

Because the pressures of injection are approximately 25 to 50 psi (172 to 345 kPa), very fragile inserts can be moulded, and mould wear is at a minimum. Some formulations for LIM also may be moulded at temperatures as low as 200°F (93°C), which permit the encapsulation of some heat-sensitive electronic components that do not lend themselves to encapsulation at conventional transfer moulding temperatures of 300°F (149°C) or higher.

LIM employs two or more pumps to move the components of the liquid system (such as catalyst and resin) to a mixing head before they are forced into a heated mould cavity. In some systems, screws or static mixers are used. Only a single pump is required for a one-part resin, but usually two (or more)part systems are used. Equipment is available to process all types of resin systems, with unsophisticated or sophisticated control systems. A very critical control involves precision mixing. If voids or gaseous by-products develop, a vacuum is used in the mould.

STRUCTURAL FOAM MOULDING (SFM)

So-called structural foam (SF) is also called integral skin forming or RIM and can overlap in performance, as well as use with the significantly larger market of the more conventional foamed plastics. SF is characterised as plastic structures with nearly uniform-density foam cores and integral near-solid skins. The definition of SF by the SF industry is a plastic product with integral skins, a cellular core, and enough strength-to-weight ratio to be classified as structural. When these foams are used in loadbearing applications, the foam bulk density is typically 50 to 90% of the plastic's unfoamed bulk density. Most SF products (90%) are made from different thermoplastics, principally PS, PE, pve, and ABS. Polyurethane is the primary thermoset. Unfilled and unreinforced plastics represent about 70% of products. The principal method of processing (75%) is modified low-pressure injection moulding. Extrusion and RIM account for about 10% each.

A great variety of foam products are available from plastic, but basically *there* are just two types: flexible and rigid. The flexible type generally identifies the very large market of principally extruded polyurethane foam for cushioning *(for* chairs, mattresses, etc.); about 5% of all plastic goes into these flexible foams. Another important flexible type can include the expandable polystyrene that is used in special injection moulding machines (steam curing). The EPS market represents about another 7% of all plastic used. Within the rigid types are the important structural foam (0.2% of plastic) and reaction injection moulding (0.3% of plastic) types, both of which are involved in basically injection moulding.

Performance

The use of SF moulding is interesting principally because it provides a three- to four-fold increase in rigidity over a solid plastic part of the same weight. (This three- to fourfold advantage, or a greater one, can be designed into many applications with solid plastic by using the basic engineering rib design for moulds). SF also permits moulding large parts with the cost advantages that injection moulding (solid parts) offers to smaller parts. Thus, large parts with a high degree of rigidity can be moulded. The self. expanding nature of SF results in low-stress parts with dimensionally stability and less tendency to warpage and sink marks. It also offers thermal and acoustic insulation.

Other advantages exist for the use of SF, but there are also disadvantages. Moulding cycle time will at least increase by the square of the thickness increase. Moreover, most SF parts are made by a lowpressure technique that causes a surface finish that visually resembles the splay marks found in injection moulding. This surface condition, called swirl, is the

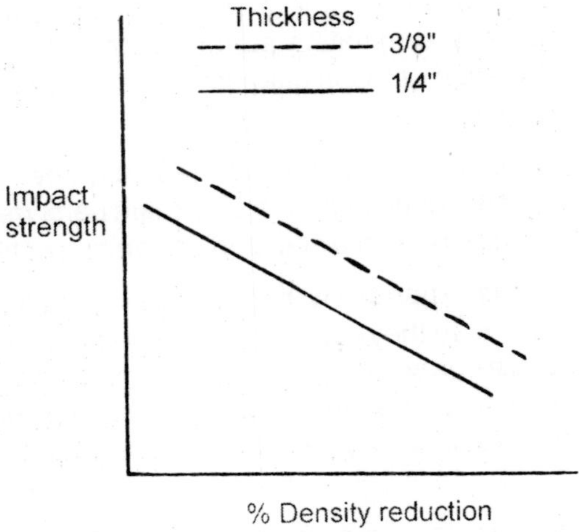

Fig. 9.6 Impact strength of structural foam based on part thickness and weight

result of broken bubbles in the surface; techniques such as counter-pressure must be used to significantly remove the swirl finish. Thus, producing conventional low-pressure SF parts can result in higher finishing costs and longer cycle times.

Plastic Materials

Polystyrene, polyurethane, ABS, and polypropylene represent about 90% of the resin used for SF. The remaining engineering resins provide the usual advantages of performance such as increased mechanical crepe resistance and heat-resistance properties. Of these engineering resins (polycarbonates, nylon, ABS, PBT, PPO, and acetal), the principal choice has usually been polycarbonate.

Applications for SF are found in computer and business machine housings, appliances, building products, etc.

Characteristics of foam

A density reduction of up to 40% can be obtained in SF parts. The actual density reduction obtained will depend on part thickness, design, and flow distance. Low-pressure structural foam parts will have the characteristic surface splay patterns; however, the utilisation of increased mould temperatures, increased injection rates, or grained mould surfaces will serve to minimise or hide this surface streaking. Finishing systems (e.g., sanding, filling, painting) for structural foam are readily available and have proved to be capable of completely eliminating surface splay. It should be noted, however, that the utilisation of techniques to minimise splay can very often result in reduced.finishing costs.

High-pressure structural foam parts have generally been found to require little or no postfinishing. Although high-pressure foam parts may exhibit visual splay, surface smoothness is maintained, and no sanding or filling is required.

Structural foam parts expanded with chemical blowing agents will exhibit increased stiffness because they are normally thicker than solid mouldings. Their lower density also provides a higher strength-to-weight ratio when compared to solid mouldings. Because of the foamed core within the part as well as its greater thickness, acoustical and insulating properties are enhanced.

Foaming a polymer does not change its chemical structure or its resistance to chemical attack, provided the proper chemical blowing agent and processing conditions are used. Mechanical properties such as tensile and impact strength (Fig. 9.6) and flexural modulus will be lower in foam parts because of their low densities.

The cell structure of structural foams varies quite widely for the various moulding processes. In the expansion cast moulding process (similar to cold compression moulding, not SF moulding), the products to be foamed are placed in a cold mould. Then the mould is heated. and expansion takes place relatively slowly, making for slow growth of the cell structure; this results in quite a uniform cell structure. This holds for not only thermoplastic foams produced by rotomoulding and the foundry process, but also polyurethanes produced by expansion cast moulding.

In injection moulding, the cell structure of moulded foam varies markedly for various processes. When the mould is filled with a short shot accompanied by low mould pressure. the cell structure shows a wide distribution in cell size across the part cross section. In fact, small random voids may occur in the structure. When the mould is filled under low pressure, the foam density shows a gradient along the flow path, with the highest density at the end of the flow path and the lowest density near the runner. When the mould is filled under high injection pressure, no foaming occurs in the mould until a solid skin has been formed. Then the mould pressure is intentionally reduced by either melt egression or mould expansion, permitting the still molten core to foam. These techniques make for uniform cell structure not only across the part thickness but over the entire part.

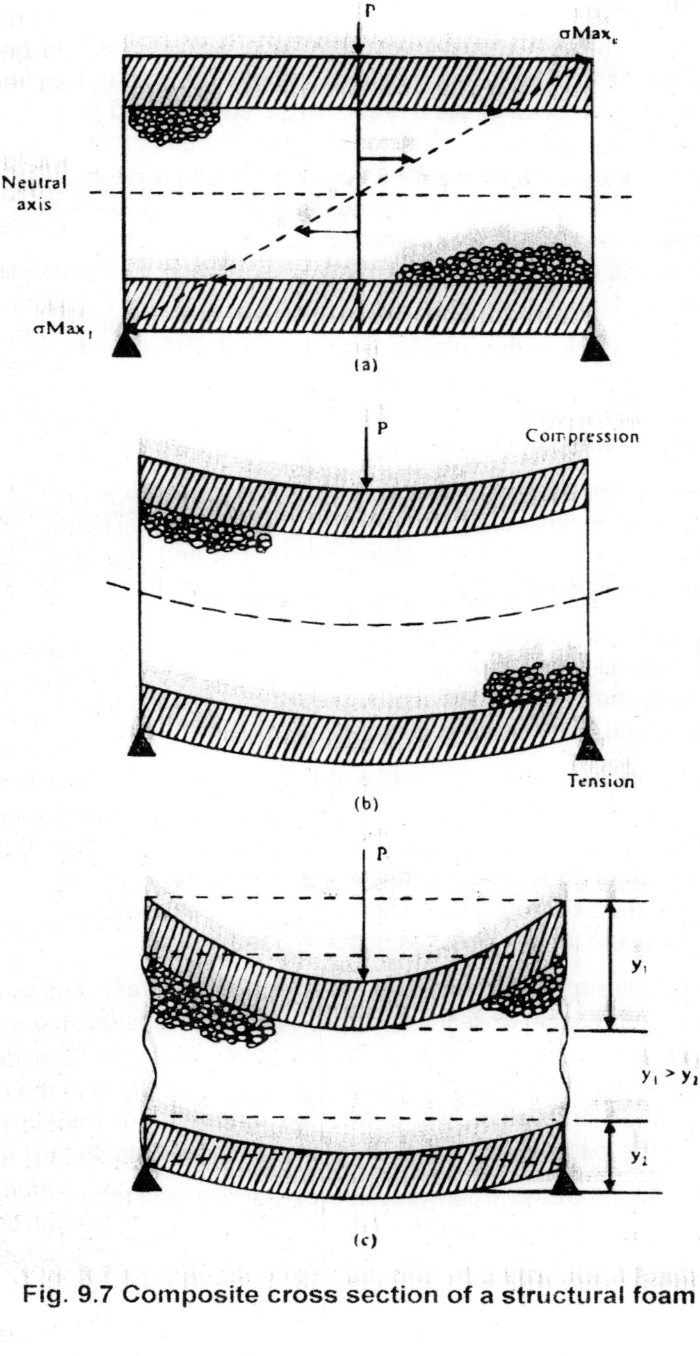

Fig. 9.7 Composite cross section of a structural foam part.

Design Analysis

For structural foam, mould pressures of approximately 600 psi (4.1 MPa) are required, compared to typical pressures of 5,000 psi and greater (34.5 MPa) in injection moulding. As a result, large, complicated parts, 50 lb and up (22.7 kg), can be produced using multi nozzle equipment, or up to 35 lb (15.9 kg) with single-nozzle equipment and hot-runner systems. Part size, in fact, is limited only by the size of existing equipment, whereas part complexity is only limited by tool design and material properties. Part cost can be kept in line through such advantages as parts consolidation, function integration, and assembly labour savings.

When an engineering plastic resin is used with the structural foam process, the material produced exhibits predictable behaviour over a large range of temperatures. Its stress-strain .curve shows a significantly linearly elastic region like other Hookean materials, up to the proportional limit.

However, since thermoplastics are viscoelastic in nature, their properties are dependent on time, temperature, and the strain rate. The ratio of stress and strain is linear at low strain levels of I to 2%, and, therefore, standard elastic design principles can be applied up to the elastic transition point.

Large and complicated parts will usually require more critical structural evaluations to allow better predictions of load-bearing capabilities under both static and dynamic conditions. Thus, predictions require a careful analysis of the structural foam cross section.

The composite cross section of a structural foam part contains an ideal distribution of material with a solid-skin outer region and foamed core. The manufacturing process distributes a thick, almost impervious solid skin, which is in the range of 25% of the overall wall thickness at the extreme locations from the neutral axis (Fig. 9.7a). These are the regions where the maximum compressive and tensile stresses occur in bending.

The simply supported beam has a load applied centrally. The upper skin goes into compression while the lower skin goes into tension, and a uniform bending curve will develop (Fig. 9.7b). However, this only happens if the shear rigidity of modulus of the cellular core is sufficiently high. If this is not the case, then both skins will deflect as independent members, thus eliminating the load-bearing capability of the composite structure (Fig. 9.7c).

The fact that the cellular core provides resistance against shear and buckling stresses implies an ideal density for a given foam wall thickness. This optimum thickness is critically important in the design of complex, stressed parts.

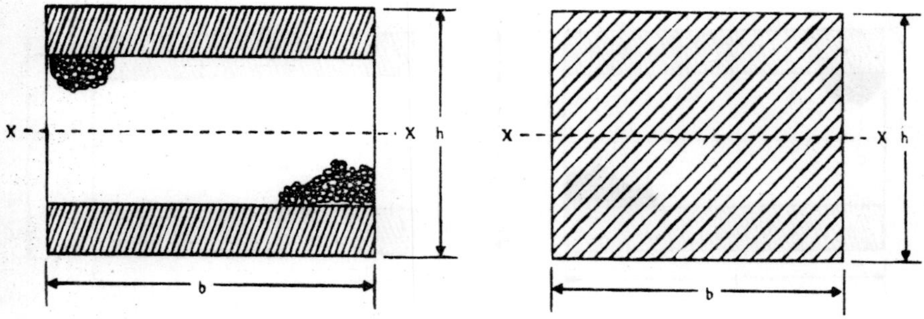

Fig. 9.8 Cross section of a solid material.

At a 1/4-in (6.4 mm) wall. for example, both modified polyphenylene oxide and polycarbonate resin exhibit the best processing. properties. and cost-in the range of 25% weight reduction. Laboratory tests show that with thinner walls. about 0.157 in. (4.0 mm), this ideal weight reduction decreased to 15%. When wall thickness reaches approximately 0.350 in. (8.9 mm), weight can be reduced 30%.

However, when the structural foam cross section is analysed. its composite nature still results in a two-fold increase in rigidity, compared to an equivalent amount of solid plastic. since rigidity is a cubic function of wall thickness. This increased rigidity allows large structural parts to be designed with minimal distortion and deflection when stressed within recommended values for a particular foamable resin. Depending on the required analysis, the moment of inertia can be evaluated three ways.

In the first approach, the cross section is considered to be solid material (Fig. 9.8). The moment of inertia I_x is then equal to

$$I_x = bh^3/12$$

where b = width; h = height.

This commonly used approach provides acceptable accuracy when load-bearing requirements are minimal-for example. in the case of simple stresses-and when time/cost constraints prevent more exact analysis.

The second approach ignores the strength contribution. of the core and assumes that the two outer skins provide all the rigidity (Fig. 9.9). The equivalent moment of inertia is then equal to

$$I_x = b(h^3 - h_1^3)/12$$

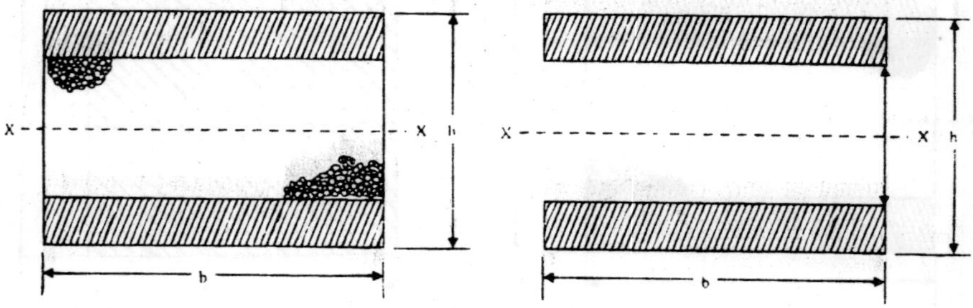

Fig. 9.9 Cross section of a sandwich structure.

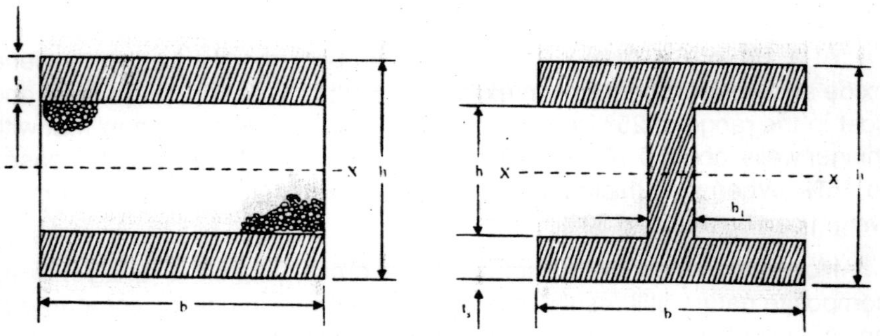

Fig. 9.10 Cross section of an I-beam

This formula results in conservative accuracy. since the core does contribute to the stress-absorbing function. It also adds a built-in safety factor to a loaded beam or plate element when safety is a concern.

A third method is to convert the structural foam cross section to an equivalent I-beam section of solid resin material (Fig. 9.10). The moment of inertia is then formulated as

$$I_x = [bh^3 - (b - b_1)(h - 2t_x)3]/12$$

where

$b_1 = b(E_c)/(E_s)$
F_c = modulus of the core
E_s = Modulus of the .skin
t_s = thickness of the skin
h_1 = height of the equivalent web (core)

This approach may be necessary when operating conditions require stringent load bearing capabilities without resorting to overdesign and thus unnecessary costs. Such an analysis produces maximum accuracy and would be suitable for finite-element analysis on complex parts. However, the one difficulty with this method is that the core modulus and the as-moulded variations in skin thicknesses cannot be accurately measured.

Blowing Agents

Blowing agents, be they solid, liquid, or gaseous substances, are used to impart a cellular structure to moulded thermoplastics. The blowing agent is a source of gas that can be used by the moulder to control sink marks, provide resins savings, or manufacture structural foam parts.

In general, blowing agents can be classified as either physical or chemical. The physical blowing agents include compressed gases and volatile liquids. The volatile liquids are generally hydrocarbons such as hexane or pentane as well as other aliphatic hydrocarbons. The materials act as a source of gas by changing their physical state from liquid to gas during processing. Volatile liquids have not been extensively used in foaming thermoplastics to date.

The most widely used blowing agent of the physical type is compressed nitrogen. Nitrogen is injected directly into the polymer melt prior to injection. Advantages of nitrogen gas are that it is inert, leaves no decomposition residue, and is not limited to a specific decomposition temperature range.

Chemical blowing agents (CBAs) are generally solid materials that decompose when heated to a specific temperature, yielding one or more gases and a solid residue. Chemical blowing agents also can be divided into the organic and inorganic types. The most common inorganic chemical blowing agent is sodium bicarbonate, which is being used to some extent in the production of foam parts. The major advantage of sodium bicarbonate is its low cost. The major disadvantage is that sodium bicarbonate decomposes over a very broad temperature range as compared to organic chemical blowing agents, so that its decomposition cannot be controlled as readily as that of the organic chemical blowing agents.

Organic chemical blowing agents are solid materials designed to decompose over specific temperature ranges. Therefore, the primary criterion used to select a chemical blowing agent is the processing temperature of the plastic to be foamed.

Methods of Processing Structural Foam (SF) with Chemical Blowing Agents (CBA)

Injection-moulded structural foam parts may be produced by both low- and high-pressure processes. In this context, low or high pressure refers to the mould cavity pressure. Nitrogen gas and chemical blowing agents are widely used in both processes.

Some of the specialised structural foam processes and equipment are patented and may require licensing. The processor is advised to ascertain the patent situation before employing any of these specialised techniques.

Low-pressure foam

Injection-moulded (structural) foam is produced by incorporating the selected chemical blowing agent with a resin and injecting a short shot (less than the volume of the mould cavity) into the tool. Gases released by decomposition of the blowing agent expand the polymer to fill the cavity. Since the mould cavity is not completely filled with resin, the pressure in the tool is only that generated by the blowing agent.

Low-pressure foam is produced on a variety of equipment with internal cavity pressures ranging from 200 to 600 psi (1.4 to 4.1 MPa).

Foam moulding on conventional machines requires some modifications to produce good-quality parts. The most important of these is the use of a positive shutoff nozzle to prevent drooling of the expandable melt, which causes a variation in part weight as well as nozzle freeze-up. The shutoff nozzle may be mechanically, spring, or hydraulically activated.

Although a shutoff nozzle is essential, other modifications can be made to improve part quality and increase "the capacity of the machine. These include an intensifier to increase injection speed and accumulator to increase shot size. Conversion kits are commercially available for all of the above modifications.

This approach allows the moulder to convert a standard injection machine from solid to foam (or the reverse) without difficulty and requires a relatively small capital investment.

Special machines, similar to high-speed two-stage injection moulding machines, have been specifically designed and built for the production of low-pressure foam mouldings. Typically, these machines offer the advantage of high-speed injection rates, large shot capacity, and large platens. Because of the lower clamp tonnages used, less expensive tooling is required. Both in-line reciprocating screw and two-stage screw-plasticating/ram-injection units are available.

A chemical blowing agent is also used in low-pressure foam systems when compressed nitrogen is the primary blowing agent. The addition ofthe CBA in this process facilitates cell formation and uniformity in the moulded parts.

High-pressure foam

Chemical-blowing-agent-expanded products can also be made on specialised foam machines using the high-pressure technique. A full shot *of* expandable plastic is injected at pressures normal for the resin involved. A skin *of* solid plastic is formed by cooling at the mould surface, and expansion *of* the core occurs by moving one or more plates to enlarge the mould cavity. This process provides a more distinct skin than the low-pressure systems, better reproduction *of* cavity detail, and a surface that may be essentially free *of* splay if the correct combination *of* chemical blowing agent and processing conditions is used. With this process, it is possible to vary density by controlling the mould expansion motion so that essentially solid sections are obtained when high strength is required and weight reduction limited to non-critical areas. Co-injection (sandwich) machines are also available that are capable *of* injecting both solid and foam polymers. Simultaneous injection occurs, resulting in a solid outer layer surrounding a foam core. Since the solid polymer forms the exterior skin, parts have an excellent out-of-mould appearance and require little or no postfinishing operations. Different resins may also be combined in the same part to maximise cost/performance. The multiple-component injection moulding process with blowing agent allows the production *of* parts are 5 to 30% lighter than compact injection-moulded parts.

Processing SF with Gas Blowing Agent

Nitrogen gas blowing agent, when introduced into a molten polymer, requires specialised equipment. Such equipment consists *of* a continuously running extruder, a gas inlet into the cylinder, one or more accumulators to hold the foam mixture, and a mould. All these are connected by suitable pipes and one or more injection nozzles that feed the mould. The multiple-nozzle arrangement is necessary because *of* the limited flow length *of* the polymer and blowing agent mixture; it facilitates the use *of* multicavity moulds and making *of* large objects.

The extruder thoroughly mixes the gas and material and feeds a prescribed volume *of* material and foam mixture into one or more accumulators, where it is kept under pressure to prevent premature expansion. When the proper volume *of* the mixture is reached, a valve opens and a piston in the accumulator quickly forces the material into the mould. The stroke *of* the piston determines the volume *of* material delivered to the mould. The mould is only partially filled. At this point, the valve closes, and the expanding gas fills the mould and exerts pressure on the forming skin to prevent skin marks. With the high melt temperature *of* the polymer, rapid delivery *of* the material

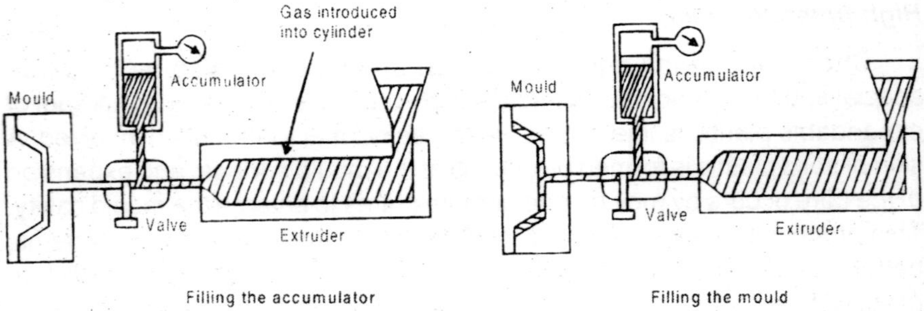

Fig. 9.11 Injection moulding SF with nitrogen gas blowing agent.

to the mould, and 25% *of* the circumference *of* the parting line devoted to equally spaced vents, a smooth surface finish can be attained (Fig. 9.11). There are other processes either in the development stage or in use for specialised applications.

Tooling

For low-pressure foam applications, moulds can be less expensive because *of* the lower clamp forces used. Moulds for low-pressure foam systems may be constructed from forged aluminium, supported cast aluminium, Kirksite, or steel. Chrome plating *of* beryllium -copper moulds has been used to reduce the degree *of* corrosion, but has not proved to be the ultimate solution.

Moulds should be designed for efficient cooling when moulding foams to minimise cycle times. This is especially important when the part has thick sections. The adequate venting of mould cavities is essential to allow excess gas to escape and enable complete filling of the mould as the plastic expands. Inadequate venting will result in unfilled parts and can also cause "burning" of the part in the vent area.

Usually, vents from 0.005 to 0.0 10in. (0.0 13 to 0.025 cm) are suitable, but actual experimentation with the mould using metal shims should be done to determine where vents should be placed and what their depth should be. Sprues, runners, and gates are usually made as generous as possible, but should not be so large as to cause an increase in cycle time or the amount of regrind generated.

Sprues are usually tapered (going from the machine nozzle to the tool) to help keep expansion of the melt to a minimum. Length should also be kept to a minimum so as not to interfere with cycles.

Runners should be generous to allow for fast injection rates. Care should be taken, however that runners be designed so that pressure will be maintained on the melt to prevent expansion. Runner systems for multicavity moulds should be designed so that fill rates to each cavity are balanced.

Gates should be sized so that fast and complete fill of the part is facilitated. Usually, the width and thickness of gates are smaller than part thickness. This provides easy removal from the moulded part, and no interference with cycle times occurs.

Whenever possible, gating of a foam part should be in the thinnest area. This allows the low-pressure melt to flow more easily into the thicker sections of the part and ensures that thin sections will be completely filled.

Startup for Moulding

Over 98% of all structural foam moulding to date has been with the low-pressure techniques, and it is likely that the major technique, and it is likely that the major technique will continue to be low pressure. Factors to consider when moulding low-pressure foamed parts are as follows:

1. Injection pressure should be set high enough to enable the maximum injection speed obtainable. High-speed injection provides improved surface quality. Back pressure should be used [100 to 200 psi (0.7 to 1.4 MPa)] for consistent, even filling during plastication. Screw speeds of 20 to 50 rpm are normally used.
2. Shot size should be adjusted to approximately 25% less than cavity volume. *Note:* Shot-sizing setting should be such that the screw completely bottoms out during injection, that is, no cushioh is used.
3. Processing temperatures should be chosen that are consistent with the polymer and blowing agent being used. An increasing profile is preferred, with the rear zone temperature set lower than the decomposition point of the blowing agent. This ensures that blowing agent efficiency will not be lost by degassing through the hopper.
4. Mould temperatures affect surface finish, skin thickness, and cycle time. Hot moulds will yield a more glossy surface, thin skins, and longer cycle time. Cool moulds, on the other hand, yield a duller finish and thicker skins with shorter cycles. Mould temperatures will normally range from 60 to 140°F (16 to 60°C), but higher or low, er temperatures are not uncommon. It is sometimes advantageous to include both heating and cooling channels in the mould to obtain an improved surface (heating) and short cycle times (cooling). Quenching the part in water immediately

upon demoulding may also be helpful in reducing post-expansion and cycle times. This is particularly true for moulded parts containing thick sections that would require a long cooling cycle.

5. Cycle times typically range from 60 to 120 sec, but are dependent on the polymer being formed, part thickness and mould temperature.
6. Venting should be determined by experimentation with the mould, using metal shims before cutting the mould.

TANDEM PROCESSING SYSTEMS

When reviewing the subject of basically using injection moulding machines to mould more than specified, there have been different approaches to moulding larger and/or more parts per machine. As an example, when a large enough machine is not available and/or limited production exists, two injection moulding machines can be set up to operate in tandem. A large mould can be built to extend across the platens of both machines. The two clamp units are linked together and operate as one. In this example, twice as much clamping force (and twice the shot volume) is available for moulding large parts as with the separate identical operating, individual machines.

To increase output and reduce the single-cavity manufacturing costs of large parts, two alternatives have been developed over the years—namely, stack moulds and two-cavity moulds running in larger machines. Both approaches have some basic technical disadvantage for moulding certain parts:

1. Either the two-cavity moulds or stack moulds would have to be injected at double the injection rate when compared to the single-cavity approach. This is especially critical on large surface parts with minimum wall thickness, such as auto body panels and bumpers. Also, it is very difficult to balance two cavities in large shot applications, particularly for short runs.
2. The two-cavity approach would need a machine of double the size, which would be slower than a machine used with the single-cavity arrangement.
3. With the stack mould approach, the same size machine could be used, however, the clamp would have to open twice as far, again resulting in a slower cycle.

Therefore, neither stack- or two-cavity moulds will double the output of two single-cavity systems.

Tandem Moulding Machines

With the limitations just reviewed, different approaches have been used. Its Tandem three-platen injection moulding complements its line of standard conventional machines. The Tandem uses two standard moulds and will almost double the output of conventional machines producing parts with relatively long cooling times. Output can be doubled for parts where inject, hold, and recovery make up less than 50% of the cycle.

The Tandem machine is a standard injection moulding machine with extended shut height and the addition of a third (central) platen. The machine also features a hot-runner system and packing cylinde in the third platen; means to independently clamp the moulds; and robot for automatic removal of parts from either mould station. The microprocessor-based control system allows customised resin processing, injection, clamping, and robotic operations for each of the two moulds. The mould cycle involves mould open, part ejection, and mould close that can take place for one mould as the other one is holding or cooling.

Operational sequence

In operation, melt is fed to a hot runner in the centre moving platen, which contains a directional valve and packing cylinder. One set of hydraulic latches holds the mould closed while the other mould is open, ejecting the moulded part. Two standard moulds can be installed in the same machine and run on overlapping cycles. While one mould is open, ejecting the part, and closing, the other mould is holding and cooling. Each mould operates independently, allowing two different parts (moulds) to be produced on the same machine.

COINING

Coining, also called injection stamping and more often injection-compression moulding, is a variant of injection moulding. The essential difference lies in the manner in which the thermal contraction of the moulding during cooling (shrinkage) is compensated. With conventional injection moulding, the reduction in material volume in the cavity due to thermal contraction is compensated by forcing in more plastic melt during the pressure holding phase. By contrast with injection-compression moulding, the melt is injected into a cavity that has a relatively short shot in a compression-type mould (male plug fits into a female mould) rather than the usual flat surface matching mould halves for injection moulding. The melt injected into the cavity is literally stress-free; it works without a holding pressure phase, and the transport of plastic melt that accompanies this action avoids stresses in the part, particularly in the gate area(s). The ICM process for thermoplastics

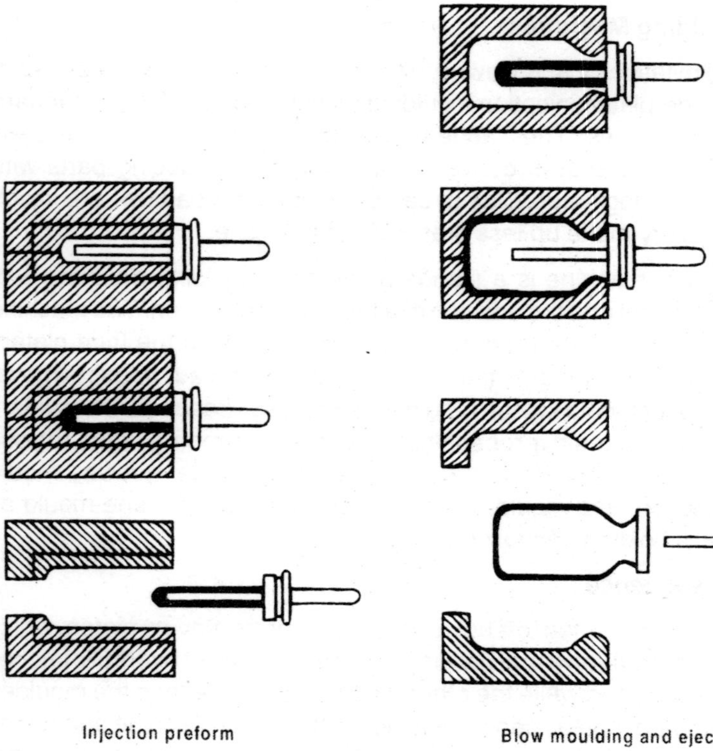

Fig. 9.12 Basic injection blow moulding process.

has been used for different-size parts, particularly for thick-walled parts with tight dimensional requirements, such as, optical lenses. When melt enters the mould. it is not completely closed. Thus, the short shot melt literally flows unrestricted in the cavity and is basically stress-free. After injection is completed, the mould is closed, with the pressure on the melt very uniform.

INJECTION BLOW MOULDING (IBM)

IBM basically has three stages, (Fig. 9.12) and (Fig. 9.13). In the first stage, hot melt is injected through an injection moulding machine nozzle into a manifold and into one or more preform cavities. An exact amount of resin is injected around a core pin(s). Hot liquid from a heat control unit is directed by hoses through mould heating channels around the preform cavity; these channels have been predesigned to provide the correct heat control on the melt within the mould cavity. The melt heat is decreased to the required amount.

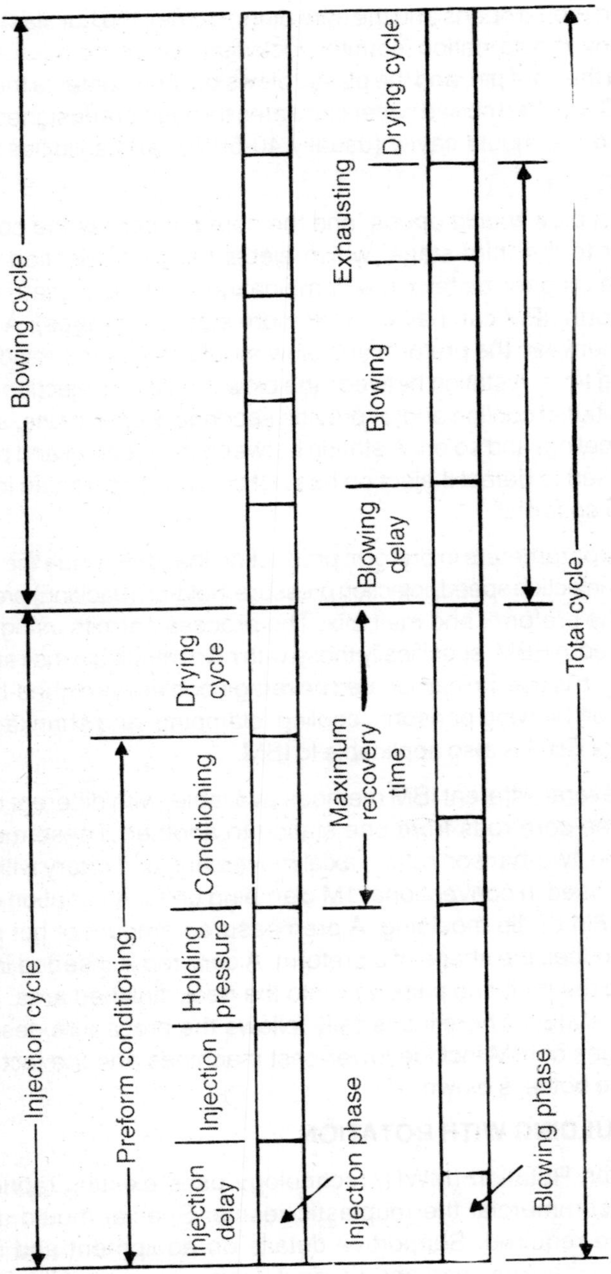

Fig. 9.13 Injection blow moulding complete cycle, starting with injection moulding the preform followed by the blowing cycle.

The two-part mould opens and the core pin(s) carries the hot plastic to the second stage blow mould station (counterclockwise). Upon mould closing, air is introduced via the core pin, and the plastic blows out and contacts the mould cavity surface. Controlled chilled water circulates through predesigned mould channels around the mould cavity (usually 40-50°F), and solidifies the hot plastic.

The two-part blow mould opens, and the core pin carries the complete blown container to the third stage, which ejects the part. Ejection can be done by using a stripper plate, air, a combination of stripper plate and air robots, and so forth. IBM can have four or more stations (stages). A station can be located between the preform and blow mould stages to provide extra heat conditioning time. A station between the blow mould and ejection stages can provide additional cooling and/or provide secondary operations, such as hot stamping, labeling, and so on. A station between the ejection and preform stages can be used to detect if ejection has not occurred, to add an insert to the core pin and so forth.

The process parameters in preform production that determine the quality of the part are the injection speed, injection pressure, hold-on (packing) pressure, heat control of the preform, and melt mix. The process permits using resins that cannot be used in EBM, specifically those with no controllable melt strength such as PET, which is used in carbonated beverage bottles (stretched-blown). The information on blowing parisons, cooling, clamping, and shrinkage that was presented for EBM is also applicable to IBM.

There are several different IBM methods available, with different means of transporting the core rods from one station to another. These methods include the shuttle, two-parison rotary, axial movement, and rotary with three or more stations used in conventional 1M clamping units. A variation of IBM is displacement 8M or dip moulding. A premeasured amount of hot melt is deposited into a cupel, the shape of a preform. A core rod is inserted into the cupel, displacing the melt and packing it into the neck finished area. It then moves to a blow station where it basically follows the procedure described above. Advantages of IBM include lower-cost machines and the fact that a nearly stress-free bottle is blown.

INJECTION MOULDING WITH ROTATION

Moulding With Rotation (MWR) technology uses existing fabrication equipment and commercial thermoplastic resins. Special mould design modifications are required. Supportive details on equipment and mould engineering, resin rheology, and end-product design are part of the license package.

This technology is most effective when employed with articles: (i) having a polar axis of symmetry; (ii) having reasonably uniform wall thickness; and (iii) whose dimensional specifications and part-to-part trueness are important to market acceptance. *Note:* Within these requirements are many parts having variable surface and wall geometries.

Initial "target" applications have been in the bottle and jar market areas. However, the use of this technology is not restricted to those particular shapes or markets. Practically any article, container, or blown or injection-moulded part having one surface reasonably rotationally symmetrical can be fabricated by MWR. The MWR process asks no sacrifice of either cycle time or surface finish. Both laboratory and early commercial runs identify good potentials for reducing cycle time; for either reducing the amount of resin required or improving properties with the same amount of resin, or both; and for substituting less expensive resin while achieving adequate properties in the fabricated part.

The MWR process is a fabrication method using a rotating mould element in the injection moulding machine. The end product can come directly from the injection moulding machine mould, or be a result of two-stage fabrication: making a parison, blow moulding the parison. The two-step process can be "integrated": in line injection blow, or separate operations for the injecting moulding of parisons with reheating and blowing at separate stations.

Orientation of the molecules within a thermoplastic mass has a direct affect on moulded end properties and is the subject of many articles and reports. Injection moulders commonly try to minimise the undirectional orientation resulting from essentially linearmould fill. Shear producers may induce lateral orientation by different stretching-tentering techniques. Blow moulders anticipate and plan for certain structural improvements that result from biaxial orientation occurring during the blowing process.

Plastic fabricators know that minimising unidirectional flow orientation usually results in better performing end products. The know-how of polymer rheology and processing temperature, implemented with varying mould fill techniques and end-product design geometries-all are used to minimise problems associated with uniaxial orientation.

The MWR process developed by Dow took a radically different approach. Instead of seeking to minimise uniaxial orientation or its adverse affects, Dow research sought a practical technique by which controlled multiaxial orientation could assure maximum properties (for the resin used) in the fabricated end product.

The MWR process permits fabricators to control molecular orientation and thus produce top performance end products.

The MWR process permits a balancing of resin temperature, resin rheology, pressures, time, and either mould core or mould surface rotation to achieve a carefully controlled degree of multiaxial orientation within the thermoplastic resin mass.

During fabrication using the MWR process, two forces act on the polymer: injection (longitudinal) and rotation (hoop). The targeted "balanced orientation" is a result' of those forces. As the part wall cools, additional high-magnitude, "cross-laminated" orientation is developed-frozen in-throughout the wall thickness. *Note:* Orientation on molecular planes occurs as each "layer" cools after injection.

This orientation can change direction and magnitude as a function of wall thickness. The result is analogous to plywood-and the strength improvements are as dramatic. In the MWR process, there are an infinite number of "layers", each of which has its own controlled direction of orientation. By appropriate processing conditions, both the magnitude and direction of the orientation can be varied and controlled throughout the wall thickness.

MWR technology produces parts having greatly increased tensile strength compared to the same parts conventionally moulded. Because MWR-type improvements are based on balanced multiaxial orientation, the gain in tensile strength also directly correlates with that in practical toughness.

In the gross sense, stress crack agents cause the failure of moulded plastic parts by attacking the chemical bonds of the molecules. Failure normally occurs as a crack perpendicular to the direction of greatest weakness. With MWR technology, the internal structurai bonding of the plastic part is greatly improved through the multi-axial "laminar" orientation of the molecules. This results often in a measurable improvement in stress crack resistance of the moulded part.

Stress crack behaviour is dependent on so many variables-resin lised, part thickness, part shape, stress crack agent, environment of use, etc.-that each part must be analysed carefully in its own right. In any case, the stress crack resistance of a part moulded with MWR technology can be improved to a commercially significant degree.

Parts moulded of polymers that normally exhibit crazes as a predecessor to catastrophic failure can be improved significantly by fabrication with MWR. For common styrenics, the yield strengths of parts having MWR-balanced orientation are significantly higher than those of conventionally moulded parts.

Additionally, the mode of failure may become shear yielding because of the high (balanced) orientation provided by MWR. When this is accomplished, crazes, as a form of failure, will not occur.

The effect of cycle time on injection moulding economics is great. With MWR, one potential for reducing cycle time relates to the ability to obtain satisfactory end-product performance with less polymer. This can result in a shorter cycle because less polymer = less heat = less cooling time = shorter cycle.

Another potential for reduced cycle time occurs because injection moulding with MWR is most effectively done when plastic melt occurs at a much lower temperature [≈ 100°F (≈ 38°C) lower for styrenics] than would be used for injection moulding without MWR.

Cycle times are dependent on not only plastic shot weight and temperature, but also all the variables in a given plant operation. It is reassuring therefore that a number of laboratory tests on cycle time have shown that the cycle time with MWR is at least equal to that of injection moulding without MWR.

As is common with conventional injection moulding, MWR also results in parts having excellent dimensional properties. In addition, MWR permits parts with high length-to-diameter ratios to be moulded without problems of core deflection and consequently thinner-thicker sections in the part wall.

With core rotation during MWR, the pin "self-centres", and part wall uniformity is excellent. The final moulded part therefore is uniformly strong about its circumference. This fact has particular value if the moulded part is a parison. Parisons fabricated with MWR can be reheated and blown without problems caused by wall eccentricity. In injection moulding with MWR, part designers and engineers should keep in mind that significant part wall thickness variation and surface geometry variation are possible, if desired, with MWR.

A basic profile of injection moulding conditions to be used with MWR is given below:

1. Any orientable injection-mouldable plastic resin.
2. Temperature at 100°F (212°C) or lower.
3. Injection pressure, high.
4. Hold pressure, high.
5. Rotation—before, during, after mould fill.
6. Rotation and injection controls.

DIP INJECTION BLOW MOULDING

Since the beginning of blow moulding hollow articles, the industry has asked for a scrap-free energy efficient process that allows one to use low-cost tooling combined with short procurement times. Extrusion blow moulding became the most common process to blow hollow articles for these reasons. However, the inherent disadvantage in finishing the neck and bottom through mechanical shear action made the industry look for other methods.

Injection blow moulding was developed to overcome this latter drawback and further to improve the tolerances required for safety neck finishes and plug fitments. However, tooling costs were high because technically two moulds are necessary to produce the hollow article: a preform mould and blow mould. Both moulds have to be constructed to very close tolerances [± 0.005 in. (0.013 Cm)]. In addition, energy requirements are substantially higher than for extrusion blow-moulding because of the need for hot-water units to condition the preform.

It allows one to inject the neck finish precisely as in injection blow moulding, but without requiring intricate preform moulds that led to the name NECK injection blow moulding. The moulds are simple and can be built in the same time as extrusion blow moulds. This process does not require energy consuming hot-water units, clamp pressure to the neck finish area only, and a high-pressure injection phase to form the preform.

Materials

Practically any thermoplastics can be blow-moulded, particularly the commodity type plastics. Different properties can be obtained with the different available and useful plastics that are now used to blow mould different size and shaped products. Properties can include strength, toughness, clarity, gas barriers, chemical resistance, heat resistance, colour, and many others. Different combinations of properties can be achieved by combining two or more plastics. Parisons can be coextruded, coated, dipped, coinjected, etc., in order to provide the combinations of different properties available in different plastics. Strength blow moulding also provides an important processing technique to offer improved properties and reduce the quantity of plastics to improve cost/performance characteristics.

Examples of properties that can be obtained with the different plastics are as follows: claritycrystal polystyrene, acrylonitrile, styrene acrylontrile, polyvinyl chloride, stretched PET, polysulphone; moisture barrier-polypropylene, low-density polyethylene, high-density polyethylene, transparent nylon, polymethylpentene; oxygen barrier-PET, polyvinyl chloride, polyacrylonitrile, polysulphone, transparent nylon; etc.

Extrusion blow moulding represents the biggest oulet for blow-moulded containers, with high-density polyethylene being the major plastic used, about 80% of all plastic consumed. There are different grades of HDPE. With increased density, the stiffness, strength, hardness, crepe resistance, softening temperature, and gloss improve. However, toughness, stress crack resistance, and permeability decrease. It resists most acids and salts but is attacked by strong oxidising agents.

Polyvinyl chloride (PVC) is one of the largest resin used today. Because of its low oxygen transmission, water-clear clarity, and relative ease of processing, it has captured the haircare, toiletries, cosmetics, household chemical, and edible oil markets. It is now being challenged by stretch blown polypropylene and PET.

This brief review of different plastics emphasises the importance of using the correct plastics to meet specific requirements. The real test of any material is that it is blown, either unoriented or stretchoriented. Unfortunately, in the past, many simulated "fast" tests to evaluate plastic bottle performance have had "bad" records. However, there are fast tests that have been developed to simulate actual performance.

METAL INJECTION MOULDING (MIM)

Over a century ago, the plastic injection moulding machine advanced the state of the art by taking advantage of machines involved in moulding die-cast/metal parts. The die-cast machines "injectionmoulded" their "melt" at above 1,000°F (538°C). In recent years, injection moulding machines have been moulding/processing metals. As an example, the "Inject alloy" combines the best of plastics processing and powder-metal technologies. This process is targeted for the production of complex precision parts.

Specifically, upper size restriction is about 2 in.In diameter (50 mm) and 0.250 in. in wall thickness (6.35 mm) on cross sections. Parts are "near net shape", at 94 to 98% of theoretical density. Tolerances are generally from 0.003 to 0.005 in.lin. (0.076 to 0.127 mmlmm).

The process uses spherical powder less than 10 μ in diameter (compared with 30 to 200 μ for conventional processing). Fine powders are said to promote rapid diffusion during sintering, producing near-complete homogenisation. In addition, smaller size allows more intricate part geometry, thinner walls, sharper edges, and low porosity.

The particles are mixed with a plastic binder and injection-moulded in commercial thermoplastics moulding equipment. The binder improves flow and assures the uniform fill of mould cavities. Binder is removed through solvent extraction or heating, and the parts are then sintered.

The alloys offered include iron with 2 to 50% nickel and Fe-Ni-Co alloy with 90,000 psi tensile strength (620 MPa) and 25% elongation. The process and machine convert these materials into a thixotropic semi-solid state. After the conversion, an all-magnesium liquid-solid slurry remains that can be injected directly into the mould. Injection moulding then yields an all-metal part with mechanical properties iimilar to those of the original alloy.

Reducing their viscosity by shearing converts the thixotropic materials (semi-solid masses) to a fluidlike condition. Shearing eliminates the dendritic structures that give rigidity to a solidifying metal. Two temperature prome methods can be used to eliminate these structures. One, the classic "hot profile", involves two steps: (i) heat the entire metal mass to a molten state; and (ii) subsequently, shear this molten mass as it cools to the semisolid state.

In general, the different MIM methods available combine the flexibility of plastic injection moulding technology with the properties of metals. Production is accomplished with standard injection moulding machines, A knowledge of the plastic moulding process can aid one in being successful with MIM. The finished moulded metal part, however, contains no plastics. For processing certain metals or to obtain particular complex moulded metal shapes, plastics are sometimes used to hold the metal powders together while they are moulded. The nature of MIM is such that it will probably never be widely used in the near future by the plastics injection moulding industry.

The MIM process is generally limited to smaller parts and is especially suitable for designs involving complex geometries. The process moulds thin wall sections, sharp corners, edges and other details never before possible in metal parts. MIM has the ability to produce parts with injection-moulded finish and geometry (threads, side core features, etc.) usually not obtainable with precision metal parts such as those using zinc die-casting. The choice of metal powders is quite broad, including stainless steel and a variety of iron and non-ferrous alloys.

Close control over the injection process must be maintained to avoid moulded-in stress, surface pitting, or voids caused by internal shrinkage. Once the feedstock is mixed, it can be extruded, pelletised, and loaded into the moulding machine.

The initial moulded piece is called a green part. Its geometry is identical to that of the finished piece, but to allow for shrinkage during sintering, it is roughly 25% larger. Average sintering time is 5 to 10 h. The time needed for the debinding process varies widely.

CERAMIC INJECTION MOULDING

In order for powder ceramic compounds to be processed through injection moulding machines, they must be specially prepared. This involves the addition of a binder. These binders usually consist of plastic blends of various compositions.

The binder is a temporary aid that makes it possible to carry out the injection moulding process. Before the injection moulding parts are fired to produce the final ceramic part, the binder must be removed as fully as possible since otherwise the parts could explode, swell (expand), or break. Drying or volatilisation (debindering) is a rather complex operation in the entire production process. Exact adherence to temperature-time curve specified according to the particular material and size, shape and wall thickness of the preform is very important for the quality of the fired part.

Thermoset binders are less suitable than thermopiastic binders because of their greater thermal stability at temperature and the resulting complications for the debindering process. In each case, the amount of plastic that is later to be decomposed should be kept as low as possible. Injection moulding of any powdered parts makes high demands on the wear resistance of different machine components, particularly screws, non-return valves, cylinders, and moulds. Efforts in powder and binder manufacture are directed toward minimising machine wear and improving end-product quality. Although a reduction in particle size brings improvements in the material and injection moulding, it also increases the difficulty of removing the binder greatly by drying. Thus, tradeoffs exist. Regardless of these, ceramics have advantages such as the following: complicated parts (with thread, undercuts, etc.) can be made, high strength of the preforms permits the following automatic production, constant shrinkage behaviour in the sintering process can be accurately controlled, and owing to the good slip properties of the binders, the injection mouldings are very highly and uniformly compacted.

FUSIBLE AND SOLUBLE CORE MOULDING

The use of fusible core technology (FMCT), as well as soluble core technology (SCT), to injection mould parts with cavities that could not be formed or released otherwise. Other forms, types, or terms used include lost-core technology. (LCT), soluble salt-core technology (SSCT), lost ice-core technology (LICT), and ceramic - core technology (CCT). LCT has been the most popular term.

More recently, fusible cores and soluble cores have been used. As an example, there are automobile engine intake manifolds moulded of glass-fibre-reinforced nylon that has been shown to be economical and technologically interesting as an application. Utilisation of the fusible core to mould the complex, curved part produced the high-quality, smooth interior surface sought. The air resistance coefficient of a 90 deg bend was reduced by more than 50% in going from a rough die-cast to a smooth plastic surface of the hollow inner spaces of the curved manifold. The die-cast aluminium parts required -extensive postmachining as assembly operations: The RP provided the design freedom required to consolidate several manifold components into one, greatly reducing assembly and finishing costs.

The basic fusible core technique makes it possible to produce simple to very complex hollow structural products (take-off of cored metal casting). It involves using a fusible core inside the plastic shape or structure. The core permits forming of the desired plastic shape, to date usually RP. Core material is a type that will not collapse or change shape during a pressure-temperature-time processing cycle. Shape is not usually the problem since the core material is restricted.

The core material used depends on actual processing requirements, particularly temperature. It can range from a wax, thermoplastic, and to different ratios of zinc-aluminium eutectic mixtures (alloys) to special fusible eutectic alloys. Core material has to melt below the temperature of the plastic. These shaped cores are usually inserted in a mould cavity where it is retained by the mould (such as used with a mould core puller) or by "spiders" (as used in certain metal core supports for extrusion dies). After processing, the core material is removed by heating it to its melt temperature. Release in via an existing opening or a hole is drilled through the plastic to the core. This technique is used in different processes, such as injection moulding compression moulding, reaction injection moulding, and various RP methods.

VACUUM MOULDING

Vacuum injection moulding has been used to meet special requirements, such as ensuring exceptionally void free parts and providing a degree of aid to meet tight tolerances on very complex moulded parts. The process involves using the conventional injection moulding machine and literally putting a mould in a vacuum box. It actually develops a vacuum around the mould cavity (via seals, etc.). Thus, the vacuum ,can remove air and gas by-products that develop when melting certain plastics or elastomers.

10

Troubleshooting in Injection Moulding

Injection Moulding Problems

In the injection moulding process, faults can appear e.q.:

1. When changing to a new material.
2. While running regular production runs.
3. While trying out a new mould.

The faults appearing while moulding components can be due to one or more factors given below:

1. Machine related.
2. Mould and mould design related.
3. Operating conditions related (Time, Pressure and Temperature).
4. Material related.
5. Component design related.

Before going to the analysis to find out reasons for the moulding faults, it must be ensured that the machine operating conditions are consistent, temperature control is maintained, moulding operation is consistent and a uniform cycle time is maintained. Now, let us see the various faults that occur during the injection moulding process and the possible solutions to solve these problems.

Problem of Short Shots

Short shots are components that are incomplete and are usually caused by the material solidifying before it completely fills the cavity.

Possible Cause	Suggested Solution
Material too cold	• Increase the cylinder temperature. Increase moulding cycle time.
Mould is cold	• Increase the mould temperature to the possible limit. Decrease the rate of flow of coolant.
Injection pressure low	• Increase the injection pressure
Insufficient injection time	• Increase the injection time.
Insufficient injection speed	• Increase the injection speed.
Insufficient feeding	• Check the material in the hopper. Check the feed throat for the bridging of the granules. Machine capacity not enough.
Melt flow restricted	• Increase the gate, runner and sprue size. Use the nozzle with a higher diameter hole. Try with a higher MFI material. Check the nozzle for blocks.
Back pressure in cavity	• Provide adequate venting. Reduce the injection rate and pressure. Reduce the clamping force.
Unbalanced runner design	• Balance the runner design/ cavity location.
Cold slug clogging gates, runners and sprue	• Increase the size of the cold slug well. Provide cold well for sub runners.
Un uniform mould temperature	• Rearrange the cooling line in the mould to provide a uniform cooling.
Un uniform melt cushion	• Maintain a uniform melt cushion. Check back the flow valve, repair if needed.
Machine capacity not enough	• Use a bigger machine.

Problem of Flashing

The parts flashing defect appears as extra material attached to the component in the parting line area and its waste material, and has to be trimmed off before use. It is usually caused by mould deficiency. Other reasons include high pressure, inadequate venting, low clamping force etc.

Possible Cause	Suggested Solution
Material is too hot	• Decrease the cylinder temperature. Reduce the overall moulding cycle time. Decrease the mould temperature.
Injection Pressure is too high	• Decrease the injection pressure. Decrease the hold

		on pressure. Decrease the injection hold time.
Insufficient clamping force	•	Use a bigger machine if available. Reduce the number of cavities. Adjust the mechanism to increase the clamping force.
Foreign matter of flash acting as high spot on mould	•	Inspect the mouldland and clean carefully wherever necessary.
Mould pattens are warped. Clearance in vents. Knockouts are too great	•	Check the overhaul, if necessary. Check the clearance and adjust.
Insufficient venting causing material from	•	Inspect vents and clean in case of blockage enlarge vents, if needed cavity to flow out.
Injection presure unevenly distributed in the mould	•	Cavity and the runner layout should be balanced.

Problem of Sink Marks

Sink marks appear as depressions on the surface of the component. This occurs due to the insufficient

Possible Cause		Suggested Solution
Gate location, size and design	•	Locate the gate at the thick section of the part. Increase the gate size and reduce the gate land.
Insufficient packing	•	Increase the injection pressure. Increase the hold pressure time. Check back the flow valve for leakage.
Not enough material in cavity	•	Increase the shot weight.
Part sections uneven	•	Redesign the part with an even wall thickness.
Product too hot when ejected	•	Decrease the cylinder temperature. Increase the cooling time in mould. Reduce the mould temperature.
Restrictions in flow	•	Increase the gate, runner and the sprue size. Provide a proper venting in the mould. Balance flow and filling in cavity.
Local hot spots in the mould	•	Redesign the cooling pattern in the mould

Problems of Bubbles and Voids

Voids are caused by insufficient plastics in the cavity. The external walls freeze the material into a solid and the shrinkage continues internally, creating a vacuum, resulting in the formation of voids in the moulded components. The piece has to be cut open in the case of coloured mouldings or can use lower weight components when compared to the good ones. If voids are seen while opening the mould, it indicates a problem in the mould. If it is seen after the cooling of the mould, it may be due to the mould or the moulding problem.

Possible Cause	Suggested Solution
Internal shrinkage after the outer surface sets	• Increase the injection pressure, rate, time. Increase the size of the gates, runner, sprue. Increase the screw forward time.
Material too hot	• Decrease the cylinder temperature. Reduce the moulding cycle time.
Insufficient venting in the mould resulting in entrapment of air	• Provide vents at the point of final fill. Decrease the injection speed. Decrease the mould clamping force improve the gate size, change location
Condensation on cavity surface mould	• Reduce the flow of the coolant through. Wipe the cavity surface with a solvent.
Moisture in material	• Preheat the material thoroughly, use hopper dryer.
Injection rate too fast	• Decrease the injection rate
Restriction to flow of material	• Eliminate restrictions, inrease the gate and the runner size.

Problem of Brittleness of Component

Brittleness is seen by poor mechanical strength of the moulded component and sometimes the component cracks during ejection itself and is usually caused due to material degradation.

Possible Cause	Suggested Solution
Material is over heated	• Reduce the cylinder temperature, Shorten, the overall cycle time, Machine is too big change to a small machine.
Material too cold	• Increase the cylinder temperature. Increase the nozzle temperature. Decrease the screw speed.
Mould surface too cold	• Avoid using regrind. Use less percentage of regrand.
Bad quality regrind	• Check regrind for contamination moisture, degraded polymer check the regrind melt index.
Rate of injection too slow	• Increase the injection rate. Maintain the minimum feed cushion.

Original part design too thin	• Redesign the part to strengthen the weak areas.
Product not conditioned	• Condition the part as per the raw material manufacturers recommendation

Problem of Discoloration

The material discoloration problem is the visible variation of colour in the moulded component, due to the degradation of the material, pigments, additive etc. This can be due to excess temperature or the hang up of the material on dean spots or contamination, etc.

Possible Cause	Suggested Solution
Contamination of material	• Check the moulding material. Purge the heating cylinder. Check the feed system and hopper.
Material not dry	• Preheat the material. Use the hopper dryer.
Degradation of material, colourant, additives	• Decrease the cylinder temperatures. Decrease the overall moulding cycle. Use a smaller machine. Check the residence-time of the material. Reduce the screw speed. Use colourants and additives which will withstand processing temperatures.
Degradation of material due to entrapment	• Provide proper venting. Relocate the gates. Decrease the mould clamping force.
Too much stress on component	• Check the ejection system.
Charred materials is in cylinder or nozzle coming out with material.	• Purge the cylinder completely, remove the clean the nozzle

Problem of Silver Streaks

The problem of silver streaks appear on the surface of the component as a streaky flow or bright specks. Usually it is the result of the wetness of the hygroscopic material, contamination etc.

Possible Cause	Suggested Solution
Moisture and volatiles in the material	• Preheat the material adequately, Use a hopper driver.
Mixture of fines in granules	• Use uniform granules and sieve out all the fines.
Material too hot	• Decrease the mould cycle time. Decrease the cylinder temperature

Contamination of foreign material	• Check the moulding powder for contamination. Check the feed system, purge the cylinder. Check the regrind content and quality.
Gates and runner too small	• Increase the size of the runner and the gates
Excessive condensate/lubricant	• Wipe the mould thoroughly. Use a lesser quantity of the lubricant. Change the lubricant and try.
Adjust injection rate	• Increase or decrease the injection rate.

Problem of Nozzle Drooling and Foaming

The problem of nozzle drooling is seen as material leaking out of the injection nozzle and is usually due to residual pressure, high temperature. and lack of positive seal for the nozzle.

Possible Cause	Suggested Solution
Nozzle temperature very high	• Decrease the nozzle temperature.
Material too hot	• Decrease the cylinder temperature. Decrease the moulding cycle time.
Nozzle orifice too large	• Use a nozzle with a small orifice. Use the reverse taper nozzle. Use a nozzle with shut off valve.
Moisture in the material	• Preheat the material. Use a hopper dryer.

Problem of Scorching

Possible Cause	Suggested Solution
Material is overheated	• Reduce the cylinder temperature. Decrease the moulding cycle time. Remove dead spots in the cylinder. Screw nozzle assembly.
Thermocouple burnt out	• Check all the thermocouples and change if necessary.
Temperature controller mulfunctioning	• Check for the sticking of relays. Check for the con troller connected to the wrong heaters. Check if the relays are functioning properly.
Regrind not of good quality	• Segregate and check regrind critically for contamination, excess moisture or degraded polymer.
Improper shut down procedures	• Purge the machine thoroughly, clean the nozzle and start moulding afresh
Moisture in material	• Preheat the material, Use a hopper dryer.
Gas entrapment	• Vent cavities properly relocate the gate position.

Rate of injection too fast	• Decrease the injection speed. Decrease the injection pressure. Increase the size of the gates.
Colourant degradation	• Use a colourant which can withstand the processing temperature.

Problem of Sprue Sticking

The sprue sticks on to the sprue bush and delays the time cycle during moulding, mostly. This is due to the sprue-nozzle non-alignment and inadequate pull back arrangement for the sprue runner system.

Possible Cause	Suggested Solution
Nozzle not alinged with sprue Sprue puller too small.	• Realign the nozzle with a sprue bush. Increse the undercut. Increase the size of sprue puller.
Material too cold at nozzle and sprue unable to breakway	• Increase the nozzle temperature until the sprue breaks from the nozzle.
Nozzle orifice greater than that sprue bush orifice	• Change the nozzle with a lower dia orifice or increase the sprue
Material too hot sprue breaking at component end	• Decrease the cylinder temperature. Increase the moulding cycle time. Increase the cooling time in the mould.
Sprue held up on sprue bush due to inadequate taper	• Give adequate taper in the sprue bush. Use mould release temporarily. Remove the burrs on the sprue.

Problem of Surface Lamination

Possible Cause	Suggested Solution
Contamination of material	• Check the feed material for contamination. Purge the injection cylinder. Clean the feed system. Check the quality of regrind added. Preheat the material.
Material wet	• Preheat the material. Use hopper dryer.
Material too cold	• Increase the cylinder temperature. Increase the moulding cycle time.
Mould surface too cold	• Increase the mould temperature.
Rate of injection too low	• Increase the injection rate.

Problem of Parts Sticking to the Mould

The injection moulded parts stick to the mould and do not come out. This phenomenon is usually due to the over packing of the material, defect in the ejection system and a wrong mould design.

Possible Cause	Suggested Solution
Rough surface of the mould	• Polish the mould well
Inadequate release taper in mould cavity	• Provide a release taper
Ejection system not designed properly	• Check the ejector systems/provide extra ejector pins.
Undercuts in the mould cavity	• Eliminate undercuts with a proper design, polish and provide sufficient draft
Misalignment of core and cavity	• Check the alignment of the core and cavity
Mould made of soft porous steels	• Replace the mould with a hardened metal
Overpacking of the plastic material	• Reduce the feed material. Reduce the screw forward time
Uneven pressure in cavities	• Maintain a constant feed cushion. Balance the gates and runners for uniform filling
Parts sticking to injection side	• Use an undercut runner to keep the parts on the ejection side. Use a mould release spray. Adjust the mould temp to retain the component on the ejection side.
Mould deposits causing sticking	• Check and clean the mould deposits.

Problem of Surface Waviness (Pits, Orange peel, Wrinkles)

The problem is seen as wrinkled surface, pits etc and is usually due to an insufficient packing of the material in the cavity.

Possible Cause	Suggested Solution
Inadequate injection pressure	• Increase the injection pressure.
Insufficient hold pressure time	• Increase the hold pressure time
Injection rate too low	• Increase the injection rate. Increase the size of the gates, runners, sprue and the nozzle.
Mould surface too cold	• Increase the mould surface temperature
Material too cold	• Increase the cylinder temperature. Increase the overall moulding cycle time.
Poor mould surface	• Polish the mould

Problem of Fractures and Cracks

Possible Cause	Suggested Solution
Internal stresses due to mould design	• Check the mould design and change
Embrittlement due to thermal degradation	• Reduce the cylinder temperature. Use a faster moulding cycle
Parts ejected too fast	• Five more cooling time in the mould
Ejector system defective	• Check the ejection system for a smooth operation
Internal stress due to cold metal insert	• Warm the insert before using. Thicken the section in the area of crack. Use toughened materials.

Problem of Warping

Warpage is seen as distortion in the shape of the moulded component and is usually caused by the wrong design of the part and the gate location.

Possible Cause	Suggested Solution
Components ejected too hot	• Reduce the cylinder temperature. Increase the mould cooling time. Place in the jig after moulding. Increase the temperature.
Part design and uneven thickness	• Design the part with an even wall thickness and strengthen it with ribs.
Mould cooling uneven	• Maintain a uniform temperature in the mould. Use a cold mould.
Distortion due to internal strain	• Increase/decrease the injection pressure, increase the mould cooling time, increase the overall moulding cycle.
Ejection knock out pins working unevenly	• Check the knockout pin levels and set evenly. Increase the knockout area.
Gate location not proper	• Gate location should be in such a way that the material flows from the thick to the thin section. Gate runner system designed for balanced filling.
Distortion of heavy section only	• Increase the mould cooling time. Maintain a uniform melt temperature slowly. Cool the part in warm water. Place in a shrink jig after injection.

Problem of Weld Lines

Weld lines are seen as lines normally opposite to the gate location or any flow divider in the mould. This is due to the weak joining of a divided melt flow in the mould.

Possible Cause	Suggested Solution
Material too cold	• Increase the cylinder temperature. Increase overall moulding cycle.
Mould too cold	• Increase the mould temperature. Throttle the flow of coolant in mould.
Injection pressure too low	• Increase the injection pressure. Increase the screw forward time. Increase the rate of injection. Increase the size of the gates, runner and sprue. Use multiple gates and runners.
Gas entrapment	• Provide vent in cavities. Relocate the gate. Decrease the mould clamping force
Pat too thin at weld	• Thicken the part at the weld
Capacity of the machine small	• Change to a bigge machine
Contamination of material	• Check the material. Check the feeding system.
Material poor flow	• Use a higher MFI material. Use an external lubricant.

Problem of Dimensional Variation

Dimension variation can be seen as deviation in the dimensions of the moulded component, compared to the standard acceptable dimensions and can be due to various reasons, including moulding conditions, etc.

Possible Cause	Suggested Solution
Inconsistent mould cycle	• Maintain uniform moulding cycle
Feeding system mulfunctioning, particularly in the plunger machines.	• Check the feed system and adjust for uniform feed.
Inconsistent melt cushion while injection	• Maintain a uniform melt cushion. Check the non return valve for wear.
Mulfunction of non-return valve	• Check the replace the valve if necessary
Uneven back pressure adjustment	• Arrange for a uniform back pressure.

Mulfunction of temperature control system	•	Check the heater bands. Check the thermocouples
Insufficient of plasticising capacity	•	Use a bigger machine.
Incorrect runner, gate dimensions	•	Check and provide a proper runner gate system
Uneven mould filling	•	Design the mould for uniform filling of cavities
Distortion during ejection	•	Check the knockout pin system and correct
Incorrect mould dimensions	•	Machine the mould cavity and core for proper dimensions with proper allowances for shrinkage
Un uniform mould temperature	•	Maintain a uniform mould temperature
Packing of cavity not enough	•	Use a higher injection pressure. Increase the screw forward time.

Problem of Jetting

The problem of jetting is seen as a snake like flow pattern in the region next to the gate. It is usually due to the material directly jetting in the cavity.

Possible Cause		Suggested Solution
Melt injected directly into the cavity	•	Direct the material flow to hit the wall and flood the cavity
Melt temperature is not enough	•	Increase the cylinder temperature. Increase the moulding cycle time.
Adjustment of the injection rate	•	Increase or decrease the injection rate
Gate size too small	•	Increase the gate size and flare the gate

Problem of Gate Smear

The problem can be seen as spray marks immediately next to the gate.

Possible Cause		Suggested Solution
Mould temperature not enough	•	Increase the mould temperature
Injection rate too fast	•	Decrease the injection rate
Gate too restricted	•	Decrease the gate size, flare the gate. Change the gate location

TECHNOLOGICAL SOLUTIONS FOR TOTAL QUALITY IN INJECTION MOULDING OF PLASTICS

Since injection moulding is an automatic mass production technique, it is meaningless to use cheaper, inferior and imperfect moulds on expensive machine. Once the mould is fixed and process parameters are set on the machine for desired quality, the production should go on and on till the production schedule is over. This can be possible only if, all concerned with operations understand the strength and significance of four 'M's i.e., Machine, Mould, Material and Man.

Machine

Machine, which gives excellent repeatability of set parameters-for which machine control is responsible. Machine should be able to reproduce machine parameters repeatedly without any error. The machine should have microprocessor controls which is capable of giving:

1. 5-10 steps of injection speeds.
2. 5-10 steps of injection follow-up pressure.
3. 3-5 steps of back pressure.
4. 3-5 steps of screw RPM.

These features of multi-step control of machine parameters, if suitably set, can have influence on quality of moulding.

The machine is not responsible for:

1. Deviations of melt flow with different velocities in the complex shaped space between core and cavity. The part design is responsible for this.
2. Uniform distribution of mould surface temperature and its consistency with, respect to time.

The design of cooling circuit in the mould and coolant temperature and circulation pump capacity are responsible for this.

There should be periodical machine preventive maintenance practice so that there should be no unscheduled interruption of production.

Mould

Mould which has to mould part :

1. Part has to be perfectly mouldable. All complex shapes need not be perfectly mouldable. Therefore, there is need for understanding the perfect mouldability of complex shapes. The constrains of moulding process can be avoided by suitable part design.

2. Mould has to be designed to achieve quick stability of the moulding process. Therefore, through understanding of injection moulding process is necessary. The good knowledge of Wanderwall's equation, PVT diagram, cavity pressure profile, characteristics of plastic melt, heat exchange in mould etc. are essential.

3. Using right steel, the mould parts are machined precisely. When above mentioned factors are considered before manufacturing mould, then only it can produce parts without interruption in production. There should be scheduled for lubrication, inspection, servicing of cooling system of mould.

Material

Material including additives of excellent quality standards and consistency are used. Knowledge of material characteristics and it's properties is essential.

Man

Man who is able to visualise and understand, what is happening inside the mould and plasticising screw assembly. He should be able to visualise forces acting and its influence on various component of mould. He should have clear understanding of fundamentals of the subject-strength of materials of metal and peculiarities of plastics.

"Plastics are more complex material than metals and therefore, are less understood (even by technical personnel) and not always successfully applied.

Normally we are familiar with metals and we tend to view plastics as a type of metals. Metals are hard, stiff and elastic, they corrode where as plastics have none of these characteristics. All metals have similar behaviour but one plastic does not necessarily behave like any other plastic.

Different types of same plastic may be totally unlike. Solid Urea-formaldehyde is a hard material while urea-formaldehyde foam is the softest material. Polycarbonate is very tough material, but it is not tough if a notch is cut in it or wipe it with a solvent. Plastics are exciting materials to use, but they are deceptive in ways that no metals are. Therefore, skilled practicing engineers should have imagination and caution in working with plastics.

Quality Related Problems

It should be realised that, every intricate shape need not be perfectly mouldable. Therefore, there exists problems which can be recurring processing problem or quality related problems. To solve these problems, we should have in-depth knowledge of plastics technology. It can be realised that, the root cause of all processing and quality related problems lies in part design and mould design.

The problems may be due to: (i) defective part design from manufacturing point of view; (ii) defective mould design from plastic melt characteristics and processing point of view; (iii) poor, machine specification or poor machine controls; and (iv) inconsistent material quality.

The problems belonging to 1, can not be solved by searching for solution in 2, 3, 4. The problems belonging to 2, can not be solved by searching for solution 1,3,4. The problems belonging to 3, can, not be solved by searching for solution 1,2,4. The problems belonging to 4, can not be solved by searching for solution 1,2,3. The solution for problems have to be in it's own domain.

All these quality problems listed below are not new. They existed right form the beginning and they continue to exist. Obviously, this shows men concerned have not applied their mind to the problems and hence, they are repeated. Computer Aided Engineering (CAE) analysis software like Mouldflow can help in detecting these problems at part design stage itself and it enables to correct the defect in computer even before mould is fabricated. The useful data obtained from the analysis can be used to design perfect mould. Problems of moulding machine and mould related are discussed below.

Problems of Moulding

Moulding problems	*Moulding Related*	*Machine Related*
Sink marks	Part design related non uniformity of wall thickness	Injection speed profile on pressure profile can minimise to some extent.
	Technique can be considered	Gas injection moulding
Warp	Use technique to improve part stiffness with part design Random distribution of mould surface temperature. Cooling circuit design related.	
Weak weld lines	Part design related	Injection speed can influ- ence
Inconsistent critical dimensions and fluctuality quality during long production run	Unequal shrinkage due to variation in mould surface temperaure. Cooling circuit design related.	Melt temperature, injection speed and hold-on pressure can have little influence.
	Core and cavity dimension	Unestablished process due

Moulding problems	*Moulding Related*	*Machine Related*
	related Correct shrinkage is not considered for core/ cavity dimension	to unbalanced heat exchange in mould and unbalanced melt flow and high percentage utilisation of shot capacity more than 3D injection stroke.
Degradation	Check dimensions of runner system for excessive shearing	Excessive residence time due to use of oversized injection unit. Lowering barrel temperature and injection speed can have some influence
Ejection difficulty	Part design related- unbalanced melt flow. Use Flow leader to reduce unbalanced in flow.	
Poor impact strength	Radius at projections and sharp corners as it act like notch from where crack propagates	
Inconsistent weight		Percentage utilisation of shot capacity is closer to 90 per cent resulting in in consistent melt quality, if melting stroke is more than 3 times screw diameter. Boarderline case for shot weight.
Inconsistent filling	Increase gate size to reduce pressure drop	Available maximum injection rate is not across the gate. Adequate for flow ra -tio of part being moulded. Boarderline case for injection rate.
Stress cracking	Melt flow is unbalanced. Part design related	Over packed part. Set correct pressure profile during pressure phase.

Moulding Problems	*Material Related Problems*
Sink marks	• Filled polymer can reduce sink mark
Poor mechanical strength	• Consider high molecular weight polymers • Consider filled polymers. Pre heat polymer in dehymidifier if required for polymer as recommended for polymer
Dimensional variation	• Check shrinkage characteristics of material.
Degradation of melt	• Check thermal stability of polymer as well as pigments and other additives if any used with material.
Difficulty in filling	• Consider polymer of higher MFI.

Perfect Mouldability

A 100 per cent balanced flow in mould results in 100 per cent perfect mouldability. If say 60 per cent balanced flow part will definitely have some area overpacked while filling unbalanced region of part. Overpacked parts have quality problems like-dimensional inaccuracy, unequal shrinkage, distortion while ejection, moulded-in stresses resulting failure due to environmental stress cracking. Since overpacked parts have quality problems, part designer should try to achieve balanced flow by using flow leader/flow deflector in the part design. It should be noted that all these major operational problems-requiring frequent alteration of process parameters on machine-have their roots in :

1. Unbalanced melt flow causing overpacked regions.
2. Unbalanced heat exchange in mould resulting in erratic quality problems related to dimensional accuracy and warpage.

Therefore, obviously if these factors are considered while freezing part design and mould design, then we can have moulds which once set on the machine will keep on producing quality parts without any intervention of supervisor or operator.

In fact production shop supervisor should be more busy with statistics of production and SQC than frequent adjustment machine settings. Therefore, it is a challenge for practicing engineers to design plastic parts, keeping in mind the:

1. Functional requirement and strength of material, creep behaviour and other characteristics of material.

2. Flow-behaviour of plastic melt while flowing and freezing resulting in moulded-in stress and weld lines-which causes failure of part in service.
3. Shrinkage behaviour during processing and thereafter resulting in warpage and dimensional variation and dimensional inconsistency in moulded part.

Keeping in mind the flow and shrinkage behaviour of plastic melt the mould has to be designed to ensure:

1. Balanced and uniform melt flow by selecting right size of runner system and type/number of gates, balancing melt flow by flow leader flow deflector.
2. Uniform mould surface temperature to take care of warpage and non-uniform shrinkage. This has to be done by designing cooling system so that heat flowing in and flowing out of mould, after the desired mould surface temperature is reached, is balanced.
3. Adequate ejection mechanism.
4. More than adequate thickness of mould plates. Cost increase on account of increase in mould plate thickness is negligible. This ensures, safety of mould and improved life of mould.

The injection mould can be considered good only if it produces consistently excellent parts without any quality problems as well as processing problems at an economic cycle time on long production run. Mould plays the highest and most important role in producing good quality parts.

Mould design and manufacturing technology has gone through many changes in the seventies and eighties from designing simple moulds with spurs and runners, moulding polypropylene and polyethylene to the present complex moulds incorporating runnerless moulding systems to produce parts from expensive engineering plastics for the automotive electronic and industrial markets.

Highest level of economic productivity with very high level of quality can be achieved when solution for all the possible quality problems are considered while designing the part and mould. This means, establishing the quality at the part design stage through the integration of Design for Functionality (OFF) and Design for Manufacturability (DFM). The possibility of achieving this objectivity is certainly a function of the knowledge of the technological process and experience knowledge database. This is possible with the help of CAE software programmes like Mouldflow.

11

Injection Moulding of Thermosets

INTRODUCTION

In the mid-1960s, about two years after the introduction of automatic transfer moulding machines and screw-preplasticising/transfer moulding machines, the concept of in-line screw injection moulding of thermosets (sometimes referred to as direct screw transfer or DST) was developed. It has long been thought that this process, already highly successful with thermoplastic materials, would be impractical for thermosetting plastics because the critical time temperature relationship would prove uncontrollable, and material would set up in the barrel. Development progressed not only on screw and barrel designs but also on stability of thermoset materials at elevated temperatures, finally leading to successful processing by screw injection moulding.

Screw type injection moulding machine is shown in Fig. 11.1 and plunger type injection moulding machine is shown in Fig. 11.2. This technique has had a significant influence on the thermoset moulding business by virtue of reduced moulding cycle time and the potential it offers for low-cost, high-volume production of moulded thermoset parts. Today, thermoset injection moulding machines are available in all clamp tonnages up to 1200 tons and shot sizes up to 20 lb.

Thermoset in-line screw assemblies are fitted to horizontal or vertical clamp machines. Most horizontal clamp thermoplastic injection machines can be converted to injection of thermoset by changing the screw, barrel, and nozzle. Because most thermoset barrels are shorter than their thermoplastic counterpart, it may be necessary to reposition the injection assembly closer to the clamp fixed platen.

The thermoset moulding materials developed specifically for injection moulding have a long shelflife in the barrel at moderate temperatures (approximately 200° F), and react very rapidly when the temperature is brought up to 350 to 400° F as the material is forced through the sprue, runners, and gates, and fills the cavities. This unique development in materials helped to gain acceptance of injection moulding as a reliable production process.

Thermosets are injection-moulded without premature curing by suitable control of heat and pressure and the use of thermosetting resins suited to the process. Plasticating screws are used. Back pressure must be controlled to prevent excessive wear of the screw by the abrasive filler materials common in thermosets. The injection process is basically faster for thermosets than for thermoplastics, especially for thick sections, because the thermosetting plastic cures more rapidly than the thermoplastic can cool in the mould. Other advantages of the thermosets in injection moulding are their lower price and their ability to be moulded in thick sections.

PROCESS OPERATIONS

A typical arrangement for in-line screw injection moulding of thermosets is shown in Fig. 11.1. The machine consists of two sections mounted on a common base. One section clamps and holds the mould halves together under pressure during the injection of material into the mould. The other section—the plasticising and injection unit-includes the feed hopper, the hydraulic cylinder which forces the screw forward to inject the material into the mould, a motor to rotate the screw, and the heated barrel which encloses the screw.

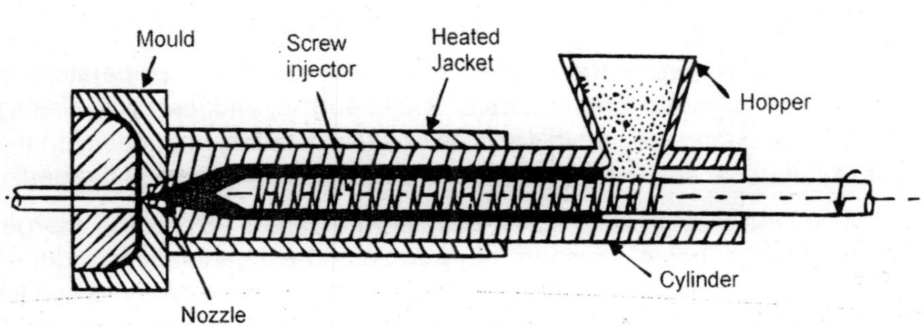

Fig. 11.1 A screw type injection moulding machine.

Basically, the injection-moulding press, whether for thermosets or for thermoplastics, is the same, utilising the reciprocating screw to plasticate the material charge. In most injection moulding of thermosets, the material, in granular or pellet form, is fed from the hopper by gravity into the feed throat of the barrel. It is then moved forward by the action of the flights of the screw. As it passes through the barrel, the plastic picks up conductive heat from the heating element on the barrel and frictional heat from the rotation of the screw.

For thermoset materials, the depth of flights of the screw at the feed-zone end is normally the same as the depth of flight at the nozzle end; this is a 1 : 1 compression ratio screw. This compression ratio is the major difference between thermoset and thermoplastic moulding machines-the latter having compression ratios such that the depth of tlight at the feed end is 1½ to 5 times that at the nozzle end, giving compression rations of 3 : 1 to 5 : 1.

As the material moves forward in the barrel, it changes from a granular to a semiviscous consistency, and it forces the screw backward in the barrel against a preset hydraulic pressure. This back pressure is an important processing variable. The screw stops turning when the proper amount of material has reached the nozzle end of the barrel, as sensed by a vernierset limit switch, This material at the nozzle end-the charge-is the exact volume of material required to fill the sprue, runners, and cavities of the mould.

The heated and plasticated slug of material at the front or nozzle end of the barrel is moderately stable for perhaps a minute or more-enough retention time for the mould to complete closing and the machine to be in the high-pressure clamp mode.

The screw is then moved forward at rapid speeds (up to 2000 inches per minute) by hydraulic pressure (up to 20,000 psi) on the plastic. The hot plastic melt is forced through the nozzle of the barrel, through the sprue of the mould, and into the runner system, gates, and mould cavities.

The temperature of the material rises from the barrel temperature of about 200°F to mould temperature of 350 to 400° F, and fast cross-linking takes place, curing the part in seconds or a few minutes, depending on the mass of material and the maximum cross-sectional thickness of the part.

When the reciprocating screw has delivered about 95% of the charge, the injection or "boost" pressure of up to 20,000 psi generally is reduced automatically to about half that value for completion of the cavity fill and for holding during cure. This secondary pressure generally is termed the "hold" pressure. Following cure, the mould opens automatically, parts are ejected, and the mould closes.

At a carefully selected time during the cycle, the plasticating process in the barrel is initiated and timed to be complete by the time that the mould is fully closed again. The moulding cycle repeats automatically.

In the process, the granular plastic is fed directly into the barrel of the press, and no external auxiliary performing or preheating equipment is required. Despite this, the temperature of the material entering the mould is higher and more uniform than that in other thermoset mould techniques because of the homogenising effect of the screw upon the plastic.

Most barrels are covered with a metal jacket designed to permit heated water to flow across and around the barrel. The water or temperature-controlled fluid not only assists in heating the thermoset material as it moves along the flight of the screw but helps prevent over heating, as the fluid will withdraw excessive internal heat should it occur because of excessive screw rpm or back pressure.

Screw check valves or sleeves, which are standard for thermoplastics (except for heat-sensitive material such as PVC), are not used with thermosets. They provide restrictions to even flow of high viscosity materials, and eventually cause the material to set up in the valves or sleeves. Some material slippage or back flow along flights of the screw does occur when the injection pressure approaches maximum. Because of this slippage, the full slug of plasticated material does not reach the cavities.

Therefore, one should not attempt to use the maximum rated shot capacity of the machine. A rule of thumb for most. materials and machines is to use up to 80% of rated capacity.

Nozzles at the end of the barrel usually are water-cooled or temperature-controlled to maintain a proper balance between a hot mould (350-400° F), and a relatively cool barrel (150-200° F).

PROCESS AND DESIGN CONSIDERATIONS

Thermoset moulding resins require curing by a chemical reaction, or polymerisation. Thus, the closer to the curing temperature the material is when it fills the cavity, the shorter will be the in-cavity cycle time. The direct screw injection process substantially reduces cure time from that of other thermoset processes, particularly for parts having 1/8 inch wall section or greater. Cycle-time reductions on the order of 20 to 30% are common; even greater reductions have been reported.

Moulding a thermoset material on an injection moulding machine involves approximately the same cost factories as moulding a thermoplastic material. Machinery costs, plant space requirements, and labour costs are about the same. Therefore, the cost that makes the differences are the basic material price and the cycle time required.

Materials

Most materials are slightly modified from conventional thermoset compounds. These modifications are required to provide the working time/temperature relationship needed for screw plasticating. Additionally, material formulations may be altered according to the geometry of the part being moulded. The new compounds are priced approximately the same as conventional materials.

Although all thermosetting materials have been moulded by this technique, the most commonly used materials are the phenolics as these materials were the first to be injection-moulded. Other thermoset materials being moulded by the process include melamine, urea, polyester, alkyd, diallyl phthalate (DAP), polyurethane, and alloys such as phenolic melamine and phenolic epoxy.

A wide variety of fillers can be used to achieve the properties required in the finished produce. Except in a few special cases, the choice of filler is of greater significance in end product properties than in the method by which the product is moulded.

The introduction of dust-free phenolic in pellet form brought additional advantages to injection moulding. The dust-free material eliminated the former

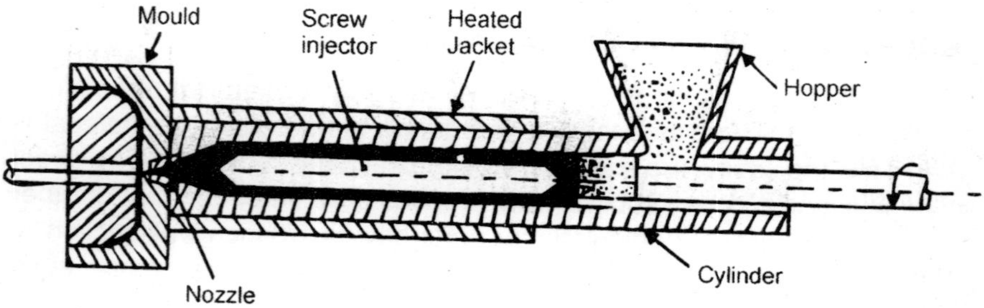

Fig. 11.2 A Plunger type injection moulding machine.

need for separate moulding areas and equipment for phenolics. Now these materials can be moulded side by side with a thermoplastic operation, with minimum danger of contamination. If fact, with a change of the barrel and screw, the same machine often can be used for both materials.

Applications particularly suited for the process are automotive power brake, transmission, and electrical parts; wet/dry applications such as in stream irons, washer pumps, and moisture vaporizers; and communications and electrical distribution parts that require dimensional stability and electrical insulation (Fig 11.2).

Process Effects on Design

Proper design of injection-moulded thermoset parts requires an understanding of the flow characteristics of material within the mould. These characteristics affect some properties of the finished parts, and they vary somewhat with the different materials. In that they have a flow pattern, such parts are more similar to transfer moulded parts than to compression-moulded parts.

Shrinkage, in most parts, occurs slightly more in the direction of flow than in the transverse direction. This difference is caused by the orientation of the filler (almost all thermoset compounds contain a filler) as the compound flows through the gate and into the cavity. Such shrinkage is particularly evident in edge-gated parts. To minimize the flow effect, centre gating, which distributes the material more evenly, is recommended where optimum shrinkage control is required, such as in moulding a round piece within dimensional tolerance. Technology is now well advanced in the use of warm runner moulds (equivalent to hot-runner moulds used with thermoplastics), which, when used with center gating, provide a substantial reduction in material consumed in the sprue and runner-a cost saving over conventional thermoset moulding.

The flatness required in the finished moulded part is another design parameter affected by process capabilities. Long, narrow parts that have to be flat may be difficult to mould because of the variation in shrinkage. Similarly, a non-uniform wall section may warp as a result of non-uniform shrinkage. The choice of gate location sometimes can compensate for such conditions; close cooperation with the mould designer is recommended at this stage. The surface finish on moulded parts also differs from that of traditionally moulded thermosets. The greater the distance of material flow required, the more likely it is that flow marks will occur. Avoiding large, flat, polished areas helps reduce rejects and keeps moulding costs down. Here, too, gate location is a factor. If large, flat areas are necessary, such areas can be textured or patterned to mask slight irregularities. A rough surface texture generally is not desirable, however, because it may cause sticking in the mould cavity.

Gates used for thermoset injection moulding usually are smaller than those needed for transfer moulding. This difference provides several advantages. A smaller gate gives a cleaner gate break that requires little or no hand finishing. A gate can be placed in an area where previously the appearance of a larger gate mark would have been objectionable. A small gate also contributes to faster cure cycles because it increases frictional heat within the moulding compound during filling. However, the impact properties of compounds containing long-fibre reinforcement degrade when the material passes through a small gate. When such materials are specified, close cooperation between the material supplier and the moulder is necessary. Other physical properties such as tensile and flexural strength can also be controlled by gate geometry.

Injection-Compression Moulding

To minimise fibre Orientation, and thereby improve the impact strength of injection-moulded fibrous compounds, the conventional injection moulding process is often modified to allow the mould to remain slightly open-perhaps ¼ inch during cavity fill. When the cavity is essentially full, the mould is closed and held under full clamp pressure until cure is completed. In this process, the final mould closing acts like compression moulding, permitting the fibres to shift from a longitudinal flow orientation to a more random orientation. The design and construction of the mould must be such that is prevents escape of the injected material to mould parting surfaces during the cavity-filling step. Frontal flanges are incrorporated to effectively close off the cavity when the mould is partially closed. The injection-compression process often reduces the clamping force required, as compared to conventional injection moulding.

Part-Design Considerations

As in most other moulding processes, wall-section uniformity is important. Moulding cycles, and therefore costs, depend upon the cure time of the thickest section. Therefore, cross sections should be as uniform as design parameters allow, with a minimum wall thickness of 1/16 inch. A good working average for wall thickness is 1/8 to 3/16 inch. Nevertheless, as part requirements dictate, heavy walls favour the use of thermosets because the cure rate of thermosetting material is consIderably faster than the cooling rate of thermoplastics. A rule of thumb for estimating cycle times for a 1/4 inch wall section is 45 seconds for thermoplastics and 30 seconds for thermosets, when injection moulding is,used.

Generous radii and fillets are recommended, as in other plastic processes, for maximum strength. Most plastic materials are somewhat notch-sensitive, also avoiding sharp corners is important. Generous fillets are less likely to cause sink marks in the low-shrinkage thermoset material than they are in some of the thermoplastics, so more freedom is available in the use *of* reinforcing fillets. .

Draft to allow the release of the moulded part from the cavity and force plug (core) should be at least 1/4° per side; greater draft is preferred if possible. Because the injection method is automatic, ease of mould release is essential for rapid ejection with minimum distortion of the part. Provision should be made in the part for the placement of ejector pins for this purpose. The use of knockout pins as large as -possible (at least 1/8 inch in diameter)' consistent with part design and aesthetic considerations will provide trouble-free processing, which ultimately is reflected lower costs.

Venting of gases from the cavity must be done in the short time available during the filling of the cavity. The most effective vent is the parting line of the mould; so try to visualise the material flow from the gate to the most distant point of the part where the gases will collect. If this point is on a mould parting line, then the part is well designed for venting. Avoid long, lead-end corridors of flow and trapped wall sections that prevent venting. Vacuum venting is readily adapted to injection moulding when complex shapes cannot be adequately vented from the parting line.

Moulded-in inserts commonly are used with thermosetting materials. However, because the injection process is automatic, the use of post-assembled inserts rather than moulded-in inserts is recommended. Moulded-in inserts require holding the mould open each cycle to place the inserts. A delay in manual placement destroys the advantage of uniformity and consistency of the automatic cycle, affecting both production and quality.

Tolerances of parts moulded by the injection method are comparable to those produced by compression and transfer methods. Tolerances have been held as low as ± 0.001 in./in., but ordinarily, tolerances of ± 0.003 to 0.005 in./in. are economically practical for production.

All mould techniques and variations such as cams and movable die sections used in other forms of moulding are adaptable to thermoset injection moulding. Therefore, parts can include such features as moulded-in side holes, threads, and undercuts. These refinements increase mould cost, of course, so the decision of how many refinements to build into a mould is usually an economics problem rather than a technical one.

COLD RUNNER MOULDING

Standard injection moulds for thermoset materials are very similar to standard mould designs for thermoplastics. Because one cannot grind and reuse the thermoset runner system, there is always interest in reducing the amount of material in a runner system required to produce parts on a production basis.

Toward this end, moulds, may be designed to maintain thermoset material in a plastic state in the runner without ejecting it from the mould. This cold runner technique is not too different from "hot runner" thermoplastic mould designs, except that heated water is used to maintain a "runner" temperature of between 150 and 210° F, and cartridge heaters are used to maintain proper cavity and force temperatures for curing. This type of mould is known as a "cold runner" thermoset mould, or sometimes 'warm runner" mould. Parts may be separated from the runners right at the part surface; or short sub runners may be ejected with the parts, leaving most of the runner material in the warm manifold, to be used in the next shot.

A multicavity standard injection mould for small thermoset parts may have 50 to 150% runner or waste material. Using a cold runner mould, this waste can be reduced to as little as 10% of the shot.

INJECTION MOULDING REINFORCED POLYESTERS

A popular material increasingly used in thermoset injection moulding is polyester reinforced with glass or other fibres. This material generally is referred to as bulk moulding compound (BMC) and as dough moulding compound (DMC). Because it is doughlike in consistency at room temperature, it does not feed from a hopper but requires a special stuffing mechanism on the injection machine for automatic moulding.

Although BMC often is moulded by using a conventional reciprocating screw, many BMC injection machines use a simple plunger to force the material from the barrel to the mould. The plunger is used to lessen shear degradation of the fibres as well as to prevent back slippage of material during the injection and hold part of the cycle.

The stuffer mechanism includes a loading chamber, which is generally manually loaded with up to several hundred pounds of compounds. The stuffer chamber has a large-diameter piston, air-or hydraulically driven, to force the room temperature material into the injection barrel upstream of the reciprocating screw or downstream of the plunger, depending on which injection method is used.

Because the BMC is already plasticised at room temperature, it needs a minimum of heating in the barrel and relatively low pressures, 6000 to 10,000 psi, for rapid injection. Also, because BMC reaches the moulder from the supplier in a fully homogenized state, no mixing in the barrel is necessary.

Injection Moulding Presses

There are a number of injections moulding presses specifically designed to handle thermoset polyester operations. All require stuffing cylinders because of the physical characteristics of the material. Most FRP is puttylike (BMC) or a fibrelike coated material, neither of which flows freely through normal hopper systems (Fig. 11.3).

On some machines the material or compound is forced from the stuffer cylinder form the top or side into the rear of a conventional screw injection cylinder. The screw acts only as a conveyor that moves the material to the front of the cylinder instead of providing a plasticating function. Then, the screw acts as a plunger. It does not turn as it pushes the material into the mould.

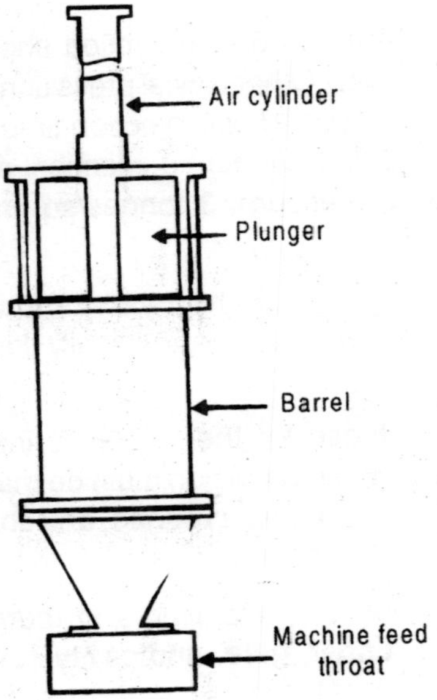

Fig. 11.3 Sketch of material stuffer for BMC materials. The stuffer usually consists of a cylinder with a plunger that maintains pressure against the polyester material while the screw is rotating. When the stuffer cylinder is nearly empty, the plunger is withdrawn and additional material is deposited into the stuffer.

On other machines a plunger instead of a screw pushes the material into the mould. This type densifies material as it pushes it into the mould cavities. Screws and plungers can be interchanged within the same machine frame, requiring only changes in electricals. Another type is the coaxial plunger machine. Material is dropped into a stuffer cylinder in line with a smaller cylinder that pushes the material into the mould. Advantages claimed for this structure include the short distance that the material has to flow. Angles and corners around which the material must move have been eliminated.

Regardless of their basic design, machines should be capable of accurately controlling temperatures and pressure throughout the moulding cycling with as little glass degradation as possible.

Temperature Control

The object of controlling temperatures is to warm the material in the barrel enough to permit free flow to preheat it as it goes though the nozzle and runners, and to cure it as fast as possible after it has stopped flowing in the cavity. Because of the temperature sensitivity of thermoset materials, control is very critical. Typical settings are; rear zone of barrel, 125° F, front zone, 150°F; cold runner, 175°F; and both halves of the mould, 335°F. As a practical limit, material coming out of the nozzle should not be more than 200°F. The mould temperatures .for most materials are between 300 and 400°F.

Experience shows that the cure time of a 1/8 inch section should be within 15 to 45 seconds, depending on part size. Other typical press conditions are screw rpm, 20 to 75; back pressure up to 100 psi; injection time 1 to 5 seconds; injection pressures, 5000 to 20,000 psi during injection, and as little as half that during cure; and clamp pressure, 3 tonnes/sq. in max. (based on cavity projected area).

Besides presses specifically designed for thermoset moulding, conversion kits also are available to change over machines originally designed for thermoplastic operations.

Tooling requirements are similar to those for thermoplastic injection moulding. The major difference is that adequate provision must be made for heating the moulds. Moulds should be fully hardened, polished, and chrome-plated. Tool steels such as AISI HI3 are recommended.

Another significant difference between thermoplastic and thermoset injecting moulds is the need for harder runner, gate, and cavity surfaces because of the extreme abrasiveness of most thermoset materials. Typical hardnesses are 56 to 58 Rock well C, and such surfaces are often hard-chrome-plated for further resistance to wear.

The low-shrinkage characteristic of BMC makes ejection of pieces more difficult than with thermoplastics. Liberal draft, where possible and provisions for positive ejection on both sides of the mould generally are required. Properly hardened moulds should wear well, but gate areas are susceptible to wear. Designing them as replaceable inserts makes their repair and replacement less costly.

Gates should be located so as to minimise effects of knit lines that form after material has flowed around an obstruction in the mould. Also, multiple gates should be avoided to reduce the number of knit lines that form where materials from gates join. Eliminating knit lines reduce chances of rejects. Larger area and short-length gates and runners give the strongest parts.

The mould should permit the material to flow so that it pushes air ahead of it into places where it can be vented out at parting lines or knockout pins. Vacuum extraction of air is another useful technique for venting. Sharp corners, restricted orifices, and gates that cause glass degradation should be avoided if possible.

Because low-shrink BMC can stick in conventional sprue bushings after curing, cold runners and spruce can be used. These elements can be oriented in different ways, but in all cases they are watercooled to somewhat below mould temperatures. A typical temperature for them is about 175°F. Thus the material actually gets a useful amount of preheating in the "cold runner". Runners should have relatively large diameters to provide for easier material flow and less degradation. Center gated. three plate mould should be considered for parts requiring maximum impact strength if cold runners are not used. Problems of flashing common to compression moulding do not occur with properly designed and maintained injection moulds. The little flash that occurs is paper-thin and easily removed.

12

Injection Moulding Machine

Injection moulding is regarded as total technology covering materials, moulds, moulding machineries, peripheral equipments and moulding technology. Modern moulding technology covers all the above aspects required to achieve:

1. Better dimensional accuracy, precision quiet running and cleanliness, stability and surface finish deal for the production of medical electronic components.
2. Saving in raw material consumption, reduction in rejects and waste, through on line SPC system.
3. Total energy consumption by use of variable speed volume pumps in barrel heating, screw drive and transfer movement is reduced by 20 per cent.
4. Better and accurate controls on various parameters and fully automatic operations.

The introduction of solid state controls made it easier to use digital setting and reading of process parameters such as pressures, speeds, timers and temperatures. This resulted in cutting down of the setting time as well as start up time, reducing wastage and increasing production. Subsequent to the solid state techniques, followed the introduction of microprocessors. The microprocessors were first introduced as an optional arrangement till the time when an Italian company sold injection moulding machines with microprocessors as standard. This step could be described as the concept of the 80's in that the injection moulding falling out of the bottom. The integrated process includes multicolours, barrel changing standard robotic programme, automatic mould changing etc., all becoming an essential facility in the middle of a machining centre.

One of the developments is the integration of a robot operated withdrawal system. An eight axis, preprogrammable electric motor driven robot takes the product to an inspection station. Here the video camera inspection techniques previously noted are used, and the result on pass and fail enables the correct storing in bins of products; the control-system of the machine forms an external network of the production.

Here then is the complete chain. The polymer is fed from off-site material storage stations; processed; the product inspected; the production distributed, and the rest of the production network informed of the local loop of events.

Klockner feromatik has developed the machine that can mould different parts with different shot weights of single giant moulding from injection moulding machines having locking force upto 40,000 KN force.

Negri Bossi has developed canbino machines that range from 400KN to 4800KN injection moulding machines. The machines may be the first to fully implement canbus for routing signals to the central control, instead of using direct wiring. The system simplifies controls, enables the use of self microprocessors to reduced wiring and using digital signals, that are less prone to interference than analog.

Many other companies developed the shifting of partial use of Canbus. Some offer digital signal transmission but direct wiring, and many expect it to gain popularity. This is the main advantage one can best exploit on large machines, which have hundreds of metres of cables. While others are waiting for signal sampling intervals to rise from current 500 micro second time.

The newer precision injection compression moulding process gives the advantage of improved dimensional activities upto + 01 -5 micron. The parts required no machining and the dimension quoted has been achieved without further finishing. The inherent advantage of the process are total automation, shorter curing time, and the possibility to mould directly from powder and a better finish without excessive deflashing.

A tiebarless system has developed from last some years. The main benefits of tiebarless systems are space and freedom at mould loading and unloading and there are no limitation at mould dimensions. Many moulds can be worked on easily while the robots have it easier in their work place by using tiebarless machine. So the machine platen is fully usable. Its prime benefit is that it can produce large parts with limited transfer.

The following are the areas where maximum work is done to improve machinery at various stages to manufacture more competent product to cater the demand from various fields.

1. The wider use of SPQC system is to cut the percentage of rejection and improve efficiency of machine and post moulding automation to speed up the production rate to achieve better dimensional accuracy. .
2. Machine design adopted to provide longer mould strokes for robot entry. It is better to provide separate robot control system.
3. Machine builders are trying to offer machine with at least 16 bit, 32 bit and more bits to control auxiliary. In the hydraulic system to reduce the requirement of oil as per the size of reservoir.
4. To change barrel automatically.
5. High aberration resistance screws and cylinders to process the typical compounded materials and then inject this material into the cavity at up to 100 MPA pressure.
6. Machine with quick and simple changing filter elements for the removal of foreign bodies from the polymer melt flow without detrimental effects on the process and therefore the product quality.

Thus the injection moulding machines have passed through the technology tunnel to regain their industrial importance. Twin screw injection unit is used in injection moulding process. The main purpose of twin screw is to make a compounding for raw materials and filler. (i.e., $CaCO_3$) and directly inject in closed mould. This process is generally used for producing garden chair armrests.

Injection moulding machines in software developments are also helping to make smart machines like demonstrating a self-learned machine. In this machine there is a trouble shooting facility in running production and mould flow with quick machine setup. Advantages of this development are being more precise control and cancelling of machine difference (i.e. the melt is transferred with minimum pressure losses).

An alternate arrangement to "push pull" injection moulding machine is twin piston arrangement. It is now integrated with hot runner system on the fixed platen. The original version is still available and is attached to the end of the injection unit, and require significant modification to the unit if it does not have long enough stroke. The new version adds around 25 mm to the thickness of hot runner manifold. The melt stream divides in two streams that enter the mould cavity through separate gates. Pressure in each stream is controlled by dedicated pistons. During the hold on pressure phase the piston oscillates in or out of phase, to orient the melt as it cools and thus improves part strength, as well as remove weld lines and prevent voids and sink marks. Tensile property can be improved by over 100 per cent.

Co-injection Moulding

Co-injection moulding or sandwich moulding as it is sometimes called, is a process that permits injection moulding of parts with a skin of one thermoplastic and a core of another compatible thermoplastic. Co-injection moulding has found application primarily as an advanced structural foam technique. Most commonly, the skin material is solid, while the core material contains a blowing agent, but any combination of foamed and/or unfoamed skin/core resins is possible.

For heavy walled parts, coating time may be substantially reduced by running skin resin at a higher melt temperature for a smooth surface and the core resin, which essentially determines cycle time, at a lower melt temperature.

Process

The co-injection moulding process has undergone three stages of development: single-channel technique (the last-named is a Battenfeld patent).

With the single channel technique, the two resins are injected into the mould sequentially by shifting a valve from one position to another. Due to the flow characteristics of the melt and because the skin resin tends to adhere to the cooler mould surface, a dense, solid skin is formed. Thickness of the skin can be influenced by varying the injection rate, melt temperature, mould temperature and flow compatibility of the two resins. A major disadvantage of the single channel technique is that under conditions necessary for thin, dense skin, the skin in the gate area may become extremely thin, or even may be flushed away completely. In addition, the shifting action in the nozzle may cause objectionable surface blemishes.

With the two-and three-channel techniques, sequential or simultaneous injection of both skin and core resins is possible as required, to achieve acceptable parts. This permits control of the wall thickness of the compact skin, especially in the gate areas on both sides of the part. The more sophisticated control, such as injection velocity profiling, available with these latter techniques permit greater control over part properties and surface appearance. The three-channel technique offers an advantage when the part to be moulded can be centre-gated, and trials have determined that the three channel technique is necessary to mould satisfactory parts. For multi-cavity moulds, the two-channel technique is preferred, since material and colour changes may be conducted much faster due to the less complex nozzle.

Machines are available with programmable controls, vented barrels, and the capabilities for co-injection, co-injection combined with the gas counter pressure process, and co-injection combined with the retractable core process.

Equipment

Co-injection moulding machines generally are offered with a reciprocating screw system. The reciprocating screw system offers the advantage that temperature sensitive resins can be processed more gently and that material and colour changes are quicker. Use of closed loop process control provides for injection velocity profiling, and thus extremely accurate control of the injection rate on a programmed basis. This programmable injection rate allows matching of the two melt flows to eliminate defects on the part surface. Where surface quality is unimportant, low-pressure injection moulding machines may be employed when processing easy-flowing resins. For more complex and thin walled parts of high viscosity melts, clamping forces must be close to those of conventional injection machines, particularly when a high quality surface is desired.

An advantage of co-injection moulding machinery is its versatility. Processes which find application include single component low pressure structural foam moulding, single component injection moulding, two component injection moulding, two-component structural foam moulding (Sandwich moulding with solid skin and core). Co-injection moulding (sandwich moulding with solid skin and foam core) and marbleizing.

Reaction Injection Moulding (RIM)

Reaction injection moulding is a process in which two or more liquid intermediates are metered separately to a mixing head where they are combined by high-pressure impingement mixing and subsequently flow into a mould where they polymerise to form a moulded part. Although automotive front and rear end components comprise the largest market, a wide variety of other applications are growing rapidly. Advantages that are inherent in RIM fall into three general categories: low pressure, low-temperatures and the use of reactive liquid intermediates.

Low pressures

Although the pressures in the mixing head are as high as 3500 p.s.i the in-mould pressures are significantly lower than in other moulding processes. When comparing a typical RIM in mould pressure of 50 p.s.i with the 5000 p.s.i or more required for thermoplastic injection moulding, it becomes apparent why RIM is particularly suitable for larger parts. Automotive bumpers are routinely produced on RIM presses with 100 to 150 tonnes of clamping force, while comparable injection moulded parts require presses of 3500 tonnes or more.

Low temperature

The temperatures used in RIM are also significantly lower. With polyurethane, the intermediates normally are processed at temperatures between 75 and 120°F and the mould is usually between 130 and 170°F. These lower temperatures obviously require significantly less energy consumption.

Liquid Intermediates

The use of liquid intermediates has additional benefits beyond the low pressures and temperatures involved. A tremendous amount of design flexibility is possible with RIM. Since the mould is filled with low viscosity liquid, very complex part configurations can be produced. Ribs, mounting bosses, slots and cut-out areas are all possible. RIM parts are being moulded with wall sections as thin as 0.1 inch and as thick as 1.5 inch. Furthermore, mouldings can incorporate variations in thickness within the same part. Incorporation of inserts for mounting or reinforcements is also possible. Since the mould is filled before polymerisation occurs, there are no moulded in stresses to cause part warping or cracking after demould.

The relative case of compounding liquid formulation allows a great deal of flexibility in fine tuning the material to the requirements of the part. By changing variables such as filler type and level, blowing agent concentration, pigment and catalyst the properties of the material can be optimised for the specific application.

Equipment

Processing equipment consists of the material conditioning system, high-pressure metering system, mix head, and mould carrier system.

Material conditioning system

Since the RIM process involves a chemical reaction in the mould after the intermediates have been mixed, if consistent parts are to be produced it is necessary that the material delivered to the mix head be consistent from shot to shot. The material conditioning system is designed to ensure such consistency. It typically includes tanks to hold the intermediates, agitators to ensure that the material in the tanks is of homogeneous temperature, and a nucleation control system that keeps the level of dissolved gases in the polyol component at the desired level. The tanks can range in size from 15 to 150 gal. or larger depending on the consumption rate. Jackets on the tanks as well as heat exchangers on circulating loops are used for temperature control.

Metering system

The metering system takes the conditioned intermediates from the supply tanks and delivers them to the mixing head at the desired rate and pressure. There are two basic types of metering system; high pressure axial or radial piston pumps, and lance displacement cylinders. The piston pumps are hydraulic pumps that have been modified to handle chemicals. They are capable of continuously metering at pressures up to 3500 psi. Lance pistons, which are driven by a separate hydraulic pump, displace the reactants from a high pressure metering cylinder. In addition to more precise metering, they have the capability of processing filled systems.

Mixing head

The mixing head contains a cylindrical chamber where the intermediates are mixed by direct impingement at pressure ranging from 1500 to 3500 psi. It also contains a cylindrical cleaning piston which after the shot is complete, moves forward to wipe the remaining materials out of the mixing chamber. In addition, there is a revolving mechanism to shift the material flow between recirculation back to the tank and flow into the mixing chamber. This allows the circulating materials to reach an equilibrium at the proper temperature, pressure, and flow rate before shifting in to the mixing position.

Mould carrier

The mould carrier holds the tool in the proper orientation for moulding, provides enough clamping force to overcome the in-mould pressure, opens and closes the mould, and position the open mould in an accessible possible for demoulding, cleaning, and preparing it for the next shot.

Tooling

Since the in-mould pressures in RIM are generally relatively low (25 to 100 psi), a variety of tooling constructions have been used. These include machined steel or aluminium, cast aluminium or kirksite, sprayed metal or electroplated shells, and filled epoxy. Although some of these constructions are relatively inexpensive when compared with other large-volume production tooling, it should be remembered that the low viscosity liquid that fills the mould will duplicate exactly the surface of the tool. Consequently, when good surface characteristics and high tolerances are required, machined tooling has generally been the chosen route, particularly for high-volume production rush. The ability to use less costly tooling methods for prototype and for short tuns, however, remains a significant advantage of the RIM process.

13

Design for Injection Moulds

INTRODUCTION

The injection mould has two functions. It forms the air space into which the hot plasticised material is injected under pressure, and it acts as a heat exchanger, removing heat from the material in the mould until it is rigid enough to be ejected so that the final part will conform to all its specifications. The quality of the part and its cost of manufacture are largely dependent on mould design, construction, and excellence of workmanship.

Over the year, as the size of the moulding machine increased, so did the cost of moulds. The two critical areas in ensuring the right mould are the design of the piece and the design of the mould. An acceptable product is not possible with an incorrect part design. An acceptable part may be possible with an incorrect mould design, but always under extremely difficult and uneconomical conditions.

The last opportunity to change the design of the part occurs when the mould is being designed. It is imperative that the user, mouldmaker, moulder, part designer, quality control department, and packaging people be consulted before designing the mould. The design of the mould is usually done by the moulder and the mouldmaker. The selection of the method of gating, location of the gate, venting, parting line, and method of ejection effect the appearance and function of the part.

Mouldmakers vary from an individual owner with several helpers to plants with hundreds of employees. The quality of the mould bears no relation to the size of the shop. In selecting a mouldmaker, it is important to use one who has the best type of equipment for the job and who has had experience in building similar moulds. Surveys have shown that mouldmakers are leaving the industry about three times faster than they are being replaced. This situation has greatly increased the use of computer aided design and manufacturing (CAD/CAM) systems in mouldmaking.

The overriding consideration in mould design is to be completely confident that the mould will work. Unfortunately, mouldmaker selection often is done on the basis of initial price with no regard for the money that may have to be spent to get the mould to work correctly after it is delivered. Because of daily lost productivity of a bad mould versus a high-quality one, the lowest-priced mould has too often turned out to be the most expensive. If there are questions, they should be resolved before the mould is built, not afterward, as it is much easier to change a design on a piece of paper than to change a completed die. If, during the course of mould construction, questions of this kind arise, the work should be stopped and the problem resolved.

The injection mould normally is described by a variety of different criteria, including the following:

1. Number of cavities.
2. Material
   (a) Steel-hardened
   (b) Stainless steel
   (c) Prehardened steel
   (d) Hardened steel
   (e) Beryllium copper
   (f) Aluminium
   (g) Epoxy-steel
3. Surface finish.
   (a) Polish (using SPI nomenclature)
   (b) Chrome plate
   (c) Electroless nickel
   (d) EDM
   (e) Sandblast

(t) Photoetch

(g) Impingement

4. Parting line

(a) Regular

(b) Irregular

(c) Two-plate mould

(d) Three-plate mould

(e) Stack mould

5. Method of manufacture

(a) Machined

(b) Hobbled

(c) Gravity cast

(d) Pressure cast

(e) Electroplated

(f) EDM (spark erosion)

6. Runner system

(a) Hot runner

(b) Insulated runner

7. Gating

(a) Edge

(b) Restricted (pin point)

(c) Submarine

(d) Sprue

(e) Ring

(f) Diaphragm

(g) Tab

(h) Flash

(i) Fan

(j) Multiple

8. Ejection
   - (a) Knockout pins
   - (b) Stripper ring
   - (c) Stripper plate
   - (d) Unscrewing
   - (e) Cam
   - (f) Jiggler pins
   - (g) Removable insert
   - (h) Hydraulic core pull
   - (i) Pneumatic core pull

Following these criteria, a typical mould might be described as follows: a four-cavity, machined, hardened steel, chrome-plated, hot-runner, stripper-plate, tumbler mould.

MOULD DESIGN FEATURES

Two-Plate Mould

Fig. 13. 1 shows a two-plate mould that certainly has more than two plates. This is the common name for a mould with a single parting line. The parting line of a mould can best be defined as that surface where a mould separates to permit the ejection of plastic (either the moulded parts or gates and runners). The part being made in the mould shown in Fig. 13.1 is a shallow dish, edge-gated. The temperature control channels are in both the cavity and the core.

This arrangement is preferable to cooling the plate, as the boundary between the cavity or core and the plate has high thermal resistance and greatly lowers the rate of heat transfer. Note also the support pillars, which prevent the support plate from buckling under the pressure of the injecting material and the knockout bar, which is attached to the machine and is the actuator for the knockout plates. A sprue puller with a reverse taper is used.

Three-plate Mould

Suppose, for example, that one had to mould several cups or similar-shaped items in one mould. It would not be possible to gate them except at the top. Otherwise, venting problems would make it impossible to mould. One way to produce such parts is to use a three-plate mould.

To do this, a runner system is developed that received its material from the nozzle and distributes it through secondary nozzles to each individual part. In order to remove this runner, an extra plate is added, which, when separated, allows the runner to be removed. The runner is trapezoidal with a 7° per side taper and is cut the runner plate and moulds between it and the pin plate. The pin plate moves on its own leader pins and bushings to prevent binding.

After moulding, the mould opens up at parting line 1, breaking the gate while both the runner and the part are contained in steel. The mould then opens at parting line 2, a step that results in the ejection of the part; and if chains or latches attach the movable side to the A plate, the stationary side opens at parting line 3. The runner had been held flush against the pin plate by small undercut pins.

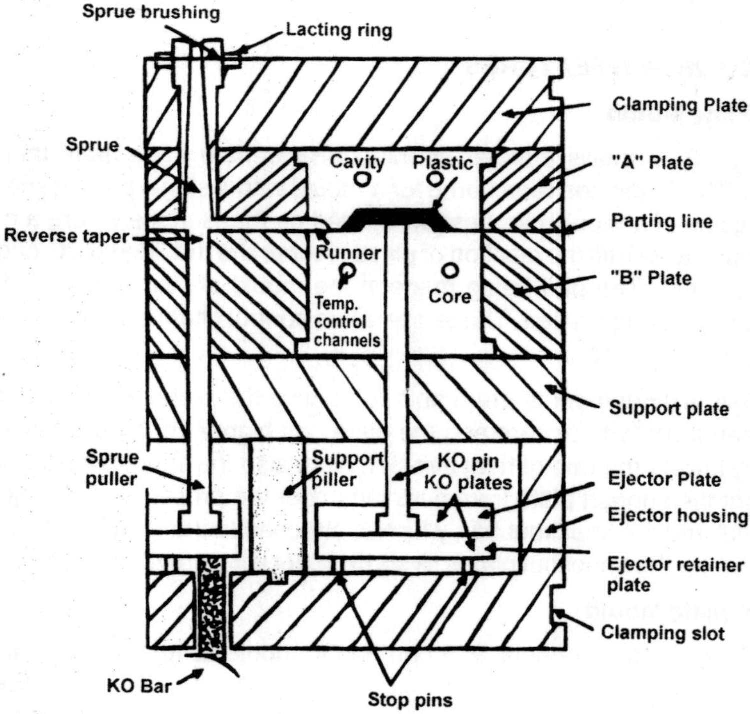

Fig. 13.1 Schematic drawing of a "two" plate mould

When the pin plate moves forward, these undercut pins remain stationary, and the runner moves forward, separating itself from them. The runner is mechanically ejected. Another way to move the A plate, without using chains or latches, is to attach air cylinders to both sides with the rods attached to the platens.

Hot Runner Moulds

In three-plate mould, the runner system must be reground and the material reused. However, it is possible to eliminate the runner system entirely by keeping the material fluid. This is done by using a hot runner mould (Fig. 13.2). The material is kept plasticised by the hot runner manifold, which is heated with electric cartridges. The block is thermostatically controlled, and heated probes, controlled by thermocouples and pyrometers, are used. The material is kept fluid at the proper temperature, and the injection pressure is transmitted through the hot runner manifold and gate into the part. A probe is inserted from the runner to the gate area. There are two kinds of probes: one has no moving parts and essentially depends on the insulating properties of

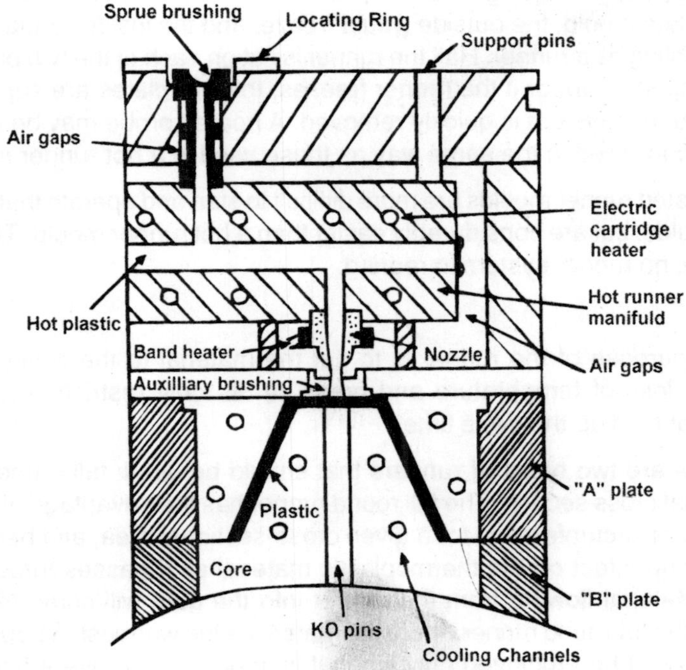

Fig. 13.2 Hot runner mould.

the plastic at the gate area to prevent it form drooling, whereas the other has a reciprocating device or other method to block the flow between each shot.

A hot runner mould is more difficult to start up than a three-plate mould. It takes considerably longer to become operational. In multicavity moulds, balancing the gate and the flow and preventing drooling can be difficult. The hot runner mould is highly susceptible to tramp metal, wood, paper, and other contaminants, which quickly clog up the nozzle. Various screen systems have been devised in attempts to prevent this. Cleaning out a plugged hot runner mould is a long process, and the moulds themselves are relatively expensive; but they offer the advantage that in a long-running job they provide the most economical way of moulding. There is no regrinding, with its cost of handling and loss of material. The mould runs automatically, eliminating the variations caused by operators. The loss of temperature and pressure experienced with a cold runner in a three plate mould is eliminated.

Insulated Runner Moulds

An insulated runner mould is a cross between a hot runner mould and a three-plate mould. If a large diameter runner, 2 inches or over, were used in a three-plate mould, the outside would freeze, and the inside would remain molten, acting as a runner. Half the runner is cut on each of the two plates so that during start-up, or if the runner freezes, the two plates are separated, and the runner system is quickly removed. A heated probe may be used. If it is, it is controlled in the same way as those used in a hot runner mould.

Insulated runner moulds are more difficult to start and operate than three-plate moulds, but are considerably easier than a hot runner mould. There is, of course, no runner system to regrind.

Runners

The purpose of the runner is to get the material to the cavity with a minimum loss of temperature and pressure. Its only restriction is that it should not hold up the cycle time.

There are two types of runners that should be used: full round and a trapezoidal cross section. The full round runner has the advantage of having the smallest circumference for a given cross-sectional area, and hence the least chilling effect on the thermoplastic material as it passes through the runner. Material flowing from the runner into the gate will come from the centre of the full round runner where the material is the warmest. A trapezoidal runner should be employed only when it is impossible to use a full round runner, or in a three-plate mould where the flat back is essential for automatic ejection. Trapezoidal runners have a taper of 7° per side, and standard cutlers are available for them. Under no condition should a half round runner be considered, as a trapezoidal shape is much superior to a half round.

Gates

The gate is the connection between the runner system and the moulded part. It must permit enough material to flow into the mould to fill out the part plus such additional material as is required to overcome the normal thermal shrinkage of the part. The location of the gate, its type, and its size strongly affect the moulding process and the physical properties of the moulded part.

There are two types of gates, (a) large and (b) restricted or pin pointed. Restricted gates usually are circular in cross section and for most material do not exceed 0.060 inch in diameter. The restricted gate is successful because the apparent viscosity of the plastic is a function of the shear rate. The faster it moves, the less viscous it becomes. As the material is forced through the small opening, its velocity increases, decreasing its viscosity. A second characteristic is high mixing, due to the Reynolds's effect. It is virtually impossible to mould a good variegated pattern without going through a large gate.

The size of the restricted gate is so small that when the flow ceases, the plastic solidifies, separating the moulded part from the runner system. Unless the cavity is completely filled before this happens, the part cannot be lacked and will be a reject. In multicavity moulds all parts must fill equally; if not, some cavities will receive more plastic than the others. This results in sticking, packing, and different-sized parts. The only way to overcome this problem is to short-shoot the shot and open individual gates carefully until all the parts fill equally.

An advantage of using the small gate is the ease of degating. In most instances, the parts are acceptable if they are cleanly broken from the runner. Also, the rapidity of gate sealing when the flow ceases tends to make it more difficult to pack the moulded part at the gate. This type of stress is a prime cause for failure. Unfortunately, this type of failure might not show up for a long time after moulding.

Fig. 13.3 shows various types of gating. A sprue gate feeds directly from the nozzle of the machine into the moulded part. It has the advantage of direct flow with minimum pressure loss. Disadvantages include the lack of a cold slug, the possibility of sinking around the gate, the high stress concentration around the gate area, and the need for gate removal. Most single cavity moulds are gated this way.

A diaphrag n gate has a sprue attached to a circular area that leads to the piece. In gating hollow tubes, flow considerations suggest the use of this type of gate. The part could be gated by a single, double, or quadruple runner coming from the sprue, but for runners, 90° apart, would give four flow or weld lines on the moulded part, which is often objectionable. Additionally, the diaphragm gate gets rid of stress concentration around the gate because the whole area is removed. The cleaning of a diaphragm gate is more difficult and time-consuming than cleaning of a sprue-gate. In some instances, gating internally in a hollow tube is not practical. Ring gates accomplish the same purpose from the outside.

The most common gate is the edge gate, where the part is gated by either a restricted or a larger gate on some point of the edge. This is an easy method from the point of view of mould construction. For many parts it is the only practical way to gate. When parts are large, or there is a special technical reason, the edge gate can be fanned out, making what is called a fan gate. If the flow pattern is required to orient in one direction, a flash gate may be used. Here the fan gate is extended to the full length of the piece but kept very thin, comparable to a piece of flash.

With some materials, gating directly the part can cause jetting or some other surface imperfection. To overcome this, a tab is extended from the part into which the gate is cut. The tab will have to be removed in a secondary operation. This approach is called tab gating.

A submarine gate goes through the steel of the cavity and forms an undercut (steel is in the way of direct plastic removal). When the mould opens the gate breaks, and the part sticks to the core. The submarine gate works because of the flexibility of the runner and judicious placement of the knockout pin. This is a highly desirable means of gating and is very often used in automatic moulds.

Venting

When plastic fills the mould, it displaces air. Unless the air is removed quickly, several things may happen. It may ignite, causing a characteristic burn. It may compress enough to restrict the flow to the point where the cavity cannot fill or will fill to a lesser extent. To remove the air from the cavity, slots are milled or ground, usually opposite the gate. The best way to find the proper vent location is to short shoot the mould and find out where the fronts of plastic meet. These slots normally vary from 0.00 I to 0.002 inch deep and from 3/8 to I inch wide. After the vents have been extended for Y:z inch, the depth is increased, usually to about 0.025 inch. The

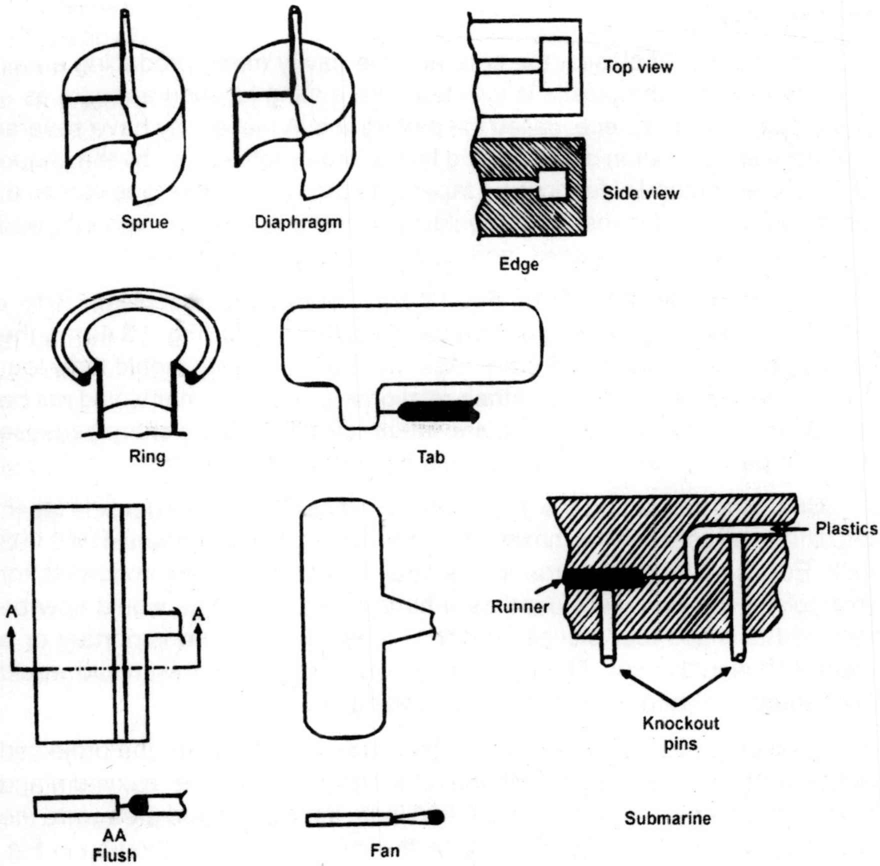

Fig. 13.3 Gating Designs

clearances between knockout pins and their holes also provide venting, though they usually cannot be relied upon. If more venting is needed, a flat can be found on the knockout pin. The gate location is directly related to venting. Often the gate cannot be located in certain places because that would make it impossible to vent the mould or prevent air entrapment. A typical example is the impossibility of gating a tumbler on the rim. The plastic would flow around the rim and then up toward the top, forcing the air into the upper part of the tumbler. No amount of vent pins or venting devices would successfully remove the air from that location because it is not on the parting line.

Parting Line

When a mould closes, the core and the cavity meet, producing an air space into which the plastic is injected. The mating junction appears as a line on the moulded piece, called the parting line. A piece may have several parting lines. Selection of the parting line is largely influenced by the shape of the piece, method of fabrication, tapers, method of ejection, type of mould, aesthetic considerations, post-moulding operations, inserts, venting, wall thickness, number of cavities, and location and type of gating.

A sample example follows: Fig. 13.4(a) shows a piece of plastic 3/16 x 1/2 x I inch. With the parting line on the 1/2 x I inch side (Fig. 13.4(b)), the projected area would be 0.5 sq. in. Assuming a four-cavity mould, only four cavities would be needed, and their relationship to each other would not be critical as the other side is a flat plate. Intersection R must be sharp because it is on a parting line, whereas, S could be round or sharp.

Changing the parting line (Fig. 13.4(c)) and assuming a 10 per side taper, the difference between the maximum and minimum dimension would be 0.003 inch. Edges on S could be round or sharp. This could be very important, for example, if the part were used as a handle. Eight cavities would now be required to make four pieces, and their location would be important or a mismatch would occur. The parts would look similar, but this mould would cost about one-third more than the preceding one.

If it were parted on the 3 /16 x ~ inch side (Fig. 13.4(d)), the projected area would be 0.093 sq. in., with the difference between the maximum and minimum dimensions of the sides 0.035 inch. If the projected area were the limitation to the number of cavities on the mould, the configuration in Fig. 13.4(d), would result in more than five times the number of cavities used in the configurations in Figs. 13.4 (b) and 13.4 (c). The cavity could be EDM'd but not polished; so it would have to be either made in two pieces or electroformed. If the part were gated at the parting line, the air would be trapped on the top; so a three-plate, hot, or insulated runner would be required. This might double the original mould cost. Additionally, the part in Fig. 13.4(d) might not even be recognised as the original part.

It thus can be easily seen that selection of the parting line, like all other mould design items, will affect the piece, its cost, its physical properties, and its appearance.

Ejection

After a part has been moulded, it must be removed from mould. It is mechanically ejected by KO (knockout) pins, KO sleeves, stripper plates, stripper rings, or air, either singly or in combination. The selection of the type and location of the ejection mechanisms affects the moulded part in ways similar to the selection of the parting line. The most frequent problem in new moulds is with the ejection of the part, as there is no mathematical way to determine the amount of ejecting force needed. It is entirely a matter of experience. The larger the area of the ejection system, the lower the pressure on the part, thus permitting lower ejection temperatures and less stress from the knockout system. It is poor practice to build a mould unless the part will eject properly. Unless a mould ejects consistently, it is impossible to produce parts economically. Mould release never should be used except in an emergency, or unless it is more economical to finish the run by using it instead of stopping and repairing the mould.

The geometry of the part, the location of the gate(s), and the plastic material are the most important parameters in ejection. It is desirable to have a minimum draft of 10 per side, though many parts will work with less draft. The quality of polishing is important. Polishing and stoning only in the direction of ejection often will solve a difficult problem. Because ejection involves overcoming the forces of adhesion between the plastic and the mould, the area of the knockout mechanism becomes important. If the area is too small, the force will be concentrated (high pressure), developing severe stresses on the part. In materials such as ABS and high impact polystyrene, this force can discolour the plastic. In other instances it may so stress the part that it will fail immediately or in later service.

Sticking in a mould often is related to the elasticity of steeL When the injection pressure is applied to the molten plastic, the steel of the mould deforms. When the pressure is relieved, the steel will return to its original position and then will act as a clamp on the plastic. Additionally, packing causes sticking by increasing even more the adhesive forces between the plastic and the mould. Very often, a reduction of the injection pressure and/ or the injection forward time will eliminate the problems. Packing is also common in multicavity moulds where the individual cavities do not fill equally. One cavity will seal off first, and the material intended for that cavity will be forced into other cavities, causing overfilling.

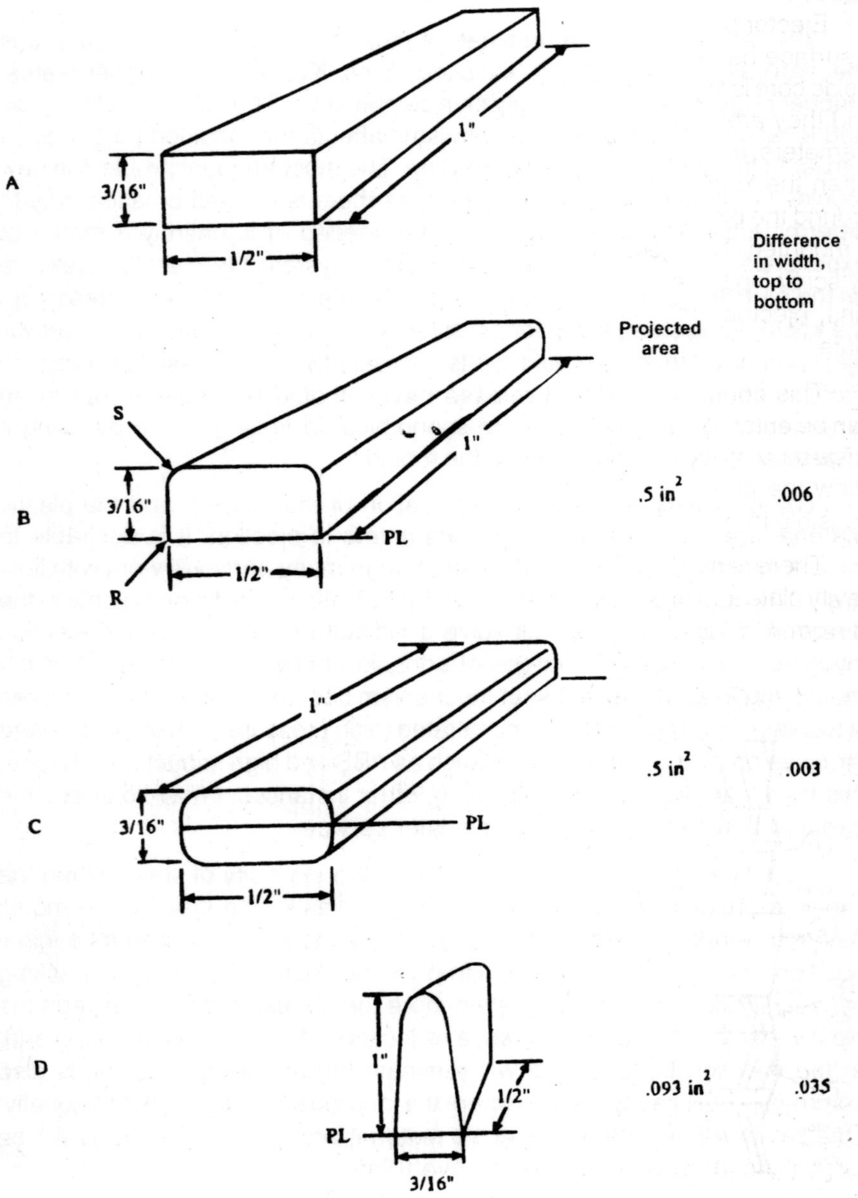

Fig. 13.4 Effect of parting line on the shape of a moulded part.

Ejector Mechanisms

Ejector pins are made either from an H-II or a nitriding steel. They have a surface hardness of 70 to 80 Rc, to a depth of 0.004 to 0.007 inch. The inside core is tough. The heads are forged and annealed for maximum strength and they are honed to a fine finish. They come in fractional and letter-size diameters, each being available in a 0.005 inch oversized pin. They are used when the knockout holes in the cavity or core are worn and flash occurs around the pins. The right side of Fig. 13.5 shows the way a knockout pin (L) is mounted. The ejector plate is drilled and countersunk. The pins are held in by screwing the ejector retainer plate (J) to the ejector plate (0). The ejector pins, ejector sleeves, sprue puller, and return pins are all located in this plate.

This construction facilitates assembly of the mould because the pins can be entered one by one into the cavity plate. It is often difficult to assemble large moulds with a great number of ejector pins if the construction does not allow the pins to be inserted individually. This construction also makes it possible to remove one or two knockout pins without removing all of them.

There is nearly always a slight misalignment between the holes and the cavity plate and the ejector plate. Therefore, it is important to leave a clearance of from *1164* to *1132* inch around the heads of the pins and at least 0.002

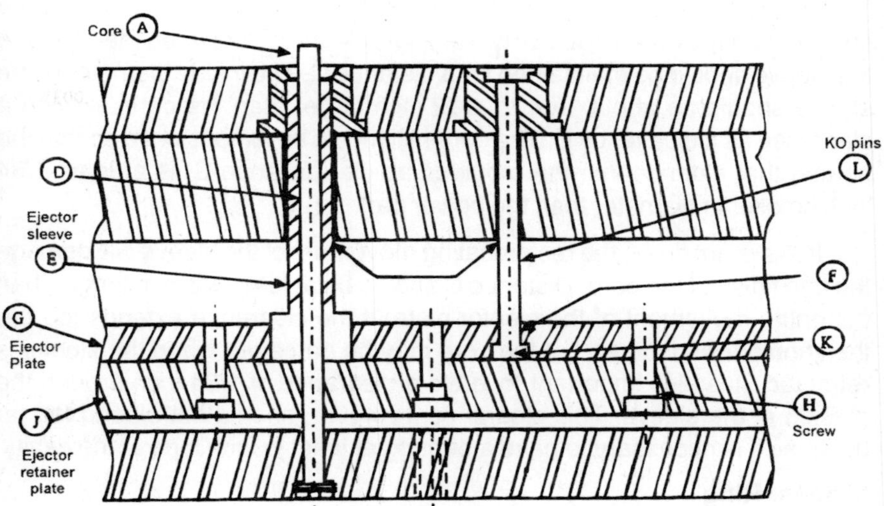

Fig. 13.5 Ejector (KO) pins, ejector plates and stripper pin and sleeves

inch clearance at K. This will permit the pins on the counterbore to find their proper location when the mould is assembled. Return pins should be used only to return the knockout plates, not to guide them. The knockout plates should be on their own leader pins and bushings. Chamfers at point I are helpful for easy insertion of the pins.

The holes for the ejector pins should be relieved to within a fraction of an inch of the face of the cavity or core to facilitate the alignment and operation of the pins. The top of the knockout pins will leave a circle on the moulded parts.

Ejector Sleeve

Ejector sleeves labeled E in Fig. 13.5 are preferred when moulded parts have to be stripped off round cores. They are subjected to severe stress and wear, so their inside and outside surfaces must be hard and finely polished. If they are not sufficiently hard and are of different hardnesses, scoring of both the cavity and the core may take place. Additionally, both the cavity and the core must be of a different hardness compared to the ejector sleeve. Two parts of equal hardness, regardless of how hard they are will scour. The lower portion of the sleeve should be drawn to obtain maximum toughness, while the upper part should be left hard for the full length of the ejector movement.

The outside diameter of the sleeve should be about 0.001 to 0.002 inch smaller than the hole in the cavity. An equal clearance between the core and the sleeve should be maintained for a distance C. The inside diameter of the sleeve should be about 1/64 to *1/32* inch larger than the core, leaving a clearance as indicated by D. The core (A) should be dimensioned so that the portion that extends into the moulded article (distance B) is at least 1/64 inch smaller in diameter than the power part.

If this is not done, the reciprocating movement of the sleeve will damage the fine finish of the core. Distance C should be at least 3/8 inch longer than the entire movement of the ejector plate. If the clearance extends too for, the shoulder and the end of the core may be damaged when the sleeve is retracted. It is also important to leave a clearance of 1/64 inch around the outside of the sleeve. This clearance, however, should not extend too far because it is necessary to have a bearing at least ½ inch long at the cavity.

Stripper Ring

The ejector sleeve requires that a core be attached beyond the ejector plates, usually to the backup plate. In many instances a stripper ring can be used (Fig. 13.6). The core then can be attached to the core retaining plate. A ring is inserted, which is directly attached by stripper bolts to the knockout plates. An advantage of the stripper ring is that other knockout devices, such as knockout pins, can be attached to the same plate. This would be useful in moulding a container and its cover at the same time.

Stripper Plates

If, instead of mounting the stripper rings directly on the knockout plate, the stripper rings were mounted in their own plate and the plate were mounted on the knockout plate, a stripper plate mould (Fig. 13.7) would result. Hardened

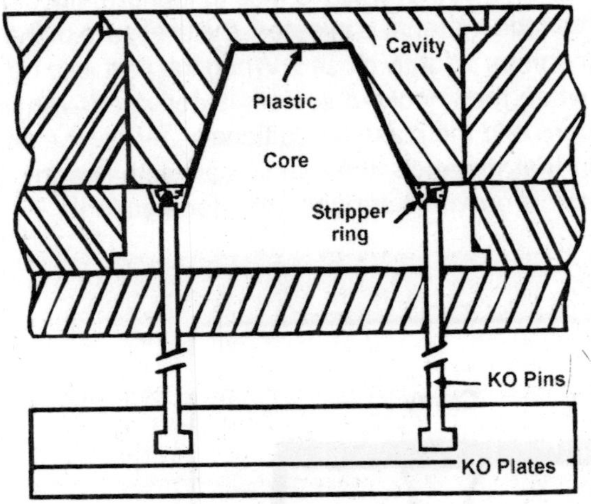

Fig. 13.6 Stripper ring type ejection

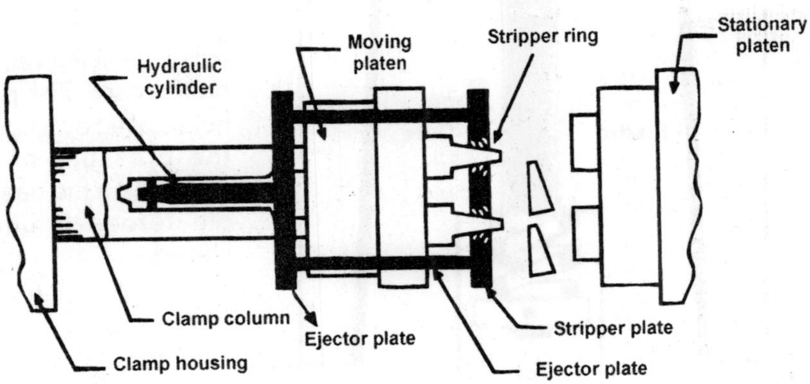

Fig. 13.7 Schematic drawing of a stripper ring ejection.

inserts should be put around the core and inserted into the stripper plate to prevent wear and for ease of maintenance. Stripper plate moulds give a larger surface area for ejection than knockout pins. Heretofore, they primarily were used for round cores. With the use of EDM equipment, irregularly shaped stripper plate moulds are economically feasible.

Vent Pins

Consider the case of moulding a deep container, as shown in Fig. 13.8. After the cavity separated from the core, the atmospheric air pressure would make it difficult, if not impossible, to remove the part. To overcome this difficulty a vent pin is used, which is held in its normally closed position by the spring. When the material is injected, the pressure of the material on the head of the pin forces it tightly closed. When the part is to be ejected, the pin will move up when the knockout system is activated, venting the interface between the core and the plastic. Additionally, air can be used to help blast the part off. In that instance, the plastic part acts like the piston of an air cylinder. Often this provides enough force for ejection.

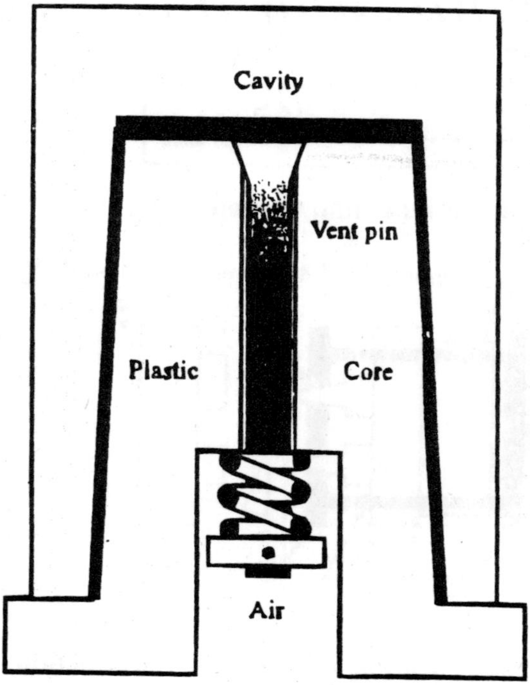

Fig. 13.8 Use of venting pin to break the vaccum on the core. The pin is held closed by a spring; the pressure of the material on the head of pin forces if tightly closed.

Cam Actions

A cam-acting mould is used to overcome the effect of an undercut, which is an interference by the mould that will prevent mechanical ejection of the part. There are two types of earn action-one moves the cams independently of the machine action, and the other moves the cam by the moulding machine action.

Fig. 13.9 shows a schematic section of a cam used to make a hole in the side of a plastic box. The cam pin is attached to the cam slide, which moves on wear plates. The slide is activated by either an air or a hydraulic cylinder. The locking device is not shown. This cylinder can be activated at any time in the cycle. For the plastic part to stick on the core, the cam pin must be retracted before the mould opens. This would be impossible in a mould where the cam action is worked by the machine opening.

Fig. 13.10 shows a standard cam action. The cam slide is attached to plate A, which is the moving side of the mould. The cam pin and the cam lock are attached to the stationary side of the mould. In the mould closed position the cam pin is held in place by the cam lock. As the mould opens, the cam slides up on the cam pin, moving toward the right. The amount of the cam slide movement will depend on the cam angle and how far the slide moves on the cam pins. By the time that the mould is opened, the cam slide has moved enough that the cam pin has been fully withdrawn from the plastic

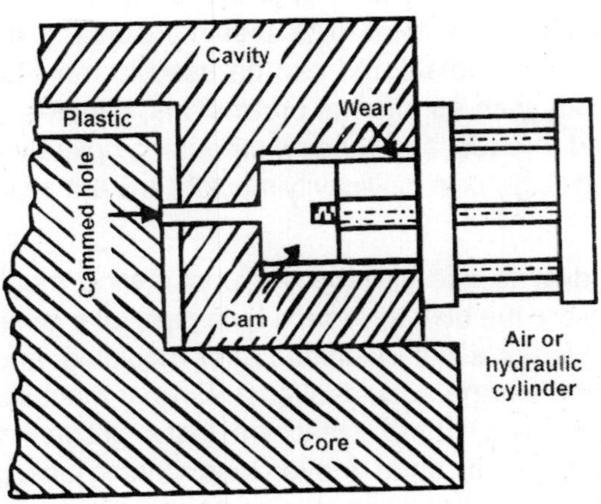

Fig. 13.9 Schematic drawing of an externally operated cam for moulding a hole in plastic.

part. Following that, the part is ready for normal ejection. There are other ways of camming mechanically, but they all work on the same principle as that of an angle pin. If the cam pin should come out of the cam slide, a method of holding the cam slide in place is required.

External threads can be moulded readily by using cam pins and slides to separate the cavities themselves. Such movement of the cavity block is a common form of cammed mould.

Moulding internal threads or external threads when cams are not used requires unscrewing devices. The usual methods include a rack and pinion, where the rack is moved by the machine action, a hydraulic cylinder, a pneumatic cylinder, or an electric motor. Unscrewing can also be obtained by the use of an individual hydraulic motor for each core, or by a gear and chain mechanism, motor-driven.

Another way to mould internal threads and undercuts is to use a collapsible core, which consists of a circular, segmented core or sleeve into which the internal threads or configuration is ground. When centre core pin, which backs up and holds the segments in the moulding position, is retracted by normal ejector plate travel, the segments collapse inwardly, because of their inherent flexibility, pulling them selves away from the moulded undercuts and allowing the part to be ejected. The segments are alternately wide and narrow, and the narrow segments collapse farther inwardly, thus "making room" for the wider segments to collapse also, freeing themselves from the moulded undercuts. A third member, a positive collapse bushing, is not shown, to allow the collapsible core detail to be seen more clearly. Besides moulding internal threads, collapsible cores can be used to mould parts with other types of undercuts such as internal protrusions, dimples, grooves for cap liners, interrupted threads, and window cutoutscompletely around the part. They can be used singly or in multicavity moulds, and are available in standard sizes.

Before deciding to use cammed or unscrewing moulds, one should determine if they are the best approach for a particular project. Some times a hole can be drilled or a slot machined after moulding, and often it can be done at the machine at no additional cost. Even if machining or assembly work has to be done away from the machine, that might be a more economical and preferred approach on short or even long running jobs, particularly if it is automated. Sometimes assembling two parts can avoid cam action; at other times threaded inserts or taping will eliminate automatic unscrewing moulds. The part should be carefully reviewed at this stage of development.

Early Ejector Return Unit

A typical mould base accessory is an early ejector return unit (Fig. 13.11). Whenever a mechanically operated cam slide passes over an ejector pin, the ejector plate must be returned "early," or before the mould is closed; otherwise the returning cam will slide and hit the ejector pins with mould damage. This is not the case if the machine or mould has air or hydraulically operated knockout plate.

To prevent this problem in other types of moulds, an early ejector return unit can be used. The unit consists of a bushing, a post with slidable cam fingers and a cam actuating pin. The bushing is installed in the B plate, the post is attached to the ejector plate, and the cam actuating pin is installed in the A plate.

In operation, the early return of the ejector plate is accomplished while the press is closing, by the cam actuating pin pushing against the projecting cams on the post (and thus returning the ejector plate) until the cams are released into a matching countersink, which happens when the ejector plate is fully back. The cam pin then passes on through as the mould continues to close. Timing is regulated by adjusting the length of the pin.

MOULD COOLING

The mould, in effect, is the containment for the molten plastic and the vehicle through which heat is removed from the plastic to solidify it to the point of ejector. It is obvious that proper selection of mould cooling channels is essential for economic operation. Mould temperature control consists of regulating the temperature and the flow rate of the cooling fluid. The functioning of the mould and the quality of the part depend in large measure on the location of the cooling channel. It is difficult to have "too much" cooling because the amount is always coagulated by the temperature and velocity of the circulating cooling fluid. If there are "too many" cooling channels, they can always be blocked off and not used.

The second factor in mould temperature control is the selection of the material itself. Beryllium copper moulds have a high thermal conductivity, approximately three times that of steel and six times that of stainless steel. Because the time required for cooling plastic in the mould is a function of heat removal, a beryllium copper cavity will remove heat more rapidly than a steel one, although not in the three-to-one ratio; one still has to wait for the heat to come out of the plastic, and the steel cooling channel can be 50% closer to the plastic because of steel's greater strength compared to beryllium cooper.

Cooling channels should be in the cavities and cores themselves, and in the retaining plate only if needed. The rate of heat transfer is lowered tremendously by the interface of two pieces of metal, no matter how close the contact. The cooling channels should be as close as possible to the surface of the plastic (taking into account the strength of the mould material), and should be evenly spaced to prevent an uneven temperature on the surface of the mould. For practical purposes, it can be assumed that the heat is removed in linear fashion; that is, equal distances from a cooling channel will

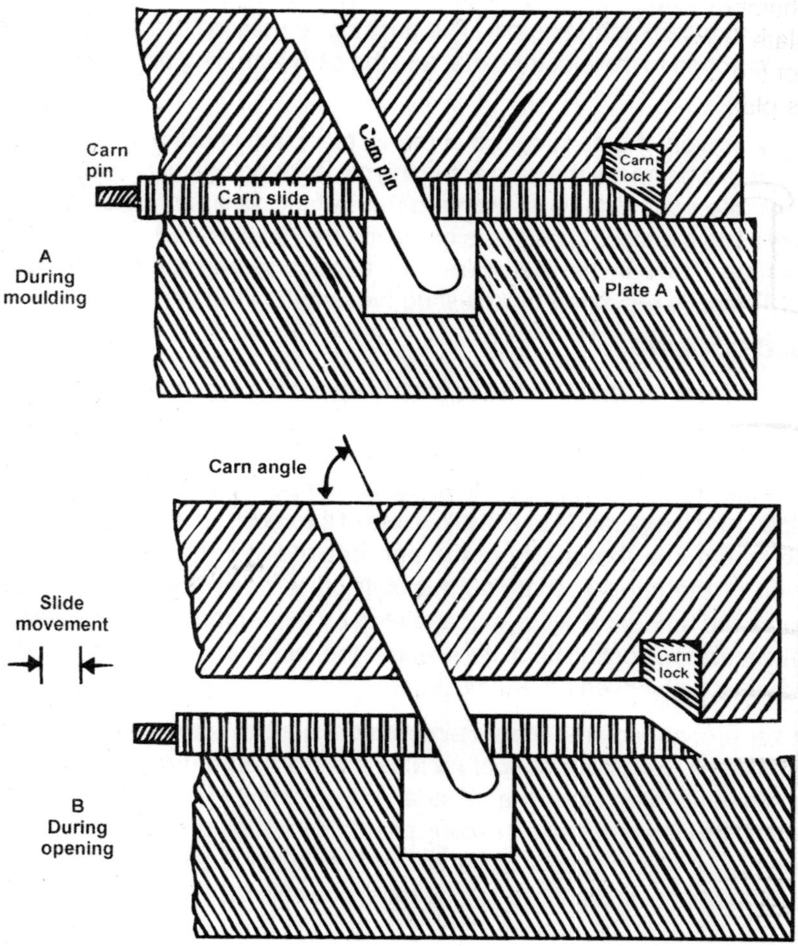

Fig. 13.10 Mechanical cam action using cam pins

be at the same temperature. The simplest means of cooling is to drill channels through the cavity or core. The minimum size should be ¼ inch pipe, with 3/8 inch pipe preferable; 1/8 inch pipe never should be used unless it's use is dictated by the size limitations of the mould. A centre distance of three to four diameters should work well.

Fig. 13.12 shows one of the simplest types of water cooling, commonly used in injection moulds for rectangular shapes such as boxes and radio cabinets. It consists of a number of channels drillied near the top of the core (the number depending on the size of the core), joined by several risers to circulate the cooling medium. The horizontal channels are drilled from one end of the core, and are drilled and counter bored to accommodate a soft brass plug, which should be a light drive fit, machined flush with the core

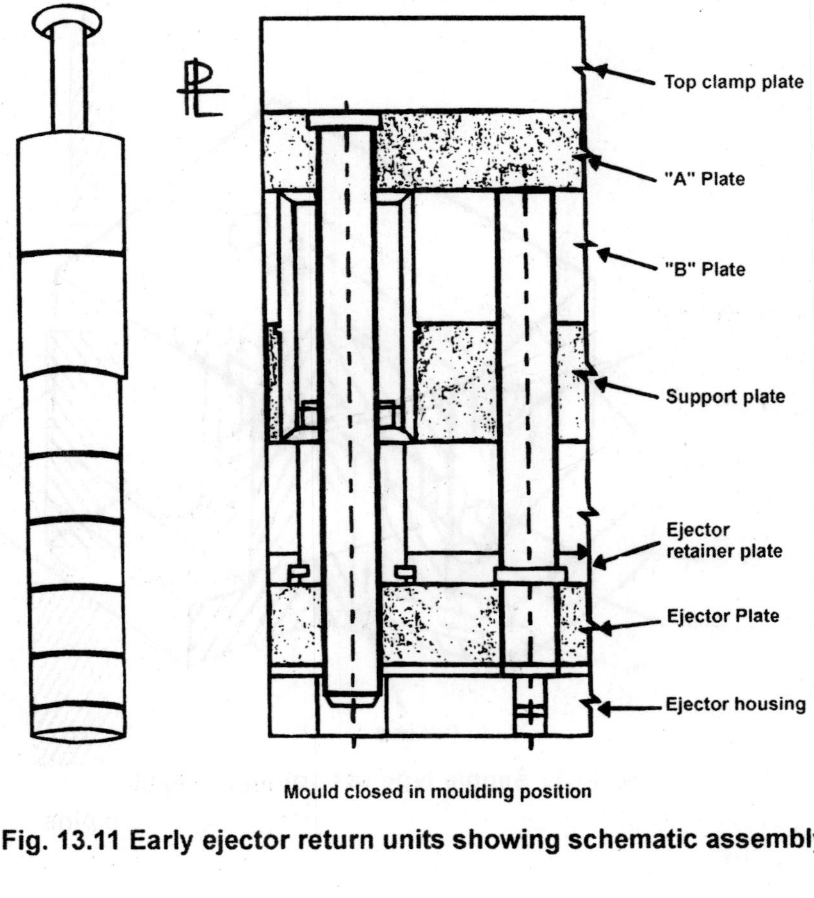

Fig. 13.11 Early ejector return units showing schematic assembly

surface and then polished. Usually a continuous flow is used through the core, and should it be necessary to cross over channels already drilled, the flow of the fluid can be directed by using blank plugs, which are drive fit in the channels.

Fig. 13.13 shows a cooling system using channelled inserts within the cavity block and core block. The cavity block and core block are machined to hold the inserts (circular, as shown, or rectangular) before the cavity and core are finished, hardened, and polished. The inserts are made to fit the spaces thus provided. Grooves for the channels are machined in the face of the inserts and then are interconnected and baffled to provide the desired route of flow. The inserts, not hardened, are fastened into place within the cavity and core blocks and sealed by O-rings. In designing the grooves, it is important to leave a sufficient area unmachined to support the cavity or core against distortion by moulding pressure.

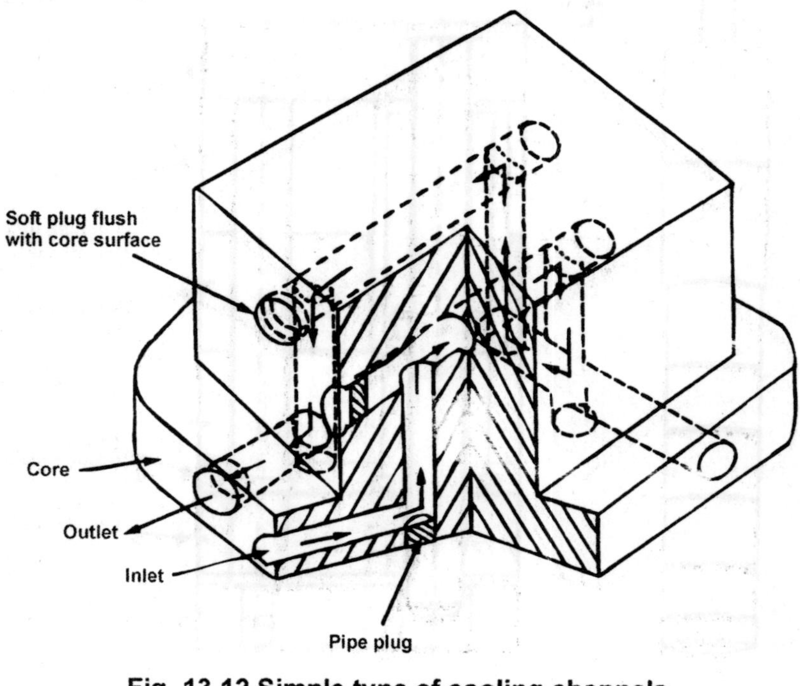

Fig. 13.12 Simple type of cooling channels

Fig. 13.14 shows a bubbler in the core and O-rings to seal off the cooling medium or confine it to each individual cavity or core in the chase. The underside of the cavity or core may have a pattern of grooves similar to that of the channeled insert in Fig. 13.13, or it may be as shown.

The two main means of directing cooling fluid in the mould, aside from cooling channels, are bubblers (Fig. 13.15) and baffles (Fig. 13.16). A baffle is a flat strip of brass or stainless steel (to prevent rusting) inserted in the core to divide the channel in the core into two separate channels so that the cooling fluid is forced to flow up one side of the baffle to the end of the core, and down the opposite side and out. The thickness of these baffles ranges from 1/32 to 1/8 inch, depending on the size of the channel in the core. The baffle is never extended to the extreme end of the core because the fluid must pass over the end of the baffle to flow down to the opposite side. The baffle may be attached by brazing or machined with a mechanical force fit. The water seals of Fig. 13.15 and 13.16 can be achieved by threading or by the use of O-rings. It should be noted, in Fig. 13.15, that if the water connection were reversed and the pressure low, the pipe would be filled, and the water might dribble over the side without ever contacting the core itself. This would result in almost no cooling. On the contrary, when the water is connected correctly, no matter how low the pressure or flow, the core has to fill with water until it reaches the top of the tube, from which it is drained.

Cooling with baffles is an excellent method if there are not too many hooked up in series. Consider ten pins, 4 inches high and ½ inch in diameter, with baffles hooked up in series (Fig. 13.17). The first pin will be cooler than the last pin. The total resistance to flow will drastically reduce the amount and velocity of the cooling fluid flowing through the system and thus will markedly decrease the cooling capacity. Additionally, if there is any blockage because of dirt, or for any other reason in one pin, the whole unit is inoperative. In practice this design would not work, and the pins would be too hot for moulding. Fig. 13.18 shows the correct way to cool the same pins, using parallel cooling. This can be done with pins or with any other series of bubbler action in a core or cavity. This type of cooling will give significantly faster moulding compared to that shown in Fig. 13.17.

The excellence of the cooling system depends on the ingenuity and the ability of the mould designer and the mouldmaker. No aspect of mouldmaking affects the cycle and the quality of the moulded part more than the selection and location of the cooling channel.

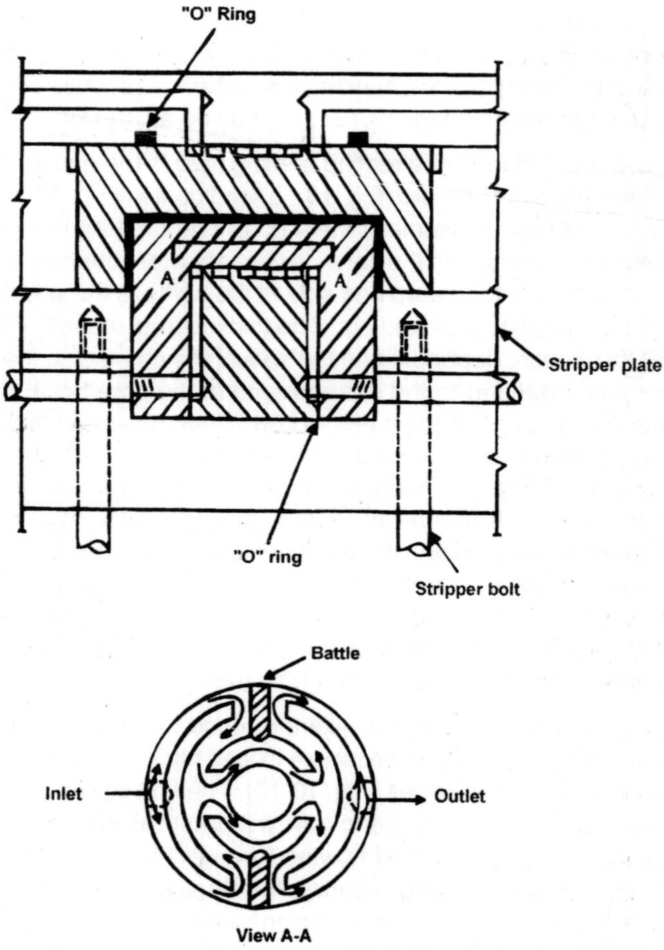

Fig. 13.13 Mould Construction showing a more elaborate cooling system.

STANDARD EQUIPMENT

Standard Mould Bases

In the early years of injection moulding mouldmakers had to build their own mould bases, a costly and inefficient process, as most mouldmakers do not have the large equipment for such machining. By standardising on the mould assembly and the component parts, especially those that come in contact with the press platens such as the locating ring, sprue, bushing, and ejector plates and housing, the mould became interchangeable among all

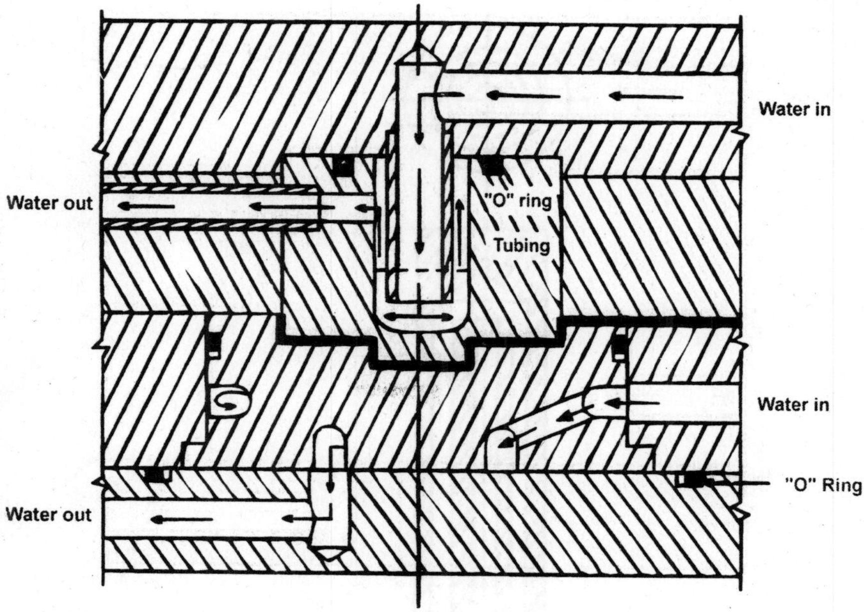

Fig. 13.14 Cooling with a bubbler and using O-rings to seal off the cooling medium.

makes of injection moulding machines. All of these parts, together, with other parts such as leader pins and bushings, return pins, sprue puller pins, and ejector pins, were made available as stock items for replacement. Standard mould base assemblies for injection moulds also could be rearranged for use in compression or transfer moulds.

All mould components incorporated in the mould base assemblies are also available as separate items so that mouldmakers can make up their own special bases. The maximum-size mould plates (A and B) are 45 3/4 x 66 x 5 7/8 inches. The plates are prefinished; that is, they are finish ground on all sides to extremely close tolerances. The plates are available in medium carbon steel, SAE 1030, mould steel; type AISI 4130 heat treated to 300 Bhn, a P 20 AISI 4130 heat treated to 300 Bhn, that also can be used for cavities and cores.

A standard injection mould base consists of a stationary part that is attached to the stationary platen, through which the material comes and an ejector or movable part attached to the movable platen, which contains the knockout mechanism. The top or stationary side has a top clamp plate and

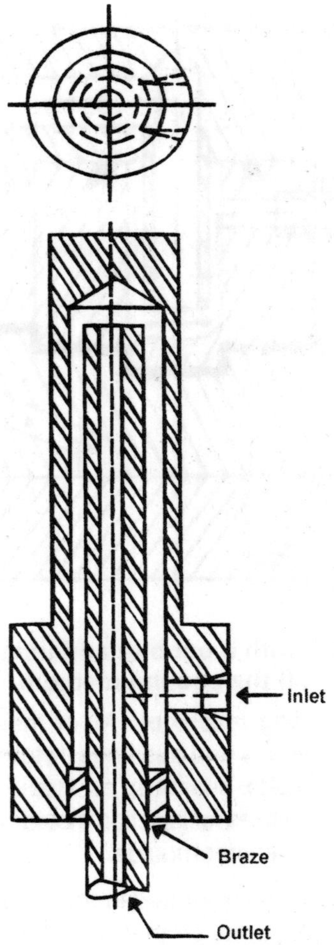

Fig. 13.15 Bubbler type cooling

a top cavity or A plate. This side contains a locating ring for positioning to the press platen so that the sprue bushing, which has an orifice through which the plastic material enters the mould under heat and pressure, is directly in front of the nozzle opening of the cylinder. Leader pins are also contained in the upper cavity plate and enter into leader pin bushings on the other side to align the mould halves.

The ejector, movable, or lower half of the mould has the lower cavity or B plate. which rests on its support plate. An ejector housing is mounted on

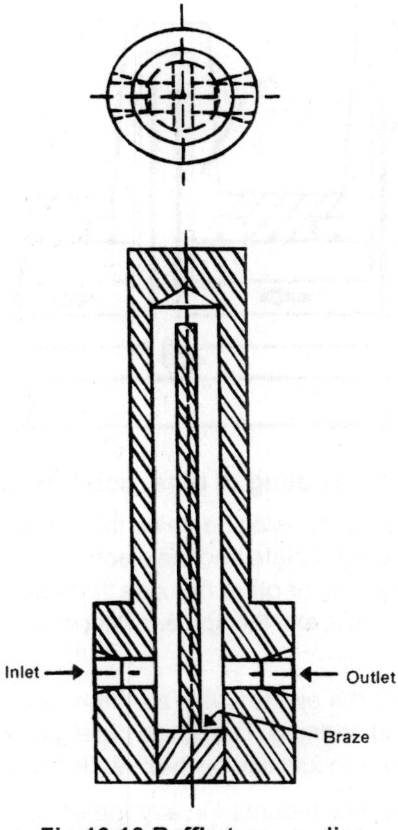

Fig.13.16 Baffle type cooling

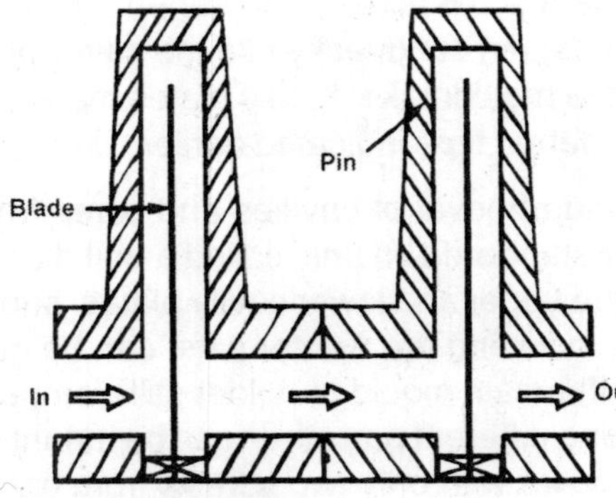

Fig.13.17 Series cooling of pins, poor design.

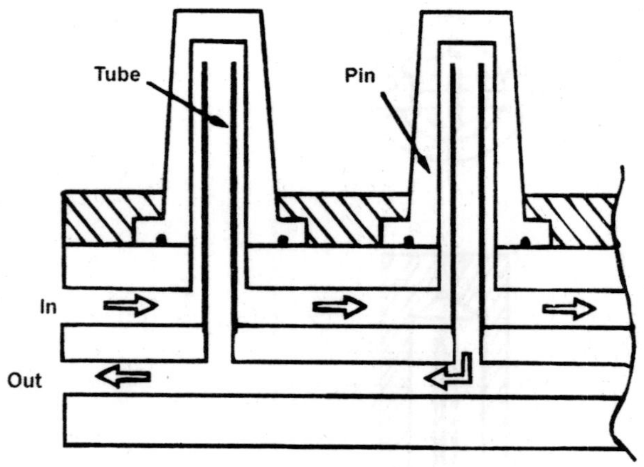

Fig. 13.18 Parallel cooling of pins, good design.

the support plate. The ejector housing contains the lower clamp slots; it also incorporates within it the ejector plate and the ejector retainer plate, between which are held the ejector pins or other devices that eject the moulded part from the mould. The return pins and the sprue puller pin also are held between these two plates.

The return pins return the ejector plate as the mould closes and pull or "break" the sprue at mould opening. The sprue puller pin is located opposite the sprue. The ejector plates should ride on their own leader pins and bushings.

Cavities and cores can be mounted in anyone of four ways: (I) surface-moulded on the A and B plate (or cavity retainer plates as they are often called); (ii) inserted about 0.015 inch above the surface in blind pockets milled partway through the A and B plates; (iii) inserted in holes cut completely through the A and B plates; (iv) cut directly into the cavity plates. In the last case, it is important for the mouldmaker to use plates made of a cavity steel, such as the P-20 prehardened type indicated earlier.

Quick installation and removal of cavities and cores from the press is incorporated in an other standardised unit, called a unit die. This is a mould base designed so that the upper and lower cavity plates. support plates and ejector plate assembly, including the ejector pins, can be quickly removed from the press, leaving the main mould or holder still clamped in position. A unit assembly for moulding different parts then can be mounted back into the holder, being fastened down with only two screws from each end for each mould half.

Large mould bases can be removed and changed in several minutes with special equipment external to and on the machine. These quick mould changers are used for "just-in-time" deliveries and are expensive.

Standard Cavity Inserts

Standard, rectangular cavity insert blocks also are available in sizes offrom 3 x 3 inches to 6 x 8 inches, and in thicknesses of from 7/8 to 7/8 inches. In addition, round cavity inserts are also available from stock in l-to 4- inch diameters in ½ inch increments, and in thicknesses of from 7/8 to 3 7/8 inches in ½ inch increments. All of the cavity inserts have a ground finish on all sides and surfaces, ready for immediate cavity cutting. The rectangular inserts come in P-20 type steel, H-13 type steel, and T- 420 type stainless steel. The rounds come in 20 and H-13 type steels.

14

Designing Moulds for Thermoset Processing

INTRODUCTION

A successful and profitable thermoset moulding operation is dependent on the selection of the proper type of moulding equipment, the plant layout, the method of moulding, and moulds that has been engineered properly and are of superior construction. A poor mould design or an inferior mould will produce a part that is costly in that it may require subsequent finishing operations before it can be shipped. Processors of thermoset raw materials must constantly keep abreast of new moulding methods and new and improved mould steels or non-ferrous alloys. They also must make sure their mould suppliers are aware of the newer, more advanced techniques for making moulds (computer-controlled machining equipment, spark or chemical erosion processes, etc.). This chapter will cover the methods of moulding and mould design for thermosets.

METHOD OF MOULDING

The trend is toward automation wherever possible. Therefore, the processor has an opportunity to select one of four methods of moulding (taking into account the geometric design of the part, the finished part tolerances, the operating conditions, the type of moulding compound (long fibre filled, bulk handling characteristics, etc.), and environmental surroundings): (i) compression; (ii) transfer; (iii) injection; and (iv) injection-compression.

Compression Moulds

Compression moulds may be designed for hand moulds or semiautomatic or automatic operations. In the early stages of moulding, hand moulds were quite popular, but in recent years they have been used principally for prototype parts or parts with limited production. The custom moulder does a large amount of moulding using the semiautomatic method. The compression moulds may be hand-loaded with loose powder, bulk moulding compound (BMC), or preforms. The preforms generally are preheated to 200 to 260°F in high-frequency preheaters. The trend being to automate, both custom and captive moulders are automatically compression moulding a wide range of thermoset parts. This is done on a variety of press equipment. Conventional single-ram hydraulic or toggle presses may range from 15- to 300-tonne capacity.

Rotary presses designed for compression moulding are used to mould closures, wiring device parts, timer cams, outlet boxes, and so on. The size of the part is limited to the clamp capacity of each individual mould station, often 10 tonnes and rarely exceeding 30 tonnes.

The automatic moulding presses for compression moulding are so designed that various methods of loading the cavities may be used. Material may be loaded with cold granular, high-frequency preheated or infrared preheated granular, preheated preforms, or a charge that is preheated by a heated barrel and reciprocating screw.

A compression mould consists of heated platens onto which are mounted the cavity and force block or blocks. A knockout system, either top, bottom, or both, is incorporated to remove the parts from the mould. A typical cycle is mould open after cure period, remove parts, clean mould, load material, close press. On closing of the mould, the excess material is forced out through the flash escapement area.

In general, when parts are moulded by compression, the part density is the same in all directions. For this reason it is recommended that parts that have very close tolerances over the face of the part be moulded by compression; there is little chance of uneven density causing shrinkage problems or out-of round conditions or differences in shrinkage from width to length.

As explained previously, in a compression mould the material is loaded into an open mould, and the excess material required to fill the part is forced out over the flash line. The least expensive compression mould is a flash

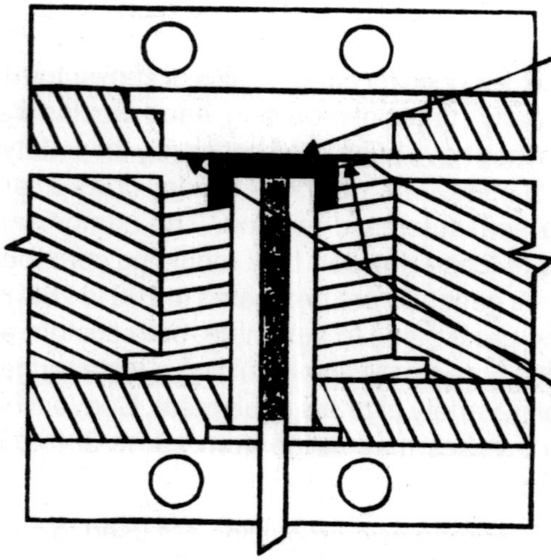

Fig. 14.1 Flash Mould

mould, as illustrated by Fig. 14.1. The greatest disadvantage of a flash mould is that there is minimum restriction to the flow of material, and very little back pressure is built up in the moulded part. The excess material is allowed to flow out horizontally with little restriction until the mould is essentially "metal to metal". The parts may lack uniform density; so they may be inferior with regard to their strength and moulded finish. It is most difficult to maintain dimensional tolerances when density variations exist. Although the mould cost may be less than for other types of compression moulds, the fact that there is no loading space except for the cavity of the part itself usually makes the material charge excessive. The percentage of flash loss may be extremely high, thus costly on a piece part basis. It is extremely difficult to maintain the centerline relationship between the force and the cavity, and if guide pins wear, the force and the cavity become mismatched. Very few semiautomatic or automatic moulds, therefore, are flash moulds.

The second type of compression mould, the semi positive horizontal flash, is illustrated by Fig. 14.2. The majority of the semiautomatic and automatic compression moulds are of this design. Ample loading space may be provided so that the percentage of flash loss may be held to a minimum. If the clearance between the force and cavity is held to 0.003 to 0.004 inch, all the material is trapped in the cavity so that the part is of maximum density. Because there may be slight differences in the volume contained within the force and the cavity in a multicavity mould, it is well to provide flash

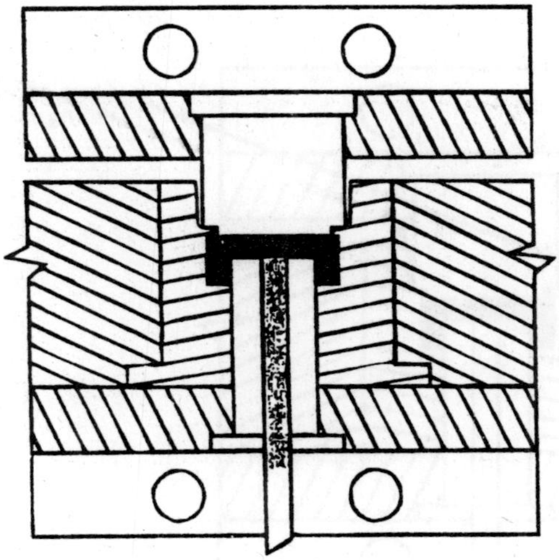

Fig. 14.2 Semipositive mould.

escapements in the form of flats or grooves 0.015 to 0.020 inch in depth. These should always be put on the force because they then can be cleaned off each shot more easily than when put into the cavity. This type of mould produces parts having maximum physical strength. If moulds are "breathed" just before final close, porosity may be eliminated by releasing the trapped volatiles. Dimensional tolerance may be closely held, especially over the face of the part.

The third type of compression mould, the semipositive vertical flash, is illustrated by Fig. 14.3. It is quite similar to the semipositive horizontal flash except that the force enters directly into the geometric design of the part itself for a distance of 1/16 to 1/8 inch. The clearance between the force and cavity at this point should be 0.005 to 0.007 inch to prevent scoring of the cavity side wall. If this is not the case, and scoring takes place, the moulded article will have a scratched appearance. Again, flash escapements should be provided on the force. A part moulded in such a mould will be of good density. The flash is vertical, which may be preferable. and can be removed easily. The moulded article, because it has good density, should have a good finish and maximum physical strength. This type of mould is quite expensive because there are two areas between the force and the cavity that must fit perfectly. There is absolutely no chance for mismatch between the force and the cavity, so concentricity of the article from cavity to for is as

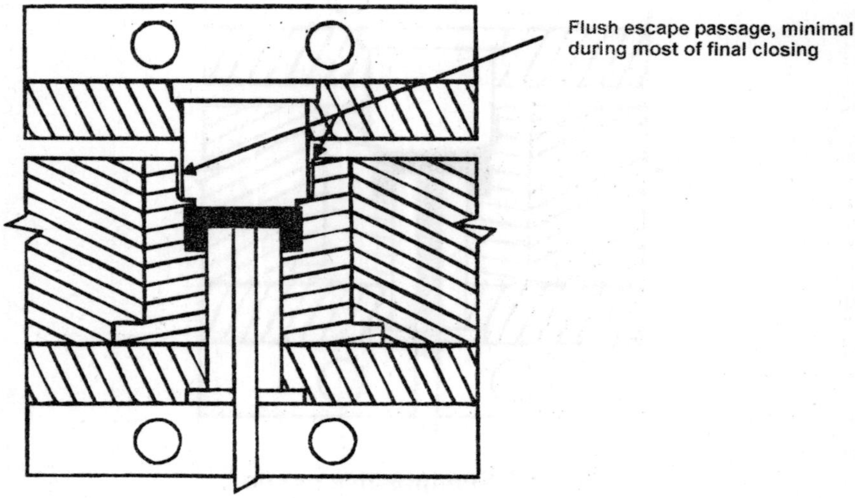

Fig. 14.3 Semipositive mould

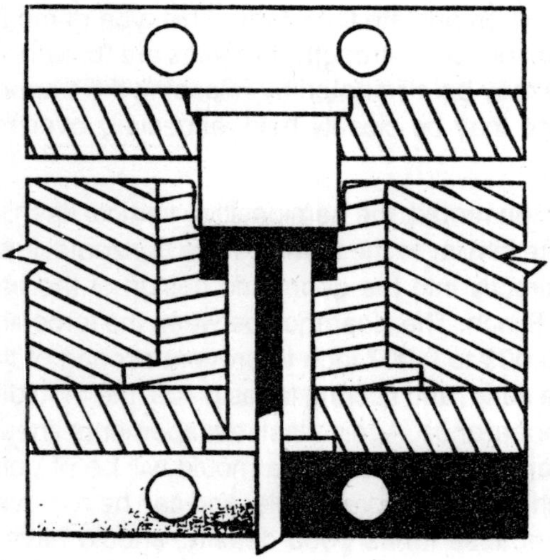

Fig. 14.4 Fully Positive mould

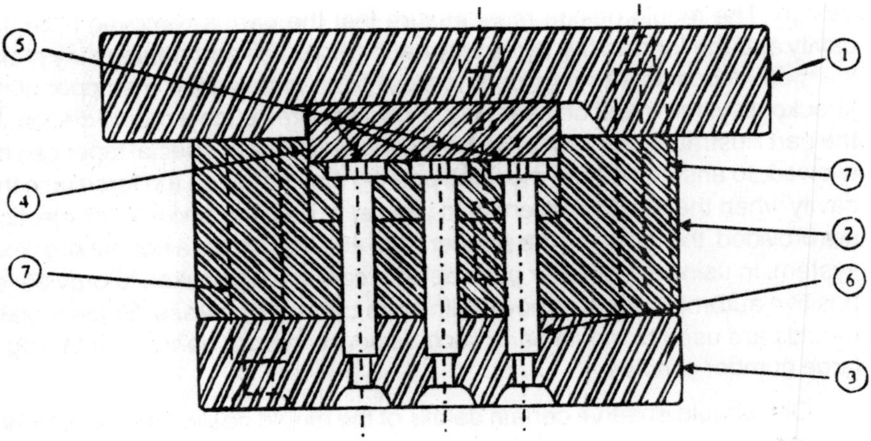

1. Force plate 2. Chase 3. Bottom plate 4. Force 5. Cavities 6. Ejector pins 7. Leader pins

Fig. 14.5 Subcavity mould

close as possible. Again, good dimensional tolerances are achieved over the face of the part.

The fourth type of compression mould, fully positive, is illustrated by Fig. 14.4. This type of mould generally is used if the materials are of high bulk, or if the filler fibre are quite long, as in glass roving. It is difficult to pinch off such fibres to a thin flash. The fully positive moulds give a vertical flash that may be easier to remove than that of other designs. It is difficult to produce parts of equal density if a multicavity mould is used. The clearance between force and cavity must be excessive, or generous flash escapements should be provided. It may be desirable also to provide a slight taper on the force to help in flash escapement. Pressure pads, away from the loading area, must be provided to ensure proper control of the thickness of the part by making the mould close to the same stopping point each time. Material or flash must be kept free from the surface of such pads.

If parts are extremely small so that it becomes difficult to charge each individual cavity, a subcavity mould can be used, as illustrated in Fig. 14.14. The mould shown is a positive mould; however, a semi positive design may be used. Only one charge is needed in a subcavity because all cavities in the subcavity are filled by the single charge.

In the design of the mould, variations of the basic design may be made to provide an improved tool design. The ejection of the part in an automatic or semiautomatic moulding operation must be considered in the final mould design. The mould design must ensure that the part is removed from the cavity and the force in the same way each cycle. The part design may make it almost impossible to provide knockout pins. In this case a stripper plate knockout system must be used. Fig. 14.6 illustrates such a mould design. In the part illustrated, we shall assume that no undercut or special taper can be allowed, to ensure that the moulded part will stay either on the force or in the cavity when the mould is opened. In this case, both top and bottom ejection are provided, the top being the stripper plate and the bottom a normal knockout system. In using the stripper plate design, care must be taken to provide for positive automatic flash removal with each cycle of the press. Stripper plate moulds are used to mould parts such as pin connector boards containing a large number of holes.

One should observe certain details of the mould design here illustrated:

1. Clearance under the dowels or leader pins to keep flash from building up in this area, preventing full entry of pins.
2. The use of a hardened dowel or leader pin bushing in a soft plate.
3. Slight positive entry action of the force into the cavity, to ensure alignment of the mould and full density of the moulded articles.
4. Flash grooves in the force.
5. Clearance between underside of stripper plate and top of cavity to allow escape of material from flash grooves.
6. Clearance holes under inserts to allow any flash to fall completely through the mould.
7. Pressure pads or blocks to control the thickness.
8. Retainer plate for top ejection pins.
9. Clearance space above stripper plate so that flash working up between the top force and the stripper plate will not be confined and can easily be blown out.
10. Inside diameter of stripper plate made slightly greater than outside diameter of the force that shapes the inside of the moulded article, in order to avoid scoring of the force, which would mar the inside surface of the moulded article.
11. Placement of lower supporting parallels to avoid blocking off the clearance holes under the dowel bushings.
12. Counterbored in underside of ejection pin holes to reduce friction and to allow flash escape.
13. Screws for holding mould parts together put in from undersides of plates, remote from the surfaces where moulding material might get into the

counterbored recesses for screw heads and cause trouble in cleaning and in screw removal for mould maintenance.

Pressure pads, illustrated as Item 7 in Fig. 14.6, are desirable on all compression moulds. This is a safety measure that assures that the land area of the mould will not be damaged in mounting the mould in the press. The landing pads (or pressure pads) should be designed to be in contact when there is approximately 0.002 inch clearance between the force and cavity at the land area or other surfaces such as pins, blades, and so on.

In the design of compression moulds, especially flash and/or semipositive types, it is important that the land area at cutoff in the outer landed area, or in the cavity itself, be carefully designed in relation to the moulding pressure.

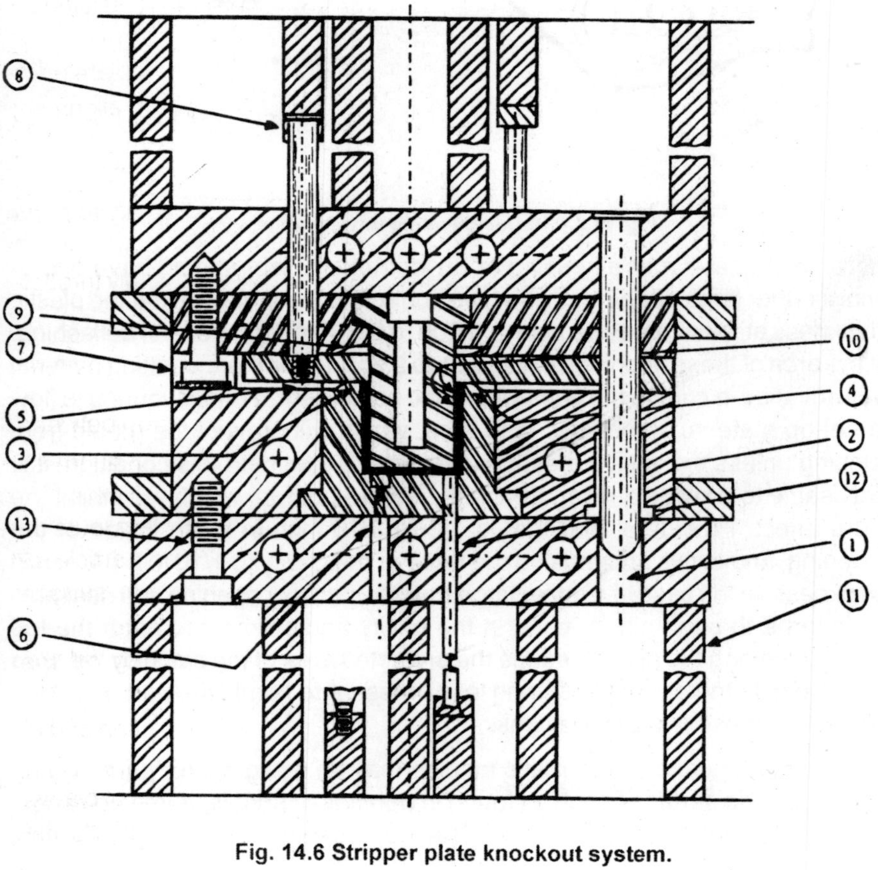

Fig. 14.6 Stripper plate knockout system.

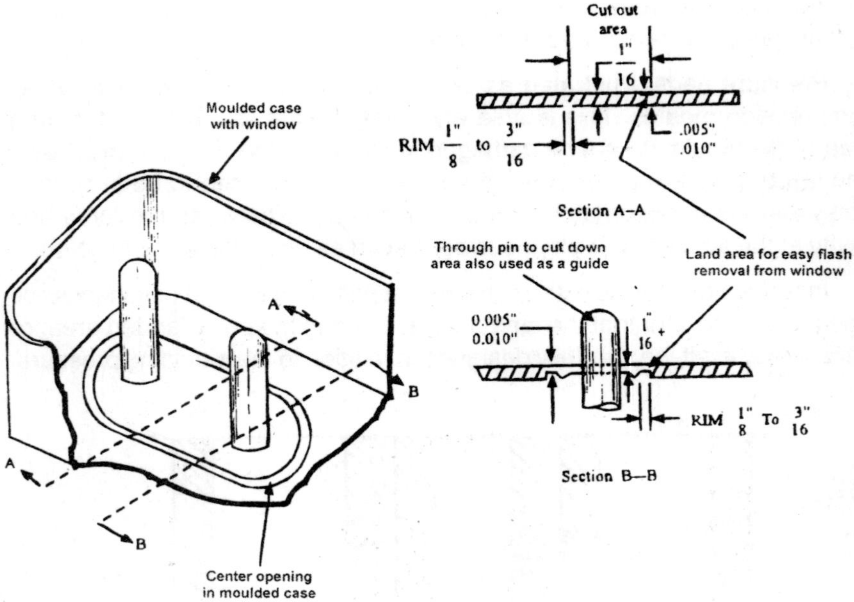

Fig. 14.7 Part Design using through pins.

If, for instance, a metre housing or an instrument door should have one or more rather large openings in the face surface, it is imperative that the plastic thickness at these areas be held to 0.005 to 0.010 inch for ease of deflashing. If the area of these openings exceeds 1 to 2 sq. in., the thermosetting material will advance in cure to the point where the equipment is endeavouring to flow a set-up material across this land area; which will prevent the mould from closing unless excessive pressure is used. To eliminate this condition, it is advisable to provide a relief area in the centre portion, which will inhibit the cure effect. Provide a land that is 1/8 to 3/16 inch in width inside of the opening, and in this area relieve the force or the cavity to 1/16 to 3/64 inch in thickness. In the case of a rather large round window or opening, it is desirable to insert a through pin, or core, in the cavity and permit it to enter the top force. Inserting the pin will reduce the projected area of the piece by the area of the pin diameter, thus requiring less pressure to mould the part. Fig. 14.7 illustrates these two part designs.

Semiautomatic or automatic moulds may be designed for parts having undercut side surfaces such as found in bobbins or spools, pump housings, automotive brake parts, and so on. The mould in Fig. 14.8 is used for such a

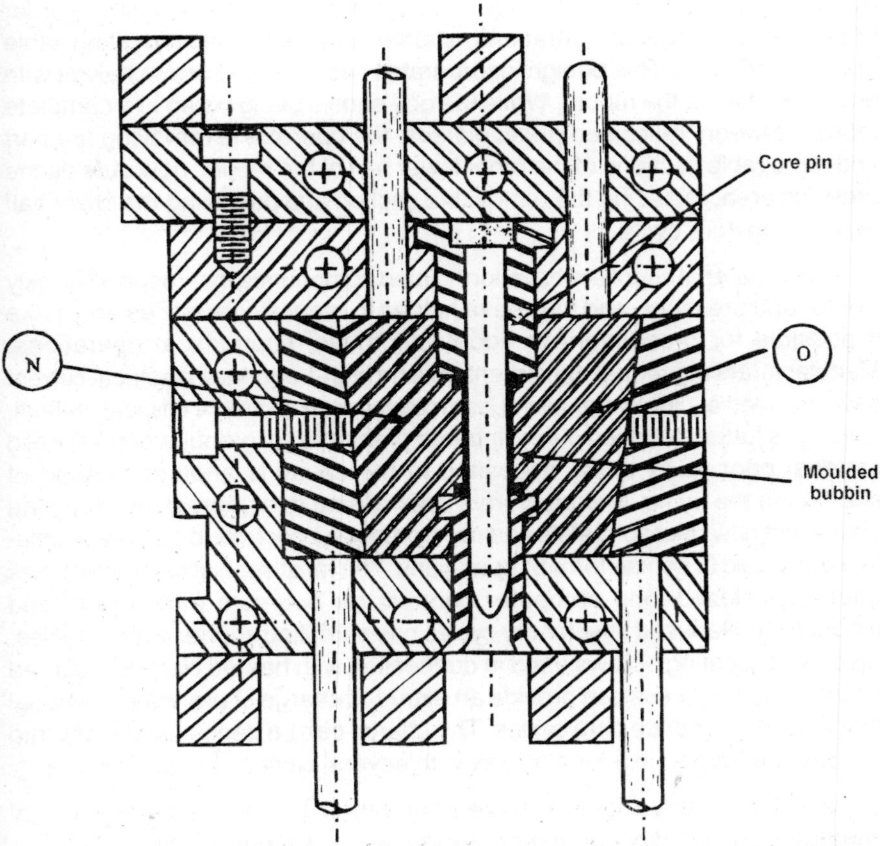

Fig. 14.8 Semiautomatic mould for part with undercuts in side walls. Mould segments N and O are automatically raised from the cavity plate when the press and mould open, and then are moved to the left and the right, respectively, to allow the moulded part to be stripped from the core pin.

part. The undercut areas may be moulded by the use of split moulds, removable pins, or sections from moulds. Side cores activated by cams or sideacting hydraulic cylinders commonly are used. In the latter case, locking devices (such as wedges) of sufficient strength must be provided to keep the cores from being forced out of position by the internal force of the material.

One of the critical aspects of this design is the flash removal; the flash must be completely removed from around the movable side cores. It is for this reason that most such moulds are operated semiautomatically. In order to provide economical operations, shuttle presses or reciprocating table presses are used. This design incorporates two or more bottom halves with one upper half of the mould. While the one shot is being cured in a complete mould between the closed press platens, the operator is removing the part and removable sections of the other lower half of the mould, now outside the pressing area, replacing the removable section and preparing the lower half for the next cure cycle.

Raw-material suppliers have formulated compounds that respond quickly to heat and pressure, and thus have helped to reduce cure cycles and make it possible for processors to adopt automatic, economical operations. Manufacturers of preheat equipment utilising high-frequency electrical current have provided equipment requiring less maintenance and more efficient preheat, which has further reduced cures. Infrared preheating of granular or preformed material prior to its being deposited in the cavity is another method of shortening the cycle. Manufacturers specialising in compression moulding equipment now offer solid state and microprocessor controls to provide trouble-free automatic or semiautomatic operations. The most sophisticated machines often use closed-loop computer controls for optimum part quality and productivity. Reduced time for dry cycles has permitted shorter overall cycles. Also, reciprocating screws used in connection with heated barrels mounted on the moulding press can provide an extruded charge of preheated material that will further reduce cure cycles. The charge can be deposited directly into the cavity or stored in a loading tray with several cavities fed at one time.

All of the above factors have contributed to the continuing use of compression moulding for making a wide range of plastic parts.

Transfer Moulds

Transfer moulds will vary in design, depending on the method of transfer moulding. There are three basic methods: (i) The original method-pot transfer-utilises a three-plate mould with the plunger retaining plate mounted to the head of the press, a floating plate containing the pot and sprue bushing and top cavity or cavities, and the third retainer plate (mounk~ on grids) containing the bottom cavity. Fig. 14.9 shows such a mould, often operated as a hand modi, the bottom plates of which are removed from the press each cycle for manual separation of the plates and removal of parts. Fig. 14.10 shows how the same mould can remain in the press each cycle, having the middle plate raised by pull- or pushrods when the press opens; (ii) The second method is known as the plunger transfer method. In this case, the plunger is activated by an independent hydraulic cylinder. The transfer cylinder may be mounted at the top of the press or at the bottom of the press, or it may incorporate a ram within a ram if the main clamp cylinder and the transfer plunger are both on the top, or both on the bottom, of the press, Fig. 14.11 illustrates the top plunger transfer; (iii) The third method is the two-stage, reciprocating screw transfer method. In this case a conventionally designed hydraulic or toggle, top clamp press (i.e., downward pressing), with a bottom transfer cylinder and plunger, is used. The reciprocating screw and barrel is mounted horizontally, and material is discharged into the transfer chamber through an opening in the transfer sleeve or pot.

There are certain design features that must.be considered for each method of transfer moulding, and each method will be discussed separately.

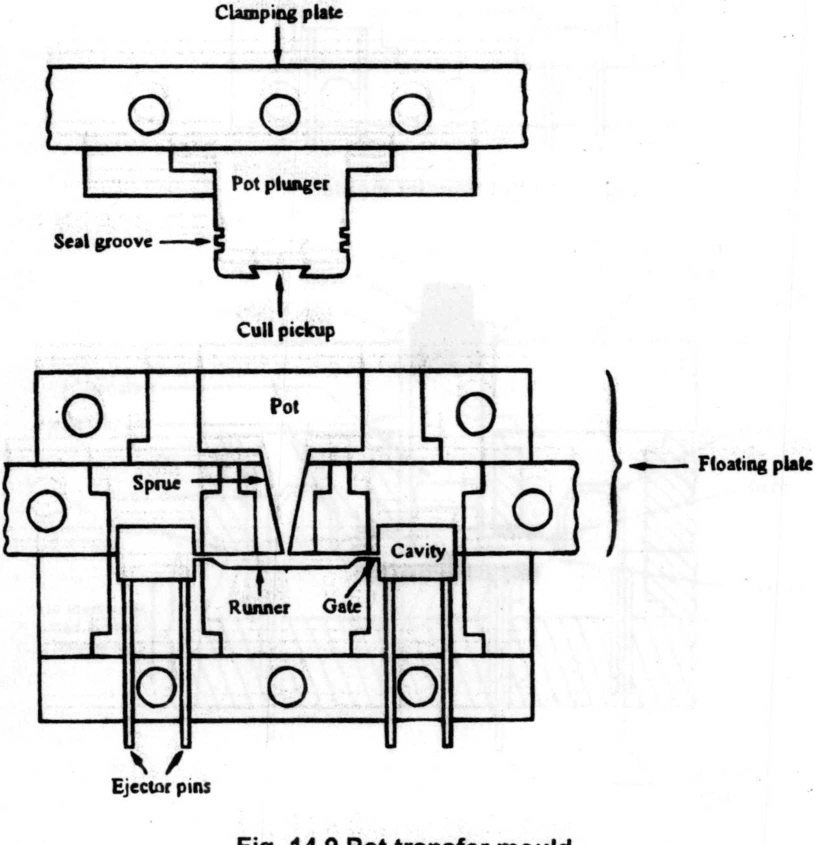

Fig. 14.9 Pot transfer mould.

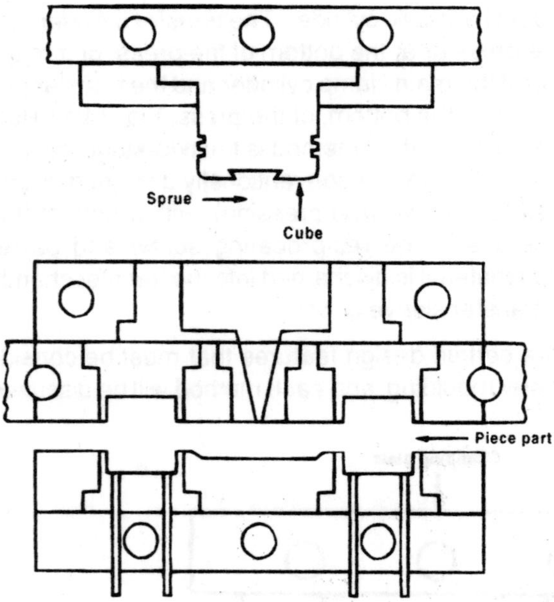

Fig. 14.10 Pot transfer mould.

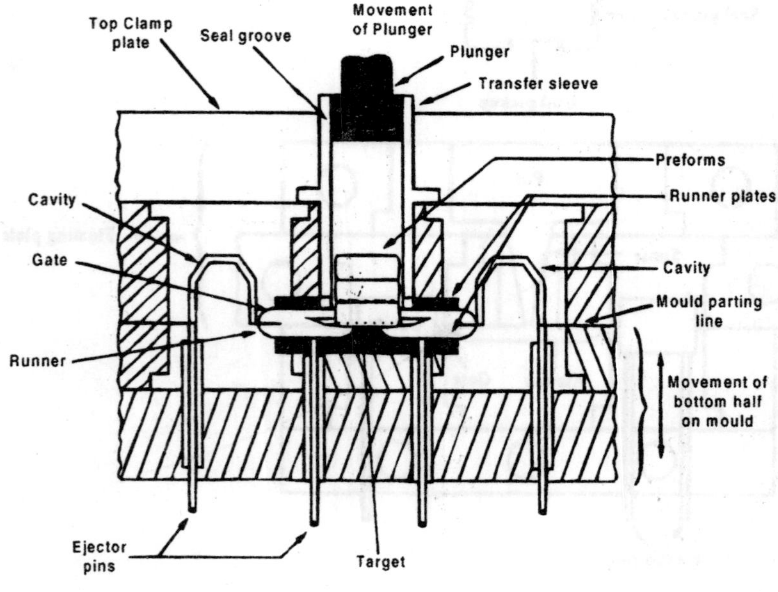

Fig. 14.11 Top plunger transfer mould

The *pot method* of transfer moulding generally is done in a conventional bottom ram clamp moulding press. The moulds usually are three-plate moulds with the centre section floating, as in Fig. 14.10.

Generally, the material is fed directly into the mould cavity or cavities from the pot through the sprue bushing. If multiple cavities are used, the sprues may come from a common pot, or multiple pots may be used. The principle may also employ a sprue into a runner system feeding one or more cavities.

After the mould layout of the individual cavity or cavities has been determined, the next step is to accurately calculate the projected area of the part or parts. If a runner system is used, its projected area must be added. The area, in square inches, of the pot or pots required to clamp the mould is subjected to discussion.

It was considered good practice to make the area equal to or slightly greater than the total projected area of all articles to be moulded, including the sprue and runners. However, because the material is advancing, it need not be treated as a hydrostatic liquid. Standard practice is to reduce the area in the pot to less than the above total area.

The next step is to determine the volume of charge to be transferred and to make the pot of sufficient depth to accept the preheated charge. It may be granules, preforms, or extruded material.

The mould design should provide for the pot or pots to be centrally located so that pressure is exerted uniformly in the centre of the press.

The design of the steel retainer or mounting plate and section of steel containing the pot should be sufficiently strong to withstand the higher transfer pressures used to transfer material from the pot to the mould cavity. In order to prevent escapement of material around the plunger, the clearance between the plunger and the pot should be held to 0.002 to 0.003 inch or smaller-diameter plungers and 0.004 to 0.005 inch on larger-diameter or rectangular plungers. To ensure that there is no escapement of material, it is well to incorporate one or two sealing grooves, which may be 5/32 to 3/16 inch in width and 1/16 to 3/32 inch in depth and are generally half-round in cross section. A small radius is desirable at the bottom of the pot to provide extra strength to the pot and to assure that the cull remains on the force.

In pot transfer moulding, the pot may have a sprue cut into the solid piece of steel; however, in most cases it is desirable to insert sprue bushings. The sprue bushing may be tapered so that the smaller opening is at the

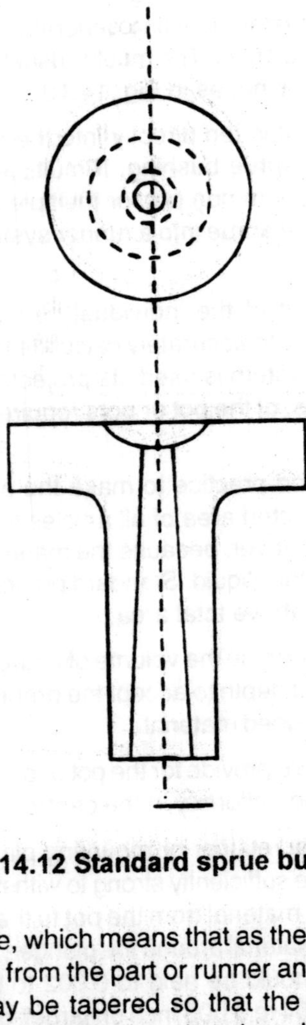

Fig. 14.12 Standard sprue bushing.

cavity or runner surface, which means that as the cull is pulled from the pot the sprue will separate from the part or runner and will remain as one piece with the cull. Or, it may be tapered so that the smaller opening is at the bottom of the pot; in that arrangement, when the cull is removed, it will separate from the sprue, leaving the sprue firmly attached to the moulded part or runner for removal with them. The length of the sprue bushing should be kept to a minimum. Fig. 14.12 illustrates a standard sprue bushing.

An undercut on the face of the plunger is provided to remove the sprue, or cull with sprue, trom the pot. Fig. 14.13 illustrates various types of cull removing grooves and sealing grooves on the plunger.

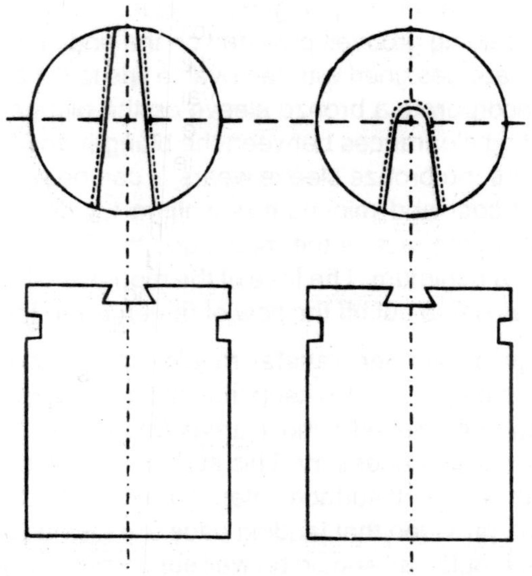

Fig. 14.13 Types of cull-removing grooves and sealing grooves on the plunger.

Because the pot method of transfer does not normally incorporate runners and gates, they will. be discussed later in this section. The second and more popular method of transfer moulding is the plunger transfer method. In this method the press may be a toggle clamp or a full hydraulic. The clamping pressure may be applied from either the top or the bottom of the moulding press, and it may vary from 25 to 500 tonnes.

Individual or multiple hydraulic cylinders are mounted in opposite direction to the clamping pressure to provide the transfer pressure. Limited presses are available that have the transfer ram within the clamp ram. The clamp force in relation to transfer force is generally three or four to one (100 tonne clamp/25-35-tonne transfer). The majority of presses are constructed with a horizontal parting line; however, horizontally moving presses are available with vertical parting lines. The advantage of the latter is that no unloading mechanism is necessary to remove parts from the mould, the parts falling from the ejector pins by gravity.

The plunger transfer method of moulding can easily be designed for automatic moulding, especially if the transfer ram is in the lower half of the mould. High-frequency preheated pills or extruded stock may be charged automatically (by the use of a loading tray) into the transfer pot. In case of a horizontal transfer cylinder, the preheated material is dropped into an opening on the upper side of the transfer sleeve or pot.

The clearance between the plunger and the transfer pot should be held to a minimum, and sealing grooves provided on the end of the plunger. Some transfer plungers are designed with removable tips to simplify maintenance. Other designs incorporate a bronze sleeve on the plunger with no sealing grooves, permitting clearances between the plunger and the cylinder to be held very close. As the bronze sleeve wears, it can be replaced with a new sleeve at limited cost and minimum downtime for changeover. The cull developed between the face of the mould and the face of the transfer ram should be held to a minimum. The face of the mould and the plunger should be designed so as not to cut off the flow of material into the runner system.

In the design of plunger transfer moulds, it is important that ample clamping pressure be provided to keep from flashing the mould. The surface of the mould should be relieved in those areas where a seal off of part, runner, gate, and plunger is not necessary. This surface should be relieved 1/32 to 1/16 inch in depth. A sealoff surface, often termed a "land area", of 3/16 inch width is sufficient, provided that landing pads are located in the area of the guide pins. Each mould half should be well supported with pillar supports to keep the centre section of the mould from bowing or opening when under pressure of material. Any flashing of the mould will result in uneven pressure in the mould cavities and may prevent full "packing" pressure on the material if the plunger "bottoms out" before the cavities are filled.

The third method of transfer moulding is known as the two-stage, reciprocal screw method. The method of transfer and the mould layout are similar to the plunger method of bottom ram transfer. Such presses have a vertical toggle clamp, and the reciprocating screw mechanism is mounted horizontally, below the mould. The reciprocating screw is used as a means of preheating the charge of material, thus eliminating need for preform equipment and preheater. The material is preheated to 220 to 260°F and fed into the transfer pot or sleeve during the curing cycle. The operation is fully automatic, with parts being removed from the knockout pins by means of a comb. The parts may be degated from the cull and runner system, and then separated in one operation. If inserts are involved, a press can be provided with a rotating table to permit loading and unloading of one section of the mould while the other section is curing.

Injection Moulding of Thermosets

Injection moulding of thermosets has become popular during the last few years, and the process is rapidly displacing many compression and transfer moulding installations. The mould design for an injection mould is similar to that of a plunger transfer or two-stage reciprocal screw transfer method. The transfer pot or sleeve is replaced by a sprue bushing.

As most injection presses have a horizontal action and vertical cutoff area, knockout systems are somewhat different in this process, in that the parts and runner system fall by gravity from the mould area. It is not uncommon to have combs installed to assure that all moulded material is removed from the mould area before the next cycle.

Faster moulding cycles are obtained and higher mould temperatures are common, making injection moulding more economical than the above-mentioned processes for a high rate of production. It is essential that more heating elements be provided to keep moulds at the desired mould temperature. This is especially true with alkyd materials because their high specific gravity and mineral filler system tend to pull considerable heat from the mould. Venting is extremely important because injection cavity fill times are faster than those in transfer moulding.

Injection-Compression Moulding of Thermosets

The process of injection-compression moulding of thermosets combines features of both injection and compression moulding. The mould contains a sprue bushing, which accepts heated moulding compound from an injection barrel and nozzle. The mould is designed somewhat like a fully positive compression mould with a force plate (also containing the sprue bushing with wide opening toward the cavity plate) that enters partly into the cavities. In operation, the mould closes partway, within about 1/4 inch of full close, and stops. The injection screw then forces material from the barrel through the nozzle and through the sprue bushing into the runner area and cavities. As soon as the full shot has flowed into the space between the mould halves, the clamp system is activated to close the mould the final 114 inch of travel. Moulding compound in the cavity or cavities thus is further densified, and, with the additional displacement of material during the final compression stroke, fibre orientation in the cavity or cavities will be less pronounced because of random movement, resulting in greater strength of the moulded part. The process is used principally with fibre-reinforced moulding compounds where optimum strength in the moulded part is desired.

Runner and Gate Design

Moulds for all types of transfer and injection moulding should be designed for the ultimate in economical operations; use of reduced transfer and injection pressure; minimum waste material in cull, runners, and gates; maximum heat buildup to obtain short cure cycles; and ease of removing parts from the cavities, and gates and runners from the parts.

Ideally, the runners should be circular in cross section because such runners offer minimum resistance to flow and the most effective insulation of the centre of the stock against the heat of the mould block, which tends to advance the cross-linking or polymerisation of the material. Advanced material can cause uneven density, warpage, and poor surface appearance. If a full round runner cannot be incorporated, a trapezoidal cross section in one mould half only may be used. Avoid a half-round runner because it offers less effective insulation of the centre of the flowing compound, and precuring may develop. Runners should be as short as possible to prevent waste and precure. One should design to avoid sudden changes in direction and with generous radii when changing direction of flow. The type of material, number of cavities, and part size and design all influence the size of the runners. In the design of the mould, it is recommended that the runner section be a separate section of the mould, hardened to 60 to 65 Rockwell C scale, and well polished. It is desirable to hard-chrome-plate this section of the mould to facilitate better flow and release and to prolong the life of the mould. Undercut wells may be provided with knockout pins below the wells to ensure holding the runner system on one side of the mould until ejection.

Gate design is extremely important when consideration is given to part density, warpage, shrinkage, weld lines, and overall physical strength. Gate size, shape and location are responsible for material orientation, the pattern of flow, time and pressure to fill the cavity, and temperature of the material as it enters the cavity. In Fig. 14.14, test specimens are being fed from constant cross-section runners through gates of various designs.

Temperature of the moulding compound rises from 270°F at the nozzle end of the barrel to as high as 351°F in the mould. The increase in temperature is caused by frictional heat developed in flow through the runner and the gate. Seven gate designs are illustrated—centre, small fan, medium fan, "Y" with two gates, large fan, side on end, and edge. The large fan and edge gate on part of this design give the most uniform flow. The "Y" gate design is not recommended, as it produces parts filled with "ball joints" and weld lines.

Fig. 14.15 shows a ring gate used to avoid weld lines and uneven density within the moulded part, which causes warpage and internal stresses.

Fig. 14.16 illustrates submarine or pinpoint gates, which are becoming quite popular in transfer and injection moulds. The main advantage of the pin-point gate is automatic degating. When pin-point gate design is used, the gate area must be a removable section of the mould. The pin-point gate will erode quite rapidly, and hardened gate sections may need to be replaced frequently. Erosion of the gate will depend on the type of filler used in the moulding compound as well as cavity fill rates.

It is a good practice to gate into the heaviest section of the moulded part, if possible. Placing gates below the surface of the part will eliminate erosion of the top surface area of the mould. If the part design permits, removable gate sections should be incorporated in gate layout. They should be very hard in order to minimise gate wear. Frequently, a special steel such as tungsten carbide is used in the gate section. Removable gate sections provided in the mould may be replaced as needed to maintain a minimum gate size. The angle of the axis of the gate should be in excess of 45° from horizontal to ensure its positive removal with the runner when the runner is lifted by the ejector pins.

Runnerless moulding or cold or warm runner systems have been developed to eliminate the large percentage of scrap material lost in sprues, culls, runners, and gates. They are applicable to thermoset injection moulds. More experience and possibly additional development work in the runner design and moulding compounds are needed for completely trouble-free moulding cycles with such moulds. In principle, only the moulded parts and secondary sprues cure, while the "cooled" moulding compound in the primary sprue and manifolded runner system remains fluid and flows into the cavities on the next cycle, where it finally cures.

Vents

Air or volatiles entrapped within a mould are the cause of many moulding problems and may be present in compression, transfer, and injection moulds. In the case of compression moulding, the location of vented knockout pins, proper venting at activated mould sections, and placement of vented activated pins at dead end sections of the mould will provide adequate venting. Fig. 14.17 illustrates vented pins. A breathe cycle, wherein the mould is opened slightly for a second or two shortly after closing and then is closed again for the cure, is not uncommon in compression moulding to allow easy escape of volatiles that otherwise would be trapped in the moulded part, creating voids.

As stated, in transfer and injection moulding the location of the gate is important; also, the location of vents is equally important. If entrapped air and volatiles are not permitted to espace, they will prevent the filling of the cavity,

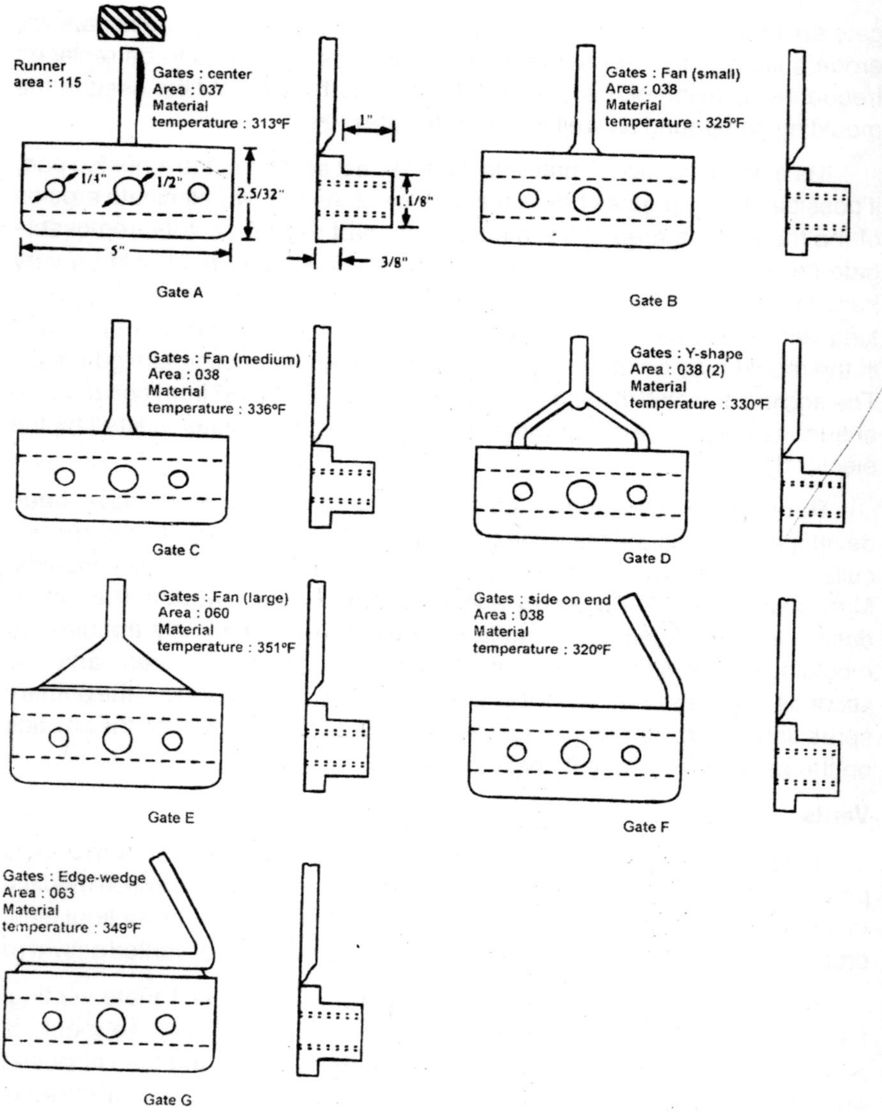

Fig. 14.14 Seven gate designs : (A) center, (B) small fan; (c) medium fan; (d) "Y" with two gates, (E) large fan, (F) side on end, (G) edge. Areas given are in square inches and refer to the trapezoidal runner cross section areas. The material temeprature is measured as soon as the cavity is full.

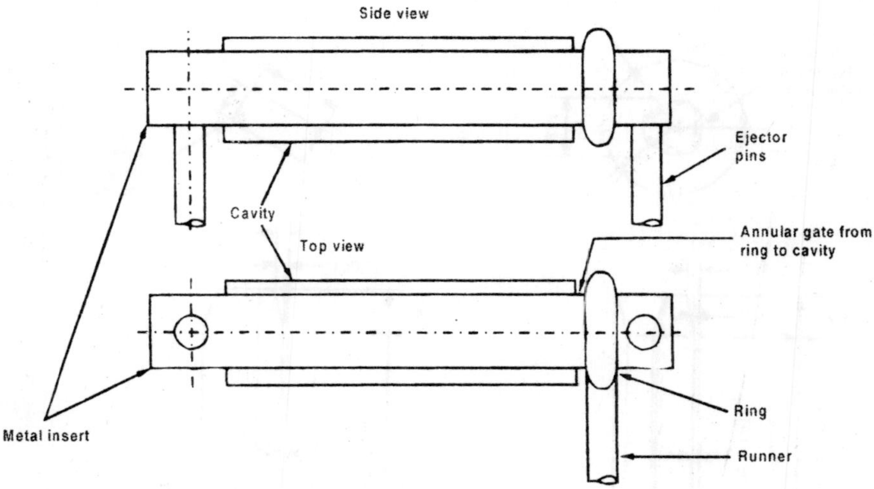

Fig. 14.15 Ring gate.

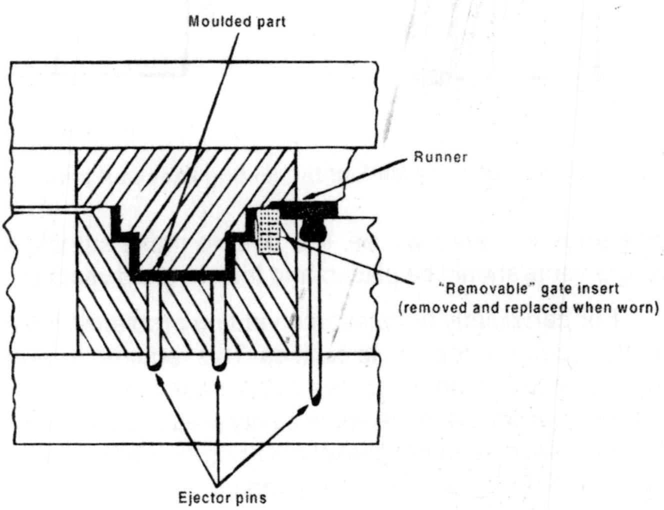

Fig. 14.16 Submarine or pin-point gate.

- will produce porosity in the part, which may cause warpage and dimensional problems, and may contain weldlines causing weak parts. The trapped air, being heated by compression causes a burning of the material. Vents a minimum 00/16 inch in width and 0.003 to 0.005 inch in depth should be ground in the face of the sealing or land area of the cavity. Unless it is obvious

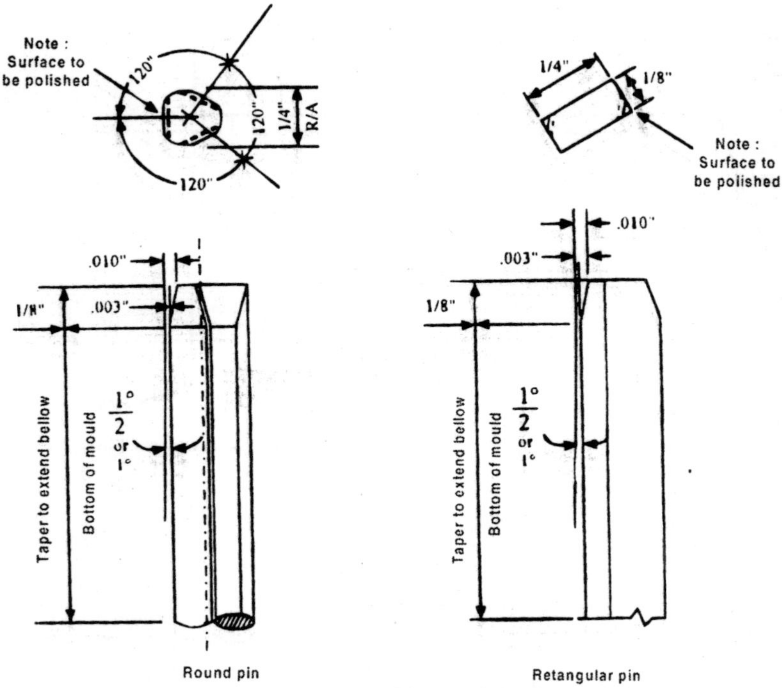

Fig. 14.17 Method for venting knockout pins.

where the knit area will be, it is best to make sample shots to determine where vents should be placed and then to grind vents on the land area.

For particularly troublesome venting problems, it may be necessary to apply vacuum to the mould cavities. This requires all vents from the cavities to discharge into an air groove or passage leading to a vacuum pump and reservoir, and to have the entire cavity area enclosed within the confines of a Teflon or silicone rubber gasket or O-ring located between parting surfaces of the mould. An ample vacuum reservoir tank must be provided to pull 15 to 25 inches of vacuum immediately as the material enters and fills the cavities.

GENERAL MOULD DESIGN CONSIDERATIONS

All mould components contacted by the moulding compound-runners, gates, cavities, land areas should be made of through-hardened carbon steels, hardened to 65 to 68 on the Rockwell C scale, highly polished, and hard-chrome-plated. Because most thermoset compounds are slightly soft at the time of ejection from cavities, ejector pins should have an adequate cross-sectional area to minimise the possibility of distorting or puncturing the moulded plastic at this point in the cycle.

In automatic moulds, it is vital to ensure, with part design, undercuts, or hold-down pins, that the moulded parts, during mould opening, consistently remain in the desired half of the mould (usually the moving half), so that when the parts and the runner system are ejected, the comb or extractor will always "find" them and effect positive removal.

Flash removal from the mould, each cycle, is critical for successful automatic moulding (the "flashfree moulds" are myths). Every effort must be made to have the flash ejected with the moulded part. An air blast. directed appropriately to cavities and land areas each moulding cycle when the mould is open, frequently is incorporated into the mould or press to further ensure the absence of flash each cycle. Should flash begin to accumulate in or on the mould, the mould should be cleaned, polished, and/or repaired.

Moulds should be of uniform temperature in the cavities, and should have adequate heating capacity to ensure maintenance of the desired temperatures despite continual heat extraction by the relatively cooler moulding compound each cycle. Temperature sensors and heating cartridges must be judiciously placed to provide this uniformity of temperature. Insulating blankets may prove helpful to minimise mould heat losses and variations due to local air currents around moulds and presses. To minimise local temperature variations in large moulds, heating cartridges often are grouped in zones, with each zone having its own temperature controller and sensor. Sensors should be positioned within 1/4 inch of heating cartridges to prevent significant temperature overswings.

It also is prudent to provide for a "mould overtemp" sensors, which will cut off power to the heating cartridges whenever it senses a mould temperature more than a few degrees over the desired mould temperature. Excessive mould temperatures not only will result in reject parts, but also may anneal the mould steels and warp critical mould components.

15

Injection Moulded Plastic Components

INTRODUCTION

Electric lights are supplied with electricity from a storage battery. When the storage battery runs down, it can be recharged from an outside source, or from a dynamo, run from the engine. The old style "carbon" filament in the electric globe consumed so much current that it was difficult to obtain a storage battery of a reasonable size and weight which would supply current from any length of time. The carbon filament lamp used a filament chemically treated and in a vacuum. The filament in the "Tungsten mazda" globe reduces the current consumption and is not liable to break with the unusual motor car vibration. There are three methods of furnishing electric current for car lighting.

1. By independent storage battery system.
2. By generator & battery system.
3. By an independent generator system.

MANUFACTURING PROCESS

Injection moulding is a multi-step process, carried out usually in a single machine, in which a thermoplastic is melted or plastic is melted or plasticized and injected into a mold farming a cavity of the shape and size of the desired article. The mould is kept at a temperature below the solidifying point of the plastic, causing the injected plasticized mass to take the form of the mold cavity, and after a sufficiently long cooling time the mold is opened and the article ejected. The injection molding process comprises four stages, each of which must be closely controlled and regulated to obtain good quality moldings. These stages are (1) Plasticizing. (2) Injection (3) after filling, and (4) Cooling and mold release.

Plasticizing :- The resin is fed from the hopper of the molding machine and heated and softened to make it plastic in a heated cylinder. To achieve a suitable state of plasticization, which will ensure a good quality product, requires closer control of temperature of the cylinder . In addition, on preplasticizing machines (screw type), the speed of rotation of screw and the applied pressure also influences the state of plasticization.

During this operation the resin compound is conveyed from one end to the other end of the during the operation.

PROCESS FLOW SHEET

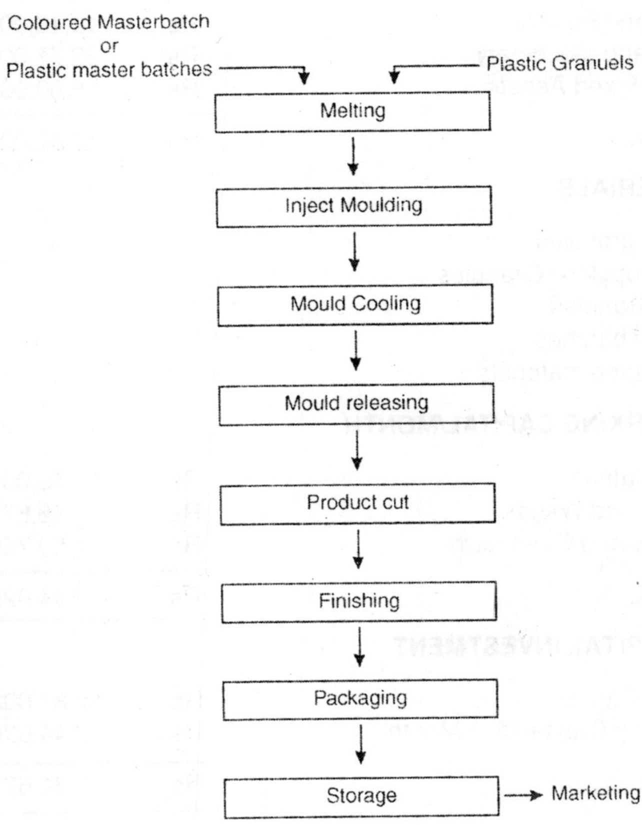

Plant Economics of Injection Moulded Plastic Components

Rated Plant Capacity = 600.00 KGS/Day

LAND & BUILDING

(Land Area 1000 Sq.mts.) =	Rs.	12,10,000.00

PLANT & MACHINERY

1. Horizontal Plastic Injection Moulding M/c.
2. Horizontal/Platic injection moulding machine
3. High speed Mixer
4. Scraps grinder
5. Working tools, testing equipments measuring instruments, fixtures
6. Dies Mould sets

FIXED CAPITAL

1.	Land and Building	Rs.	12,10,000.00
2.	Plant and Machinery	Rs.	32,77,000.00
3.	Other Fixed Assets	Rs.	6,00,000.00
	TOTAL	Rs.	50,87,000.00

RAW MATERIALS

1. HDPE granules
2. Polypropylene Granules
3. C.P. Granules
4. Master batches
5. Packaging materials

TOTAL WORKING CAPITAL/MONTH

1.	Raw Material	Rs.	10,45,000.00
2.	Salary and Wages	Rs.	48,875.00
3.	Utilities and Overheads	Rs.	1,50,750.00
	TOTAL	Rs.	12,44,625,00

TOTAL CAPITAL INVESTMENT

Total Fixed Capital	Rs.	50,87,000.00
Total Working Capital for 3 Month	Rs.	12,44,625.00
TOTAL	Rs.	63,31,625.00

TURN OVER/ANNUM

By sale of HDPE Injection Moulded
By sale of P.P. Injection Moulded
By sale of C.P. Injection Moulded

TOTAL	Rs.	1,88,85,600.00

PROFIT SALES RATIO = Profit / Sales x 100 = 12.00%
RATE OF RETURN = Operating profit / T.C.I x 100 = 35.79%
BREAK EVEN POINT (B.E.P) = 53.53.83%

16

Plastic Moulded Toys

INTORUDCTION

Plastic toy is nothing but s simple toy made of plastic either by injection moulding process or blow moulding process, for the entertainment of children. Actually, from very beginning the toys made of various materials are main source of entertainment for children. Initially the toys were made only from clay, wood or other conventional metals. Clay toys are brittle in nature and colouring on them is cumbersome. Moreover, they are not appealing due to lack of finishing, but are not appealing due to lack of finishing. But clay toys are cheap and are popular even today in rural areas. With the introduction of plastic the market of clay toys have reduced very much and various types-colours, finishing and cheaper of costly plastic

toys are available today. Since the plastic toys are more durable and have good eye appeal, they have replaced the toys which are more or less of same cost as that of plastic toys.

Plastic toys may be made from L.D.P.E. H.D.P.E., P.V.C. and Polystyrene. But only L.D.P.E. and Polystyrene are used in general due to cost as well as finishing factors. These plastic raw materials are indigenously and readily available. The plant and machinery for plastic toys manufacture are quite simple. Injection moulding and injection blow moulding bath hand operated as well as power operated are indigenously available in different sizes and capacity.

The setting of a small-cottage scale unit for the manufacture of plastic toys is not a cumbersome job. Moreover all the facilities granted by Government of India for S.S.I. Units may be available to a new enterpreneur of thid field.

The present project report envisages the manufacture of plastic toys using L.D.P.E. and polystyrene as raw material, with the capacity of 16 lakhs of various weight on annual basis, which is well feasible technicaly as well as on economic grounds.

PROCESS OF MANUFACTURE

Blow moulding machines are used for the production of hollow toys. The principle is to produce a "Pariston" - a tube of malten material - and close a mould around it, and introducing air to expand the Parison into the shape of the mould. A measured quantity of the moulding powder is put in cylinder, the feed and being at a sufficiently row temperature to present clogging nd the highest temperature being at the nozzle. The material should issue from the nozzle as a smooth slimy mass free from bubbles and lumps. A mould is closed around it and by introducing air it is expanded to the shape of the mould. The mould is opend and the piece thus formed is removed and given for finishing.

In injection moulding, the cylinder which is heated electrically is filled with the material and a mould is clamped tightly after centering it around the nozzle. The article is ejected after cooling. Usually solid toys are produced by the moulding process. But hollow toys can also be produced by first making two halves to a hollow toy and then joining them by a suitable cement.

Injection Moulding Process In Detail :

Injection moulding is a multi-step process, carried out usually in a single mchine, in which a themoplastic melted or plasticized and ijected into a mold forming a cavity of the shape and size of the desired article. The mold is kept at a temperature below the soldifying point of the plastic, caustic, causing the injected plasticized mass to to take the form of the mold cavity, and after a sufficiently long cooling time the mold is opened and the article ejected. The injection mouiding process comprised for stages, each of which must be closely controlled and regulated to obtain good quality moldings. These stages are :

1. Plasticizing.
2. Injection.
3. After-filling and
4. Cooling and mold release.

Plasticizing :

The resin is fed from the hopper of the machine and heated and softened to plasticization which will ensure a good quality product, requires close control of temperature of the cylinder and the residence time of the resin in the cylinder. In addition, on preplasticizing machines (screw type) the speed of rotation of screw and the applied pressure also influences the state of plasticization. During this operation, the resin compound is conveyed from one end to the other end of the cylinder and is heated, melted and plasticized during the operation.

Injection :

In the injection stage a correct amount of plasticized melt is injected from the plasticizing cylinder into the relatively cold mold, while colosed, under controlled pressure. The amount material injected into a mold is controlled by the machine feed mechanism. On piston of plunger type molding machines this is achieved by a volumetric measurement of unmelted granules or resin itself : on a screw preplasticizing machine, however, the control is very volumetric measurement of molten material - the latter method being more accurate. To minimize errors on the plunger type machines, especially in the case of difficult moldings, it is sometimes necessary to fit feed weighing devices of a vibratory feeder operating on a time cycle.

After Filling :

The solidification of the plasticized melt begins in the cold mold soon after its injection in the mold from the walls of the mold. The injected material is kept under pressure for some ime to ensure adequate filling of the mold and prevent the backflow of the polymer, and to compensate for the decrease in volume due to solidification. The quality of the article very much depends upon the temperature and pressure of material in the mold cavity at the moment it starts solidifying in the gate. When the mold is being filled, the temperature of the plasticized melt starts falling and there are two opposing tendencies taking place - the thermal contraction tries to reduce the volume of the molding and residual pressure in the melt tries to expand it. The above two tendencies exist simultaneously and in an ideal case they must counter - balance each other.

PROCESS FLOW SHEET

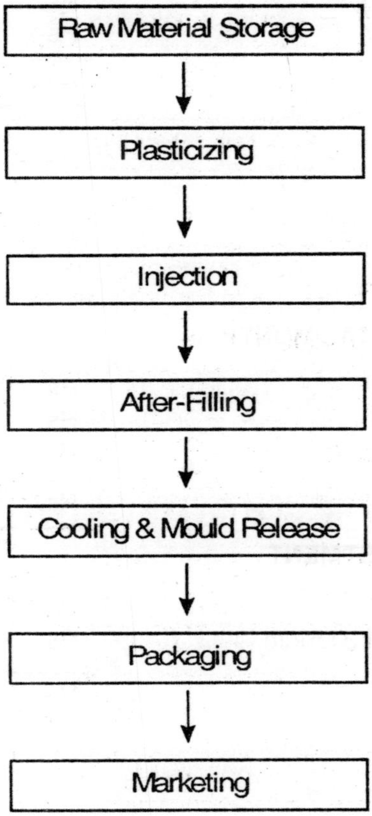

Plant Economics of Plastic Mould Toys

Rated Plant Capacity = 6000.00 KGS/Day

LAND & BUILDING

(Land Area 500 Sq.mts.) = Rs. 11,25,000.00

PLANT & MACHINERY

1. Automatic Injection Moulding
2. Moulds & dies
3. Other miscellaneous equipments

FIXED CAPITAL

1.	Land and Building	Rs.	11,25,000.00
2.	Plant and Machinery	Rs.	11,05,000.00
3.	Other Fixed Assets	Rs.	6,00,000.00
	TOTAL	Rs.	22,50,000.00

RAW MATERIALS

1. LDPE Moulding
2. Polystyrene moulding
3. Colours & Dyes
4. Packaging Materials

TOTAL WORKING CAPITAL/MONTH

1.	Raw Material	Rs.	4,28,775.00
2.	Salary and Wages	Rs.	86,500.00
3.	Utilities and Overheads	Rs.	65,000.00
	TOTAL	Rs.	5,80,275.00

TOTAL CAPITAL INVESTMENT

Total Fixed Capital	Rs.	22,50,000.00
Total Working Capital for 3 Month	Rs.	5,80,275.00
TOTAL	Rs.	28,30,275.00

TURN OVER/ANNUM

Receipt by sale of
3,00,000 pcs of 1 oz, 3,00,000 pcs of 2 oz, 3,00,000 pcs of 3 oz
Polystyrene Balls :
3,00,000 pcs of 1 oz, 3,00,000 pcs of 2 oz, 3,00,000 pcs of 3 oz

TOTAL	Rs.	94,50,000.00

PROFIT SALES RATIO = Profit / Sales x 100 = 19.09%
RATE OF RETURN = Operating profit / T.C.I x 100 = 63.75%
BREAK EVEN POINT (B.E.P) = 43.86%

17

Plastic Injection Moulding Products

Injection moulding is one of the most important used in plastic articles manufacture bath in terms of volume thermo-plastics handled and the range of articles manufacured.

The original injection moulding machines were similar in design to metal die casting machines, when this process was developed in 1934 for the rapid moulding of thermoplastics. During the subsequent years, especially as experience and increase in understanding of processing chracteristics of plastics led to the improvements in the design of such machines, this technique has proved highly success full and to the bulk of thermoplastics are manufactured by this technique. The injection moulding machine is now a sophisticated integrated piece of equipment and includes all the machanisms and centralls required to carry out successfully each step of the injection moulding process completely in a single unit. During the past two decades the damand has grown for larger capacity machines and today its is possible to inject as much as 5 Kg of material at one 'shet'.

Injection moulding process has inherent advantages of high degree of repititive accuracy and adaptability for the production of a wide range of components. The process of injection moulding can be applied with modifications to thermosetting materials also and differs from transfer moulding in that the plasticizing chamber contains enough material to fill the mould several times.

The thermoplastics material in general used for injection moulding in clude polyethylene PVC polystyrene, polypropylene polymethyl metacrylate PTFFZ polyamides, cellulose, derivatives polyurethanes, CAB and polycarbonates.

PROCESS OF MANUFACTURES

For the manufacture of injection moulded articles mostly, screw guided injection moulding machine is used. The advantage of this machine is that thermoplastics as well thermosets can be processed with the same machine using different dies for defferent product. The injection moulding process comprises four stages, each of which must be closely controlled and regulated to obtain good quality mouldings.

The re stage are :-

1. Plasticizing
2. Injection
3. After filling and
4. Cooling and mould release.

Plant Economics of Platic Injection Moulding

Rated Plant Capacity = 923.00 KGS/Day

LAND & BUILDING

(Land Area 200 Sq.mts.) = Rs. 5,50,000.00

PLANT & MACHINERY

1. Injection Moulding Machine
2. Scrap Grinder
3. Extruder, Mixer
4. Acrylic Cutter, Grinder, Heater

FIXED CAPITAL

1.	Land and Building	Rs.	5,50,000.00
2.	Plant and Machinery	Rs.	4,10,000.00
3.	Other Fixed Assets	Rs.	1,40,000.00
	TOTAL	Rs.	11,00,000.00

RAW MATERIALS

1. Plastic Moulding Power
2. Plastic scrap

3. Acrylic Plastic Sheet
4. Packaging Expencess

TOTAL WORKING CAPITAL/MONTH

1.	Raw Material	Rs.	1,71,250.00
2.	Salary and Wages	Rs.	27,060.00
3.	Utilities and Overheads	Rs.	57,300.00
	TOTAL	Rs.	2,55,610.00

TOTAL CAPITAL INVESTMENT

Total Fixed Capital	Rs.	11,00,000.00
Total Working Capital for 1 Month	Rs.	2,55,610.00
TOTAL	Rs.	13,55,610.00

TURN OVER/ANNUM

By sale of Patras 72000 Pcs.
Ice Trays 50000 Pcs.
Fridge Mats 25000 Pcs.
Small Plastics Misc. Parts 50000
Small Plastic Kits 50000
Plastic waste paper baskets 30000
Misc. items of Stationary

TOTAL Rs. 42,84,000.00

PROFIT SALES RATIO = Profit / Sales x 100 = 21.98%
RATE OF RETURN = Operating profit / T.C.I x 100 = 69.45%
BREAK EVEN POINT (B.E.P) = 41.94%

18

Plastic Injection Moulding Items (like Bucket, Plastic Chairs, Bathing Tub)

Plastic Injection Moulded Items have got tremendous demand now-a-days especially Plastic chairs, Buckets, Bathing Tubs etc. Injection molding is somewhat unusual among production methods in that essentially the entire process in carried out on the injection molding machines were similar in general design to metal die casting machines, but the processing characteristics of plastic have led to change in design & evolution that are still going on. The product injection molded plastic furnitures are the products produced by these injection molding machines with varied shape & size along with different colour & shades according to the choice of customers & even according to the pattern as per the modern society such as office culture, drawing rooms of houses, which give style & likingness of consumers.

At present, these injection molded plastic furnitures frequently used at every mode of the social occasions & places.

MANUFACTURING PROCESS

Injection moulding is a multi-step process, carried out usually in a single machine, in which a thermoplastic is melted or plastic is melted or plasticized and injected into a mold farming a cavity of the shape and size of the desired article. The mould is kept at a temperature below the solidifying point of the plastic, causing the injected plasticized mass to take the form of the mold cavity, and after a sufficiently long cooling time the mold is opened and the article ejected. The injection molding process comprises four stages, each of which must be closely controlled and regulated to obtain good quality moldings.

These stages are (1) Plasticizing. (2) Injection (3) after filling, and (4) Cooling and mold release.

Plasticizing :- The resin is fed from the hopper of the molding machine and heated and softened to make it plastic in a heated cylinder. To achieve a suitable state of plasticization, which will ensure a good quality product, requires closer control of temperature of the cylinder . In addition, on preplasticizing machines (screw type), the speed of rotation of screw and the applied pressure also influences the state of plasticization. During this operation the resin compound is conveyed from one end to the other end of the during the operation.

PROCESS FLOW SHEET

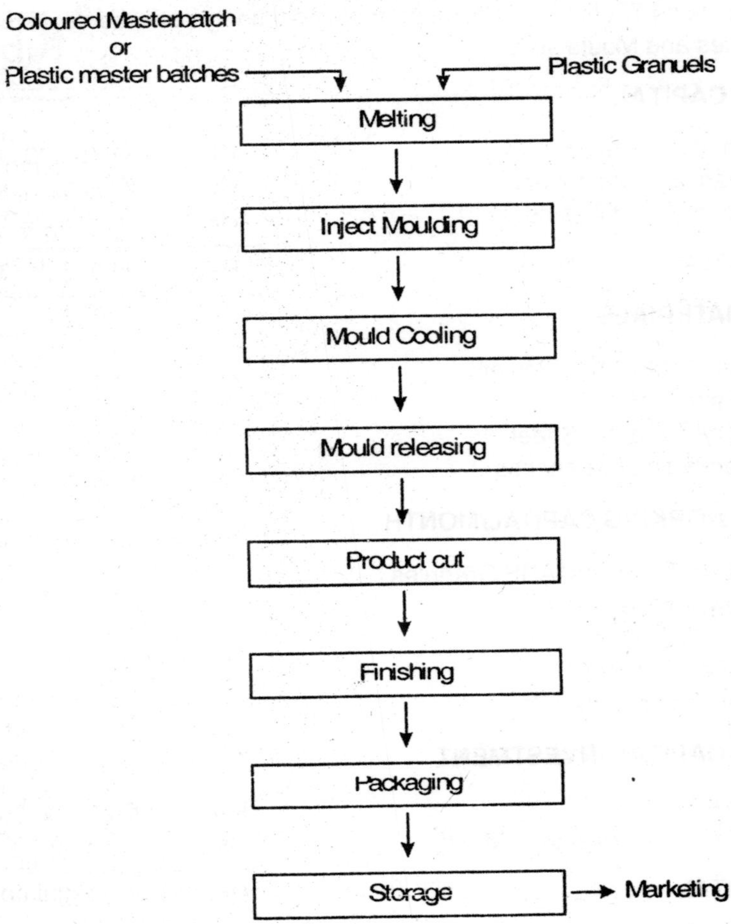

Plant Economics of Platic Injection Moulding

Rated Plant Capacity = 619.20 KGS/Day

LAND & BUILDING

(Land Area 1000 Sq.mts.) =	Rs.	32,75,000.00

PLANT & MACHINERY

1. Horizontal Plastic Injection Moulding Machine.
2. Horizontal /Plastic injection Moulding Machine
3. High Speed Mixer
4. Scraps Grinder
5. Working Tools, Testing equipments measuring instruments, fixtures
6. Dies and Mould sets

FIXED CAPITAL

1.	Land and Building	Rs.	32,75,000.00
2.	Plant and Machinery	Rs.	49,80,000.00
3.	Other Fixed Assets	Rs.	8,37,000.00
	TOTAL	Rs.	90,92,000.00

RAW MATERIALS

1. Plastic Moulding Power
2. Plastic scrap
3. Acrylic Plastic Sheet
4. Packaging Expencess

TOTAL WORKING CAPITAL/MONTH

1. HDPE Granules/ ABS Granules
2. Polypropylene Granules
3. C.P. Granules
4. Master batches
5. Packaging materials

TOTAL CAPITAL INVESTMENT

Total Fixed Capital	Rs.	90,92,000.00
Total Working Capital for 1 Month	Rs.	17,87,522.00
TOTAL	Rs.	1,05,79,522.00

TURN OVER/ANNUM

By sale of Plastic Injection Moulding Products i.e. Plastic Chairs, Small Child bathing Tub & Plastic Buckets etc. 185760 Kgs.	
TOTAL	Rs. 2,32,20,000.00

PROFIT SALES RATIO = Profit / Sales x 100 = 11.62%

RATE OF RETURN = Operating profit / T.C.I x 100 = 25.50%

BREAK EVEN POINT (B.E.P) = 62.31%

LIST OF THE READY AVAILABLE DETAILED PROJECT REPORTS

AUTOMOBILES, MECHANICAL & METALLURGICAL

1. AGRICULTRAL EQUIPMENTS
2. AGRICULTRAL EQUIPMENTS INCLUDING THRESHERS
3. AIR BRAKE HELICAL COIL
4. AIR COOLER
5. AIR FILTERS(FOR SCOOTER CAR & EXCAVATORS ETC.)
6. ALUMINIUM & ALUMINIUM ALLOYS FROM ALUMINIUM SCRAP TO MAKE UTENSILS (INDUCTION FURNACE MELTED)
7. ALUMINIUM ALLOY WHEELS
8. ALUMINIUM ALLOYS FROM ALUMINIUM SCRAP TO MAKE UTENSILS (INDUCTION FURNACE)
9. ALUMINIUM HOT & COLD ROLLING MILL
10. ALUMINIUM BOTTLE MANUFACTURING (COLD EXTRUSION OF ALUMINIUM)
11. ALUMINIUM/COPPER CABLE LUGS
12. ALUMINIUM CANS FOR BEER PACKAGING
13. ALUMINIUM CANS FOR CAPACITORS
14. ALUMINIUM CAPS FOR INJECTION VIALS
15. ALUMINIUM EXTRUSION
16. ALUMINIUM FURNITURE & HARDWARE
17. ALUMINIUM SHEET ROLLING MILL
18. ALUMINIUM UTENSILS
19. ALUMINIUM UTENSILS & SCHOOL BOXES
20. ALUMINIUM WIRE DRAWING AND SUPER ENAMELLING FOR WINDING
21. ANODISED ALUMINIUM UTENSILS
22. ANODIZING OF ALUMINIUM
23. ANTIMONY OXIDE FROM LEAD SCRAP
24. ARC WELDING FILTER GLASS
25. ALUMINIUM FOIL CUTTING & ROLL MAKING
26. AUTO FLAPS FOR TRUCKS & BUSES
27. AUTOMOBILE WORKSHOP (GARAGE & SERVICE CENTRE)
28. AUTO GEARS
29. AUTO HORNS
30. AUTO LEAF SPRING
31. AUTO TUBES
32. AUTO PISTON RING
33. AUTO PISTON
34. BAKERY AND BISCUITS EQUIPMENTS FABRICATION
35. BALL POINT PEN REFILLS
36. BALL ROLLER & TAPER BEARING
37. BAND SAW BLADES
38. BARBED WIRE
39. BICYCLE SPOKES
40. BRAKE LINING ASBESTOES/ RESIN BASED & ASBESTOES FREE
41. BRASS ARTWARE/HOLLOW WARE CASTING (WITH THE HELP OF PHENOLIC RESIN)
42. BRASS CASTING
43. BRASS PIPES FROM BRASS SHEET WITH LONGITUDINALLY WELDING
44. BRASS WARE BY CASTING METHOD (BRASS ARTICLES VIZ. BRASS POOJA LAMPS AND OTHER CASTED)
45. BRIGHT BARS
46. BUFFING AND POLISHING INDUSTRY (JOB WORK)
47. BUTT HINGE (BRASS SHEET)
48. CARBON BRUSH HOLDER & SLIP RING
49. CO_2 WELDING WIRE ELECTRODES (COPPER/ COPPER ALLOY COATED M.S.WIRE)
50. CARBON FILM RESISTORS
51. CARBURETTORS
52. CAST STEEL PANES FOR MELTING FURNACE
53. CHEMICAL ETCHING OF STAINLESS STEEL
54. CHEMICAL RESISTANT IRON & STEEL
55. COLD FORM SECTION MILL
56. COLD ROLLED FORMING OF SECTION AND OTHER SECTIONS
57. COLD ROLLING OF MS STRIP
58. COLD TWISTED DE-FORMED RIBBED STEEL
59. COMPRESSOR (HERMETIC) FOR AIR CONDITIONERS
60. COMPRESSED NATURAL GAS (CNG KIT) FOR AUTOVEHICLE
61. CONTINUOUSLY CAST STEEL WIRE RODS (5 mm)
62. CONTINUOUS CASTING COPPER WIRE RODS
63. CONVEYOR BELTINGS
64. CONVEYOR BELT, TRANSM -ISSION BELT & V BELTS
65. COOKING RANGES
66. COPPER/BRASS SHEETS, CIRCLE & UTENSILS
67. COPPER FOIL
68. COPPER INGOTS, RODS MAKING & WIRE DRAWING
69. COPPER PRODUCTS FROM COPPER SCRAP
70. COPPER SMELTING PLANT
71. COPPER WIRE RODS FROM COPPER SCRAP
72. CORRUGATED BOX MAKING MACHINERY AND OTHER THEIR PARTS
73. CYLINDER LINER FOR AUTOMOBILES
74. DOOR LOCKS/PAD LOCKS
75. DRILL BITS & TOOL BITS
76. DRUM CLOSURES
77. ERW STEEL CONDUIT PIPE
78. EARTH MOVING EQPT.
79. ENGINE VALVES FOR AUTOMOBILES
80. FABRICATION OF HEAT EXCHANGER
81. FABRICATION OF STORAGE TANKS AND M.S. DRUM
82. FERROUS ALLOY NI-HARDY I.V CASTING
83. FERROUS Mn ALLOY CASTING BY ALUMINA THERMIC PROCESS
84. FERRO ALLOYS
85. FERRO SILICON & FERRO MANGANESE FROM DOLOMITE (SMS GRADE)
86. FIRE EXTINGUISHERS
87. FLIP-TONE CANS
88. FORGED CONECTING ROD
89. FORGING UNIT
90. FOUNTAIN PEN NIBS
91. FOUNDRY SAND
92. FUEL INJECTION SYSTEM
93. GALVANIZED M.S.STRIPS
94. GALVANIZING PLANT
95. GALVANIZED IRON WIRE
96. GAS WELDING TORCHES AND NOZZLES
97. GASKET SHEET
98. GATE GRILLS & WINDOW FRAMES
99. GENERATING SET (DIESEL)
100. HARD ANODISED ALUMINIUM
101. HOSPITAL WARES
102. HOSPITAL FURNITURES
103. HOT DIP GALVANIZING
104. HOT FORGED FASTENERS
105. HOT MIX PLANT
106. INJECTION MOULDED PLASTIC COMPOUNDS WITH TOOL ROOM
107. INJECTION MOULDED PLASTIC COMPONENTS AND METAL PIPE SPINNING UNIT
108. INVESTMENT CASTING
109. IRON/STEEL WIRE GAUGE
110. IRON TAWA
111. KNIVES (S.S.KNIVES)
112. KITCHEN SINK (S.S.)
113. L.P.G REGULATORS
114. MACHINE SCREWS & SELF TAPPING SCREWS
115. MARUTI WORKSHOP CUM SERVICE STATION
116. MAGNESIUM INGOTS & BULLETS CASTING

359. DI ETHYL OXALATE
360. DI METHYL ORTHOPHTHALATE
361. DI-METHYL PHTHALATE
362. DICLOFENAC GEL
363. DIOCTYL PHTHALATE (DOP)
364. DI PHENYL GLYCERINE
365. DI PHENYL OXIDE
366. DINITRO-CHLORO BENZENE
367. DISTILLED WATER
368. DODECYL BENZENE SULPHONATE
369. DUSTLESS CHALK
370. EDTA & ITS SALTS
371. ELECTROLESS NICKEL PLATING ON PLASTICS
372. ENDOSULFAN
373. EPOXY RESIN BASED COMPOUND
374. ETHYL ACETATE
375. EHTYL ETHER
376. ETHYL ALCOHOL (POTABLE LIQUOR)
377. ETHYL HEXANOL
378. EXTRACTION OF ESSENTIAL OILS BY SUGAR CRITICAL FLUID (CARBON DIOXIDE) METHOD FROM FLOWERS, HERBAL & SPICES
379. FERRIC ALUM
380. FERRO CHROME LIGNO SULPHONATE
381. FERRO MANGANESE
382. FERRO SILICONE
383. FERRO VANADIUM FROM VANADIUM SLUDGE
384. FERROUS SILICATE
385. FERROUS SULPHATE
386. FERTILIZER FROM ANIMAL BLOOD & LEATHER WASTE
387. FLUORESCENT TUBE LIGHT POWDER
388. FOAMED PVC COMPOUNDING & ITS PRODUCTS
389. FORMALDEHYDE
390. FRACTIONAL DISTILLATION OF D.M.O (DEMENTHOLIZED OIL)
391. FRACTIONAL DISTILLATION OF ESSENTIAL OIL & MEDICINAL PLANT EXTRACT
392. FRICTION DUST (LIQUID & POWDER) FROM CNSL
393. FRUIT FLAVOURS
394. FURFURAL FROM RICE HUSK
395. GARLIC ACID
396. GASKET SHELLAC COMPOUND
397. GEAR OIL
398. GIBBERELLIC ACID
399. GLASS PUTTY
400. GLYCERINE
401. GOSSYPOL (POLY PHENOL) FROM COTTON SEED OIL
402. GUAR GUM POWDER
403. HAIR FIXER (HAIR GEL TYPE)
404. H - ACID
405. HENNA PASTE MAKING
406. HEPTAL DEHYDE
407. HIGH CARBON FERRO CHROME
408. HYDRATED CALCIUM SILICATE BRICK
409. HYDRATED LIME FROM SEA SHELL
410. HYDROCHLORIC ACID
411. HYDRO FLUORIC ACID
412. HYDROGEN PEROXIDE (BY AUTO-OXIDATION PROCESS)
413. ICE PACKS (SOLUTIONS TYPE, WHITE GEL TYPE, VIOLET SEMI SOLID POLYMER TYPE)
414. IMPROVING DROP POINT PARAFFIN WAX FROM 45-50ºC TO 75-80ºC
415. INDUSTRIAL ALCOHOL
416. INTEGERATED COMPLEX OF EASTER & ALLIED PRODUCTS (D.O.P, D.B.P, ETHYL ACETATE WIRE ENAMEL & CABLE JELLY)
417. IMFL (WHISKY) & COUNTRY LIQUOR
418. IRON OXIDE FOR MAKING FERITTE
419. IRON SULPHIDE
420. JUTE BATCHING OIL
421. KESH KALA TEL (HAIR DYE LOTION) (VASMOL 33, BLACK NITE TYPE)
422. L-LYSINE MONOHYDROCHLORIDE
423. LACTIC ACID FROM WHITE SUGAR BY FERMENTATION PROCESS
424. LDPE GRANULES FROM VIRGIN (LDPE RESIN)
425. LEAD EXTRACTION FROM BATTERY SCRAP
426. LEAD OXIDE (A) LEAD MONOXIDE
(B) LEAD TETRA OXIDE
(C) GREYLEAD OXIDE
427. LIQUID GLUCOSE & ITS BY PRODUCTS
428. LIQUID OXYGEN BOTTLING PLANT
429. LIQUID SHOE POLISH
430. LIQUID FLOOR POLISH
431. LUBE OIL VISCOSITY IMPROVED FOR P.P.G/P.E.G
432. LUBRICANTS ASHLESS 100% COMBUSTION
433. MAGNESIUM CARBONATE AND MAGNESIUM BICARMONATE
434. MAGNESIUM HYDROXIDE POWDER
435. MAGNESIUM SILICATE
436. MAGNESIUM SULPHATE
437. MALACHITE GREEN
438. MALEIC ANHYDRIDE
439. MANGANESE SULPHATE
440. MANUFACTURING OF CARBON MONO-OXIDE WATER GAS
441. MENTHOL BOLD CRYSTALS FROM FLAKES
442. MENTHOL CRYSTAL & MENTHA OIL
443. MERCURIC OXIDE
444. METAL PRE-TREATMENT CHEMICALS
445. METHANE GAS BY SODIUM ACETATE & SODA LIME
446. METHYL ACETYL RICINOLATE
447. METOL
448. METOL FROM HYDROQUINONE & METHYLAMINE
449. MICANITE
450. MICRO NUTRIENT MIXTURE
451. MINERAL WATER
452. MINERAL WATER AND PET BOTTILNG PLANT
453. MINERAL WATER IN BOTTLES, GLASS AND POUCHES
454. MINI CEMENT PLANT (BY ROTARY KILN PROCESS)
455. MIXED FERTILIZER
456. MOSQUITO & FLIES REPELLENT AGARBATTI (INCENSE STICKS)
457. MONO CHLORO ACETIC ACID
458. MONOCROTOPHOS (TECHNICAL)
459. MOSQUITO COIL
460. MOSQUITO COIL & MAT
461. MOSQUITO MAT
462. MOTHER TINCTURE & BIO CHEMIC MEDICINES
463. NAPHTHALENE & PHENYL (INTEGRATED UNIT)
464. NATURAL MINERAL WATER BY REVERSE OSMOSIS PROCESS
465. NICKEL PLATING BRIGHTNER (PRIMARY OR CARRIER BRIGHTNER & SECONDARY BRIGHTNER)
466. NICKEL SULPHATE
467. NICOTINE FROM TOBACCO WASTE
468. NICOTINE SULPHATE FROM TOBACCO WASTE
469. NITRO BENZENE
470. NITRO CELLULOSE SANDING SEALER/LACQUER
471. NITRO MUSK
472. NITROGEN & OXYGEN GAS PLANT
473. NON-IONIC SURFACTANT (WETTING AGENT)
474. NO-CARB PASTE
475. OCTANOL
476. ORTHO NITRO PHENOL
477. OXALIC ACID FROM MOLASSES
478. OXALIC ACID FROMRICE HUSK
479. OXALIC ACID FROM TREE BARK
470. OXALIC ACID FROM WASTE VEGETABLES
471. OXYGEN GAS PLANT
472. OXYGEN GAS PLANT (AIR SEPERATION METHOD)
473. PARA-AMINO BENZOIC ACID
474. PARA-AMINO PHENOL
475. PARA TOLUENE SULPHONIC ACID
476. PECTIN FROM RAW PAPAYA
477. PERFUME (LEMON & OTHERS)

CRUDE NAPHTHA

570. TRIMETHYL AMMONIUM CHLORIDE
571. TRIPHENYL PHOSPHITE (T.P.P)
572. ULTRAMARINE BLUE (LIQUID)
573. UREA FORMALDEHYDE & MELAMINE FORMALDEHYDE POWDER
574. UNDECYLINIC ACID
575. VINYL ACETATE MONOMER
576. VITAMIN C
577. VITAMIN E
578. WASTE WATER TREATMENT PLANT FOR INDUSTRIAL SECTOR IN INDIA (ONLY MARKER SURVEY)
579. WIRE DRAWING LUBRICANT
580. WIRE ENAMEL
581. XANTHATES
582. YELLOW DEXTRIN
583. ZINC CHLORIDE
584. ZINC OXIDE
585. ZINC PHOSPHATING BY COLD PROCESS
586. ZINC SILICATE
587. ZINC STEARATE
588. ZINC SULPHATE
589. ZINC SULPHATE MONOHYDRATE
590. ACID BLACK
591. AURAMINE'O'
592. AZO DYES STUFF
593. DYE & DYE INTERMEDIATE
594. DYE INTERMEDIATES
595. MALACHITE GREEN
596. METHYLENE BLUE
597. PHTHALOCYANINE BLUE
598. PHTHALOCYANINE BLUE & GREEN
599. REACTIVE DYES
600. SULPHUR BLACK DYE
601. VAT DYES
602. WATER CHILLING PLANT
603. WADDING OIL (100%) FOR WADDING OF COTTON HOSIERY CLOTH IN THE DYEING PROCESS
604. WHITE OIL
605. WAX FLOOR POLISH

ELECTRICAL, ELECTONICS, COMPUTERS AND INFOTECH/IT PROJECTS

606. AIR CONDITIONING
607. ALUMINIUM ALLOY CONDUCTOR
608. ALUMINIUM CABLE
609. ALUMINIUM ELECTROYTIC CAPACITORS
610. AUDIO CASSETTE ASSEMBLING & RECORDING
611. AUDIO CASSETTES DUPLICATING RECORDING
612. AUDIO CASSETTES & AUDIO STUDIO
613. AUDIO CASSETTES PLANE & RECORDED
614. AUDIO MAGNETIC HEADS
615. AUDIO MAGNETIC TAPE
616. AUDIO/VIDEO CASSETTES
617. AUTO BULB/LAMPS
618. AUTOMATIC VOLTAGE STABILIZER
619. BATTERY PLATES
620. BACK OFFICE (Rs. 5000/-)
621. B/W TV & COMPUTER MONITOR PICTURE TUBE
622. BREAD BOARDS
623. CALL CENTRE
624. CAMERA (35 MM)
625. CAPACITORS
626. CARBON ELECTRODE USED FOR BATTERY CELL
627. CARBON POTETIOMETERS
628. CEILING FAN
629. CERAMIC INSULATOR
630. CHILDREN INFOTECH TRAINING INSTITUTE (Rs. 5000/-)
631. CHOKE AND PATTI
632. CHOKE AND STARTER
633. CHOKE USED FOR FLUORESCENT LAMPS
634. COLOUR TELEVISION
635. COLOUR AND BLACK & WHITE TELEVISION
636. COMPACT DISC
637. COMPACT DISC PLAYER (AUDIO/VIDEO)
638. COMPUTER EDUCATION INSTITUTE
639. COMPUTER ASSEMBLY
640. COMPUTER HARDWARE
641. COMPUTER KEYBOARD
642. COMPUTER PERIPHERALS
643. COMPUTER PRINTERS
644. COMPUTER RIBBON
645. COMPUTER RIBBON REINKING OR REFILLING
646. COMPUTER STATIONERY
647. COMPUTER STATIONERY & IMPORTED HARDWARE PARTS

648. COMPUTER TERMINALS
649. COMPUTERISED WASHING MACHINE (AUTOMATIC)
650. COMPUTER SOFTWARE
651. CONDENSER FOR MOTOR USING MPP FILM
652. CONTENT DEVELOPMENT CENTRE (EOU) (Rs. 5000/-)
653. CONTROL PANEL BOARD
654. COOLING COIL FOR AIR CONDITIONERS
655. COPPER STRIP COIL FROM SCRAP
656. CORDLESS TELEPHONES
657. CYBER CAFE
658. CYBERKIOSK (Rs. 5000/-)
659. DATA PROCESSING CENTRE (Rs. 5000/-)
660. D.C. MICRO MOTORS
661. D.G.SETS
662. DISH ANTENNA AND CABLE T.V. NETWORK EQUIPMENT
663. DISTRIBUTION TRANSFORMERS & REPAIRS
664. DOMESTIC ELECTRICAL APPLIANCES- ROOM COOLER, WASHING MACHINE, WATER HEATER, ELECTRIC ROOM HEATER
665. E-SCHOOL
666. E-COMMERCE/BUSINESS
667. ELECTRIC ENERGY METER
668. ELECTRIC FANS
669. ELECTRIC HORN FOR AUTOMOBILE
670. ELECTRIC LAMP/GLS (INCANDESCENT LAMP)
671. ELECTRIC MIXER
672. ELECTRIC MOTORS UP TO 10 HP. REWINDING OF ALL TYPES OF MOTORS WATER PUMPS
673. ELECTRIC MOTOR WINDING (FOR FAN, MIXIES, ETC.)
674. ELECTRIC STEAM IRON
675. ELECTRICAL APPLIANCES
676. ELECTRICAL FIXTURES
677. ELECTRICAL STAMPING
678. ELECTROLYTIC CAPACITORS
679. ELECTROMAGNETIC RELAY
680. ELECTRONIC BALAST/CHOK
681. ELECTRICAL CHOKE
682. ELECTRONIC DIGITAL WATCHES
683. ELECTRONIC DIGITAL WEIGHING MACHINE
684. ELECTRONIC FIRE ALARM
685. ELECTRONIC GAS STOVE LIGHTERS
686. ELECTRONIC PRESSURE INDICATORS, ELECTRICALS, ELECTRONIC LIQUID LEVEL INDICATORS, ELECTRONIC TEMPERATURE INDICATOR, DIGITAL TACHOMETER
687. ELECTRONIC TELEPHONE INSTRUMENTS
688. ELECTRONIC TOYS
689. ELECTRONIC WATCHES & CLOCKS
690. FAX MACHINES
691. F.H.P MOTORS
692. FLOPPY DISKETTES
693. FLUORESCENT LAMP STARTER
694. FLUORESCENT TUBULAR

LAMPS WITH INTRODUCTION TO MERCURY VAPOUR LAMP
695. FRANCHISEE COMPUTER EDUCATION CENTRE (Rs. 5000)
696. GAS DETECTOR (L.P.G)
697. GENERATOR SET & PUMP SETS
698. GENERATOR (BATTERY OPERATED)
699. GIS SERVICE CENTRE (GEOGRAPHICAL INFORMATION SYSTEMS)
700. HARDWARE FITTING FOR TRANSMISSION LINE OVERHEAD LINE MATERIAL
701. HEADERS FOR TRANSISTOR ICS SEMI CONDUCTOR
702. H.T & L.T INSULATORS
703. H.T & M.V INDUSTRIAL CUBICAL SWITCH BOARD
704. INFORMATION MOVING DISPLAY (L.E.D TYPE)
705. INSURANCE CLAIM PROCESSING CENTRE (EOU) (Rs. 5000/-)
706. INTEGRATED CIRCUITS
707. INTERNET BASED STOCK TRADING (Rs. 5000/-)
708. INTERNET SERVICE PROVIDER (I.S.P.)
709. JELLY FILLED TELEPHONE CABLES
710. LAP TOP COMPUTERS
711. LEAD ACID BATTERIES
712. LEAD ACID BATTERY PLATES AND ASSEMBLING OF BATTERY
713. LEGAL TRANSCRIPTION & SECRETARIAL SERVICES CENTER (EOU)(Rs. 5000/-)
714. LIGHT EMITTING DIODES (L.E.D)
715. LINEAR ICS TRAINER KIT
716. LOUD SPEAKER
717. L.T TRANSFORMER REPAIRING
718. MEDICAL TRANSCRIPTION CENTRE
719. METAL FILM RESISTORS
720. METALLISED POLYPROPYLENE, POLYESTER FILM CAPACITOR
721. MICA BASE ELECTRONIC COMPONENTS
722. MICA PAPER WASTE PAPER FROM MICA WASTE
723. MICRO PROCESSORS TRAINER KITS BASED ON MICRO PROCESSORS
724. MINI COMPUTER (PERSONAL COMPUTER)
725. MINIATURE CIRCUIT BREAKER (M.C.B)
726. MINIATURE WATCH BATTERIES (BUTTON CELL)
727. MIXER/GRINDER (MIXI)
728. MONO CHROME COMPUTER MONITOR
729. MOTOR START ELECTROLYTIC CAPACITOR
730. MULTI LAYER P.C.B
731. MULTIPLE RELAY FOR LOW VOLTAGE
732. NEON INDICATOR
733. NEON SIGN MANUFACTURE
734. OPTICAL FIBRE CABLES
735. ON LINE SHOPPING MALL (Rs. 5000/-)
736. OPTO MECHANICAL & ELECTRICAL EQUIPMENTS
737. PHOTO COLOUR LAB
738. PICTURE TUBE (B/W)
739. PLAIN PAPER COPIER
740. PLASTIC FILM CAPACITORS
741. POLYESTER CAPACITORS
742. PORTABLE GENERATOR SET
743. PORTAL
744. PORTABLE TELEVISION(TV)
745. POWER CAPACITORS
746. POWER INVERTERS
747. POWER PLANT
748. POWER TRANSFORMERS UP TO 600 KVA
749. PRINTED CIRCUIT BOARD
750. PVC WIRES & CABLES
751. RE-CONDITIONING OF PICTURE TUBE
752. RESIN CAST CT & PT (1 KV)
753. SEMI CONDUCTOR DEVICE
754. SEMI CONDUCTORS FOR TRANSISTORS & DIODES
755. SETTING UP OF A VIDEO STUDIO
756. SMOKE DETECTORS
757. SOLAR CELLS
758. SOLAR MODULES
759. SOLAR PHOTO VOLTAIC SYSTEM
760. SOLDER FLUXES
761. SOLAR WATER HEATING PANELS
762. STEEL FURNITURE & ELECTRICAL APPLIANCES
763. STEREO AMPLIFIERS
764. STEREO CASSETTE RECORDERS/PLAYERS
765. STREET LIGHT FITTINGS SURGE SUPPRESSOR
766. TANTALUM CAPACITORS
767. TEFLON COATED ELECTRIC CABLE
768. TELEMEDICINE (DISTANCE HEALTH CARE) (Rs. 5000/-)
769. TELEPHONE CORD/CABLE
770. TELEPHONE (PUSH BUTTON TYPE)
771. TELEPHONE (PUSH BUTTON & CORDLESS)
772. TELEVISION (CTV & B/W)
773. TELEVISION (3-D)
774. TELEVISION DEFLECTION COMPONENTS
775. TELEVISION SIGNAL BOOSTERS
776. TELEVISION TUNERS
777. TRACTION BATTERIES
778. TRAINING INSTITUTE OF MEDICAL TRANSCRIPTION
779. TRANSFORMER FOR B/W TV
780. TRANSFORMER FOR VOLTAGE STABILIZER & E.H.T
781. TRANSMISSION POWER LINE FITTING
782. TRANSMISSION TOWER FITTING
783. TV AUDIO EQUIPMENT CABINETS & THEIR ASSEMBLING UNIT
784. UN-INTERRUPTED POWER SUPPLY (U.P.S)
785. VARIABLE FREQUENCY
786. VARIABLE VOLTAGE A.C. DRIVE
787. VIDEO CASSETTES (COMPLETE MANUFACTURING & ASSEMBLING)
788. VIDEO CASSETTES RECORDER (V.C.R)
789. VIDEO FILM STUDIO
790. VOLTAGE REGULATOR FOR AUTOMOBILES
791. VOLTAGE STABILIZERS
792. VOLTAGE STABLIZER & T.V. GAIN BOOSTER
793. WAX AND CHEMICAL COATED, BRAIDED TINSEL WIRE
794. WEBSITE DESIGN & E-MAIL REGISTERING
795. WELDING ELECTRODES
796. WIND ENERGY POWER PROJECT (10 MW) WIRE WOUND POTENTIOMETERS

FOOD, AGRO FOOD, PROCESSED FOOD, AGRO PLANTATION, CULTIVATION, FARMING, DAIRY/MILK, TOBACCO/PAN MASALA, BREWERY & DISTILLERY, EDIBLE OILS, EOU FOOD PRODUCTS AND ALLIED PRODUCTS

797. ALCOHOLIC BEVERAGES & VENEGAR FROM COCONUT WATER
798. ALCOHOL DRINKS FROM ETHYL ALCOHOL BY MIXING OF VARIOUS FLAVOURS
799. ANTI SCALE COMPOUND FOR ADDING INTO SUGAR JUICE BOILING
800. APPLE JUICE CONCENTRATED & DEHYDRATED FRUIT & VEGETABLES
801. ARTIFICIAL FISH MEAL FOR POULTRY FEED
802. AUTOMATIC BISCUIT PLANT
803. BABY CEREAL FOOD AND MILK POWDER
804. BACTERIA FOR CANE JUICE
805. BAKER'S YEAST
806. BAKERY INDUSTRY
807. BANANA PUREE
808. BEER & WINE
809. BEER PLANT (BREWERY)
810. BIDI
811. BIDI & CIGARETTE
812. BISCUIT PLANT

813. BREAD (AUTOMATIC PLANT)
814. BLACK PEPPER (SPICES)
815. BREAD AND BISCUITS
816. BREEDING FARM
817. BROILER CHICKEN
819. BUTTON MUSHROOM CULTIVATION & PROCESSING
820. CANNING OF RASAGULLAS IN METAL CANS
821. CAFFEIN FROM TEA WASTE
822. CANNING OF FRUITS & VEGETABLES
823. CASEIN AND BY-PRODUCTS
824. CASHEW FRUIT JUICE FROM CASHEW FRUIT APPLE
825. CASHEWNUT KERNEL EXTRACTION FROM CASHEWNUT FRUIT
826. CASHEWNUT SHELL LIQUID & KERNEL PROCESSING
827. CASHEW FENI
828. CATECHEU (BY CHEMICAL PROCESS)
829. CATTLE FEED FROM TAPIOCA
830. CHEWING & BUBBLE GUM
831. CHICKEN/SHEEP MEAT PROCESSING
832. CHOCOLATE (MILK)
833. CIGARETTE AND BEEDIES
834. COCOA BUTTER FROM COCOA MASS
835. COCONUT PRODUCTS & BY PRODUCTS PROCESS COMPLEX
836. COLD/SOFT DRINKS
837. COLLECTION OF MILK AND MILK MAKING POWDER
838. COLLECTION OF MILK AND PACKING IN POLYTHENE POUCH (1/2 KG.1 KG. & 2 KG.)
839. CONDENSED MILK (SWEETNED)
840. CONFECTIONERY INDUSTRY (TOFFEE & CANDY, SEMI-AUTOMATIC PLANT)
841. COUNTRY LIQUOR FROM MOLASSES
842. CIGARETTE
843. DAIRY FARM AND DAIRY (MILK) PRODUCTS (PASTEURISED MILK, BUTTER, GHEE, PANEER)
844. DAIRY FARM TO PRODUCE MILK & PACKING IN POUCHES (50%) & CAN(50%)
845. DAIRY FOR MILK PROCESSING
846. DAIRY FARM (BUFALO)
847. DAL (PULSE) MILL UNIT
848. DEHYDRATION OF CARROT & GARLIC
849. DEHYDRATION & CANNING OF FRUITS & VEGETABLES
850. DEHYDRATION OF FIGS
851. DEHYDRATION OF FRUITS AND VEGETABLES
852. DEHYDRATED ONIONS AND ONION POWDER
853. DRY ICE BY BREAKING OF AIR
854. DRYING OF RED CHILLIES, HALDI, DHANIA, AND GREEN PEAS
855. EGG POWDER (40,000 EGGS PROCESSING PER DAY)
856. EXPORT OF PROCESSED FOODS AND MARINE PRODUCTS
857. FISH CANNING & POUCHING
859. FISH FARMING (PRAWN & OTHER MARINE PRODUCTS)
860. FISH MEAL
861. FLOUR MILL AND MUSTARD OIL
862. FOOD COLOUR & ORASTED GROUNDNUT GRAM PEAS, ETC IN POUCHES
863. FROG LEGS PROCESSING
864. FROZEN MEATS PROCESSING
865. FOOD FLAVOURS (WHISKY) VODKA, GRAPE, BUTTER SCOTCH)
866. FOOD PRODUCTS COMPLEX (DEHYDRATED ONIONS, GARLIC POWDER & FLAKES, CATTLE FEED, TOMATO POWDER, TOMATO PRODUCTS, CANNED FRUITS & VEGETABLES, TOMATO PURE, GROUN NUT OIL, REFIND OIL, DEHYDRATED GRAPES, BANANA POWDER & WAFFERS)
867. FRUIT JUICE, JAM, JELLIES & ALLIED PRODUCTS
868. FRUIT JUICE, PICKLES PROCESSING AND CANNING
869. FRUIT JUICE MAKING & PACKING IN PLASTIC CONTAINER/POUCHES
870. FRUIT PROCESSING (JAM & JELLIES)
871. FRUIT PULP & JUICE CONCENTRATES
872. FRUIT & VEGETABLE DRYING (FREEZE DRYING METHOD)
873. GOAT & SHEEP FARMING
874. GRAM DALL/PULSE MILL
875. GRAPE DEHYDRATION
876. HARD BOILED CANDY (TOFFEE & CANDY)
877. HERBAL CIGARETTES
878. HONEY PROCESSING & PACKAGING
879. ICE CREAM OF DIFFERENT FLAVOURS
880. ICE CREAM STABILIZER
881. ICE MAKING PLANT
882. INDIAN MADE FOREIGN LIQUOR (I.M.F.L)
883. INSTANT FOOD (IDLI MIX, DOSA MIX, GULAB JAMUN MIX)
884. INSTANT FOOD (INSTANT FOOD & FAST FOOD PARLOUR)
885. INSTANT NOODLES
886. INSTANT TEA
887. INSTANT TEA FROM BLACK TEA
888. INTEGERATED STARCH BAKING POWDER/YEAST INDUSTRY
889. IODIZED SALT
890. IODIZED SALT (ORDINARY MOISTURE-LESS/FREE FLOWING IN PLASTIC BAGS AND CONTAINERS)
891. JAM, JELLIES, FRUIT JUICE & ALLIED PRODUCTS
892. KATHA AND CUTCH
893. KHANDSARI SUGAR
894. KHANDSARI SUGAR & IMFL
895. LACTIC ACID FROM WHITE SUGAR BY FERMENTATION PROCESS
896. LACTOSE & BY PRODUCTS PROCESSING FROM MILK
897. LIQUID GLUCOSE AND ITS BYE PRODUCTS
898. MACRONI AND VERMICILLI
899. MALT EXTRACTION FROM BARLEY
900. MANGO PROCESSING (MANGO PULP, JUICE & SLICES)
901. MAYUR BRAND TYPE CHEWING TOBACCO
902. MINERAL WATER
903. MILK PRESERVATION & MARKETING TO WHOLE SELLERS (INPOUCH PACKING BY UHT TECHNOLOGY)
904. MILK PROCESSING AND PACKAGING OF MILK PRODUCTS
905. MILK PRODUCTS (CASEIN, LACTOSE, GHEE & WHEY POWDER)
906. MILK TOFFEE
907. MINI FLOUR MILL
908. MINI SUGAR PLANT
909. MISRI (PEARL SUGAR CANDIES)
910. MODERN RICE MILL
911. MURABBA
912. MUSTARD OIL EXTRACTION & REFINING
913. MUTTON TALLOW
914. NAMKEEN INDUSTRY (BHUJIA, CHANA CHUR ETC.)
915. NAMKEEN & SWEETS
916. NON-BASMATI RICE FROM PADDY
917. OLEORESIN, ESSENTIAL OIL, DYES & POWDER OF SPICES
918. OLEORESIN EXTRACTION FROM DIPTERO-CARPUT TURMINATUS AND PINUS KHASYANA
919. OLEORESIN EXTRACTION FROM CHILLI
920. PAN MASALA AND POUCH

1059. BUFFALO HORN TIP, HOOF
1060. BANQUET HALL
1061. BUTTON
1062. CALCINED PETROLEUM (C.P) COKE
1063. CANVAS SHOES
1064. CANVAS SHOES, JUNGLE BOOTS
1065. CARBON BRUSH, BRUSH HOLDER & SLIP RING
1066. CEMENT SHEETS WITH COIR FIBRE & OTHER SEGMENTS
1067. CERAMIC TILES (GLAZED) BY DOUBLE FIRING/HEATING
1068. CHILDREN RECREATION CENTRE
1069. COAL BRIQUETTES
1070. COLD STORAGE & ICE
1071. COLD STORAGE FOR FRUITS AND VEGETABLES
1072. COMPRESSOR (HERMETIC) FOR AIR CONDITIONER
1073. COSTUME JEWELLERY/ IMITATION JEWELLERY
1074. DECORATIVE LAMINATED SHEET (SUNMICA)
1075. DIAMOND CUTTING & EXPORTS
1076. DRINKING STRAW FROM PROPYLENE
1077. ENGINEERING COLLEGE
1078. ENTERTAINMENT CLUB
1079. FASHION TECHNOLOGY INSTITUTE
1080. FAST FOOD PARLOUR
1081. FAST FOOD (INSTANT FOOD & FAST FOOD PARLOUR)
1082. FIRE EXTINGUISHERS (SODA ACID TYPE)
1083. FISH NET
1084. FLORICULTURE (CUT FLOWER ROSE) WITH GREEN HOUSE
1085. FLOOR COVERING SHEET
1086. FILM STUDIO (VIDEO)
1087. FLUSH DOOR, CHIP BOARD, WOOD WOOL & OTHER INSULATING BOARDS
1088. GAS DETECTORS OF L.P.G
1089. GEMS MANUFACTURING
1090. GLASS BOTTLE BY SCRAP
1092. GOAT & SHEEP FARMING
1093. GOLD ELECTROPLATING
1094. GOLD JEWELLERY (E.O.U)
1095. GOLD PLATED SILVER JEWELLERY & CUTLERY
1096. GRANITE SLAB AND TILES
1097. GREEN HOUSE
1098. HARD CHROMIUM PLATING
1099. HEALTH CLUB AND BEAUTY PARLOUR CUM HAIR SALOON WITH SONA BATH
1100. HEALTH CLUB CUM BEAUTY PARLOUR TRAININGINSTITUTE
1101. HORN TIP, HOOVE BUTTON
1102. HOSPITAL
1103. HOSPITAL (100 BEDS)
1104. HOSPITAL (200 BEDS)
1105. ICE MAKING PLANT
1106. IMITATION AND COSTUME
1107. JEWELLERY (NECKLACE, EARRINGS EAR TOP ETC.)
1108. INITMATE SCENT CHEMICALS FROM ALL TYPES OF FLAVOUR
1109. INVESTMENT CASTING
1110. JUTE, COIR, GLASS ROPE/ SUTLI
1111. JUTE TWINE
1112. L.P.G BOTTLING PLANT
1113. L.P.G REGULATOR (DOMESTIC PURPOSE)
1114 LAMINATED PARTICLE BOARD & HARD BOARD
1115. LAMINATED SAFETY AND TOUGHENED GLASS
1116. LEASING & HIRE PURCHASE
1117. LICHEN (CHARILA)
1118. MANILA ROPES
1119. MEDICAL COLLEGE
1120. MATCH UNIT FROM WAXED PAPER
1121. MEDIUM DENSITY FIBRE BOARD
1122. MELAMINE CROCKERY
1123. MINERAL WATER
1124. MINI CEMENT PLANT
1125. MIRROR SILVER, GOLDEN, PINK, BLACK & SMOKES
1126. MODERN ADVERTISING AGENCY WITH DTP & FILM STUDIO
1127. MOTEL/SMALL HOTEL
1128. MULTI COLOUR PRINTING
1129. MULTI STOREY COMMERCIAL COMPLEX ALONGWITH RESIDENTIAL AND DELUX FLATS FOR FOREIGN TOURISTS & REVOLVING RESTAURENT AT THE TOP
1130. MULTIPLE LAMINATION INDUSTRY
1131. MUSHROOM GROWING AND PROCESSING (BY DEEP FREEZING METHOD)
1132. NEWS PAPER PRINTING
1133. NICKEL LINED INDUSTRIAL SCREEN
1134. OFFSET COLOUR PRINTING PRESS (SIX COLOUR)
1135. OFFSET PRINTING PRESS
1136. P.C.C ELECTRIC POLES
1137. PHOTOGRAPHIC DEVELOPER & FIXER
1138. PVC EXTRUSION PROFILE (DOOR & WINDOWS)
1139. POP-CORN
1140. PHOTO ETCHING OF S.S.
1141. PRE STRESSED CEMENT CONCRETE PIPES
1142. PILFER PROOF CAPS
1143. PILFER PROOF CAPS AND CROWN CAP
1144. POUCH MAKING & GRAVURE PRINTING (ROTO PRINTING)
1145. POULTRY & FISH FARMING (INTEGERATED UNIT)
1146. PRINTING OF TIN SHEETS
1147. READYMADE GARMENTS
1148. RESTAURANT
1149. ROSE PLANTATION AND ROSE OIL EXTRACTION
1150. ROTOGRAVURE PRINTING
1151. SAFETY BELTS
1152. SAFETY MATCHES
1153. SHOE LACES
1154. SILK COCOON CULTIVATION (GROWING OF SILK COCOON WARM)
1155. SILK SCREEN PRINTING FORMULATIONS FOR PLASTIC, PAPER & CLOTH
1156. SPIKENARD (JATAMANSI)
1157. STENCIL COATING SOLUTION
1158. SUGAR CANDY (MISRI)
1159. SUGAR CANE PLANTATION
1160. SUGAR CANE JUICE PRESERVATION
1161. SURAT ZARI
1162. SYNTHETIC SHOES & SOLES
1163. TEA PACKAGING INDUSTRY
1164. TENNIS BALLS
1165. THREE STAR HOTEL
1166. TRAVELLING AGENCY
1167. TRAYS, TROLLEYS FOR HOSPITAL WITH SCRATCHLESS COATING
1168. WAX EXTRACTS (TANNING POWDER)
1169. WIRE ROPE SLINGS
1170. WOOD WOOL SLAB
1171. WOODEN CANE FURNITURE WITH EXPORT POTENTIAL
1172. WOODEN FURNITURE
1173. WOODEN PANEL INCLUDING KILN SEASONING
1174. WOODEN FURNITURE
1175. WATCH CASE BUFFING
1176. WATCH DIAL
1177. WRIST WATCHES
1178. WATCHES (ELECTRONIC)
1179. ZEDOARY (KACHUR)

EDIBLE OILS, ESSENTIAL OILS LURICATIING OILS, GREASES, VEGETABLE OILS, WAXES, CAMPHOR, PERFUMES & PERFUMERY COMPOUNDS AND REFINED OILS ETC.

1180. AROMATIC PERFUMERY COMPOUND
1181. AEROSOL
1182. AGARBATTI PERFUMERY COMPOUND
1183. BEES WAX MANUFACTURE
1184. CAMPHOR
1185. CARDANOL FROM CASHEW NUT SHELL LIQUID
1186. CASTOR OIL
1187. CASTOR OIL DERIVATIVE OLEORESINS
1188. CHILLI OIL
1189. CITRONELLA OILS
1190. CLOVE OIL
1191. CONCENTRATE OF ROSE JASMINE & LILY ETC.
1192. COLOURED FLAME CANDLE

1193. CANDLES (SEMI-AUTOMATIC)
1194. CORN OIL (MAIZE OIL)
1195. DEHYDRATED CASTOR OIL
1196. EUGENOL FROM CINNAMON LEAF OIL
1197. EXTRACTION OF ESSENTIAL OIL (CARDAMON, JEERA, AJOWAN, GINGER OILS ETC. & PACKAGING OF GROUND SPICES)
1198. EXTRACTION OF JASMINE ESSENCE
1199. EXTRACTION OF ESSENTIAL OILS BY SUPER CRITICAL FLUID METHOD FROM FLOWERS, HERBS & SPICES
1200. EUCALYPTUS OIL
1201. EXTRACTION OF OIL FROM OIL SEED EXPANDEREXTRUSION TECHNOLOGY)
1202. FAT LIQUOR SULPHATED OIL
1203. FLAVOURS FOR FOOD
1204. GARLIC OIL & POWDER
1205. GINGER OIL, SANDALWOOD OIL AND NAGARMOTHA OIL
1206. GINGER OIL
1207. GINGER OIL & GINGER DUST
1208. INTEGERATED WAX COMPLEX
1209. IONONE FROM LEMON GRASS OIL
1210. JASMINE & LILLY FLOWER OIL
1211. LEMON GRASS OIL
1212. LIQUID PARAFFIN
1213. LUBE OIL & GREASE
1214. LUBRICATING OIL
1215. MENTHOL CRYSTALS
1216. MENTHOL OIL & CRYSTAL
1217. MICRO CRYSTALLINE WAX
1218. MUSTARD OIL (EDIBLE OIL)
1219. OIL FROM ARTEMISIA HERBS
1220. PALM OIL CRUSHING UNIT
1221. PAN MASALA
1222. PARAFFIN WAX
1223. PARAFFIN WAX FROM SLACK WAX
1224. REFINED OIL-SUN FLOWER OIL, GROUNDNUT OIL, STAFF FLOWER OIL & COTTON SEED OIL
1225. REFINED VEGETABLE OIL
1226. RECLAMATION OF USED ENGINE OIL
1227. RICE BRAN OIL (R.B.O)
1228. ROSE OIL EXTRACTION
1229. SMOKE LESS CANDLE
1230. SPICE OIL & OLEORESINS
1231. SOLVENT EXTRACTION PLANT (OIL CAKE BASED)
1232. SYNTHETIC ALMOND OIL
1233. SYNTHETIC TALLOW
1234. SYNTHETIC GHEE
1235. VEGETABLE OIL EXTRACTION & REFINING
1236. WADDING OIL (100%) FOR WADDING OF COTTON HOSIERY CLOTH IN DYEING PROCESS
1237. WAX EMULSION FOR TEXTILE
1238. WAX FLOOR POLISH

PAINT, ENAMEL, SOLVENTS, THINNERS, INKS & VARNISH

1239. ACRYLIC EMULSION PAINTS
1240. ALUMINIUM PAINT
1241. AUTOMOBILE PAINTS
1242. BALL POINT PEN REFILL INK
1243. BITUMINIOUS ROAD EMULSION
1244. BITUMEN
1245. BITUMINIOUS FELTS FOR WATER & DAMP PROOFING
1246. BITUMINIOUS ROAD EMULSION RAPID MEDIUM & SLOW SETTING
1247. BUFFING & POLISHING
1248. CEMENT PAINT FOR WHITE & GREY CEMENT

1249. DISPERSANT
1250. DRY DISTEMPER
1251. DRY DISTEMPER & CEMENT PAINT
1252. DUPLICATING INK BLACK FOR GESTNER DUPLICATOR
1255. EMULSION PAINTS (WATER BASED)
1256. HAMMERTONE PAINT
1257. INSULATING VARNISH & WIRE ENAMEL
1258. IRON OXIDE PIGMENTS
1259. INSULATING VARNISH (POLY VINYL BUTYRAL BASED, FFC GRADE)
1260. LIME COLOUR (CEMENT COLOUR)
1261. SYNTHETIC RED OXIDE FOR FLOORINGS
1262. SOLVENT & THINNERS
1263. MARKING INKS (WATER PROOF)
1264. METAL NAPHTHANATE (AS DRIER FOR PAINTS)
1265. N.C.PUTTY
1266. OFFSET PRINTING INK
1267. OIL BOUND DISTEMPER PAINT
1268. PAINT BRUSHES
1269. PAINT REMOVERS
1270. PAINT INDUSTRY
1271. PAINT & VARNISH
1272. PICTURE VARNISH
1273. POWDER COATING PAINT
1274. PRINTING INKS (OFFSET, FLEXO & ROTO GRAVURE)
1275. PRIMER PAINT & ENAMEL PAINT
1276. PUTTY & WATER PROOFING PAINT
1277. PRINTING INKS (FLEXO-GRAPHIC INK)
1278. PUTTY (METAL CASEMENT)
1279. RED OXIDE PRIMER (ANTI CORROSIVE)
1280. REFRECTORY PAINT (GRAPHITE BASED)
1281. SCREEN PRINTING INKS
1282. SILK SCREEN PRINTING INK FORMULATION FOR PLASTIC, PAPER, CLOTH
1283. STAMP & PAD INK
1284. STOVING PAINT
1285. SPIRIT SOLUBLE MALEIC RESIN
1286. TEXTURE PAINT
1287. THINNERS AND ITS ALLIED PRODUCTS
1288. TONER INK
1289. VARNISH THINNER (SOLVENT)
1290. VACUUM METALLIZING LACQUERS
1291. WOOD PRIMER

PHARMACEUTICAL, DRUGS, AYURVEDIC/HERBAL COSMETICS & MEDICINES, HOMOEOPATHIC MEDICINES, DISPOSABLE SYRINGE, DENTAL COLLEGE & FINE CHEMICALS ETC.

1292. AROMATIC PILLS
1293. ASPIRIN
1294. AYURVEDIC PAIN BALM OINTMENTS
1295. AYURVEDIC CHURAN AND TABLETS
1296. AYURVEDIC TABLETS (HAJMOLA TYPE)
1297. AYURVEDIC/HERBAL PHARMACY
1298. AYURVEDIC SHERBATS
1299. AYURVEDIC PRODUCTS
1300. BULK DRUGS (E.O.U)
1301. BLOOD BAGS
1302. CALCIUM GLUCONATE
1303. CAPSULE, TABLET & INJECTION WITH MODERN INSTRUMENTS
1304. CASHEW FENI
1305. CHLOROQUINONE PHOSPHATE (BULK DRUGS)
1306. CLINICAL THERMOMETER
1307. DENTAL CLINIC

1308. DENTAL COLLEGE
1309. DENTAL GRADE EUGENOL
1310. DEXTROSE MONOHYDRATE, LIQUID GLUCOSE
1311. DEHYDRATED ONION & ONION POWDER
1312. DEXTROSE POWDER (ANHYDROUS FROM STARCH)
1314. DEXTROSE SALINE SOLUTION
1315. DISTILLERY (I.M.F.L)
1316. DISPOSABLE NEEDLES FOR SYRINGES
1317. DISPRIN
1318. DISTILLED WATER
1319. EMPTY HARD GELATINE CAPSULES
1320. FILLING & PACKING OF CAPSULES
1321. GLUCOSE - D - POWDER
1322. GLYCERINE
1323. HERBAL COSMETICS
1324. HERBAL SHAMPOO
1325. HERBAL HAIR OILS (AYURVEDIC)
1326. HOMOE & BIO-MEDICINES WITH MOTHER TINCTURE
1327. HOMOEPATHIC MEDICINES
1328. HYPODERMIC NEEDLES
1329. I.V. FLUIDS
1330. IBUPROFEN
1331. INFUSION & TRANSFUSION SETS (I.V. SET)
1332. INJECTABLE FOR PHARMACEUTICALS
1333. INJECTION AMPOULES PACKAGING BOX
1334. INTEGERATED SURGICAL COTTON
1335. ICE MAKING PLANT
1336. ICE & COLD STORAGE
1337. LACTOSE & BY PRODUCTS PROCESSING FROM MILK
1338. LICHEN (JATAMANSI CHARILA)
1339. LIQUID GLUCOSE AND ITS BY-PRODUCTS
1340. L-LYSINE MONOHYDRO CHLORIDE
1341. LIQUID GLUCOSE FROM POTATOES
1342. MEDICAL COLLEGE
1343. NICOTINE FROM TOBACCO WASTE
1344. OINTMENT-AYURVEDIC (YELLOW & WHITE)
1345. PHARMACEUTICAL AND FOOD GRADE GELATINE
1346. PHARMACEUTICAL INDUSTRY (TABLETS, CAPSULES, LIQUID, GEL, OINTMENT POWDER INJECTABLE)
1347. PHARMACEUTICAL UNIT (EOU) WITH FORMULA TIONS, INJECTABLES, ETC. PYRIDINE & DERIVATIVES
1348. SALT (IODIZED SALT)
1349. SALINE & INJECTION WATER
1350. SALINE WATER & DEXTROSE SOLUTION (I.V.FLUID IN PLASTIC BOTTLES)
1351. SORBITOL
1352. STARCH (MAIZE)
1353. SURGICAL ADHESIVE PLASTER
1354. SURGICAL BANDAGES
1355. SURGICAL GLOVES
1357. SURGICAL COTTON
1358. SURGICAL COTTON AND BANDAGE
1359. SYNTHETIC CAMPHOR POWDER
1360. TABLETS & CAPSULES
1361. TISSUE CULTURE
1362. TINCTURE FROM RECTIFIED SPIRIT
1363. TRIMETHOPIME
1364. VETERENARY MEDICINES (ONLY FORMULATIONS)
1365. VITAMIN 'C', SORBITOL' ANHYDROUS DEXTROSE, STARCH

PULP, PAPER, STRAW/GREY BOARD, KRAFT PAPER, PACKAGING, PAPER CARRY BAGE, PAPER FROM AGRO WASTE & STATIONERY ETC.

1366. AMMONIA PAPER
1367. AUTOMATIC BOOK BINDING
1368. ADHESIVE (FEVICOL TYPE)
1369. ALL PIN & GEM CLIPS
1370. CARBON PAPER
1371. CARD BOARD
1372. CARBON LESS PAPER
1373. CELLPHANE PAPER
1374. COMPUTER FORMS & SECURITY PRINTING PRESS
1375. CORRUGATED BOARD & BOX (PRINTED & LAMINATED)
1376. CORRUGATED BOARD AND BOXES FROM FROM CARD BOARDS
1377. CORRUGATED CARTONS FROM PLAIN PAPERS
1378. CORRUGATRED PACKING & MATERIAL (BULB & TUBES PACKING)
1379. DESK TOP PUBLISHING
1380. DEFOAMING AGENT FOR PAPER PLANT
1381. DRINKING STRAW PAPER
1382. D.T.P CUM OFFSET PRESS
1383. EGG TRAYS
1384. EXERCISE NOTE BOOK, REGISTER AND PAD
1385. FLEXOGRAPHIC INK
1386. GREETING CARD BY OFFSET PRESS
1387. HAND MADE PAPER FILTER PAPER
1388. HARD BOARD
1389. INJECTION AMPOULES PACKAGING BOXES
1390. INSULATIING PAPER
1391. KRAFT PAPER
1392. KRAFT PAPER FROM BAGASSE
1393. LAMINATED PACKAGING PAPER WITH PRINTING
1394. LAMINATION & COATING ON PAPER
1395. M.G. PAPER FROM WASTE PAPER
1396. MILL PAPER FROM WASTE PAPER
1397. MILL BOARD FROM RICE & WHEAT STRAWS
1398. MILL BOARD FROM WASTE PAPER
1399. MINI PAPER PLANT FROM SISAL
1400. MINI PAPER PLANT
1401. MULTI WALL PAPER SACKS
1402. NEWS PAPER FOR CHILDREN
1403. NEWS PRINT PAPER FROM RICE STRAW BAGASSE
1404. NEWS PAPER CHILDRENS
1405. NEWS PRINT PAPER
1406. OFFSET AND TREADLE TYPE PRINTING PRESS
1407. MILL BOARD BASED ON RICE STRAW
1408. PAPER AND BOARD FROM STRAW
1409. PAPER & PAPER PRODUCTS
1410. PAPER ENVELOPES
1411. PAPER CARRY BAGS
1412. PAPER BOARD CARTON
1413. PAPER CONES FOR LOUD SPEAKERS
1414. PAPER FROM AKRA
1415. PAPER FROM BAGASSE WITH CORRUGATED BOARD & BOXES
1416. PAPER FROM BAMBOO
1417. PAPER GLASSES FOR BEVERAGES
1418. PAPER FROM RICE HUSK & WHEAT HUSK
1419. PAPER FROM TREE BARK, EUCALYPRUS WOOD
1420. PAPER PRODUCTS
1421. PAPER PLANT (WHITE WRITING & NEWS PAPER FOR PULP & WASTE PAPER)
1422. PAPER PLATES, PAPER GLASS
1423. PAPER CONES & TUBES
1425. PAPER PLANT WITH DTP & PRINTING & PUBLISHING UNIT
1426. PAPER BASED PHENOLIC SHEET
1427. PAPER CUP FOR ICE CREAM
1428. PAPER TUBES SPIRAL WINDING COMPOSIT CONTAINER
1429. PAPER LABLE FOR BEER BOTTLES
1430. PARTICLE BOARD & BLACK BOARD WITH SANDING & LAMINATION OF PARTICLE BOARD
1431. PARTICLE BOARD FROM RICE HUSK
1432. POUCH FILLING & MAKING FOR TOMATO SAUCE
1433. POUCH MAKING &

GRAVURE PRINTING
1434. PROCESSING OF PAPER FOR FEEDING IN COMPUTER
1435. PULP FROM BAMBOO & WOOD
1436. PAPER FILES
1437. PLAYING CARDS
1438. ROSIN SIZING AGENT (FOR PAPER PLANT)
1439. SAND PAPER
1440. SANITRY NAPKINS
1441. SILICON COATED PAPER
1442. STENCIL PAPER
1443. STRAW BOARD AND GREY BOARD
1444. STRAW BOARD & MILL BOARD
1445. STRAW BOARD AND PAPER BOARD
1446. TISSUE PAPER FACIAL
1447. TISSUE MOIST TOILETERY CLEANSING TISSUE AND RELATED PRODUCTS
1448. TISSUE PAPER ROLLS
1449. TETRA PACK FOR MILK PACKAGING, GHEE & OTHER LIQUIDS
1450. TOILET PAPER ROLLS
1451. TOILET PAPER & NAPKINS
1452. WAX COATED PRINTED PAPER
1453. WET FACE FRESHNER TISSUE
1454. WHITE WRITING & PRINTING PAPER
1455. WRITING & PRINTING PAPER (PAPER MILLS)

PLASTIC, B.O.P.P, ACRYLIC, DISPOSABLE PLASTIC PRODUCTS, PET PRODUCTS, P.V.C, H.D.P.E, P.P, L.D.P.E., P.U, A.B.S, THERMOFOARMING, MASTER BATCHES, & POLYMER AND RUBBER PRODUCTS, TYRE, TUBE, ADHESIVE, SHEET, COIR & MANY OTHERS

1456. ABS GRANULES FROM ABS SCRAPS FROM OLD T.V. CABINETS, WHITE GOODS ETC.
1457. ACRYLIC BEADS
1458. ACRYLIC COPOLYMER EMULSION
1459. ACRYLIC LATEX
1460. ACRYLIC SHEET
1461. ACRYLIC SHEET & MOULDED PRODUCTS
1462. ACRYLIC TEETH
1463. AUTO TUBES
1464. AUTO FLAPS FOR TRUCKS & BUSES
1465. AUTO TYRES & TUBES
1466. BABY BOTTLES (PLASTIC) WITH WHITESILICON RUBBER NIPPLES
1467. B.O.P.P. FILM
1468. B.O.P.P. PRESSURE SENSITIVE SELF ADHESIVE TAPE
1469. BABY NIPPLE (SILICON)
1470. BABY NIPPLE (BIG SIZE)
1471. BALLOON PLASTIC ADVERTISING
1472. BLISTER FILM PVC
1473. BLISTER PACKAGING & POUCH PAKAGING
1474. BLOW MOULDING PLASTIC CONTAINER
1475. COATING ON METALIZED POLYESTER FILM/METALISED PAPER/ ALIMINIUM FOIL
1476. COATING ON PLASTIC (ELECTROLYSIS) & GLASS
1477. COIR FOAM (RUBBERISED)
1478. COLOUR COATING ON PLASTICS
1479. COLOUR MASTER BATCHES FOR VARIOUS PLASTICS
1480. CYCLE TYRES AND TUBES
1481. DISPOSABLE PLASTIC CUPS GLASSES, ETC.
1482. DISPOSABLE PLASTIC SYRINGES & NEEDLES
1483. DISPOSABLE PLASTIC SYRINGES
1484. DOUGH MOULDING COMPOUND (D.M.C)
1485. EPOXY RESIN
1486. EXPANDED POLYESTRENE MOULDING (THERMOCOLE)
1487. F.R.P AUTO, SCOOTER ROOFS & CEILINGS
1488. F.R P PRODUCTS (HELMET, WASHBASIN SHEETS, ROOFING SHEETS)
1489. FIBRE REINFORCED PLASTIC (HIGH PRESSURE MOULDING WITH SMC BMC AND DMC)
1490. FIELD RUBBER CONVERTED TO THE 60% LATEX RUBBER
1491. FLEXIBLE P.U. FOAM
1492. FORMALDEHYDE CROCKERY & OTHER ITEMS
1493. FORMALDEHYDE RESIN (UREA, PHENOL, MELEMINE)
1494. GASKET SHEET
1495. GUM BOTTLE (PVC)
1496. GLASS BEADS
1497. HDPE COATED PAPER SACK
1498. H.D.P.E. BAGS
1499. H.D.P.E. CONTAINERS (BLOW MOULDING)
1500. H.D.P.E. CONTAINER, POLY JARS BY INJECTION MOULDING (FOOD GRADE)
1501. H.D.P.E. JERRY CANS
1502. HDPE MANUFACTURING FROM ETHYLALCOHOL
1503. H.D.P.E PIPE AND FITTINGS
1504. H.D.P.E. PIPES
1505. H.D.P.E PRINTED BAGS
1506. H.D.P.E TWINES AND ROPES
1507. H.D.P.E. & L.D.P.E PIPES AND FITTINGS
1508. H.D.P.E/PP BOX STRAPPING
1509. H.D.P.E/PP WOVEN SACKS
USING PLAIN LOOMS
1510. HOLOGRAM STICKERS-3D
1511. H.M BAG PLANT WITH PRINTING UNIT
1512. HAWAI CHAPPALS (RUBBER)
1513. I.V PLASTIC BOTTLE
1514. ICE CREAM CUP (PLASTIC)
1515. INJECTION MOULDED AUTO COMPONENTS
1516. INJECTION & BLOW MOULDED PLASTIC PRODUCTS
1517. INJECTION MOULDED PLASTIC PRODUCTS
1518. INTEGERATED COMPLEX ESTER'S & ALLIED PRODUCTS (D.O.P, D.B.P, & ETHYL ACETATE, BUYTL ACETATE, WIRE ENAMELS, JELLY CABLE COMPOUND)
1519. L.D.P.E. (LOW DENSITY POLY ETHYLENE) GRANULES FROM VIRGIN (L.D.P.E. RESIN)
1520. INTEGERATED SURGICAL RUBBER GOODS INDUSTRY
1521. INJECTION MOULDED PLASTIC BALLS
1522. L.D.P.E FROM ETHYL ALCOHOL
1523. LDPE MOULDED PRODUCTS
1524. LAMINATION OF COEXTRUSION MULTILAYER FILM IN ROLL FORM
1525. LATEX RUBBER
1526. LATEX RUBBER CONDOM
1527. MASTER BATCHES (COLOURED, P.V.C, L.D.P.E, H.D.P.E, ETC.)
1528. MELAMINE FORMALHYDE RESIN
1529. MOULDED LUGGAGE
1530. MULTI-LAYER (3 LAYER BAGS)
1531. MULTI-LAYER (3 LAYER) FILM WITH LAMINATION & PRINTING
1532. OIL SEAL
1533. PET BOTTLE/CONTAINERS
1534. PET BOTTLES FROM PRE FORM
1535. PET BOTTLE & MINERAL WATER
1536. PET PRE-FORM FROM PET RESIN
1537. PET PRE-FORM CUM PET BOTTLES
1538. PET PRE-FORM PET BOTTLES CUM MINERAL WATERS
1539. POLY CARBONATE RESIN
1540. PTFE COMPONENTS
1541. PU/PVC SOLE FOR SPORT SHOE BY IMPORTED M/C.
1542. PVC BATTERY SEPARATOR
1543. P.V.C COMPOUNDS (FRESH)
1544. P.V.C COMPOUNDS (SCRAP)
1545. P.V.C ELECTRICAL INSULATING TAPE
1546. P.V.C. EXTRUSION PROFILES
1547. P.V.C FITTINGS
1548. P.V.C FLEXIBLE FUSIBLE POWDER HEAT FUSIBLE POWDER
1549. P.V.C GRANULES (FOR

INSULATION & SHEETS GRADES)
1550. P.V.C GRANULES FROM PVC SCRAPS (WITH POLLUTION CONTROL)
1551. P.V.C HOSES
1552. P.V.C LEATHER CLOTH
1553. P.V.C FLEXIBLE PIPES
1554. P.V.C PIPES AND FITTINGS
1555. POLYTHENE BAGS (PRINTED)
1556. PVC PLASTICS FILM SHEET SOFT/RIGID
1557. PVC RESIN AND COMPOUND
1558. PVC RULAR
1559. PVC STABLIZERS (SINGLE PACK SYSTEM)
1560. PVC WIRE AND CABLES
1561. PAPER BASED PHENOLIC SHEET FOR ELECTRICAL
1562. PHENOL FORMALDEHYDE RESIN
1563. PHENOLIC RESIN
1564. PLASTIC BEADS FROM PLASTIC SCRAPS
1565. PLASTIC BUTTONS
1566. PLASTIC CANS
1567. PLASTIC COLLAPSIBLE TUBE
1568. PLASTIC CORRUGATED SHEET & BOXES
1569. PLASTIC FILM AND SHEETS WITH PRINTING FLEXO & ROTO/LDPE/HDPE/PP/HM/PVC
1570. PLASTIC FILTER MASTER BATCH & OTHER MASTER BATCHES FOR VARIOUS PLASTICS
1571. PLASTIC JERRY CANS
1572. PLASTIC GRANULES OR POWDER FROM PLASTIC SCRAP
1573. PLASTIC INJECTION MOULDED T.V. CABINETS
1574. PLASTIC ITEMS MANUFAC TURE FROM POWDER MELAMINE
1575. PLASTIC GOODS
1576. PLASTIC PIPES & TARPAULINES
1577. PLASTIC SHEET FROM SCRAP
1578. PLASTIC PLANT (BLOW MOULDING & INJECTION MOULDING)
1579. PLASTIC PRODUCTS (GOLD, SILVER, NICKEL)
1580. PLASTIC TOYS
1581. POLYESTER BEADING
1582. POLYESTER FILM
1583. POLYTHENE BAGS & AUTOMATIC PRINTING
1584. POLYTHENE PRINTED BAGS
1585. POLYURETHANE FOAM AND ITS PRODUCTS
1586. PROPYLENE FILM (PRINTED) & BAG MANUFACTURING
1587. PLASTIC MATS
1588. RAINBOW COLOUR ON PVC FILM & SHEET
1589. RED MUD PVC PIPES AND FITTINGS
1590. RE-RUBBERISED OF SOLID TYPE
1591. RESIN COATED SAND REXINE
1592. REXINE CLOTH & ALLIED PRODUCTS
1593. RUBBER ADHESIVE
1594. RUBBER AUTO PARTS
1595. RUBBER BELTING
1596. RUBBER MOULDING UNIT INCLUDING LINING RUBBER SHEETING
1597. RUBBER RECLAIMING
1598. RUBBER ROLLERS FOR TEXTILE MILLS & PAPER INDUSTRIES
1599. RUBBER & PLASTIC SHEETS, MATS & FLAPS
1600. RUBBER SHEET AND ALLIED HOSPITAL RUBBER GOODS
1601. RUBBERIZED PVC GASKET
1602. RUBBERISED COIR
1603. RUBBER COMPOUND FOR AUTOMOBILES
1604. SAFETY BELTS
1605. SILVER AND GOLD PLATING ON PVC AND NYLON-6
1606. SILICONE RUBBER NIPPLES/ TEATS
1607. SPECTACLE FRAMES (PLASTIC)
1608. SPUNGE RUBBER
1609. SURGICAL EXAMINATION GLOVES
1610. SYNTHETIC PEARL COATING ON POLYSTYRENE BEADS
1611. SYNTHETIC RUBBER ADHESIVE
1612. TEFLON MANUFACTURING
1613. TEFLON TAPE
1614. TEFLON TAPES & CABLES
1615. THERMOCOLE SHEET AND MOULDED PRODUCTS EXPANDED POLYESTERENE EXTRUSION PROFILES
1616. THERMOFORMED PACKAGING (BLISTER PACKAGING & POUCH PACKAGING)
1617. THERMOPLASTIC POLYURETHANE
1618. THERMOFORMED CUPS, PLATES & GLASS WITH HIPS SHEET
1619. THERMOCOLE
1620. THERMOCOLE BASED DISPOSABLE GLASS, CUPS & PLATES
1621. TOOTH BRUSHES
1622. TOY BALLOON, DECORA TIVE & INDUSTRIAL BALLOONS
1623. TREAD RUBBER
1624. TYRE RETREADING (HOT)
1625. TYRE RETREADING BY COLD PROCESS
1626. TYRE TUBES & FLAPS
1627. TYRE & TUBES
1628. UNSATURATED POLYESTER FOR REXINE
1629. V-BELT AND FAN BELT
1630. VINYL ASBESTOS AND PVC WALL PAPER
1631. VITON (FLUORO ELASTOMER)

SOAP, COSMETICS & PERFUMES

1632. ACID SLURRY, SYNTHETIC DETERGENT POWDER
1632. ACID SLURRY
1633. AGARBATTI SYNTHETIC, PERFUMERY COMPOUND
1634. AFTER SHAVE LOTION
1635. ANTISEPTIC CREAM
1636. BETA IONONE
1637. BLEACHING POWDER
1638. BLUE DETERGENT POWDER
1639. CLEANING POWDER (VIMTYPE)
1640. COLD CREAM
1641. COLOURED FLAME & PERFUMED CANDLES (RED, BLUE, GREEN FLAME)
1642. COSMETIC INDUSTRY (MODERN)
1643. COSMETIC INDUSTRY (SHAMPOO, SPRAY PERFUME, TALCUM POWDER
1644. DETERGENT POWDER (ARIEL TYPE)
1645. DETERGENT POWDER (NIRMA TYPE) FULLY AUTOMATIC PLANT
1646. DETERGENT WASHING POWDER
1647. FISH OIL SOAP
1648. GLYCERINE TRANSPARENT SOAP
1649. HAIR REMOVING CREAM
1650. HERBAL COSMETICS
1651. HERBAL SHAMPO & CREAM
1652. HERBAL/AYURVEDIC COSMETICS
1653. INCENSE POWDER, INCENSE STICKS & INCENSE CAKE
1654. OPTICAL WHITENERS
1655. ROSE OIL EXTRACTION
1656. SHAMPOOS (COCONUT OIL BASED COLD PROCESS)
1657. SHAVING CREAM
1658. SINDUR (KUMKUM)
1659. SOAP COATED PAPER
1660. SPRAY DRIED DETERGENT POWDER
1661. STAIN REMOVER
1662. TALCUM POWDER (FACE & TOILET POWDER)
1663. TOILET AND HERBAL SOAP
1664. TOOTH PASTE & POWDER
1665. WASHING DETERGENT POWDER AND WASHING SOAP
1666. WASHING POWDER LIQUID DETERGENTS, LOTION & SHAMPOO

TEXTILE INDUSTRIES, READYMADE GARMENTS, COTTON, DYEING, BLEACHING, CLOTH, HOSIERY, POWER LOOM, HAND LOOM, WOOLLEN, SILK, SOCKS, SURGICAL COTTON & MANY OTHERS

1667. ANGORA RABBIT WOOL
1668. BUCKRAM
1669. CANVAS SHOES, JUNGLE BOOT, BOOT RUBBER KNEES & BOOT COMBAT
1670. CARPET FROM COTTON WASTE
1671. CERAMIC THREAD GUIDE
1672. COTTON BUDS/SWABS
1673. COTTON FROM WASTE YARN
1674. COTTON ROLLS
1675. COTTON SPIDERS FOR LOUD SPEAKERS
1676. DENIM CLOTH
1677. DENIM CLOTH (INTEGERATED UNIT WITH BLEACHING, DYEING AND PRINTING)
1678. DISPERSENT FOR TEXTILE
1679. DYEING & BLEACHING
1680. DYEING OF HANK YARN
1681. EMULSIFIER FOR WOOL BATCHING OIL
1682. EMBROIDERY ON FABRICS
1683. GARMENT DYEING, WASHING & STITCHING (JEANS, JACKETS, SKIRTS & SHIRTS)
1684. GOVES KNITTING
1685. GUNNY BAGS
1687. HDPE WOVEN SACKS
1688. HDPE TARPAULINS USING PLAIN LOOM WITH LAMINATION
1689. HDPE/PP WOVEN SACKS USING CIRCULAR LOOMS
1690. HOSIERY CLOTH (COTTON) PROCESSING (BLEACHING, DYEING, FINISHING OF CLOTH)
1691. HOSIERY INDUSTRY
1692. HOSIERY MERCERISING
1693. HOSIERY PRODUCTS LIKE VEST, BRIEF, T-SHIRTS & SOCKS
1694. JACQUARD FABRICS
1695. JUTE COIR, GRASS ROPE/ SUTLI MAKING
1696. JUTE FELT
1697. JUTE TWINES
1698. KNITTED FABRICS
1699. LAMINATED JUTE BAGS
1700. LAMINATION OF HDPE WOVEN CLOTH (JUTE, COTTON, PAPER)
1701. NYLON YARN CRIMPING, DOUBLING AND BLEACHING
1702. PIGMENT BINDER FOR TEXTILE PRINTING
1704. POLYESTER RESIN FOR WIRE ENAMEL
1705. POLYESTER RESIN
1706. POLYESTER YARN FROM WASTE POLYESTER ZIP FASTENERS
1707. POWER LOOM
1708. READYMADE GARMENTS & HOSIERY
1709. READYMADE GARMENTS MERCHANDISE
1710. READYMADE GARMENTS & COVERS
1711. READYMADE GARMENTS & EMBROIDERY OF GOWNS, SHIRTS, BLOUSES, T-SHIRTS ETC. (ONLY LADIES)
1712. READYMADE SALWAR SUIT
1713. RECOVERY OF NYLON FROM NYLON WASTE
1714. ROTARY PRINTING AND DYEING ON COTTON, SYNTHETIC TEXTILE
1715. SANITARY NAPKINS
1716. SCREEN PRINTING ON COTTON CLOTH
1717. SEWING THREAD REELS & BALLS MAKING INDUSTRIES
1718. SCREEN PRINTING ON COTTON, POLYESTER & ACRYLIC
1719. SHAWLS (WOOLLEN)
1720. SHOE LACES
1721. SILK FABRICS ON HANDLOOM
1722. SOCKS KNITTING
1723. SPINNING, DOUBLING DYEING MERCERISING & BLEACHING OF COTTON YARN
1724. SPINNING & CARDING OF WOOL INTO YARNS
1725. STARCH BOOK BINDING CLOTH
1726. SURAT JARI
1727. SURGICAL COTTON & BANDAGE
1728. SYNTHETIC TEXTILE INDUSTRY(SUITING, SHIRTING, SAREES) TERRY CLOTH
1729. T-SHIRTS
1730. TOWELS, BED SHEET COVERS
1731. TERRY TOWEL
1732. TERRY FABRICS WEAVING UNIT
1733. TEXTILE AUXILLIARIES & CHEMICALS
1734. TEXTILE BLEACHING, DYEING & FINISHING & PRINTING OF COTTON FABRICS
1735. TEXTILE (HOSIERY)
1736. TEXTILE MILL
1737. TEXTILE DYEING & PRINTING
1738. TEXTILE PRINTING (JOB WORK)
1739. TEXTILE PIGMENT PRINTING BINDER
1740. TOWEL (TERRY)
1741. VELVET CLOTH BY FLOCKING PROCESS
1742. VISCOSE STAPLE FIBRE
1743. WADDING OIL (100%) FOR WADDING OF COTTON HOSIERY CLOTH IN THE DYEING PROCESS
1744. WEAVING OF DASUTI CLOTH WITH PRINTING, DYEING, EMBROIDERY & FINISHING
1745. WASHING OF JEANS & OTHER GARMENTS
1746. WORSTED WOOLLEN YARN CLOTH
1747. ZARI GLITTER SALMA SITARA OF PLASTIC FILM

INFOTECH/IT, HOSPITALITY, HOSPITAL, COLLEGE, SCHOOL, MEDICAL, ENTERTAINMENT CLUB, WARE HOUSING & REAL ESTATE, PROJECTS

1748. AMUSEMENT PARK
1749. AMUSEMENT PARK CUM WATER PARK
1750. BANQUET HALL
1751. CALL CENTER (DOMESTIC)
1752. CALL CENTER (INTERNATIONAL)
1753. CHILDREN RECREATION CENTRE
1754. COLD STORAGE
1755. COMMUNITY HALL
1756. COMPUTER EDUCATION INSTITUTE
1757. COMPUTER SOFTWARE
1758. COLLEGE
1759. CYBER CAFE
1760. DENTAL CLINIC
1761. DENTAL COLLEGE
1762. DIAGONOSTIC CENTRE
1763. E-COMMERCE/BUSINESS
1764. E-SCHOOL (Rs. 5000/-)
1765. ENGINEERING COLLEGE
1766. ENTERTAINMENT CLUB
1767. ENTERTAINMENT CLUB, HOLIDAY RESORT, 4 STAR HOTEL, AMUSEMENT PARK CUM WATER PARK, MUSHROOM & ITS PRODUCTS, FISH FARMING, LAKE FOR BOATING, DEER PARK
1768. FASHION TECHNOLOGY INSTITUTE
1769. FAST FOOD PARLOUR
1770. FIVE STAR HOTEL
1771. FOOD PARLOUR
1772. FRANCHISE TRAINING PROGRAMME FOR IIT & ENGINEERING ENTRANCE EXAMS
1773. GOLF COURSE
1774. HEALTH CLUB, BEAUTY PARLOUR
1775. HEALTH CLUB AND FITNESS CENTER
1776. HEALTH RESORTS
1777. HOLIDAY RESORTS
1778. HOLIDAY RESORT CUM

ENTERTAINMENT CLUB WITH 4 STAR HOTEL
1779. HOSPITALS
1780. ICE CREAM PARLOUR
1781. INTERNET SERVICE PROVIDER (I.S.P.)
1782. MEDICAL COLLEGE
1783. MEDICAL COLLEGE, HOSPITAL & RESEARCH INSTITUTE
1784. MEDICAL TRANSCRIPTION CENTRE
1785. MENTAL RETARDATION HOSPITAL & CEREBRAL PALSY
1786. MOTEL/SMALL HOTEL
1787. MULTISTOREY COMMERCIAL COMPLEX
1788. MULTISTOREY RESIDENTIAL COMPLEX
1789. NURSERY SCHOOL
1790. NATURE CARE CENTRE
1791. NURSING HOME
1792. ONLINE SHOPPING MALL (RS. 5000/- REPORT)
1793. PORTAL
1794. REHABILITATION CENTRE FOR AGED & NEEDY PERSONS
1795. RESIDENTIAL CUM COMMERCIAL COMPLEX
1796. RESTAURANT
1797. RESTAURANT WITH PUB
1798. SCHOOL (PRIMARY)
1799. SCHOOL (HIGHER SECONDARY)
1800. THREE STAR HOTEL
1801. TOURIST CLUB
1802. TRAINING INSTITUTE FOR MEDICAL TRANSCRIPTION
1803. VIDEO FILM STUDIO
1804. WARE HOUSE
1805. WEBSITE DESIGN & E-MAIL REGISTERING

AGRO BASED INDUSTRIES

1806. COAL BRIQUETTES FROM AGROWASTE
1807. FURFURALFROM RICEHULL
1808. MUSHROOM CULTIVATION & PROCESSING (BUTTON)
1809. MUSHROOM GROWING & PROCESSING WITH AIR CONDITIONING
1810. MUSHROOM CULTIVATION & PROCESSING UNIT DEHYDRATION & PACKAGING OF OYSTER & PADDY STRAW MUSHROOMS
1811. ORGANIC MANURE
1812. PAPAYA CULTIVATION
1813. PAPAYA & TOMATO CULTIVATION
1814. PROCESSING & UTILISATION OF COCONUT
1815. PROCESSING OF SHEEP HAIR TO PRODUCE WOOL

BAKERY, CONFECTIONERY & FOOD PRODUCTS

1816. AGROLACTOR SOYA MILK
1817. APPLE FRUIT JUICE WITH CANNING BOTTLING
1818. AYURVEDIC SHARBAT
1819. BAKERY UNIT (PASTRIES, BREAD, BUNS, CAKE, TOFFEE ETC.)
1820. BAKING POWDER
1821. BANANA & ITS BY PRODUCTS
1822. BANANA POWDER
1823. BANANA WAFERS
1824. BANANA CULTIVATION
1825. BEER INDUSTRY
1826. DEHULLING OF JAUN FOR BEER
1827. BEER & WINE
1828. BEER, ALCOHOL, IMFL
1829. BESEN PLANT
1830. BISCUIT PLANT
1831. BREAD & BISCUIT PLANT
1832. BOTTLING PLANT COUNTRY LIQUOR FROM RECTIFIED SPIRIT
1833. BRANDY
1834. BREAD RUSKS
1835. CANNED FRUITS & VEGETABLES
1836. CANNING & PRESERVATION OF MEAT
1837. CANNING & PRESERVATION OF VEGETABLES
1838. CANNING OF MANGO PULP & MANGO SLICES
1839. CARBONATED BEVERAGS
1840. CASHEW FENI
1841. CASHEW NUT (DRIED & FRIED)
1842. CATTLE BREEDING
1843. CATTLE BREEDING & DAIRY FARM TO PRODUCE MILK
1844. CATTLE FEED FROM TAPIOCA
1845. CHEWING GINGER & AMLOKI
1846. CHEWING GUM
1847. CHILLI SAUCE
1848. CHILLI POWDER
1849. CHOCOLATE
1850. CIDER PLANT
1851. COCOA POWDER
1852. COCOA BUTTER & COCOA POWDER
1853. COCONUT SHELL POWDER
1854. COCONUT WATER
1855. COCONUT SWEET (WATERY)
1856. COCONUT MILK POWDER (DEHYDRATED)
1857. COCONUT PRODUCTS & BY PRODUCTS (INTEGRATED PLANT)
1858. COLD DRINK
1859. CURRY POWDER
1860. DAIRY FOR MILK PROCESSING (GHEE, BUTTER & PANEER)
1861. DAIRY PRODUCTS
1862. DAIRY PRODUCTS MILK PACKAGING IN POUCH (GHEE, BUTTER, ETC.
1863. DAIRY FARM TO PRDUCE MILK WITH PACKAGING (COW)
1864. DAIRY FARM TO PRDUCE MILK WITH PACKAGING (BUFALLOE)
1865. DAIRY FARM & MILK PRODUCTS
1866. DAL MOTH, CHANACHUR & BHUJIYA
1867. DEHYDRATION OF FRUITS & VEGETABLE
1868. DESICCATED COCONUT POWDER FROM COCONUTS
1869. DEHYDRATION & CANNING OF FRUITS & VEGETABLES
1870. DRY FRUIT ROASTING & PACKAGING
1871. DRYING OF RED CHILLIES, HALDI, DHANIYA, PEAS & GROUND NUT
1872. EGG POWDER
1873. FISH CANNING IN TIN & POUCHES
1874. FISH DEHYRATION (DRYING OF FISH)
1875. FISH MEAL
1876. FISH PROCESSING (BEAST FREEZING PROCESSES)
1877. FLAVOURS FOR FOOD INDUSTRIES
1878. FLOUR MILL (ROLLER)
1879. FROZEN MEAT
1880. FOOD DEHYDRATION (FRUITS & VEGETABLES)
1881. FRIED & ROASTED GROUND NUT, GRAMS, PEAR ETC.
1882. FRUIT JUICE MAKING & PACKAGING IN PLASTIC CONTAINER
1883. FRUIT JUICE IN TETRA PACK (DRINKS)
1884. FRUIT JUICE, SQUASHES, SAUCE & KETCHUP, JAM, JELLY, VINEGAR ETC.
1885. GARLIC FLAKES
1886. GARLIC POWDER
1887. GHEE & BUTTER
1888. GINGER (PULVERISED)
1889. GINGER GLAZING & PRESERVATION
1890. GINGER STORAGE
1891. GINGER PROCESSING
1892. GINGER OIL & GINGER DUST
1893. GINGER POWDER (DRY) & OLEORESIN
1894. GRAPE DEHYDRATION
1895. GRAPE CULTIVATION
1896. GRAPE JUICE
1897. HONEY PROCESSING & PACKAGING
1898. ICE CREAM & ICE CANDY
1899. ICE CUBE
1900. INVERT SUGAR
1901. IDLI MIX, DOSA MIX SAMBHAR MIX, VADA MIX, GULAB JAMUN MIX
1902. INSTANT COFFEE & INSTANT TEA

1903. INSTANT NOODLES
1904. INSTANT SOUPS
1905. IODIZED SALT FROM CRUDE SALT
1906. JAM CHUTNEY PICKLES & SQUASHES
1907. KATHA MANUFACTURING
1908. LECITHIN (SOYA BASED)
1909. LEMON & ITS PRODUCTS
1910. MACARONI MANUFACTURING
1911. MACARONI, SPAGHETTI, VERMICELLI & NOODLES
1912. MAIZE & ITS BY PRODUCTS MALTING PLANT
1913. MANGO PAPPAD (AAM PAPPAD)
1914. MANGO POWDER RIPE
1915. MANGO POWDER
1916. MANGO PROCESSING & CANNING (MANGO PULP)
1917. MEAT PROCESSING (CHICKEN MUTTON)
1918. MEAT PROCESSING (BUFFALO)
1919. MENTHOL BOLD FROM MENTHOL FLAKES
1020. MILK POWDER
1921. MILK POWDER & GHEE
1922. MILK POWDER, GHEE & SPICES
1923. MILK PRESERVATION & MARKETING TO WHOLE SELLERS
1924. MILK PRESERVATION & MARKETING TO WHOLE SELLERS (IN POUCHES)
1925. MILK TOFFEE MANUFACTURES
1926. MINERAL WATER
1927. MINERAL WATER IN POUCHES
1928. MINI FLOUR MILL ATTA MAIDA, SUJI & WHEAT BRAN
1929. MITHAI/HALWAI (SWEET & NAMKEEN)
1930. MUTTON PROCESSING
1931. PAN MASALA (MEETHA, SADA, ZARDA) MAKING & PACKING
1932. PAN MASALA AND POUCH MAKING
1933. PANEER (CHEESE)
1934. PAPAD & BARIYAN
1935. PAPAD PLANT
1936. PEPSICOLA IN POLYTUBES
1937. PETHA PACKAGING
1938. PICKLES
1939. PIGGERY/MEAT/CHICKEN PROCESSING
1940. PINE APPLE JUICE CANNING
1941. POTATO & ONION POWDER
1942. POTATO & ONION FLAKES
1943. POTATO CHIPS
1944. POTATO GRANULES
1945. POUCH FILLING FOR SAUNF SUPARI ILAICHI ETC.
1946. PRESERVATION OF RAWS MANGO JUICE
1947. PROCESSED CHEESE & MARINE PDTS.
1948. PULP FROM TARMARIND
1949. READYMATE PROCESSED FOOD
1950. RICE & CORN FLAKES
1951. RICE BASMATI (TRADING)
1952. RICE POLISHING & PACKAGING IN POUCH
1953. ROASTED/SALTED/MASALA/ CASHEW NUTS ALMONDS & PEA NUT
1954. ROLLER FLOUR MILL

INFOTECH/IT PROJECTS

1955. MEDICAL TRANSCRIPTION
1956. E-COMMERCE
1957. CYBERCAFE
1958. INTERNET SERVICE PROVIDER (ISP)
1959. COMPUTER EDUCATION CENTRE
1960. PORTAL (WEBSITE DESIGN)
1961. CALL CENTRE

TERMS AND CONDITIONS

FOR INDIA

1. Please ask for Quotations/ Proforma Invoice for Each *Market Survey Cum Detailed Techno Economic Feasibility Report.* Payable in advance through Draft/M.O./Cash in favour of 'ENGINEERS INDIA RESEARCH INSTITUTE', Delhi. Delivery by Regd.Post/Courier within 2 Days. (Postage Free)

2. Ask for a Hi Tech Projects, monthly magazine. Each issue covers approx. 75 project profiles.

FOR OVERSEAS

1. Please ask for Quotations/ Proforma Invoice in US $ for Each *Market Survey Cum Detailed Techno Economic Feasibility Report.* Payable in advance through Bank Draft in favour of 'ENGINEERS INDIA RESEARCH INSTITUTE', Delhi. (Payable in India). Delivery by Regd. Air Mail Post/Courier within 3 Days. (Postage Free)

2. Ask for a Hi Tech Projects, monthly magazine. Each issue covers approx. 75 project profiles.

ENGINEERS INDIA RESEARCH INSTITUTE

4449, Nai Sarak (D), Main Road, Delhi - 110 006 (India)

Phones: 91-11- 2391 8117, 2391 6431, 2384 0361

Fax: 91-11- 2391 6431 E-Mail : eirisidi@bol.net.in Website:www.eiriindia.org

Also at : 4/54, Roop Nagar, Delhi - 110 007 (India)

Ph:. 23840361 Mob: 098114 37895

PATRON: YOU CAN ALSO DEPOSIT THE AMOUNT IN "EIRI" ACCOUNT WITH UTI BANK LTD. CA-05401020006248 OR ICICI BANK LTD. CA-022705000598 OR UNION BANK OF INDIA CA-307201010015149 AND JUST SMS US ON PH. 09811437895

PHARMACEUTICALS & DRUGS TECHNOLOGY WITH FORMULATIONS

ISBN. 81-86732-52-7 # Rs. 950/-

Tablet & Capsules, Lubricants & Disintegrants, Pan Coating, Oral Preparations Mixtures, External Preparations, Ear Drops, Mouth Washes, Nasal Drops, Ointments, Creams & Eye Preparations, Antibiotics, Formulations, Packaging, Tablets including Amoxycillin, Analgin, Ibuprofen, Injectables, Liquid Orals, Capsules & Dry Syrups, Eye & Ear Preparations etc.

MODERN PACKAGING TECHNOLOGY FOR PROCESSED FOOD, BAKERY, SNACK FOOD, SPICES & ALLIED FOOD PRODUCTS

ISBN. 81-86732-28-4 # Rs. 600/-

Latest methods of Packaging Technology of fruits/veg. growers, Spices mfrs., Snack food mfrs., Bakery Mfrs., and Edible oil mfrs. etc. Suppliers of Plant and Machinery have also been incorporated.

BOOKS ON SYNTHETIC DETERGENTS, SOAPS & DETERGENTS

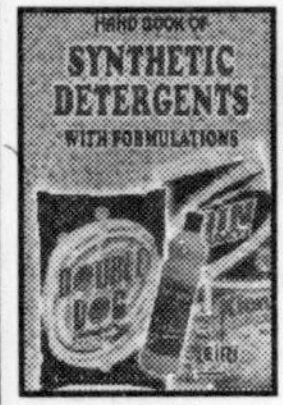

HAND BOOK OF SYNTHETIC DETERGENTS WITH FORMULATIONS

ISBN. 81-86732-43-8 # Rs. 900/-

Group of Synthetic Detergents, Synthesis of Detergents, Manufacture of Synthetic Detergents with Formulae, Testing of Detergents and Soaps, Project Profiles, Suppliers of Machinery and Raw Materials, Acid Slurry, Sirf Excel Type Detergent, Ariel Type Detergent, Dry Mix Process, Dry Clean Unit and much more others etc.

MANUFACTURE OF HOUSEHOLD SOAPS, TOILET SOAPS & OTHER SOAPS WITH FORMULATIONS

ISBN. 81-86732-53-5 # Rs. 750/-

Soap base manufacture, Solid, household and toilet soaps manufacture, Production of soap base, Perfuming, Manufacturing process & formulations, Miscellaneous formulae, Scourig bar, Detergent cake & powder, Toilet & herbal soap, Laundry soap, Liquid soap, Complete plant Suppliers, Suppliers of chemicals, Present manufacturers etc.

BOOKS ON ESSENTIAL OILS, PERFUMES & FLAVOURS

MODERN TECHNOLOGY OF ESSENTIAL OILS

ISBN 81-86732-71-3 # Rs. 850/-

Essential Oils Technology, Essential Oils and Flavours, Production of Essential Oils & Oleoresins, Herb & Oil Yield in Different Ocimum Species, Kewda Essential Oil and Attar, Mint Oil, Lemongrass, Palmarosa Oil, Musk, Java Citronella, Bio-Chemical Studies, Patchouli Oil, Rose-Scented Geranium, Basil Oil etc.

ESSENTIAL OILS PROCESSES & FORMULATIONS HAND BOOK

ISBN. 81-86732-39-X # Rs. 650/-

Essential Oils by Steam Distillation, GC-MS studies, Essential Oil from Cinnamomum, Kewda flower distillation, Composition of essential oil frombottle brush, Composition of essential oil from flowers of Keora, Manufacturers/ Exporters of Essential oils & Aromatic Chemicals with Machinery.

HAND BOOK OF ESSENTIAL OILS MANUFACTURING & AROMATIC PLANTS

ISBN. 81-86732-27-6 # Rs. 450/-

Rose oildistillation, extraction of essential oils, Uses of indigenous aromatic plants, essential oil bearing plants status, fractionation of essential oil, essential oil of hyptis suaveolens poit, super critical fluid extraction, ginger oil, Jasmine, rose etc..

HAND BOOK OF PERFUMES WITH FORMULATIONS

ISBN. 81-86732-42-X # Rs. 750/-

Creating a Perfume, Flower Perfumes, Colognes, Raw Materials, Classification, Packaging of Perfumes, Testing of Perfumes, Aromatic Perfumery Compounds, Scent & Perfume, Spray Perfume, Suppliers of Raw Materials.

HAND BOOK OF PERFUMES & FLAVOURS

ISBN. 81-86732-30-6 # Rs. 600/-

Perfume, Formulary of Perfume & Flavour, Natural Odours Simulated with Aromatic Chemicals, Simulated Flower Scents, Simulated Marine Scents (Algae), Plant & Equipment Suppliers, Suppliers of Raw Materials, Suppliers of Perfumes. Project profiles etc.

HAND BOOK OF FLAVOURS TECHNOLOGY

ISBN 81-86732-98-5
Rs. 750/- or US $ 100/-

The book cover flavour analysis, Chemistry of flavours, Off-flavours in foods, Manufacturing processes of flavours, Plant materials used in flavouring, Principal Essential Oils used in Flavourings, Application of flavourings in food processing, Quality control, Non-Alcoholic Flavours, Flavours fruit (whiskey, vodka, Grape, Butter Scotch & Rum), Terpeneles Menthol Crystals.

ENGINEERS INDIA RESEARCH INSTITUTE Mobile : 9811437895

4449, Nai Sarak, Main Road, Delhi - 110 006 (INDIA) Ph./Fax : 91-11- 23918117, 23916431, 23840361

Hand Book of
FIBRE GLASS MOULDING
EIRI

HAND BOOK OF
POLYMER
AND
PLASTICS TECHNOLOGY
EIRI